Talons of the Eagle

Talons of the Eagle

Dynamics of U.S.–Latin American Relations

Peter H. Smith

New York   Oxford
OXFORD UNIVERSITY PRESS
1996

Oxford University Press

Oxford   New York
Athens   Auckland   Bangkok   Bombay
Calcutta   Cape Town   Dar es Salaam   Delhi
Florence   Hong Kong   Istanbul   Karachi
Kuala Lumpur   Madras   Madrid   Melbourne
Mexico City   Nairobi   Paris   Singapore
Taipei   Tokyo   Toronto

and associated companies in
Berlin   Ibadan

Library of Congress Cataloging-in-Publication Data
Smith, Peter H.
Talons of the eagle : dynamics of U.S.-Latin American relations /
Peter H. Smith.
p.   cm.   Includes bibliographical references and index.
ISBN 0–19–508303–2. — ISBN 0–19–508304–0 (paper : alk. paper)
1. Latin America—Foreign relations—United States.   2. United
States—Foreign relations—Latin America,   I. Title.
F1418.S645   1996
327.7308—dc20   95–13877

1 3 5 7 9 8 6 4 2

Printed in the United States of America
on acid-free paper

For My Students

Preface

This book is a personal statement.

It reflects my belief that historical perspective is absolutely essential for the comprehension of contemporary international realities. Over the past few years there has been much discussion, often naive and short-sighted, about the end of the Cold War and its presumably benevolent impact on U.S.–Latin American relations. In my opinion we can assess the novelty and significance of the current situation only by comparing it with previous epochs—not only with the time of the Cold War itself but also with the era stretching from the American Revolution up through World War II.

It reflects my commitment to interdisciplinary scholarship. The analysis attempts to blend insights from political science and international relations with the study of diplomatic, intellectual, cultural, and political history—of Latin America, the United States, and other parts of the world. There has been remarkably little communication between these apparently disparate fields. This volume seeks to draw some new connections.

It reflects my conviction that U.S. citizens—commentators, policy-makers, investors, and others—must pay close attention to Latin American viewpoints. Too often the study of inter-American relations deteriorates into the study of U.S. foreign policy. One of my central arguments is that there has existed a coherent logic, at times infernal and perverse, in the conduct of U.S.–Latin American relations; an understanding of that logic requires an understanding of Latin American feelings, attitudes, and actions.

It expresses my appreciation for the task of intellectual synthesis, as distinct from original research. This book does not present an exhaustive chronology of U.S.–Latin American relations. My goal is to offer a conceptual framework for the comprehension of changing patterns of inter-American relations over a span of nearly two centuries, and to substantiate that analysis with solid factual evidence. The result is interpretive history (or, if one permits, historical political science). Of necessity, many topics and episodes receive cursory description. As a scholar, I am acutely aware that colleagues have published entire books on subjects that warrant only a paragraph or single sentence here. As a writer, I have sought to achieve the benefits of brevity without incurring costs of superficiality. (For the sake of readability, I have placed all statistical tables in an appendix to the text.)

Finally, the volume fulfills an obligation—to the students, under-graduate and graduate, North American and Latin American, who have stimulated, provoked, challenged, and refined my thinking on U.S.–Latin American relations. Over the past quarter century it has been my privilege to work together with outstanding young men and women—at Dart-mouth College, the University of Wisconsin–Madison, the Massachusetts Institute of Technology, the University of California, San Diego, and various institutions throughout Latin America. To all of them I dedicate this book.

La Jolla   P. H. S.
May 1995

Acknowledgments

Years of reading, observation, and reflection on U.S.–Latin American relations have left a mountainous accumulation of intellectual debts. Here I can acknowledge only a few.

From the initial conception of this book Nancy Lane, of Oxford University Press, consistently offered support, advice, and encouragement.

A remarkable corps of students at the University of California, San Diego worked with me throughout the process of research and writing. Cynthia Alvarez, Ken Maffitt, Dan Nielson, Lara Slater, and Marc Stern supplied crucial information on specific topics. Over extended periods Armando Martínez and Julie Grey gathered multitudinous materials on an infinite variety of subjects with relentless efficiency and boundless cheer. In the meantime my administrative assistants at UCSD, Deborah Ortiz and Patricia Rosas, made countless contributions to my peace of mind and to my progress on the manuscript.

Gracious colleagues, among them Gary Gereffi, Joseph Grunwald, and David A. Lake, were kind enough to furnish helpful clues to sources, data, and ideas. Paul W. Drake and Manfred Mols read the entire manuscript with care and a constructive spirit, as did graduate students in my UCSD seminar on Latin American politics; I have benefited greatly from their comments and suggestions.

I close on a personal note. During the course of this project Jennifer L. Troutner became my closest friend, partner, counselor, critic, companion, comrade-at-arms (and spouse). It is she who made the whole thing possible.

Contents

Talons of the Eagle

Introduction: International Systems and U.S.–Latin American Relations

Relations between the United States and Latin America face unprecedented uncertainty. World events since 1989 have shattered long-held assumptions about international order. The ending of the Cold War—from the collapse of the Berlin Wall to the liberation of Eastern Europe to the implosion of the Soviet Union—has led to epochal rearrangements in the distribution of power, terms of conflict, and patterns of alliance. Early optimism about the creation of a "new world order" has given way to widespread apprehension about ethnic strife, religious war, economic rivalry, and international chaos. As the United States has sought to define its interests and its role in this fast-changing panorama, nations of Latin America have attempted to identify their own options and alternatives. All countries of the hemisphere confront perplexing questions: What is the effect of the end of the Cold War on U.S.–Latin American relations? What will be the governing principles of inter-American relations in the years ahead?

Widespread expectations envision the optimistic possibility that the United States and Latin America will be able to pursue shared interests in a spirit of cooperation. The Cold War exercised an essentially distorting influence on relationships within the hemisphere, according to this argument, and in its absence nations of the Americas can recognize and act upon a natural harmony of interests. Increasing trade and investment will lead to a convergence of economic purposes, the liberalization of markets will promote political democracy, and the emergence of like-minded leaders will eliminate sources of unnecessary conflict between the United States

3

and Latin America. As officials in Washington are wont to proclaim, the post–Cold War environment offers an unprecedented opportunity to forge a "community of democracies" throughout the Western Hemisphere.

Will this prediction prove correct? Examination of this question necessarily requires exploration of the Cold War itself. Otherwise there is no way of assessing the impact of its disappearance. From the late 1940s to the late 1980s the United States and the Soviet Union engaged in a bilateral struggle for power, and the U.S. government launched an anticommunist crusade around the world. Within Latin America the United States encouraged (or compelled) friendly governments to outlaw communist parties, to crush working-class movements, and to maintain pro-U.S. foreign policies. On occasion the United States resorted, overtly or covertly, to political or military intervention. Fear of the "communist threat" may have been greatly exaggerated, as now appears in retrospect, but it had far-reaching consequences: it shaped Washington's policy toward Latin America during the entire period. The U.S.–Soviet contest also defined the parameters of plausible policy options for Latin American countries.

The duration and pervasiveness of the Cold War also raise possibilities about potential legacies: even though it is over, the Cold War might still exert considerable influence on patterns of U.S.–Latin American relations. Is the post–Cold War environment fundamentally different from the pre–Cold War period? In what ways? Or will the hemisphere simply return to the status quo ante? Consideration of these questions requires extended examination of the pre–Cold War period. Only then will it be possible to identify long-term patterns of continuity and to pinpoint fundamental differences between U.S.–Latin American relations before and after the Cold War.

Speculation over the changing nature of U.S.–Latin American relations thus provokes complex questions of historical causality. Of logical necessity, it also requires exploration of apparently remote and distant eras. One hesitates to invoke a shopworn cliché about the need to comprehend the present through the prism of the past. The fact is that it applies to this case.

Such concerns determine the structure of this book. To examine long-term trends and transitions, this volume offers an interpretive synthesis of U.S.–Latin American relations from the late eighteenth century to the present, from the Monroe Doctrine through the Cold War to the North American Free Trade Agreement and beyond. It is my contention that U.S.–Latin American relations have displayed recurring regularities. In other words, the dynamics of the hemispheric connection reveal an *underlying logic*. Inter-American relations have not been the product of whimsy, chance, or accident. Nor have they resulted from individual caprice or personal idiosyncrasy. They have responded to the interaction of national and regional interests as interpreted within changing international contexts.

Accordingly, the goal of this study, is to concentrate on the *struc-*

tural relationship between the United States and Latin America. Rather than focus exclusively on U.S. foreign policy or on Latin American developmental predicaments, I examine the linkages between the two. Three related questions will be central to this inquiry:

- What has been the stance of the United States toward Latin America?
- What has been the response of Latin American countries? And what have been the variations in response?
- What have been the consequent forms of interaction?

In this fashion I seek to reveal not only structural patterns in U.S.–Latin American relations but also the transformation of those patterns over time.

Concepts and Approaches

This book draws heavily upon a central insight from the study of international relations—the idea that interplay among actors in the international arena constitutes a "system," that the system entails tacit codes of behavior, and that these rules can be thought of as comprising a "regime." As defined by political scientist Stephen Krasner, a regime consists of "implicit or explicit principles, norms, rules and decision-making procedures around which actors' expectations converge in a given area of international relations. Principles," he continues, "are beliefs of fact, causation, and rectitude. Norms are standards of behavior defined in terms of rights and obligations. Rules are specific prescriptions or proscriptions for action. Decision-making procedures are prevailing practices for making and implementing collective choice."[1]

My usage of the concept of regime entails an adaptation of its meaning. As currently applied, the idea usually applies to specific and limited issue-areas—such as trade, environment, petroleum ("in a given area of international relations," in Krasner's phrase). In this study, by contrast, I am referring to norms and principles that establish patterns of behavior within broad and general *international systems,* not just with regard to particular issues. Construed in this fashion, the logical content of norms and principles for international systems depends upon a variety of factors: the number of major powers, the nature of resources available to them, and the scope of competition.[2]

Systems and their codes are global in scope; they pertain to all actors in the international arena. They are of relatively long duration; individual powers might rise and fall, but rules of operation tend to stay the same. They are nonetheless subject to change, especially if leading powers arrive at the conclusion that maintenance of a given system will be more costly than its alteration.[3] For implementation states depend upon subjective perceptions, especially mutual perceptions of major powers, as well as upon objective realities.

My interpretation of inter-American relations stresses both the *charac-*

ter and the *transformation* of international systems and their corresponding codes. Given the subject of this volume, however, I make no pretense of examining all variations and types of international systems.[4] Instead I focus on those systems which have provided relevant frameworks for the conduct of U.S.–Latin American relations.[5]

There have been, in my view, three broad systems which have guided the management of inter-American relations. The first stretched from the 1790s to the 1930s, when the prevailing regime corresponded to the logic of balance-of-power competition and multilateral rivalry. Imperialism— the quest for land, labor, and resources—provoked rivalry between major European powers and defined the relationship between metropolitan centers and subordinate colonial holdings. It was this logic that shaped the "great war of the mid-eighteenth century," culminating in the Seven Years' War, and it was this logic that determined the rules of international engagement throughout the nineteenth and early twentieth centuries. The United States entered this contest shortly after achieving independence. United States leaders would seek to extend territorial reach at the expense of former European colonies, to prevent other powers from challenging this expansion, and to establish a sphere of uncontested influence within the Western Hemisphere. In effect, the fledgling United States was working out the logic of the eighteenth-century wars.

The second system lasted from the late 1940s through the 1980s, corresponding to the Cold War. The prevailing logic of this regime reflected the preeminence of bilateral rivalry between the United States and the Soviet Union on a global scale, intensified by mutual capacity for nuclear destruction. The Cold War altered the basis of inter-American relations, elevating the concept of "national security" to the top of the U.S. agenda and turning Latin America (and other Third World areas) into both a battleground and a prize in the conflict between communism and capitalism, East and West, the Soviet Union and the United States. The doctrine of "containment" led the United States to extend and consolidate its political supremacy throughout the hemisphere. By the early 1950s Washington laid down policy lines in accordance with the terms of this regime, and they persisted through the 1980s.

Third is the contemporary era of the post–Cold War. The defining characteristic of this period, in my judgment, is the absence of clear-cut rules of the game. The United States has remained the world's only military superpower, especially in the wake of the Soviet collapse, and after the Gulf War of 1991 the United States appeared to enjoy a "unipolar moment." At the same time U.S. relative strength appears to be declining in the economic arena, where the rise of Japan and Europe has fostered multilateral competition. The distribution of military power does not bear a clear relationship to the distribution of economic power. This disjuncture creates uncertainty.

Within the Western Hemisphere, by contrast, the United States has acquired what might be called "hegemony by default." The Soviets/

Russians have withdrawn (from the modest extent to which they were ever there), Europeans have turned their attention elsewhere, Japanese have been slow to enter the Americas.[6] At the moment U.S. supremacy is therefore uncontested and complete. And while Latin America is becoming less important as a political asset for the United States, it may be becoming more important as an economic asset.

United States–Latin American relations are now unfolding within a context of multiple power arrangements. On a global level, there exist unipolar supremacy with regard to security matters (though contemporary problems are less and less amenable to military solutions) and a multipolar rivalry with regard to economic matters. Within the Americas, however, the United States wields unilateral hegemony. How these various configurations interact is, of course, one of the central questions of our time.

This broad shift in international contexts has continually shaped and revised the terms and nature of inter-American diplomacy. A central interpretation of this book thus takes counterintuitive form: the fundamental determinants of U.S.–Latin American relations have been the role and activity of *extrahemispheric* actors, not the United States or Latin America itself. In other words, the inter-American relationship has formed a subsystem with the global system as a whole.

To understand internal dynamics within the Western Hemisphere, a second conceptual concern focuses upon the distribution of power. Ever since the early nineteenth century, the United States has been stronger and richer than its Latin American neighbors. The nature and degree of this asymmetry have varied over time, but it has been a pervasive and persistent reality. This means, among other things, that the United States has usually held the upper hand: there has been little bargaining between equals, and the sovereignty of Latin nations has been under constant threat. In this light it seems wholly implausible to depict U.S. involvement in the region as the result of suction into a "whirlpool."[7] Throughout recent history, the United States has enjoyed by far the most freedom of action among countries in the Americas. And precisely for this reason, the study of U.S.–Latin American relations offers insight into the character and conduct of the United States: it provides an opportunity to examine, over time, how the United States has chosen to apply and exercise its perennial predominance.

This dual focus—on regimes and power—leads directly to another question: the response of nations and groups. In this account I concentrate not on intricate details of decision-making processes or on the personal psychology of decision makers, but on the formulation and pursuit of broad, long-term strategies. I assume that nations—and their leaders—seek to advance practical interests. Fundamental interests are either geopolitical, the pursuit of military security, or economic, the pursuit of prosperity. These two sets of interests often overlap. Security interests are typically advanced by governmental bureaucracies; in capitalist societies, economic interests usually represent the goals of private sectors, which might have direct or indirect representation within the apparatus of the state. While national interests are often cloaked in the uplifting idiom of moral purpose, it is the quest for geopolitical and economic advantage—not idealism—that provides the driving force behind foreign policy and international behavior.

Without assuming that nation-states always act in coherent and rational fashion, I maintain that the articulation of a long-term national strategy depends upon some form of cost-benefit calculation. Policy choices respond to logical evaluation of likely outcomes, of predictable losses and gains. Within the context of the prevailing international system and their own power capability, countries and their leaders behave in reasonable ways. There is method in what often appears to be madness.

Yet the definition of strategy depends not only on the objective nature of prevailing conditions but also upon the subjective perception of those conditions by decision-making elites. For this reason I place significant emphasis on the social construction of reality—on general worldviews or *weltanschauung*. In the argot of contemporary social science, rationality tends to be "bounded" by ideology. Prevailing assumptions are often unstated, partly because they are presumed to be self-evident, and they do not always lead to formulation of explicit ideology. Cultural and attitudinal factors play a fundamental part in international relations, however, and they require occasional excursions into the field of intellectual history.

Elite decision makers interpret and represent national interests in accordance with their own biases and outlooks. For this reason it is essential to explore the ulterior motivations of policy-making groups within the nation-state and of nonstate actors as well. As often as not, public policy represents the interests of the ruling classes, not the "nation" as a whole, and policy outcomes reflect the power and effectiveness of dominant alliances. This factor is especially pertinent to Latin America, where patterns of socioeconomic development resulted in wide discrepancies between social classes and their respective interests; as a general rule, dictatorial governments in Latin America have tended to serve and support privileged elites. And even in democratic settings, official policy does not necessarily represent the greatest good for the greatest number of national citizens.

Interests can vary over time. Among U.S. policymakers, for instance, the relative weight of economic and geopolitical motivations has undergone cyclical change. During the nineteenth and early twentieth centuries economic considerations were more important; during the Cold War, political considerations were uppermost; and now, in the post–Cold War period, economic considerations once again are coming to the fore.

In response to the presence and power of the United States, Latin America has conducted a persisting and creative search for policy options. Leaders from the region—statesmen and politicians, economists and businessmen, students and revolutionaries, poets and essayists—all have attempted to define, expand, and implement the range of plausible policy options. For the most part they have done so in a realistic fashion. United States observers frequently comment, derisively, on the curious "psychology" of Latin America, on its love-hate relationship with the United States and on its emotional penchant for populistic nationalism. This condescension utterly misses a fundamental point: for weaker participants in an unequal world, nationalism may be one of the few options available.

I am painting here with a very broad brush. My central concerns focus on the character of international systems, on the distribution of power, on the perception and pursuit of national interests, and on the resulting interaction between Latin America and the United States. My goal is to uncover recurrent regularities within the inter-American relationship, to identify long-term trends and transitions, to analyze continuity and change. Only in this fashion will it be possible to assess the prospects for U.S.–Latin American relations in this new era of uncertainty.

I

THE IMPERIAL ERA

And by and by comes America, and our Master of the Game plays it badly—plays it as Mr. Chamberlain was playing it in South Africa. It was a mistake to do that . . . he played the European game, the Chamberlain game. It was a pity; it was a great pity, that error; that one grievous error, that irrevocable error.

Mark Twain (1901)

1

The European Game

Of all characters, I think, that of a conquering nation least becomes the American people. . . . Shall she, like another Phaeton, madly ascend the chariot of empire and spread desolation and horror over the world?
  Speech in U.S. Congress (1803)

I have always wished that this country should exhibit to the nations of the earth the example of a great, rich, and powerful republic which is not possessed by a spirit of aggrandizement.
  Daniel Webster (1845)

Yes, more, more, more! . . . till our national destiny is fulfilled and . . . the whole boundless continent is ours.
  John L. O'Sullivan (1845)

Imperialism established a framework for the conduct of international relations throughout the nineteenth and early twentieth centuries. As a fledgling power, the United States took active and increasing part in the global competition that provoked continuous rivalry between major European powers and defined the relationship between metropolitan centers and subordinate colonial holdings. Over time this imperial contest developed an implicit logic that shaped the international system as a whole and the roles of contending nations in particular. Recurrent episodes of conflict led to rearrangements of power relations. Until the 1800s this system reflected both dominance and competition among leading powers of Europe, which continually sought to expand their holdings in Africa, Asia, and the New World.

13

The United States entered this contest shortly after achieving independence ("playing the European Game," as Mark Twain would acidly observe). Having established national sovereignty, U.S. leaders would seek to extend territorial reach over European colonies and prevent other powers from challenging this expansion. As a result, U.S. relations with Latin America during the nineteenth century represented a continuation and culmination of European incursions into and struggles over the New World that dated back to the late fifteenth century.

From the outset, in other words, the United States was an aspiring imperial power. It entered the international arena as a relatively minor, almost insignificant actor; within a century the young nation became a formidable contender. The United States embarked on its imperial course neither by impulse, miscalculation, or accident. Its behavior represented long-term policy and national purpose. As historian William Appleman Williams has observed, "Americans thought of themselves as an empire at the outset of their national existence. . . . Having matured in an age of empires as part of an empire, the colonists naturally saw themselves in the same light once they joined issue with the mother country."[1] In an ethical sense, U.S. conduct was neither better nor worse than that of other ambitious powers. All played by the same rules of the game.

Once engaged in this contest, the United States adapted its policy in accordance with conditions and circumstances particular to the New World. While European powers engaged primarily in colonization of overseas possessions, the United States tended to rely, first, on territorial acquisition and absorption, and, second, on the establishment and preservation of informal spheres of influence. The means thus varied, but the ends were much the same.

European Rivalry in the New World

European powers began to compete for control of the New World almost immediately after Christopher Columbus announced his earth-shattering "discovery" in 1492. Protesting Spanish claims to total monopoly over the Americas, King João II of Portugal convinced the "Catholic kings" in 1494 to modify the original ruling of Pope Alexander VI and accept the Treaty of Tordesillas, which ceded to Portugal dominion over the eastern half of South America—much of present-day Brazil. Theoretically, Spain and Portugal thus possessed exclusive title to the newly found territories. According to the terms of papal endorsement, it was the religious obligation of Spain and Portugal to spread the Catholic gospel to the heathen. So long as they fulfilled this missionary duty, Spain and Portugal would have complete control of lands and peoples of the New World. From 1580 to 1640, when Portugal fell under Spanish control, this claim belonged to Spain alone.

The Iberian monopoly did not last long. Protestantism took hold throughout much of Europe as a result of the Reformation, and its anti-

Catholic adherents saw no reason to respect the Treaty of Tordesillas or any papal declaration. Seeking economic access to the riches of the New World, merchants and buccaneers from rival European countries initiated a thriving trade in contraband. According to then-prevailing mercantilist theory, moreover, the goal of economic activity was to enhance the power of the nation-state. The accumulation of power was to be measured through the possession of precious bullion—that is, gold or silver. Mercantilist policymakers thus sought to run a favorable balance of trade, with exports exceeding imports, since this would increase the storage of coinage or bullion. (The emphasis on trade gave the doctrine its name.) Mercantilist theory tended to assume that nations engaged in a "zero-sum" game, with one state's gain entailing a loss for another state. Discovery of the New World gravely threatened prevailing power relations, since it placed massive and unforeseen quantities of gold and silver at the disposal of Spain and its crusading Catholic monarchs, Charles I and Philip II. Given the assumptions of the time, other powers had no choice but to react.

By the mid-sixteenth century England emerged as Spain's principal rival. Legendary pirateers John Hawkins and Francis Drake made raids on ports around the Caribbean. Philip II decided to retaliate by invading England. Drake roared into the harbor of Cadiz and destroyed a number of ships, "singeing the beard of the king of Spain," and the English fleet then crushed the Spanish armada in 1588. War extended beyond Philip's death and peace finally came in 1609, when the Netherlands were divided in two: the north was set free from Spain and became Holland; the south remained under Spanish control and is now Belgium.

Spain's setbacks in Europe were soon reflected in the New World. The English settled at Virginia in 1607 and at Massachusetts in 1620. The Dutch reached New York in 1612. The French began moving into Canada in the 1620s. More significantly, from the standpoint of the era, English, French, and Dutch settlements appeared in the Antilles—in the middle of what had been up to then a Spanish lake. In 1630, moreover, the Dutch seized control of the Brazilian northeast—with its extensive sugar plantations—an acquisition that for Holland vastly overshadowed the purchase of Manhattan Island a few years before. The Dutch remained in Brazil until 1654.

By the late seventeenth century Europe was seeking to establish an effective counterweight to France. In 1700 Louis XIV's efforts to impose a family relative on the Spanish throne prompted a coalition of three partners—England, Holland, and the Holy Roman Emperor—to respond with a declaration of war. The War of the Spanish Succession dragged on until 1713. At the war's end Austria gained control of Milan, Naples, Sicily, and Belgium; Philip V (Louis XIV's nephew) was made King of Spain, under the stipulation that the crowns of France and Spain would never be held by the same individual; and England, the biggest winner, gained control of Gibraltar, Newfoundland, Nova Scotia, and—most important—the commercial contract *(asiento)* for the African slave trade with Spanish colonies in the New World. This lucrative privilege gave Britain a secure foothold in Spanish America.

Competition for empire intensified throughout the eighteenth century. A series of skirmishes stretched from 1739 to 1763 (with an uneasy truce from 1748 to 1756) and comprised what has come to be known as "the great war of the mid-eighteenth century." The first part of the contest, usually known as the War of the Austrian Succession, ground to a halt in 1748 when England and France reached agreement to restore the status quo ante bellum. The second stage came with the Seven Years' War, in which Britain and Prussia joined forces against the combined strength of the Hapsburgs and Bourbons. This war had multiple fronts, stretching from Europe to Canada to India. When the dust finally cleared in 1763, the Treaty of Paris codified the results: Britain remained in India; France ceded to Britain all French territory on the North American mainland east of the Mississippi River; France retained its slave stations in Africa plus the cash-producing Caribbean islands of Guadeloupe and Martinique (leading one observer to exult, in classic confirmation of mercantilist economic doctrine, "We may have lost Canada, but we have retained Martinique!"); and Spain retained its North American holdings west of the Mississippi and at the river mouth. The Seven Years' War thus achieved a new political and economic equilibrium. England replaced France as the preeminent colonial power, a position she would extend and consolidate through the *pax britannica* of the nineteenth century.

As England was celebrating its diplomatic triumph, Prime Minister George Grenville took a series of steps to consolidate British rule in North America and to improve imperial finances. His most notorious measure was the Stamp Act, which in 1765 imposed taxes on all legal documents, newspapers, pamphlets, and almanacs. Eventually, and in many instances reluctantly, British colonists rose up in protest against these impositions and against the monarchy. Proclaiming their independence in 1776, they finally achieved sovereignty and recognition in 1783. The emergence of their new nation would have fundamental and far-reaching impacts upon the international arena.

Imperial Order: The Rules of the Game

Imperialism entailed the policy, practice, or advocacy of the extension of control by a nation over the territory, inhabitants, and resources of areas that lay outside the nation's own boundaries. Typically, nations engaged in imperialistic behavior for two basic reasons: first, to gain access to economic benefits—such as land, labor, and minerals; and second, to increase political strength and military capability—often through the improvement of geopolitical position in relation to other contending powers. Almost always, the pursuit of imperial advantage evoked elaborate ideological justification ranging from the religious mission of sixteenth-century Spain to the civilizing mission of eighteenth-century France and the "white man's burden" that would be borne by nineteenth-century England.

As it evolved over time, imperialism spawned an informal but coherent code of international rules. The keystone of this system was the idea of a balance of power. First articulated by the Peace of Westphalia in 1648, this principle assumed that international politics would consist of relations among nation-states. The ultimate purpose of a balance of power was to prevent domination by any single European nation. In practice the principle led to a constantly shifting pattern of alliances and coalitions, as weaker nations often sought to achieve an appropriate balance by combining their forces in opposition to the stronger ones. Alignments would be based not on religion, ideology, culture, or values. They would respond to momentary contingencies and power calculations.

Second, this international system supported the sovereignty of established European nation-states and accepted the state as the primary actor in the global arena. Indeed, the whole idea of a "balance" among nations tended to assume and assure their individual survival. By definition, equilibrium precluded the possibility of elimination or extinction. Of course this stipulation applied only to recognized powers in Europe, not to other parts of the world.

Third, and partly as a result of this understanding, European nations focused much of their competitive energy on imperial expansion. Preservation of a balance among metropolitan powers tended to limit the scale and scope of wars within the European theater. During the seventeenth and eighteenth centuries, battlegrounds shifted from the European continent itself toward the colonized areas. In effect, the extension of imperial possessions provided nations with an opportunity to enhance their power positions without having always to engage in direct hostilities with other European states. Colonization created a "positive-sum" game, or so it seemed at the time, a means of tilting the balance of power without upsetting the system as a whole.

Fourth, imperial holdings became integral elements in the calculation of the power balance. Especially under the mercantilist doctrines of the period, the ultimate rationale for imperial possessions was to strengthen the economic and political position of the metropolitan state. European powers consequently went to considerable lengths to maintain monopolistic control over their dominions, from Spain's elaborate complex of legalisms and regulations to England's maritime enforcement of its *pax britannica*. The point was not only to maximize direct exploitation of the dominions. It was to make sure that no other rival power would seize part of the booty and in so doing revise the prevalent balance of power.

Various methods existed for the pursuit of imperialistic advantage. One was the conquest and incorporation of territory, leading to effective enlargement of the boundaries of the nation-state. After the Peace of Westphalia most European powers tended to shy away from this method, at least in regard to each other's terrain, since it threatened to violate the whole idea of a balance of power. And with regard to overseas territories, the prospect of incorporation raised complex juridical and philosophical questions about the relationship of colonial inhabitants to metropolitan society. Even so, it became the policy of France to regard its imperial possessions in Africa, Asia, and the New World as integral parts of the nation—as *départements d'outre mer,* in theoretical possession of the legal rights and obligations pertaining to the provinces of France.

A second technique involved subjugation and colonization. Through this method, imperial dominions attained special status as subordinate appendages to the metropolitan nation and, usually, to its central government. While adding to the power of the metropole, colonization did not lead to effective enlargement of national boundaries. Nor did it raise awkward questions about the rights or roles of colonial subjects. For such reasons this approach was favored by most European competitors in the imperial contest. The British empire and its contemporary remnants (the so-called Commonwealth) offer perhaps the most notable and elaborate example of this option.

A third alternative entailed the creation of a "sphere of interest," or sphere of influence, over which an imperial power would exert de facto hegemony through informal means. This could stem from economic domination or, in politics, the installation of client regimes or protectorates. One advantage of this approach was economy of effort: it did not entail the enormous expenditures of military, administrative, and financial resources that formal colonies required. (Indeed, there now exists substantial doubt about the net profitability of colonial possessions for European powers.) A central disadvantage was, of course, insecurity: precisely because they were informal, spheres of influence were subject to intrusion by rival powers. Stability could prevail only if major powers agreed to recognize each other's spheres of domination. Such was the case in nineteenth-century Africa, where European rivals agreed to a "partitioning" of the continent, and to a lesser extent in turn-of-the-century China, where European nations attempted to carve out exclusive spheres of influence. It also applied to locations where the ever-resourceful British constructed what have come to be known as "informal empires."[2]

Enter the United States

The newly independent United States joined the contest for imperial extension soon after achieving constitutional stability in the late 1780s. Two schools of thought quickly emerged with regard to foreign policy. One, championed by George Washington, held that the United States should avoid "entangling alliances" with European powers and should separate itself as much as possible from the Old World. The other, associated with Alexander Hamilton, argued that the United States should actively take advantage of European conflicts: if the new nation were to develop a

powerful navy, he wrote, "a price would be set not only upon our friendship, but upon our neutrality. By steady adherence to the Union we may
hope ere long to become the Arbiter of Europe in America; and to be able
to incline *the balance of European competitions* in this part of the world as our
interest may dictate" (emphasis added). Despite these differences, however, U.S. policymakers were in full agreement on one fundamental premise: European influence in the Americas should be reduced and restricted.
It was this concern that directed their attention toward Spanish America.
As Rufus King said of South America in a letter to Hamilton in 1799: "I
am entirely convinced if it [South America] and its resources are not for us
that they will speedily be against us."

American statesmen employed several strategies to prevent this negative outcome. First was to insist, at least in the short run, that these
colonies remain in possession of Spain, which had the desirable quality of
being a weak and declining power. Spain presented no threat; France or
England, by contrast, would represent a powerful challenge. As a result,
the United States vigorously and consistently opposed the transfer of
Spanish dominions in the New World to any other European power.

Second, U.S. leaders would support campaigns for independence by
Spanish American colonies in the 1810s and 1820s. They reached this
position after a substantial amount of controversy and debate. One concern was that newly independent nations of Spanish America might forge
diplomatic and commercial ties with England or France. A second preoccupation was that the resulting nations would be susceptible to instability,
authoritarianism, and, as a result, extrahemispheric intervention. Another
was that it would be politically difficult for the United States to take
territory away from sister republics in the hemisphere. In the end, the
United States faced little practical choice—and concluded that Spanish
American independence would promote long-term national goals. As
Thomas Jefferson wrote in 1808, "We consider their interests and ours as
the same, and that the object of both must be to exclude all European
influence from this hemisphere."

Third, U.S. policymakers sought to establish their own hegemony
within the region. Without the power to back up their statements, they
brazenly asserted that the continents of the Americas comprised a U.S.
sphere of interest—to the exclusion of European powers. As Secretary of
State John Quincy Adams declared, the United States was willing to leave
Great Britain in "indisputed enjoyment" of all her colonial possessions so
long as Britain would accept "every possibility of extension to our natural
dominion in North America, which she can have no solid interest to prevent, until all possibility of her preventing it shall have vanished." In a
similar vein, Jefferson insisted that Europe comprised "a separate division
of the globe," while "America," he contended, "has a hemisphere to itself.
It must have a separate system of interest which must not be subordinated
to those of Europe. The insulated state in which nature has placed the

American continent should so far avail that no spark of war kindled in the other quarters of the globe should be wafted across the wide oceans which separate us from them."

Claims to hemispheric hegemony became full-fledged policy with proclamation of the Monroe Doctrine in 1823. Partly aimed at czarist Russia's territorial claims in the American northwest, the doctrine asserted that the American continents "are henceforth not to be considered as subject for future colonization by any European power." It did not condemn colonization as a matter of principle; it inveighed only against colonization by European powers in the Americas. Taking note of an apparent design by the Holy Alliance to help Spain regain her colonies, President Monroe in addition warned against reinstatement of monarchical rule:

> We owe it, therefore, to candor, and to the amicable relations existing between the United States and those powers, to declare that we should consider any attempt on their part to extend their political system to any portion of this hemisphere as dangerous to our peace and safety. . . . We could not view any interposition for the purpose of oppressing [the newly independent nations], or controlling in any other manner their destiny, by any European power in any other light than as the manifestation of an unfriendly disposition toward the United States.

In one sense this statement declared the United States to be the guardian of independence and democracy throughout the hemisphere. But in another, more fundamental sense, it was an assertion of *realpolitik*. Not only would the United States oppose colonization by Europe in America; it would also oppose political *alliances* between newly independent nations of Spanish America and European powers.

U.S. Imperialism I: Territorial Expansion

The first phase of U.S. imperialistic policy involved territorial acquisition and absorption. Circumstances were propitious in the early nineteenth century. England and France were distracted by internal strife and by continental wars. Spain was in a process of precipitous decline. New nations in the hemisphere, especially in Spanish America, would be unable to offer much resistance. As Thomas Jefferson prophesied as early as the 1780s, it would eventually become possible for the United States to take over remnants of Spain's once-formidable empire "peice by peice [*sic*]."

Pocketbook Diplomacy

The acquisition of Louisiana marked U.S. entry into the imperial contest. In 1763 France lost its possessions west of the Mississippi to Spain— fortunately for the United States, the weakest of the European powers. In 1795 the United States obtained commercial rights along the Mississippi

River. In 1800 Napoleon suddenly took title to Louisiana on behalf of France. Thomas Jefferson expressed shock and dismay over this development.[3] "It completely reverses all the political relations of the U.S.," he declared. Shortly afterward Jefferson emphasized the importance of "one single spot" on earth—the port of New Orleans—the possessor of which would necessarily become "our natural and habitual enemy." The United States and France were on a collision course.

England came to the rescue, at least indirectly, as British–French tensions threatened to erupt in war. A beleaguered Napoleon decided to sell off the Louisiana territory: better it go to the United States, he must have calculated, than to the English. By the terms of the 1803 purchase arrangement, the United States paid about $15 million in exchange for a massive span of land, one that not only included the present-day state of Louisiana but that almost doubled the territorial size of the then United States.

Florida came next, through a combination of guile and force. In 1817 Secretary of State John Quincy Adams opened talks with the Spanish minister, don Luis de Onís, after which General Andrew Jackson seized Spanish forts at St. Marks and Pensacola. Instead of reprimanding Jackson, as one might have expected, Adams demanded reparations from Spain to cover the cost of the military expedition—allegedly undertaken against Indians whom the Spaniards could not control. Unable to obtain diplomatic support from Great Britain, the king of Spain agreed in 1819 to cede "all the territories which belong to him situated to the eastward of the Mississippi and known by the name of East and West Florida." In return the U.S. government would assume the claims of its citizens against the Spanish government in the amount of $5 million. This money was to be paid to American citizens, not to the Spanish government: technically speaking, the United States did not "purchase" Florida, as is often said. In addition Spain renounced her claim to territory north of the forty-second parallel from the Rockies to the Pacific, while the United States gave up its claims to Texas. America's renunciation of interest in Texas did not, of course, endure the test of time.

England's refusal to support Spanish claims in the New World resulted from political calculations about the European theater. In the mid-1820s, with French troops occupying parts of a much-weakened Spain, British foreign minister George Canning began to worry about the possibility that France might assume control of Spain's holdings in the New World. That would upset the balance of power. To prevent this outcome he extended diplomatic recognition to the struggling republics of Spanish America, a gesture that earned accolades and gratitude throughout the continent. But Canning's motive was less than charitable, as he immodestly declared in 1826: "Contemplating Spain, such as our ancestors had known her, I resolved that if France had Spain, it should not be Spain with the Indies. I called the New World into existence to redress the balance of the Old." Rarely had the logic of the Imperial Era found such pristine expression.

Military Conquest

In the 1820s Mexico won independence from Spain and jurisdiction over the province of Texas, then a largely unpopulated wilderness. (Presumably Mexico's achievement of sovereignty freed the United States from its 1819 commitment to Spain.) After its long and bitter struggle for independence, Mexico was in a greatly weakened state. Economic production was anemic, especially in the mining and agricultural sectors; governmental budgets ran consistent deficits, taxes were steadily raised, properties were confiscated, old currencies were recalled and new ones issued; politics fell prey to chronic instability. Between 1821 and 1860 the country had more than fifty presidents, approximately one per year, and the military comprised by far the nation's strongest political force. Through this turmoil there emerged the mercurial Antonio López de Santa Anna, hero of Mexico's rejection of Spain's attempted *reconquista* in 1829 and of the expulsion of French troops during the so-called *guerra de los pasteles* in 1838. Santa Anna would both precipitate and personify Mexico's disintegration and vulnerability during its first quarter-century of independence.

Recognizing their inability to protect the country's northern frontier, Mexican leaders in the 1820s permitted colonists, most of them slaveholding planters from the United States, to settle in the province of Texas. A group led by Stephen F. Austin agreed to profess the Roman Catholic religion, to conduct official transactions in Spanish, and to abide by Mexican law. Yet the colonists soon began chafing under Mexican rule. They particularly complained about the fact that Texas was appended to the state of Coahuila, where the provincial delegation was in a small minority, and demanded that Texas should become a state within Mexico, with its own legislature and local government. Publicists in the United States began to clamor for Texan independence. Afraid that its control of Texas was slipping, the Mexican government attempted first to discourage immigration (by emancipating slaves in 1829) and then to prohibit it altogether (through a proclamation in 1830). Shortly afterward Santa Anna annulled the federalist constitution of 1824 and sought to concentrate effective power in the central government.

Texans rebelled in the name of independence. In March 1836 Santa Anna overwhelmed Texan forces in the Battle of the Alamo; later, captured and defeated, he consented to the secession. When word of his capitulation reached Mexico City, nationalist intellectuals and politicians expressed outrage and disbelief. The Mexican legislature refused to receive a peace commission from Texas or to extend recognition to the Lone Star Republic.

The United States recognized Texas as a sovereign polity in 1837. And in 1845, after the expansionist James K. Polk became president, it annexed the republic of Texas. This was a direct affront to Mexico, which still regarded Texas as an outlaw province of its own. Mexico and the United States severed diplomatic relations.

A boundary dispute fanned the flames of contention. While North

Americans claimed that the southern border extended to the Rio Grande, Mexicans insisted that the limit should end, as it always had, at the Nueces River. In 1846 President Polk dispatched U.S. troops under General Zachary Taylor to the disputed area, in what many historians interpret as a deliberate move to provoke a fight. In hopes of relieving tension the harried Mexican president, José Joaquín Herrera, agreed to receive a diplomatic mission so long as the discussions "should appear to be always frank, and free from every sign of menace or coercion." Polk withdrew a U.S. naval force from the coast of Veracruz but authorized the U.S. mission under John Slidell to discuss not only Texas but the acquisition of New Mexico and California as well. As bitterness mounted in Mexico General Mariano Paredes overthrew the hapless Herrera, installed himself as president, and refused to accept Slidell's credentials.

Polk was now looking for war. On May 9, 1846, he called a cabinet meeting to discuss "definite measures" to be taken against Mexico. That same evening news arrived of military hostilities at a place called Matamoros, on the southern bank of the Rio Grande. Seizing upon this excuse, Polk promptly called for war. In his message to Congress he praised the United States for its "strong desire to establish peace" and condemned Mexico for treachery. The Mexican government had broken its "plighted faith" by refusing to receive the Slidell mission, and had responded without reason when "Texas, a nation as independent as herself, thought proper to unite its destinies with our own." Tacitly confessing his predetermination for war, Polk insisted that "the cup of forbearance had been exhausted" even prior to the skirmish at Matamoros—which he described as a Mexican invasion of U.S. soil. "As war exists, and, notwithstanding all our efforts to prevent it, exists by the act of Mexico herself," Polk urged Congress to "recognize the existence of the war" and give him full authority to wage the necessary campaigns.

Although the logic of his message was preposterous, Polk received approval for his war. General Zachary Taylor swept into the city of Monterrey, rebels in California took sides with the United States, and in 1847 American troops under General Winfield Scott advanced from Veracruz to Mexico City, seizing the capital after subduing the resistance of young Mexican cadets. The following year, in the Treaty of Guadalupe Hidalgo, Mexico was obliged to surrender a huge span of land—from New Mexico and Colorado to California, as revealed in Figure 1, more than a million square miles—in exchange for a modest $15 million. Several years later the United States extended its holdings by obtaining an additional section of New Mexico and Arizona through the Gadsden Purchase—a transaction remembered in Mexico for the application of American pressure, and therefore known as "the imposition of Mesilla" (*el tratado impuesto de la Mesilla*), so named after the valley that passed to U.S. hands.

Ironically, one eventual consequence of the U.S. defeat of Mexico was a flagrant breach of the Monroe Doctrine. Humiliated by the "war of the North American invasion" and unable to achieve a semblance of stability,

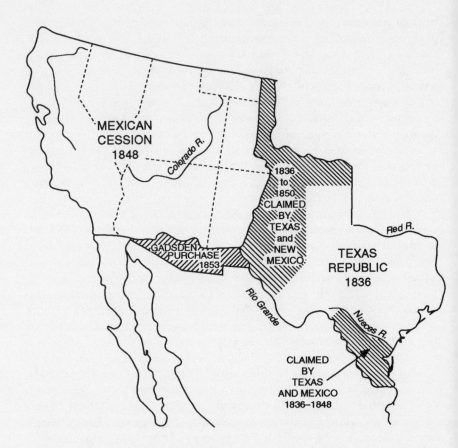

Figure 1. U.S. territorial acquisitions from Mexico, 1836–1853. [*Source:* Map from *Mexican Americans/American Mexicans* by Matt S. Meier and Feliciano Ribera. Copyright © 1972, 1993 by Matt S. Meier and Feliciano Ribera. Reprinted by permission of Hill and Wang, a division of Farrar, Straus & Giroux, Inc.]

political conservatives in Mexico came to the unhappy conclusion that the country could achieve national unity and strength only through a vigorous reassertion of Hispanic, Catholic, and royalist tradition. They also maintained that Mexico would be able to resist further encroachments by the United States only with protection from a European power—in this case France. (It was in this context, incidentally, that the whole concept of "Latin America" emerged: it was a deliberate effort by France to emphasize its solidarity with nations of the region.) In the 1860s Mexican representatives conspired with European sponsors to bring an Austrian prince, Maximilian von Hapsburg, to occupy a newly created "imperial" throne. The ill-starred reign of Maximilian and Carlota led to the exacerbation of an already bitter civil war between "conservatives" and "liberals" in Mexico and concluded with the emperor's execution in 1867.

Eyes upon Cuba

The United States coveted Cuba throughout the nineteenth century. With its tobacco and sugar production, its thriving commerce, and—especially—its strategic location in the Caribbean, "the pearl of the Antilles" offered numerous and tempting advantages. Over time, the United States developed a two-pronged policy: one goal was to prevent the transfer of Cuba to any European power other than Spain; the other was to take over the island directly.

Thomas Jefferson confidently regarded Cuba as a proper limit for U.S. territorial expansion, proposing the erection of a sign at the southern tip of the island saying *Nec plus ultra* ("Not beyond here"). And as Secretary of State John Quincy Adams viewed the hemisphere in 1823, he observed that Cuba and Puerto Rico comprised "natural appendages to the North American continent. . . . It is scarcely possible," he wrote, "to resist the conviction that the annexation of Cuba to our federal republic will be indispensable to the continuance and integrity of the Union itself." Eventually, Adams surmised, this would occur as a result of natural forces:

> . . . there are laws of political as well as physical gravitation; and if an apple severed by the tempest from its native tree cannot choose but fall to the ground, Cuba, forcibly disjoined from its own unnatural connection with Spain, and incapable of self-support, can gravitate only towards the North American Union, which by the same law of nature cannot cast her off from her bosom.

In other words, the United States had only to await Cuba's liberation from Spain. Once that occurred, laws of political gravitation would bring the island naturally and inevitably into the fold of the United States.

Campaigns for outright annexation surged in the 1840s and 1850s. Celebrating the conclusion of the Mexican War, journalist John L. O'Sullivan wrote to Secretary of State James Buchanan in March 1848:

> Surely the hour to strike for Cuba has come. . . . Fresh from our Mexican triumphs, glories and acquisition, the inevitable necessity for which the United States must sooner or later have Cuba, will force itself on the minds of the Spanish Ministry. . . . We will give great moral force to the party whose measure it will be, as contributing to prove to be the true American party, the party entrusted by God and Nature with the mission of American policy and destiny.

Having staked his presidency upon expansionist principles, President Polk promptly authorized negotiations for the purchase of Cuba.

Complications ensued. A Venezuelan adventurer, General Narciso López, proposed to conquer the island and present it to the United States. Though López was defeated by Spanish forces, England and France ex-

pressed alarm over American filibustering and proposed a tripartite agreement to guarantee that Cuba would stay under Spain. Serving as secretary
of state under President Millard Fillmore, Edward Everett not only declined to participate but seized the opportunity to reflect upon the situation of the hemisphere. English and French acquisitions in Africa and
elsewhere "have created no uneasiness on the part of the United States,"
Everett explained, just as U.S. accessions "have probably caused no uneasiness to the great European powers, as they have been brought about by the
operation of natural causes, and without any disturbance of the international relations of the principal states." To this extent, Europeans and
Americans were complying with the informal codes of the imperial contest.
Everett contended that the transfer of Cuba to any European power other
than Spain would disturb this equilibrium, however, since "it would indicate designs in reference to this hemisphere which could not but awaken
alarm in the United States." The destiny of Cuba was therefore "mainly an
American question," and the idea of a tripartite convention was wholly
inappropriate:

> The project rests on principles applicable, if at all, to Europe, where interna-
> tional relations are, in their basis, of great antiquity, slowly modified, for the
> most part, in the progress of time and events; and not applicable to America,
> which, but lately a waste, is filling up with intense rapidity, and adjusting on
> natural principles those territorial relations which, on the first discovery of the
> continent, were in good degree fortuitous.

While Europe should refrain from pronouncements or actions on Cuba,
the United States was unwilling to renounce all possibility of future claims.
The island was of such strategic importance, Everett insisted, that annexation someday "might be almost essential to our safety." In modern par-
lance, Cuba was a national security issue.

The United States continued its search for opportunities. In 1854 the
otherwise undistinguished President Franklin Pierce instructed the U.S.
minister to Spain, Pierre Soulé of Louisiana, to make a new offer to purchase the island or, if unsuccessful, to initiate efforts to "detach" Cuba from
Spain. Consequently plotting to overthrow the Spanish monarchy, Soulé
received instructions to consult with U.S. ministers to England and
France. This ebullient threesome embodied its recommendations in a dispatch known as the Ostend Manifesto. The ministers began with a solemn
vow that the United States should make every effort to acquire Cuba with
Spanish "consent," presumably through purchase. If this could not be
accomplished, however, "we shall be justified in wresting it from Spain if
we possess the power; and this upon the very same principle that would
justify an individual in tearing down the burning house of his neighbor if
there were no other means of preventing the flames from destroying the
home." As demonstrated by Haiti's continuing intimidation of the Dominican Republic, a slave revolt in Cuba could also pose a menace to racial
purity.[4] "We should," the ministers continued,

be recreant to our duty, be unworthy of our gallant forefathers, and commit base treason against posterity, should we permit Cuba to be Africanized and become a second St. Domingo, with all its attendant horrors to the white race, and suffer the flames to enter our own neighborhood shores, seriously endanger or actually to consume the fair fabric of our Union.

To maintain the "fair fabric" of American society and to protect its shores from hostile intrusions, the United States must acquire Cuba without delay. If Spain stubbornly rejected U.S. overtures, it would bear responsibility for the result. The Ostend Manifesto was an ultimatum.

Confronted by news leaks and anxious to maintain good public relations with Spain, the Pierce administration promptly disavowed the document. Yet the ensuing embarrassment proved to be short-lived: one of its signatories, James Buchanan, became the next president of the United States.

By the late 1850s the whole question of Cuba became embroiled in domestic sectional controversy, as the North objected to the prospect of admitting a new slave state. The U.S. Civil War and its outcome temporarily removed the issue from the political agenda. Cuba returned to the forefront in the late 1860s, when rebels launched the Ten Years' War against Spanish colonial rule and prompted Ulysses S. Grant to proclaim in 1869 what came to be known as the "no-transfer principle." Casting a nervous eye on England and France, the president huffed: "These dependencies are no longer regarded as subject to transfer from one European power to another." The issue faded with Spain's defeat of rebels in the Ten Years' War. It was not until the 1890s that Cuba would recapture national attention.

U.S. Imperialism II: Commercial Empire

Toward the end of the nineteenth century the United States shifted its strategy toward Latin America. After intense soul-searching and debate over principles and methods of expansion, Washington turned principally from the acquisition of territory to the creation of a sphere of interest, extending U.S. hegemony through an informal network of economic and political relations. There were several reasons for this change. One was demographic reality: these new areas were either unsuitable for European immigration or already populated by peoples of indigenous, African, or Iberian heritage. According to the racist doctrines of the era, to be explored in chapter 2, this made them unfit for incorporation into the predominantly Anglo-Saxon society of the United States. Second was a reevaluation of the global imperial contest, with its growing emphasis on commercial advantage instead of territorial reach. Third was a realization that imperialism, in the European sense, was an expensive proposition: as the British would discover in India and elsewhere, it required substantial expenditures of military and administrative capacity. By the late nineteenth century it was becoming apparent that with foresight and fortune it might be possible to obtain the benefits of imperialism without assuming all its costs.

United States leaders confronted two key challenges within the hemisphere. One was Europe's political domination of the Caribbean Basin. In the mid-1890s, as shown in Figure 2, the Caribbean was essentially a European lake. With the exception of Hispaniola (shared by Haiti and the Dominican Republic),[5] every single island was a European colony. Spain still held possession of Cuba and Puerto Rico; Britain held Jamaica, part of the Virgin Islands, Grenada and several of the leeward islands, as well as the mainland dominions of British Honduras and British Guiana; France held Martinique, Guadeloupe, and French Guiana; the Dutch held several islands, including St. Maartens, plus Dutch Guiana on the northern fringe of South America. No wonder European leaders ridiculed the Monroe Doctrine.

The second challenge came from Europe's commercial position. The United States had a strong presence around the greater Caribbean Basin, especially in Cuba and Mexico, but Europe was preeminent in South America (see Table A1 in the statistical appendix). As of 1913 Great Britain was the leading overall trade partner for Argentina, Chile, and Peru, and it was the largest source of imports for Brazil. Germany and France both had important commercial relations with Argentina and Brazil. Throughout southern South America, the United States was a relatively minor source of commerce—and of political influence. As writer and publicist William Eleroy Curtis would exclaim to the U.S. Congress in 1886, the benefits of economic growth in that southernmost region were going almost exclusively to "the three commercial nations of Europe"— England, France, and Germany—which "have secured a monopoly of the trade of Spanish America . . . [and] the Englishmen," Curtis gravely warned, "have the Brazilians by the throat." In the 1890s Benjamin F. Tracy, secretary of the navy, sounded a similar alarm: "Commercial supremacy by a European power in . . . the Western Hemisphere means the exclusion of American influence and the virtual destruction, as far as that state is concerned, of independent existence. With the great maritime powers it is only a step from commercial control to territorial control."

Investments offered a similar picture. During the nineteenth century the United States, itself a debtor nation, was in no position to export much capital to Latin America. England had taken up the slack, making long-term investments in Brazil and Argentina—and following through with spurts of new investment in the 1870s and the 1890s. By 1914 Britain alone held more than half of all foreign investments in Latin America. France supplied substantial capital during the 1880s and after the turn of the century; during the period 1910–13, in fact, over 45 percent of French overseas investments were directed toward Latin America. Germany joined the race in the 1890s, and by the turn of the century Latin American investments represented over one-third of all Germany's assets abroad.

In the meantime, U.S. policymakers insisted on the need to expand export markets. As the post–Civil War economy continued its headlong rush toward industrial growth, U.S. exports had grown from a minuscule $392 million in 1870 to $1.3 billion by 1900. This was only a promising start. "But today," cried Senator Albert J. Beveridge of Indiana in 1899, "we are raising more than we can consume. Today, we are making more than we can use. Therefore, we must find new markets for our produce, new occupation for our capital, new work for our labor." The hope was that increased trade would sustain steady growth, thereby avoiding the cycles of depression that had devastated the economy in 1873–78, 1882–85, and 1893–97.

To achieve this goal, polemicists and politicians called upon the U.S. government to develop and sustain a clear-cut economic policy, rather than laissez-faire reliance on the workings of the market. They argued that it was up to the Department of State to represent American commercial and financial interests in foreign lands, especially in Latin America. As the New York *Commercial Advertiser* asserted in 1898, we can now speak of "a new Monroe Doctrine, not of political principles, but of commercial policy. . . . Instead of laying down dogmas, it figures up profits."

A Sphere of One's Own: The Pan-American Community

In the late nineteenth century the United States began making vigorous efforts to institutionalize its rising claim to hegemony within the Western Hemisphere. In 1881 Secretary of State James G. Blaine, the "Plumed Knight" from Maine, issued invitations for an international conference to consider "the means of preventing war among the nations of America." (During 1865–70 countries of the Southern Cone had fought the long and bitter Paraguayan War, and in 1879 Chile and Peru had initiated their War of the Pacific.) As Blaine would later describe his intent, he had two purposes in mind: "first, to bring about peace . . . ; second, to cultivate such friendly commercial relations with all American countries as would lead to a large increase in the export trade of the United States. To obtain the second object the first must be accomplished." To assuage concern among Latin Americans and to distinguish the United States from England, Blaine explained that "Our great demand is expansion" but only of trade, rather than of territory. What he was seeking, in other words, was "what the younger Pitt so well called annexation of trade."

After President James A. Garfield's assassination Blaine was replaced as secretary of state, and his successor, Frederick T. Frelinghuysen, expressed open skepticism about any meeting where Latin American nations might outvote the United States. Yet Frelinghuysen supported the basic idea of consolidating a U.S. sphere of influence: "I am thoroughly convinced," he said in 1884, "of the desirability of knitting closely our relations with the States of this continent . . . in the spirit of the Monroe Doctrine, which, in excluding foreign political interference, recognizes the common interest of the States of North and South America." Commenting on recently

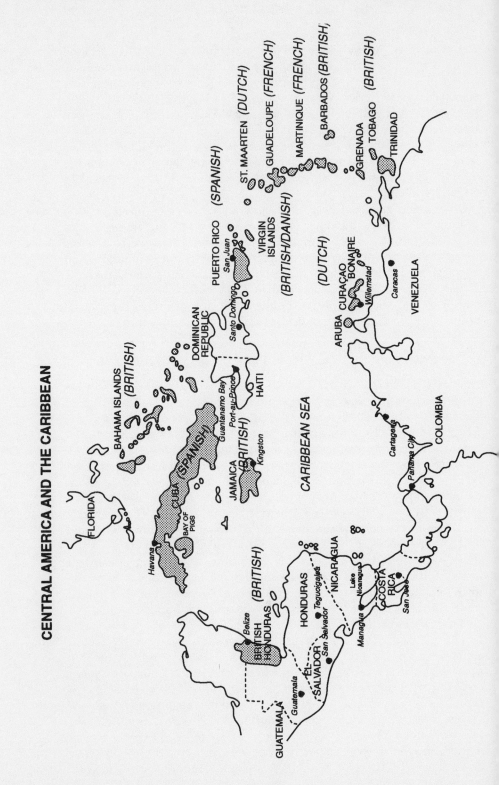

CENTRAL AMERICA AND THE CARIBBEAN

FLORIDA

BAHAMA ISLANDS (BRITISH)

Havana
CUBA (SPANISH)
BAY OF PIGS
Guantanamo Bay
Port-au-Prince

DOMINICAN REPUBLIC
Santo Domingo
HAITI

JAMAICA (BRITISH)
Kingston

PUERTO RICO (SPANISH)
San Juan

VIRGIN ISLANDS (BRITISH/DANISH)

ST. MAARTEN (DUTCH)
GUADELOUPE (FRENCH)
MARTINIQUE (FRENCH)
BARBADOS (BRITISH)
GRENADA
TOBAGO (BRITISH)
TRINIDAD

CARIBBEAN SEA

ARUBA
CURAÇAO (DUTCH)
BONAIRE
Willemstad

Caracas
VENEZUELA

Cartagena
COLOMBIA
Panama City

BRITISH HONDURAS (BRITISH)
Belize

GUATEMALA
Guatemala

HONDURAS
Tegucigalpa

EL SALVADOR
San Salvador

NICARAGUA
Managua
Lake Nicaragua

COSTA RICA
San José

30

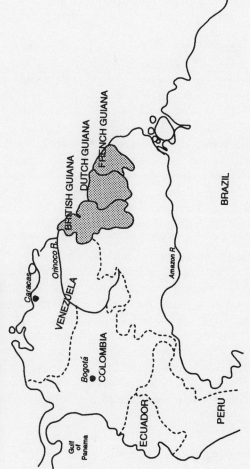

NORTHERN SOUTH AMERICA

Figure 2. European possessions in Latin America, mid-1890s. (The Falkland Islands, off the southern coast of Argentina, were also held by the British.)

concluded reciprocity pacts with Spain for increased trade with Cuba and Puerto Rico, Frelinghuysen expressed satisfaction that the accord would bring "those islands into close commercial connection with the United States [and] confers upon us and upon them all benefits which would result from annexation were that possible." The secretary also looked forward to a series of comparable agreements with nations of Latin America that "opens the markets of the west coast of South America to our trade and gives us at our doors a customer able to absorb a large portion of those articles which we produce in return for products which we cannot profitably raise." Like Blaine, Frelinghuysen saw the principal goal of U.S. policy toward the region as expansion of trade.

With Benjamin Harrison elected to the presidency in 1888, Blaine returned as secretary of state and took the opportunity to issue a second invitation for what had come to be known as a "Pan-American" conference. The agenda included not only the preservation of peace within the hemisphere but also commercial development and economic integration. Topics ranged from construction of a Pan American railway to the adoption of a common monetary standard. There was to be no contemplation of political or military alliances. At the conference itself considerable discussion focused on the possible formation of a customs union—which would oblige nations of the hemisphere to erect common tariffs on commercial products from outside the region. The idea was voted down, however, as delegates expressed concern over potential threats to national sovereignty.

The conference yielded scant material results. One was the creation of a Commercial Bureau of the American Republics—parent of the Pan American Union and, much later, the Organization of American States. Another, indirect consequence was a series of bilateral reciprocity treaties between the United States and nations of Latin America. Yet another outcome drew little notice at the time. During congressional debates over reciprocity Eugene Hale, a U.S. senator from Maine, proposed a measure that would have included Canada as well as Latin America in a common zone for free trade in raw materials. The idea gained few adherents, and Hale himself quietly withdrew it from consideration. It would reemerge in the century ahead.

Obtaining John Bull's Acquiescence

During the 1890s America's principal rival in Latin America was Great Britain. A number of episodes heightened tensions between the two powers. In the Chilean port of Valparaíso, for instance, two American sailors from the vessel *Baltimore* were stabbed to death during a saloon brawl in 1891. At first unable to obtain full satisfaction from Chilean authorities, President Benjamin Harrison threatened to take military action. But the real issue was not so much financial indemnity; it was international power. Chile was in the midst of political upheaval, and the United

States and Britain found themselves on opposite sides: Washington sided with the existing government, while the British supported anti-American rebels. The New York *Tribune* offered a clear view of the interests at stake:

> The danger to the United States in these crises arises from the disposition of Europeans to interfere, the while pretending that they are merely defending their own commercial interests. In Chili and the Argentine, the most progressive commercial countries of South America, we have permitted England to obtain monopoly of trade. We have talked lustily about the "Monroe Doctrine" while Great Britain has been building ships and opening markets. British subjects to-day hold a chattel mortgage over Chili and the Argentine. . . . No American who wishes his country to possess the influence in commerce and affairs to which its position among nations entitles it can be pleased with this situation.

The *Baltimore* affair was eventually settled in early 1892 when the Chilean government paid $75,000 as indemnity, but the implications lingered on: the United States and Britain were wrestling for supremacy in the Americas.

Subsequent encounters took place in Brazil and Nicaragua, but the most serious British-American confrontation resulted from the Venezuelan crisis of 1895–96. The precipitating conflict was a boundary dispute between Venezuela and British Guiana. At specific issue was control over the mouth of the Orinoco River, the trade artery for the northern third of South America. Venezuela requested international arbitration. Great Britain responded by augmenting its claims—now to include a region rich in gold deposits. Venezuela broke off diplomatic relations with England and appealed to President Grover Cleveland in Washington.

The United States had two major interests in this controversy. One was access to the Orinoco River. The other was political influence. In February 1895 the U.S. Congress announced its opposition to the British claims. In July 1895 Secretary of State Richard Olney couched a message to Whitehall in unusually blunt and provocative language:

> Today the United States is practically sovereign on this continent, and its fiat is law upon the subjects to which it confines its interposition. Why? It is not because of the pure friendship or good will felt for it. It is not simply by reason of its high character as a civilized state, nor because wisdom and justice and equity are the invariable characteristics of the dealings of the United States. It is because, in addition to all other grounds, its infinite resources combined with its isolated position render it master of the situation and practically invulnerable as against any or all other powers.

This passage has earned for Olney a dubious reputation in the history of inter-American relations. It is rarely remembered that after all this bluster the note concluded with a call for peaceful arbitration.

The British foreign minister, Lord Salisbury, responded with two separate messages. One refuted the assertion by Olney that the Monroe Doctrine comprised a part of international law; the other consented to the principle of arbitration. Ongoing crises in Europe, South Africa, and the Middle East finally compelled Lord Salisbury to consent to the creation of an arbitration board—with two Americans, two British citizens, and one Russian authority on international law. (No one had consulted Venezuela in the meantime.) After protesting, Venezuela was reluctantly allowed to have one member of the board.

By accepting arbitration, Great Britain was tacitly recognizing Olney's claim to American preeminence throughout the Western Hemisphere. And from that point forward, Britain would tend to align itself on the side of the United States, using U.S. power whenever possible to protect British interests in Latin America. Through the Venezuelan controversy, the United States had taken a major step toward the achievement of de facto hegemony in the Americas.

Securing the Caribbean

The Caribbean Basin remained a focal point for U.S. policy. As always Washington was eager to reduce, if not eliminate, the European presence in the area. The United States wanted to take advantage of promising opportunities for investment and trade. A related goal was the creation and protection of shipping lanes for U.S. commerce. Also compelling was a long-standing desire to construct a canal in Central America that would establish a link between the east and west coasts of the United States and, equally important, provide access to the alluring markets of the Far East. In view of widely accepted military doctrine, this plan bore geopolitical significance as well: as historian-publicist Alfred Thayer Mahan forcefully argued in such magisterial books as *The Influence of Sea Power upon History* (1890), naval power was the key to international influence, which meant that the United States required a two-ocean navy. A transisthmian canal would make this possible.

Spanish-Cuban-American War

The Cuban question returned to the fore largely because of efforts by anti-Spanish forces. The U.S. response to the depression of 1893 had major repercussions on the island: when the protectionist tariff of 1894 removed provisions for reciprocity, the Cuban economy collapsed. Plantations discharged workers in 1894 and 1895, owing to loss of the North American market, and rebellion quickly ensued. Led by the Maceo brothers in Cuba and inspired by writings of the exiled José Martí in New York, Cuban forces mounted a determined drive for independence from Spain. Chaos resulting from the military campaigns offered a short-lived pretext for intervention by the United States. In 1896 Congress declared that the U.S. government "should be prepared to protect the legitimate interests of our citizens, by intervention if necessary." By this time North Americans had invested more than $30 million in the island, including $8 million in mines and $12 million in plantations. A clamor for war was steadily intensifying. William Randolph Hearst, the creator of "yellow journalism," reportedly warned an overly scrupulous newspaper artist: "You furnish the pictures, and I'll furnish the war."

Resisting popular opinion, President Grover Cleveland refused to intervene. In June 1895 the White House issued a declaration of neutrality, tacitly acknowledging a state of belligerency in Cuba. And in April 1896, going one step further, Secretary of State Olney offered to mediate the conflict. The move was rejected by Spain, which then sought support from other European powers to forestall U.S. intervention. Madrid's overture fell on deaf ears: Britain was reevaluating its American policies in light of the Venezuelan crisis, France was unconcerned, and Russia was attempting to consolidate its growing influence in Korea and Manchuria.

As events unfolded, this became a triangular conflict—involving Spain, the United States, and the Cuban independence movement. The United States initially supported autonomy for Cuba under a reformed colonial regime, but this was not acceptable to Spain or to the Cubans. Spain wanted to maintain its empire, but this was not acceptable to the Cubans or to Washington. And the Cubans fought for independence, but this was not acceptable to Spain or the United States. In fact Madrid and Washington firmly agreed on denial of power to the Cubans. As the American consul wrote to the State Department in 1897, "All classes of Spanish citizens are violently opposed to a real or genuine autonomy because it would throw the island into the hands of the Cubans—and rather than that they prefer annexation to the United States or some form of American protectorate." He later observed that upper-class supporters of the Cuban rebellion were apprehensive as well: "They are most pronounced in their fears that independence, if obtained, would result in the troublesome, adventurous, and non-responsible class" seizing power.

By late 1897, with William McKinley as president, prospects for a negotiated settlement seemed fairly bright. Then struck two thunderbolts in early 1898. First, the White House came into possession of a confidential but careless letter from the Spanish consul, Dupuy de Lôme, who delivered himself of the opinion that McKinley was a weak, venal, and vacillating politician. Second, an explosion ripped through the U.S. battleship *Maine* in Havana harbor and took the lives of more than 260 American seamen. McKinley responded with an ultimatum, demanding an immediate cessation of hostilities by Spain and full reparations for the sinking of the *Maine*. As Madrid was preparing to accede, McKinley proceeded to recommend war anyway—"in the name of humanity, in the name of civilization, on behalf of endangered American interests." To his other terms McKinley now added a call for Cuban independence, which he knew the Spanish government could not accept.

As McKinley declared war on Spain, the question immediately arose as to whether Washington should extend recognition to the rebel forces. The president finally proclaimed, with uncommon clarity:

To commit this country now to the recognition of any particular government in Cuba might subject us to the embarrassing conditions of international obligation toward the organization so recognized. In case of intervention our conduct would be subject to the approval or disapproval of such government. We would be required to submit to its direction and to assume to it the mere relation of friendly ally.

Recognition of an independent government might impose unwelcome restrictions upon the United States. Like his predecessors, McKinley wanted to preserve complete freedom of action in Cuba.

Under orders from Theodore Roosevelt, assistant secretary of the navy, Commodore George Dewey promptly launched an attack on the Spanish fleet at Manila harbor in the Philippines. The rambunctious Roosevelt himself joined the fray, leading his "Rough Riders" in a much-publicized assault upon Cuba's San Juan Hill. The exhausted Spaniards proved to be no match for their American opponents, and the "splendid little war" lasted only a matter of months. According to the peace terms, Cuba attained independence from Spain. The United States assumed outright control of Puerto Rico and Guam and, for a payment of $20 million, the Philippine Islands as well (in these specific cases the United States established European-style colonies). What had started as a war to liberate Cuba, in the eyes of many, became a war to expand the American empire.

Cuba's independence from Spain did not mean independence from the United States. As the hostilities faded, Cuba fell under the direct administration of the U.S. War Department. And as Cuban leaders worked to establish a government, the United States in 1901 attached to Cuba's new constitution the so-called Platt Amendment, permitting the United States to intervene in the affairs of the island "for the preservation of Cuban independence, and the maintenance of a government adequate for the protection of life, property, and individual liberty." This provision was also ratified in a treaty of 1903. A sovereign nation in name, Cuba was in fact a protectorate of the United States.

Taking Panama

Major powers had long contemplated the possibility of constructing a canal through Central America that would connect the Atlantic and Pacific Oceans, eliminate the need for time-consuming and dangerous voyages around Cape Horn, accelerate commerce and trade, and revise the prevailing distribution of geopolitical influence. Initial plans dated back to the seventeenth century. By the middle of the nineteenth century, the United States and Britain sought to minimize friction resulting from their own competing claims by concurring, in the Clayton-Bulwer treaty of 1850, that any such canal would be a joint Anglo-American project. Like so many diplomatic accords, this one was made to be broken.

Attention focused principally on Nicaragua, whose lakes and rivers offered a promising site, and on Panama, a province of Colombia at the narrowest point on the isthmus. In 1878 the Colombian government authorized a French group under Ferdinand de Lesseps, builder of the Suez Canal, to dig a route through Panama. United States engineers continued to favor Nicaragua, and a North American firm received a contract to begin excavation in that country. Then came the financial Panic of 1893, when both groups ran out of money and quit.

Popular interest in Central America quickened as a result of the Spanish-American War. As a bitter internal struggle within Colombia was nearing its end in 1903, Washington dispatched troops to quell disorder in Panama. The resulting crisis eventually led to the Hay-Herrán treaty, an agreement that authorized the United States to build a canal in Panama. The U.S. Congress eagerly approved the document—but the Colombian legislature, unwilling to compromise national sovereignty, refused to go along.

The United States then fomented insurrection. With Roosevelt's full knowledge, Philippe Buneau-Varilla (the de Lesseps chief engineer) started laying plans for a separatist rebellion in Panama. As the uprising began, U.S. ships prevented Colombian troops from crossing the isthmus to Panama City. Within days Washington extended recognition to the newly sovereign government of Panama, and received Buneau-Varilla (still a French citizen) as its official representative. United States Secretary of State John Hay and Buneau-Varilla hastily signed a treaty giving the United States control of a ten-mile-wide canal zone "in perpetuity . . . as it if were sovereign." A pliant Panamanian legislature soon approved the document. As TR would reportedly boast: "I took the Canal Zone."[6]

Opened in 1914, the canal immediately became a major international waterway, and the Panamanian government began receiving steady annuities. The Canal Zone became a de facto U.S. colony, an area of legal privilege and country-club prosperity that stood in sharp and conspicuous contrast to local society. Outside the Zone, Panama developed the characteristics that typified Central America as a whole: dependence on agricultural exports (especially bananas), reliance on the U.S. market, and domestic control by a tightly knit landed oligarchy. Washington had established a protectorate that would help promote, protect, and extend its commercial empire. With the taking of the canal, the United States completed its century-long efforts to gain territorial footholds around the Caribbean Basin.

Recipe for Intervention

Effective maintenance of the U.S. sphere of influence required the exclusion of powers external to the hemisphere. In flagrant contravention of the Monroe Doctrine, however, naval forces from Germany and Great Britain launched an armed intervention against Venezuela in December 1902 to collect debts due their citizens. Italy soon joined the assault. As fighting intensified the Argentine foreign minister, Luis María Drago, urged Washington to proclaim its opposition to the use of armed force by any European power against any American nation for the purpose of collecting debts. It was Drago's intention, however naive, that this stipulation would become a multilateral inter-American policy, not a unilateral U.S. assertion.

The Roosevelt administration was unhappy with the European incursion, especially after an arbitral court decided largely in favor of the interventionist powers, but was also cool to Drago's idea of multilateral consultation. In 1904 the president finally responded with a proclamation: "Any country whose people conduct themselves well," Roosevelt asserted,

> can count upon our hearty friendship. If a nation shows that it knows how to act with reasonable efficiency and decency in social and political matters, if it keeps order and pays its obligations, it need fear no interference from the United States. Chronic wrong-doing, or an impotence which results in a general loosening of the ties of society, may in America, as elsewhere, ultimately require intervention by some civilized nation, and in the western hemisphere the adherence of the United States to the Monroe Doctrine may force the United States, however reluctantly, in flagrant cases of such wrong-doing or impotence, to the exercise of an international police power.

To avoid any pretext for intervention by Europe, in other words, the United States would assume responsibility for maintaining order in the hemisphere. And despite Drago's hopes, the United States would act on a unilateral basis.

This statement of policy became instantly known as the "Roosevelt Corollary" to the Monroe Doctrine. It was aimed at major extrahemispheric powers, assuring them that the United States would guarantee order (and fulfillment of obligations on debts) throughout the region, and also at the governments of Latin America, warning them that the United States would take military action in the face of "wrong-doing or impotence." The United States thus proclaimed itself a hegemon.

Roosevelt's bellicose stance gained widespread support from commentators and politicians throughout the United States. In 1909 one of the most distinguished journalists of the era, Herbert Croly, argued that hemispheric cooperation and solidarity would necessarily require interference and expansion:

> In all probability no American international system will ever be established without the forcible pacification of one or more centers of disorder. . . . Any international American system might have to undertake a task in states like Venezuela, similar to that which the United States is performing in Cuba. . . . The United States has already made an effective beginning in this great work, both by the pacification of Cuba and by the attempt to introduce a little order into the affairs of the turbulent Central American republics.

United States tutelage and power would bring development and democracy throughout the Western Hemisphere. Fittingly enough, Croly's book was entitled *The Promise of American Life*.

The mere proclamation of U.S. hegemony throughout the Western Hemisphere did not, of course, bring it into effect. Throughout the early twentieth century European interests would continue to play a major role throughout the region. Great Britain maintained colonies in the Caribbean and close commercial ties with Chile and especially Argentina. Germany would attempt to lure Mexico to its side during World War I through the Zimmerman Telegram, offering to restore lands lost during the "war of the North American invasion" in return for diplomatic and logistical support. With possessions of its own in the Americas, France would nurture cultural and intellectual ties throughout the region. Ultimately, it was a chain of events and processes in the global arena at large, not boisterous declarations of U.S. intent, that led to the eventual fulfillment of America's hegemonic pretensions.

2

The Gospel of Democracy

*We must Consider that we shall be a City upon a Hill, the eyes of all
people are upon us.*
    John Winthrop (1630)

*Cabalistic phrases [are designed to hold the citizenry] spell bound, as if
the lies of magic were realities and a syllable or two of gibberish could
reverse all the laws of nature and turn human intelligence into
brutishness. One of these is "Our manifest destiny," a shallow and
impious phrase. Who shall assure that it is not of the "Devil's
fetching." . . . Oh, miserable humbug of History!*
    National Intelligencer (1848)

A central tenet in America's national creed has endowed the United States
with a political mission: spreading the gospel of democracy throughout the
world. During the nineteenth century this belief served to legitimize imperial behavior and dignify unseemly conquests, at least in the eyes of the
beholders. Implicitly, the credo sustained the argument that Europe, monarchical and unrepublican, should stay out of the Western Hemisphere.
During the twentieth century it also provided a rationale for intervention
in the affairs of sovereign nations of Latin America.

    The basic purpose of this intellectual activity was to provide an expla-
nation and *justification* for U.S. imperialism, territorial and commercial.
Though ideas can acquire a life of their own, the driving goals of U.S.
policy toward Latin America were economic and political expansion. In

this context the role of ideology was to provide a cohesive interpretation of U.S. behavior, to imbue it with a higher purpose, and to present the issues at hand in satisfying and self-serving terms.

This was not merely an academic exercise. The persistent invocation of the ideals of democracy represented efforts to redefine the substance of conflict, to seize control of the agenda, to capture the terms of debate, and to shape the outcome of the struggle itself. Ideology tends toward simplification. By providing a "cognitive map" of reality, ideology reduces complex issues to straightforward and usually simplistic terms that not only provide a pleasing and coherent explanation but also suggest a prescription for action.

Regarding U.S. relations with Latin America, this rhetoric was aimed at three main audiences. One consisted of domestic society. For national leaders, the definition of U.S. policy as fulfillment of a higher mission could assist in the mobilization of resources. Everything else being equal, citizens preferred to believe that their efforts were serving some noble purpose rather than material self-interest. Ideology could also provide leaders with weapons for weakening and silencing domestic opposition. Objections to official policy would not merely express disagreement on tactics or strategy; they would constitute disloyalty.

The second audience consisted of rival powers, especially in Europe. The deployment of ideological rhetoric served to emphasize the importance of the matter at hand, warning outside rivals that interference on their part would tread on hallowed ground. Ideology underlined national purpose and will. At the same time it presented would-be rivals with an intellectual challenge. Unless they could produce an ideological rationalization of their own, one that was plausible if not superior, they would be discouraged from action. Throughout history, of course, imperial powers justified their actions in terms of a higher mission. Either they struggled for monopoly over claims to a single shared mission, as in the case of sixteenth-century Portugal and Spain; or they confronted each other and the international community with alternative declarations of purpose. In either event, ideological disputation remained part and parcel of imperialistic rivalry and contestation.

A third audience consisted of the subjugated societies. In this context, the role of ideological indoctrination—epitomized by missionary activities and educational campaigns—was to engender a rationale for acceptance by local peoples of new power arrangements. The colonized could interpret the new situation not so much as national (or societal) defeat but as a march toward higher truth. Special emphasis was placed on leadership groups and those who could serve as go-betweens (and who would usually benefit handsomely as a result). Ultimately, the achievement of voluntary acquiescence within the subordinate society was crucial to imperial power and to the imposition of durable hegemony. Otherwise rule must rest on the perpetual use or threat of force—which was costly, inefficient, and counterproductive. Ideology was serious business.

The Meaning of Manifest Destiny

Every nation has its own mythology. For the United States, the capstone idea has defined American purpose as a quest for national greatness and the promotion of political democracy. As Thomas Paine declared in *Common Sense,* his famous call for independence in 1776, "We have it in our power to begin the world all over again." This was not a modest claim. In the eyes of British (and other European) observers of the time, such brash expressions of self-importance must have looked preposterous.

America's emerging ideology drew a fundamental distinction between the New World and the Old, between America and Europe. These were to be two separate spheres. An early exponent of U.S. views on the world, Paine gave explicit formulation to this credo by stressing, first, the fact that immigrants had crossed the ocean precisely to escape from Europe: "this New World has been the asylum for the persecuted and the lovers of civil and religious liberty from *every* part of Europe." Second, Paine took notice of geography, especially the Atlantic Ocean, observing that "even the distance at which the Almighty has placed England and America is a strong and natural proof that the authority of the one over the other was never the design of heaven." And third, he combined historical with religious interpretation: "The time likewise at which the continent was discovered adds weight to the argument, and the manner in which it was peopled increases the force of it. The Reformation was preceded by the discovery of America—as if the Almighty meant to open sanctuary to the persecuted."

A central element in this mythology was belief in providential benediction. It was God in Heaven, not just earthly mortals, who endowed American society with its virtues and its purposes. The pursuit of national greatness therefore could not be a matter of choice. It was a sacred *obligation.* Just as sixteenth-century Spaniards persuaded themselves that they were performing God's will, so did eighteenth-century Americans and their descendants. It was incumbent upon them to act as they did; otherwise they could be committing sacrilege as well as treason.

This sense of heavenly mission led to an emphasis on national uniqueness, a fundamental belief in the exceptionalism of the United States. Not only was America distinct from Europe; as the bastion of democracy, it stood apart from other nations as a City on a Hill. With regard to foreign policy, this conviction encouraged contradictory impulses. On the one hand, it gave rise to the notion that the United States was exceptional, superior, a truly chosen land whose political ideals and institutions could (by definition) never flourish anywhere else. This was an isolationist idea. On the other hand, the sense of uniqueness shaped and defined the political obligation to spread the gospel of democracy. This was an activist idea. Imbued with this conviction, many American leaders could not rest content with the construction of a working democracy at home. They felt charged to *extend* the virtues of this idea to other parts of the globe, thus carrying out the divine task of political civilization.

Territorial expansion in the nineteenth century required and reinforced a righteous definition for U.S. national purpose. As President James K. Polk contested Britain's claim to the Oregon territory and prepared for war in Mexico during the 1840s, a young newspaper editor named John L. O'Sullivan invoked providential will. The U.S. claim, he asserted in the *New York Morning News,* "is by the right of our manifest destiny to overspread and to possess the whole of the continent which Providence has given us for the development of the great experiment of liberty and federated self-government entrusted to us." Cast in these terms, it was America's mission to democratize the continent.

Thus emerged the idea of "manifest destiny." This was more than a catchphrase or slogan. It was a concept that crystallized a sense of national purpose, providing both an explanation and a rationalization for U.S. territorial expansion. The seizure of lands represented not avarice but "destiny," a Heaven-sent fate that mere mortals could neither prevent nor ignore. This destiny was moreover clearly "manifest," a self-evident truth that was plain for all to see. Of course this assertion was not subject to empirical proof or verification. It was held to be transparently true, and it was therefore not a subject for argumentation.

O'Sullivan's newspaper eagerly applied the implications of the doctrine to the Texas question. As debate mounted over the possible incorporation of Texas into the Union, the *New York Morning News* in 1845 blithely interpreted its annexation as a logical expression of historical processes:

> From the time that the Pilgrim Fathers landed on these shores to the present moment, the older settlements have been constantly throwing off a hardy, restless and lawless pioneer population, which has kept in advance, subduing the wilderness and preparing the way for more orderly settlers who tread rapidly upon their footsteps. . . . As their numbers increased, law and order obtained control, and those unable to bear constraint sought new homes. These latter have rolled forward in advance of civilization, like the surf on an advancing wave, indicative of its restless approach. This is the natural, unchangeable effect of our position upon this continent, and it must continue until the waves of the Pacific have hemmed in and restrained the onward movement.

Thus did the *Morning News* resolve doubts about the validity of annexation. Tongue in cheek, the editorial also proffered an olive branch to Mexico: if the country permitted itself to be overtaken by the "Anglo-Saxon race," it, too, would become able to apply for admission to the United States.

Recurring themes in these debates were the invocation of divine purpose and the spreading of democracy. As Illinois congressman John Wentworth is recorded to have said in 1845:

> He did not believe the God of Heaven, when he crowned the American arms with success [in the Revolutionary War], designed that the original States

should be the only abode of liberty on the earth. On the contrary, he only designed them as the great center from which civilization, religion, and liberty should radiate and radiate until the whole continent shall bask in their blessing.

Expansion of the nation and the diffusion of democracy over the "whole continent" represented God's will and therefore the national mission. At issue was not the acquisition of territory, land, and natural resources; it was fulfillment of a divine plan.

Not surprisingly, there existed some uncertainty about precise boundaries for the extension of this enterprise. Some commentators cast longing eyes on Canada; others claimed that the United States should take all of Mexico. As Daniel S. Dickinson of New York proclaimed in the Senate, during deliberations over the Treaty of Guadalupe Hidalgo, the United States still had some way to go: "New territory is spread out for us to subdue and fertilize; new races are presented for us to civilize, educate and absorb; new triumphs for us to achieve for the cause of freedom. North America presents to the eye one great geographical system. . . . And the period is by no means remote, when . . . [North America] shall be united . . . in one political system, and that, a free, confederated, self governed Republic." Others went even farther. Editor James Gordon Bennett would assert in the *New York Herald,* in 1845, that "the arms of the republic . . . must soon embrace the whole hemisphere, from the icy wilderness of the North to the most prolific regions of the smiling and prolific South." Anglo-Saxons and their "free institutions" were plainly on the march.

The prospect of manifest destiny encompassed significant subthemes. One stressed the notion of America's youth, in implicit contrast to the decrepit Old World of Europe. "Too young to be corrupt," in the words of the *United States Journal,* "it is Young America, awakened to a sense of her own intellectual greatness and her soaring spirit." Fresh, eager, innocent, the United States was coming into its own as a power. Another subtheme challenged European principles of international law, codes that had arisen to regulate intercourse among nations and to sustain the post-Westphalian balance of power. Indeed, O'Sullivan explicitly dismissed "all those antiquated materials of old black-letter international law" in his initial promulgation of the doctrine. Within the Western Hemisphere, in short, the United States would not be constrained by classical rules of law. They applied only to Europe, not to the Americas.

Yet another subtheme stressed not only democratic principles in abstract form but the particular virtues of states' rights. According to O'Sullivan and his cohorts, governmental federation offered an ideal formula for territorial expansion through the incorporation of new states, one at a time: "How magnificent in conception!" O'Sullivan exclaimed. "How beneficent in practice is this system, which associates nations in one great family compact, without destroying the social identity, or improperly constraining the individual genius of any; and cements into elements of strength and civilization those very sources of difference which have heretofore destroyed the peace of mankind!" New states could join the Union without upsetting the structure of government. Added a writer in the *Democratic Review,* the discovery of such a benevolent prescription could only be "an emanation from Providence." God spoke in clear as well as mysterious ways.

Despite its vigor, the summons to manifest destiny contained a good deal of ambiguity. One source of uncertainty concerned the question of inevitability versus agency, passivity versus activism. To what extent was the American future already foreordained, and therefore bound to occur as the result of automatic processes? Or would it require decisive action on the part of leaders and citizens? Characteristically, the issue acquired its most explicit form in debates over the need for military action. In discussions over the Oregon question, John C. Calhoun, soon to oppose the war with Mexico, gave clear expression to the passive school of thought:

> *Time* is acting for us; and, if we shall have the wisdom to trust its operation, it will assert and maintain our right with resistless force, without costing a cent of money, or a drop of blood. . . . Our population is rolling toward the shores of the Pacific with an impetus greater than what we realize.

After all, one might have argued, if the nation truly had a "destiny," and a "manifest" one at that, why not simply await its arrival?

On the other side, war hawks expressed no apprehensions about military intervention. Destiny was something to be seized, not passively awaited. As hostilities mounted with Mexico, the definition of national purpose broadened in scope. In his annual message of 1847 Polk declared that U.S. action now had a political goal, the prevention of monarchy in Mexico. That same year the *Boston Times* proclaimed that military conquest by the United States would bring untold benefits to Mexico:

> The "conquest" which carries peace into a land where the sword has always been the sole arbiter between factions equally base, which institutes the reign of law where license has existed for a generation; which provides for the education and elevation of the great mass of people, who have, for a period of 300 years been the helots of an overbearing foreign race, and which causes religious liberty, and full freedom of mind to prevail where a priesthood has long been enabled to prevent all religion save that of its worship,—such a "conquest," stigmatize it as you please, must necessarily be a great blessing to the conquered. It is a work worthy of a great people, of a people who are about to regenerate the world by asserting the supremacy of humanity over the accidents of birth and fortune.

Echoed Moses Y. Beach, editor of the New York *Sun:* "The [Mexican] race is perfectly accustomed to being conquered, and the only lesson we shall teach is that our victories will give liberty, safety, and prosperity to the vanquished, if they know enough to profit by the appearance of our stars.

To *liberate* and *ennoble*—not to *enslave* and *debase*—is our mission." War thus offered the key to fulfillment of national purpose.

The greater the degree of military action, in other words, the more expansive the definition of national purpose. At the outset of the Mexican War, the concept of manifest destiny applied to areas of Mexico—ultimately from Texas to California—that would be taken from the country and incorporated into the United States. As U.S. troops hammered their way into Mexico City, however, there emerged yet another intention, the liberation and democratization of Mexico. Years later a sophisticated and skeptical observer, James Russell Lowell, would neatly capture this relationship: the deeper and deeper the military penetration, he wrote in the *Biglow Papers,* "our Destiny higher an' higher kep' mountin'."

Obstacles to Democracy: History and Character

Spreading the gospel of democracy would be no easy task, as U.S. leaders clearly recognized. And in nineteenth-century perspective, Latin America looked like unpromising soil. One line of reasoning focused on the trajectory of Latin America's history, on the forces giving shape to what would now be called political culture. Prominent among these were the character of Spain, the influence of Catholicism, and the effects of climate. And absolutely crucial, as explained below, was the difficult question of race.

A skeptical view of Latin America's capacity for democracy came from Thomas Jefferson as early as 1811, as he reflected on the wars for independence from Spain. "Another great field of political experiment is opening," Jefferson wrote to Dupont de Nemours, and yet

> I fear the degrading ignorance into which their priests and kings have sunk them, has disqualified them from the maintenance or even knowledge of their rights, and that much blood may be shed for little improvement in their condition. Should their new rulers honestly lay their shoulders to remove the great obstacles of ignorance, and press the remedies of education and information, they will still be in jeopardy until another generation comes into place, and what may happen in the interval cannot be predicted, nor shall you or I live to see it. In these cases I console myself with the reflection that those who will come after us will be as wise as we are, and as able to take care of themselves as we have been.

It would take at least a generation to uproot the legacies of monarchism and Catholicism. Jefferson was particularly harsh on the impact of the Catholic Church. In 1813 he would surmise that "History, I believe, furnishes no example of a priest-ridden people maintaining a free civil government. This marks the lowest grade of ignorance, of which their civil as well as religious leaders will always avail themselves for their own purposes."

John Quincy Adams, eventual author of the Monroe Doctrine, advocated a constructive but cautious stance toward Spanish American independence. The promotion of democracy "by all the moral influence which we can exercise, whether by example, of friendly counsel, or of persuasion, is among the duties which devolve upon us in the formation of our future relations with our southern neighbors." Faced with pressure to extend diplomatic recognition to the new republics, the secretary of state expressed doubt that U.S. influence would have much positive effect: "I wished well to their cause," he carefully explained,

> but I had seen and yet see no prospect that they would establish free or liberal institutions of government. . . . They have not the first elements of good or free government. Arbitrary power, military and ecclesiastical, was stamped upon their education, upon their habits, and upon all their institutions. Civil dissension was infused into all their seminal principles. War and mutual destruction was in every member of their organization, moral, political, and physical. I had little expectation of any beneficial result to this country from any future connection with them, political or commercial.

The less the contact, the better for the United States. Intercourse could only bring contamination.

A more optimistic assessment came from Henry Clay of Kentucky, who consistently promoted the granting of diplomatic recognition to the newly independent countries of the region. His argument had two contentions. One focused on the international arena, maintaining that new governments throughout the region "would be animated by an American feeling, and guided by an American policy," even if dictatorial in form. They would thus provide a bulwark against European influence. The other focused on domestic political processes, holding that cooperation would lead to democratization in Spanish America through a kind of demonstration effect. By granting diplomatic recognition, Clay predicted,

> We should become the center of a system which would constitute the rallying point of human wisdom against all the despotism of the Old World. Did any man doubt the feelings of the South toward us? In spite of our coldness toward them, of the rigor of our laws, and the conduct of our officers, their hearts still turned toward us, as to their brethren; and he had no earthly doubt, if our Government would take the lead and recognize them, that they would become yet more anxious to imitate our institutions, and to secure to themselves and their posterity the same freedom which we enjoy.

Recognition would lead to diplomatic cooperation, which would in turn promote democracy. When all was said and done, however, Clay's grandiose formula called for relatively modest measures by the United States.

Territorial expansion, especially the war with Mexico and anticipations of Cuba, required an activist doctrine. It was essential, in light of national mythology, for newly acquired lands and peoples to experience the blessings of democracy. In 1854 one enthusiastic legislator justified a potential military takeover of Cuba as an uplifting missionary enterprise:

> We absorb to elevate; we rule by bestowing on the governed a share of political power. Sir, we are destined to expand by assimilation, and by elevating those who have been misgoverned and oppressed to the rank of free-

men. . . . We conquer that we may raise the conquered to an equality with ourselves; we annex to assimilate others with us on a higher scale of humanity.

Acquisition was thus an act of liberation for the "misgoverned and oppressed." Once incorporated into the United States, they would be free to climb upward to "a higher scale of humanity." Others saw persisting problems with the pearl of the Antilles. "The people of Cuba speak a different language," one congressman later recounted, "they profess a different religion, and they are of different extraction from us; and our people have regarded them as aliens and outlaws from the pale of humanity and civilization. . . . I think I have been at more respectable weddings than it would be to bring her into the household [Laughter]."

In the late 1890s the imminence of the Spanish-American War prompted denunciation of Spain's historical record and, particularly, its cruelty to native populations thus reviving the "black legend" espoused by rival imperial powers in the sixteenth and seventeenth centuries. As one war hawk proclaimed:

> Spain has been tried and convicted in the forum of history. Her religion has been bigotry, whose sacraments have been solemnized by the faggot and the rack. Her statesmanship has been infamy: her diplomacy, hypocrisy: her wars have been massacres: her supremacy has been a blight and a curse, condemning continents to sterility, and their inhabitants to death.

This condemnation possessed a double edge. On the one hand, it provided a rationalization for war against Spain. On the other, it suggested that the legacy of such perfidious rule would severely impede the installation of democracy. This confronted U.S. leaders with an unsolvable dilemma: the worse the qualities of the opponent, the greater the need for military intervention—and the less the chance for democratic rule.

Climate presented yet another obstacle. Carl Schurz and other respected authorities forcefully argued that the tropics were unfit for democracy; instead they were conducive to laziness, licentiousness, and irresponsibility. When the U.S. Congress was considering how to deal with new territorial acquisitions, Richard F. Pettigrew, senator from the temperate state of South Dakota, rejected annexation of Hawaii in 1898 on the ground that "republics cannot live" in "tropical countries." And in subsequent debates on Puerto Rico, Representative James L. Slayden of Texas took it upon himself to formulate pseudoscientific principles, observing that "The Tropics seems to heat the blood while enervating the people who inhabit them." People who live within twenty degrees of the equator, Slayden solemnly concluded, "neither comprehend nor support representative government constructed on the Anglo-Saxon plan."

Obstacles to Democracy: The Problem of Race

More pervasive than concerns about historical formation and national character were preoccupations about race. These issues were closely interrelated, since racial composition was interpreted as a central feature of national character. In the view of nineteenth-century Americans (and many of their descendants), the conviction was unshakeable: nonwhite peoples were incapable of responsible self-government and were therefore unsuited to democracy.

The intellectual foundation for this conclusion rested not only on racial prejudice, as it did, but also upon a hierarchical notion of competence that reflected and expressed God's manifest will. At the top of this pyramid were Anglo-Saxons, the hardiest and strongest of all whites: "Out of all the inhabitants of the world," one polemicist boasted in the late nineteenth century, "a select stock, the Saxon, and out of this the British family, the noblest of the stock, was chosen to people our country." John W. Burgess, a well-known professor at Columbia University in this same era, confirmed as indisputable fact the contemporary notion that "there are vast differences in political capacity between the races, that it is the white man's mission, his duty, and his right to hold the reins of political power in his own hands for the civilization of the world and the welfare of mankind."

Asians of pure heritage, Chinese and Japanese, fell in the middle of this scheme; so did Spaniards and other southern Europeans. At the bottom were blacks and Indians, widely regarded as hopelessly beyond redemption. Mixed-bloods occupied an ambivalent position. Some observers regarded the mixture of races as a means of uplifting character and quality over generations; others denounced it as a path to degradation and perdition. In 1848 the *Cincinnati Gazette* expressed its considered opinion that, in general, mixed races "unite in themselves all the faults, without any of the virtues of their progenitors; as men they are generally inferior to the pure races, and as members of society they are the worst class of citizens." Standards for judgment involved not only racial background; they also demanded racial purity.

War with Mexico raised the problem of racial assimilation in clear and forceful fashion. Early in his career James Buchanan had denounced "the imbecile and indolent Mexican race." And as debate mounted in the late 1840s over ratification of the Treaty of Guadalupe Hidalgo, the *New York Evening Post* went straight to the heart of the problem:

> The Mexicans are *Indians*—Aboriginal Indians. Such Indians as Cortez conquered three thousand [*sic*] years ago, only rendered a little more mischievous by a bastard civilization. The infusion of European blood whatever it is, and that, too, infused in a highly *illegitimate* way, is not enough, as we see, to affect the character of the people. They do not possess the elements of an *independent* national existence. . . . Providence has so ordained it, and it is folly not to recognize the fact. The Mexicans are *Aboriginal Indians,* and they must share the destiny of their race.

Whatever its longevity, European and Spanish influence was negligible. As Indians, the Mexican people were beyond redemption—and therefore suitable only for conquest and servitude.

At the same time, racist formulations provided arguments for opposition to the war. John C. Calhoun, that redoubtable champion of states' rights and slavery, foresaw nothing but trouble in the annexation of Mexico, proclaiming that "we have never dreamt of incorporating into our Union any but the Caucasion race—the free white race. To incorporate Mexico, would be the very first instance of the kind, of incorporating an Indian race. . . . I protest against such a union as that! Ours, sir, is the Government of a white race." Only the "free white race" was capable of democratic government. The United States should therefore resist the temptation to seize control of Mexico.

Departing from similar racist premises, others came to advocate a compromise: their solution was to take as much land from Mexico with as few people as possible. The purpose of the Treaty of Guadalupe Hidalgo was acquisition of territory, according to the *Louisville Democrat,* not incorporation of citizens:

> Besides, we have by this treaty, not the best boundary, but all the territory of value that we can get without taking the people. The people of the settled parts of Mexico are a negative quantity. We fear the land, minus the people, is not worth much. We think all Mexico will fall, piece by piece, into this government; but then it must first be settled by a different population, and the union effected by other means than the sword.

In the long run, the United States could confidently await alteration of the ethnic composition of Mexican society. With this accomplished the entire country would fall, "piece by piece," into the control of the United States. Racial rearrangements would provide the key to imperial expansion.

Decades later the issue would again emerge. In reference to potential annexation of the Philippines, John W. Daniels, a senator from Virginia, expressed horror in 1899 over the prospect of assimilating "this mess of Asiatic pottage" into American society. Unfazed by such logic, annexationists turned the racist argument to their own advantage. Filipinos were indeed "a decadent race," according to Senator Albert J. Beveridge, but this simply defined the nature of the imperialist challenge. After Rudyard Kipling's notorious ditty on the "White Man's Burden" appeared in *McClure's Magazine* in 1899, Teddy Roosevelt concluded that it was "very poor poetry but made good sense from the expansion point of view." As Roosevelt and others saw it, the task was to provide tutelage for inferior races to prepare them for eventual democracy and civilization:

> The problem presented to us in the Philippine Islands is akin to, but not exactly like, the problems presented to the other great civilized powers which have possessions in the Orient. There are points of resemblance in our work to the work which is being done by the British in India and Egypt, by the French in Algiers, by the Dutch in Java, by the Russians in Turkestan, by the Japanese in Formosa.

Empires around the world were engaged in the task of uplifting inferior races. In this respect, Roosevelt conceded, the United States was just like any other imperial power.

As Beveridge asserted, the key political issue in the Philippines and elsewhere went far beyond the design of constitutions or the creation of competitive parties. "It is racial," he said with finality:

> God has not been preparing for the English speaking and Teutonic peoples for a thousand years for nothing but vain and idle self-contemplation and self-admiration. No! He has made us the master organizers of the world to establish system where chaos reigns. . . . He has made us adept in government that we may administer government among savage and senile peoples.

Here was, indeed, the White Man's Burden.

Fulfillment of divine obligation nonetheless raised a fundamental question: how to incorporate the newly subjugated peoples. The prospect of eventual citizenship ran directly into the problem of race. As Senator Henry M. Teller of Colorado explained, "I would a great deal rather make the Philippine Islands a colony, a province, a dependency, or whatever you may choose to call it, than to make their inhabitants citizens of the United States . . . that they shall stand before the law on an equality with all other citizens of the United States." Cuba, with its large black population, posed an even greater challenge. Southerners were especially quick to express apprehensions. Benjamin F. Tillman, a rural populist from South Carolina (fondly known as "Pitchfork Ben"), explained his opposition to outright annexation after the Spanish-American War in frankly racist terms:

> It was not because we are Democrats, but because we understand and realize what it is to have two races side by side that cannot mix or mingle without deterioration and injury to both and the ultimate destruction of the civilization of the higher. We of the South have borne this white man's burden of a colored race in our midst since their emancipation and before.

The burden, he warned colleagues from the North, would be heavier than they might expect.

Senators were listening. Orville H. Platt, author of the Platt Amendment, expressed fervent opposition to the incorporation of Cuba because "The people of Cuba, by reason of race and characteristic, cannot be easily assimilated by us. . . . Their presence in the American union, as a state, would be most disturbing." A few years later John W. Foster, who had served as secretary of state in 1892–93, would draw a clear connection between domestic and foreign policies: "With the negro problem in our Southern States pressing upon us for solution . . . do we desire to aggravate the situation by adding a million more of the despised race to our voting population?" Partly in response to such concerns, Cuba was granted independence—of the most nominal kind—in 1902. There continued to be occasional talk of annexation or incorporation after a due process of "Americanization," but the racial barrier presented a persisting obstacle. Commenting on an insurrection by Cuban blacks in 1911, one observer noted that "Cuba may need us, but we do not need the Cubans. They, as a mass, are a degenerate race lacking in all the instincts of civic pride or honor and utterly disregarding all moral obligations to themselves." Better to keep a safe distance.

In the end, racism bore a paradoxical relationship to U.S. imperialism. On the one hand, prejudicial disdain for colored peoples offered justification for the forceful acquisition of influence and territory. Since the resident nonwhite population was (by definition) unsuited to develop the land and construct a civilized society, that obligation—that "burden"—fell to members of the more highly endowed Anglo-Saxon race. On the other hand, the presence of nonwhite peoples in newly dominated lands posed the unwelcome possibility that they might have to be incorporated into American society, thus altering its racial composition and lowering its quality. Racism thus *promoted* imperialist expansion by the United States but also *restricted* it as well.

It was largely because of these ideological contradictions that, by the turn of the century, U.S. leaders turned away from the outright annexation of territory toward the construction of protectorates and colonies, which offered a permanent source of influence; or toward periodic episodes of military intervention, which provided regular (if intermittent) sources of influence. A commercial empire did not necessarily require a permanent military or administrative presence. By contrast, invasions and protectorates would prove cost-effective.

Intervention for Democracy

Between 1898 and 1934 the United States launched more than thirty military interventions in Latin America. (According to one quaint but telling definition, a military intervention consists of the dispatch of armed troops from one country to another "for other than ceremonial purposes.") There were varied motivations for these actions. One was the protection of U.S. economic interests, especially private loans to local governments. Another was the assertion of geopolitical hegemony, in keeping with the Roosevelt Corollary, thus assuring European powers that they need not meddle in the hemisphere; during and after World War I, protection of the Panama Canal assumed special importance. In all cases, the perpetual rationalization was that the judicious application of military force by the United States would lead to the promotion of democracy throughout the region.

This component of U.S. policy focused exclusively on the greater Caribbean Basin, including Mexico and Central America. As shown in Table 1, the United States launched major operations during this period in Cuba, the Dominican Republic, Haiti, Honduras, Mexico, Nicaragua, and Panama. (There were threats of intervention on other occasions as well.) Some of these, as in Mexico, were relatively short-lived episodes. Others led to military occupations of several years in duration. In Nicaragua, American forces occupied the country almost constantly from 1909 to 1934; in Haiti, U.S. troops lingered from 1915 to 1934; in the Dominican Republic, they established military rule from 1916 to 1924. The basic goal

Table 1. U.S. Military Interventions in the Caribbean Basin, 1898–1934

Country	Interventions
Costa Rica	1921
Cuba	1898–1902, 1906–1909, 1912, 1917–1922
Dominican Republic	1903, 1904, 1914, 1916–1924
Guatemala	1920
Haiti	1915–1934
Honduras	1903, 1907, 1911, 1912, 1919, 1924, 1925
Mexico	1913, 1914, 1916–1917, 1918–1919
Nicaragua	1898, 1899, 1909–1910, 1912–1925, 1926–1933
Panama	1903–1914, 1921, 1925

Source: Adapted from William Appleman Williams, *Empire as a Way of Life* (New York: Oxford University Press, 1980), pp. 136–142, 165–167.

of U.S. policy, as commentators repeatedly said at the time, was to convert the Caribbean into an "American lake."

At the same time, Washington insisted that it was fulfilling a high-minded political mission. The principal exponent of this view was Woodrow Wilson, who eventually defined his purpose in World War I as making the world safe for democracy. As for the hemisphere, Wilson would exclaim: "We are the friends of constitutional government in America; we are more than its friends, we are its champions." And then he sternly vowed: "I am going to teach the South American republics to elect good men!" Viewing democracy as a universal possibility, the southern-born Wilson was implicitly rejecting prejudicial theories about historical, religious, geographical limitations on the spread of political civilization. Through instruction, example, and the judicious application of force, even Latin Americans could learn the rules of democratic conduct.

Yet the conception of Latin American democracy, even for Wilson, had clear-cut limits. This was a period, it should be remembered, of substantial constraints on American democracy: women acquired the right to vote only in 1919, organized labor was struggling to assert itself, and racial segregation meant the virtual exclusion of blacks from political life. And in view of popular skepticism about the political capability of Latin American peoples, the United States had precious little interest in promoting highly participative politics throughout the region. Instead the preference, as political historian Paul W. Drake has pointed out, was for an "aristocratic republic."[1] The insistence was on the maintenance of law and order. The one thing to avoid was mass-based social revolution. One of the nation's leading diplomatic experts on the region, Adolf A. Berle, Jr., would sum up this point succinctly: "I don't like revolutions on principle."

Most U.S. interventions displayed a consistent pattern. Military forces would arrive amid considerable fanfare; depose rulers, often with minimal force; install a hand-picked provisional government; supervise national elections; and then depart, mission accomplished. The political key to these operations was the holding of elections—which, as tangible signs of democracy at work, justified both the fact of intervention and the decision to lift the occupation. United States supervision of these contests was often overbearing, sometimes to the point of preselection of the winner, but the holding of elections was an essential step in the process. As one U.S. ambassador explained to his bewildered British counterparts, the United States would intervene as necessary in Latin America to "make 'em vote and live by their decisions." If rebellions follow, "We'll go in and make 'em vote again."

This sequence first took clear shape in 1906, when Teddy Roosevelt used the Platt Amendment as justification for dispatching troops to Cuba and installing William Howard Taft as provisional governor. The United States undertook to annul the elections of 1905, enact electoral legislation, and monitor a vote in 1909. As TR defined the mission to Taft in 1907: "Our business is to establish peace and order on a satisfactory basis, start the new government, and then leave the island." The United States followed a similar course in Panama, diligently overseeing elections in 1906, 1908, and 1912 (at this point dispatching troops for this purpose). Nicaragua received the same treatment and provided an opportunity for expostulation of U.S. policy toward the region as a whole. According to an official declaration in 1912: "The full measure and extent of our policy is to assist in the maintenance of republican institutions upon this hemisphere, and we are anxious that the experiment of a government of the people, for the people, and by the people shall not fail in any republic on this continent." Tacit reminiscence of the rolling cadences in Lincoln's Gettysburg Address could only serve to emphasize the point.

There were efforts to enshrine promotion of democracy as hemispheric principle. In 1907 an Ecuadorean diplomat named Carlos Tobar proposed the so-called Tobar Doctrine, under which American nations would refuse recognition to de facto regimes that had entered office by deposing constitutional governments. And in 1913 the United States would propound the Wilson Doctrine, which went one step farther by calling for the nonrecognition of all unconstitutional governments in Latin America. The U.S. stand was resisted by former Argentine foreign minister Estanislao Zeballos, among others, who saw it as a pretext for continuing and arbitrary North American intervention in domestic affairs of the region. Multilateralism did not flourish in this political arena.

Taking Sides: The Mexican Revolution

The outburst in 1910 of a revolutionary movement in Mexico was deeply disturbing to Washington. American investors had profited handsomely under the decades-old government of Porfirio Díaz, which had, under the slogan of "peace and administration," promoted economic growth and political stability. Mexico was a source of special concern to the United

States—because of its size, its importance, and its geographical proximity. And as a result of its presence and power, the United States exerted considerable influence in Mexican affairs. Uncertain and hesitant, Washington first resisted the Mexican Revolution and then took halting steps to direct its political course.

Ambassador Henry Lane Wilson (no relation to Woodrow) began overtly meddling in Mexican national politics as early as July 1911. Expressing his contempt for the newly installed government of Francisco Madero, the U.S.-educated idealist who had prompted the overthrow of Díaz, Wilson complained bitterly of "disrespect for constituted authority . . . a defiance of the law . . . lack of respect for property rights, violence, and rapine. . . . The laboring classes have quit work," the diplomat said, "and are making demands . . . a formidable opposition is springing up against Mr. Madero [who] lacks in that decision of character, uniformity of policy, and close insight which is so essential."

In September 1912 the United States officially protested crimes against American citizens in Mexico. Ambassador Wilson avidly sought Madero's resignation from the presidency and threatened U.S. military intervention in the event that he refused (President Taft would not, however, endorse this act of blackmail). Unchastened, the ambassador then undertook negotiations with Madero's counterrevolutionary opponents, Victoriano Huerta and Félix Díaz. Shortly thereafter Huerta deposed and murdered Madero. While not directly responsible for this assassination, an accredited U.S. diplomat had campaigned actively against an elected president of Mexico and expressed no palpable remorse over his demise. This is not remembered as a happy chapter in U.S.–Mexican relations.

To its credit, the Taft administration withheld recognition from Victoriano Huerta. Woodrow Wilson continued this policy after his election in November 1912, vowing: "I will not recognize a government of butchers." When Huerta refused to succumb to U.S. pressure, President Wilson in April 1914 lifted an embargo on arms shipments to Mexican rebels, secured British cooperation for economic sanctions against the Huerta regime, and authorized a naval occupation of the port of Veracruz. His ultimate goal, Wilson proclaimed, was the installation of "an orderly and righteous government in Mexico."

The action proved counterproductive, as political groups throughout Mexico denounced the invasion as an unwarranted assault on national sovereignty. Huerta resigned in July 1914, more as a result of his deteriorating military position than because of U.S. pressure, and Wilson seized the face-saving opportunity to withdraw the troops from Veracruz. Perhaps as a result of this experience, Wilson began to comprehend the complexity of the Mexican situation and the logic behind its revolutionary imperative. A year later the U.S. president observed, "The first and most essential step in settling the affairs of Mexico is not to call general elections. It seems to me necessary that a government essentially revolutionary in character should take action to institute reforms by decree before the full forms of the constitution are resumed." In Mexico, social justice would become a necessary prelude to democracy.

At a later stage in the Mexican Revolution Wilson would dispatch another military mission. In March 1916 armed forces under Pancho Villa, who was feeling betrayed by lack of U.S. support, conducted a raid on the otherwise insignificant town of Columbus, New Mexico, killing eighteen American citizens and burning the town beyond recognition. In retaliation Wilson launched a punitive expedition under General John J. ("Black Jack") Pershing, who scoured the unhospitable countryside for months in an unsuccessful effort to apprehend the villainous Villa. The goal of this expedition was not to overtake a government or oversee elections, however; it was simply to capture and punish Villa. In early 1917 the fruitless expedition was withdrawn, and Pershing was rewarded for his failure with promotion to leadership of U.S. forces in Europe after Wilson finally entered World War I.

United States military responses to the Mexican Revolution had three related goals: inflicting punishment on transgressors Huerta and Villa, and weakening their political position; protecting U.S. interests; and promoting political stability. What is perhaps most striking about these episodes, in light of the high stakes involved, was the timidity of U.S. incursions. They were profoundly offensive to Mexican patriots, understandably so, but they were remarkably limited in scope. But as other countries in the Caribbean were discovering, the pursuit of "dollar diplomacy" by the United States could result in long-term military occupations.

Dollar Diplomacy I: The Dominican Republic (1916–24)

As implied by the Roosevelt Corollary, the United States expressed continuing concern over the prospect that European creditors would persuade their governments to take military action against financially delinquent countries of the Caribbean Basin in order to permit collection on debts. In this sense, economic instability threatened U.S. designs on consolidation of an "American lake." Military incursions by British, German, or French forces would clearly undermine U.S. hegemony. To forestall such possibilities, Washington encouraged U.S. banking concerns to assume the debts of these countries, usually in conformance with explicit treaties, and promised to assist the financiers in the collection of their payments. A standard procedure was for U.S. representatives to take charge of customshouses, which guaranteed timely payment on the rescheduled debts; a common corollary was long-term military occupation.

The Dominican Republic became one site for this scenario. In 1903 the San Domingo Improvement Company, a New York–based concern, purchased a public debt owed by the Dominican government to the Netherlands and, according to the agreement, obtained the right to collect customs. When the Dominican president decided to appoint his own customs board, the American company appealed to the State Department. As a result of ensuing negotiations, the Dominican Republic bought back its debt for $4.5 million—but if it was unable to pay, the United States could appoint a financial agent to take over the customs. When payments stopped, rumors began circulating that French and Italian vessels were on their way to collect their own debts by force. Accordingly, Secretary of State John Hay instructed the U.S. minister in Santo Domingo, Thomas C. Dawson, to suggest to the Dominican government that it "request" the United States to take over management of the customshouses. The Dominicans reluctantly assented, and Teddy Roosevelt eventually reached an "executive protocol" in February 1907 stipulating that the U.S. president would appoint a customs collector for the Dominican Republic, the U.S. government would afford military protection, and the Dominican government would neither increase debts nor lower taxes without the consent of the United States. Moreover, the American receiver-general was to pay off the Dominican debt with $20 million borrowed through the brokerage firm of Kuhn, Loeb & Co. To assure its payments to Kuhn, Loeb, the United States was entitled "to collect customs for fifty years." Under the terms of this 1907 agreement, the National City Bank of New York agreed to float a subsequent loan of $1.5 million to the Dominican government in 1914.

American financial control led to close political supervision. An uprising in 1911–12 led U.S. representatives to propose, for the sake of stability, the resignation of a provisional president. In September 1913 William Jennings Bryan, Wilson's secretary of state, assured Dominican rulers that the United States would uphold the country's "lawful authorities." If rebellious factions took power Washington would withhold diplomatic recognition and impound the Dominican share of customs receipts. Amid mounting tension the American minister in Santo Domingo arranged for new elections, which were held under the watchful eye of U.S. naval warships.

In 1916 a major insurrection prompted the landing of U.S. marines. The Dominican congress elected Francisco Henríquez y Carvajal as temporary president, but Washington refused to recognize his government unless he signed a new treaty granting U.S. control not only of customs but also of the treasury, the army, and the police. Henríquez y Carbajal refused, customs payments stopped, and deadlock ensued. In November 1916 Captain H. S. Knapp, in command of the U.S. marines, declared outright martial law. Knapp summarily ousted Dominican officials, dissolved the legislature, forbade elections, levied taxes, imposed censorship, and declared himself "supreme legislator, supreme judge, and supreme executor." This was, in fine, a military dictatorship.

Under the U.S. regime additional bonds followed in 1921 and 1922. Invoking the 1907 agreement, U.S. naval authorities took it upon themselves to assure American bankers that customs duties "shall be collected and applied by an official appointed by the President of the United States and that the loan now authorized shall have a first lien upon such customs duties." Since the 1922 loan was repayable over a twenty-year period, this implied that the United States would retain control of the Dominican customshouses until 1942. After another election U.S. troops withdrew from the country in 1924, but only when the new Dominican leaders agreed to ratify the acts of the military government and to place the command of local armed forces under American officers.

Dollar Diplomacy II: Nicaragua (1909–25)

A special consideration about Nicaragua was the ever-present issue of a transisthmian canal. There were questions about financial stability and American loans, as in the Dominican Republic, but the prospect of a waterway tended to dominate the bilateral agenda. Even after completion of the Panama Canal, Washington continued to express interest in Nicaragua—if for no other reason than to prevent an extrahemispheric power from winning a rival concession. United States authorities were also eager to secure a naval base in the Gulf of Fonseca. Nicaragua entailed security interests.

The Taft administration frequently conveyed displeasure over the rule in Nicaragua of José Santos Zelaya, a Liberal who strongly resisted foreign control in negotiations over a canal route. In 1909 the capricious Zelaya ordered the execution of two North American adventurers. Secretary of State Philander C. Knox denounced Zelaya as "a blot upon the history of his country" and expelled Nicaragua's ambassador from the United States. The following year U.S. support for an anti-Zelaya revolt helped force the president to resign. Nicaragua was in chaos; the treasury was empty; European creditors were clamoring for payment on their bonds.

In October 1910 the State Department appointed Thomas C. Dawson, fresh from his exploits in the Dominican Republic, as a special agent to Nicaragua with instructions to rehabilitate the nation's finances and "to negotiate a loan secured by a percentage of the customs revenues to be collected according to agreement between the two Governments, but in such a way as will certainly secure the loan and assure its object." Brown Brothers offered to float the Nicaraguan loan. Aboard an American warship, anti-Zelaya leaders consented to the so-called Dawson Pact, under which the United States would recognize their new Conservative government under several conditions: a constituent assembly would elect Juan José Estrada president and Adolfo Díaz vice president; a U.S.–Nicaraguan mixed commission would arbitrate outstanding financial questions; and a loan would be guaranteed by administration of the customshouse in ways "satisfactory to both governments." News about the Dawson Pact unleashed a storm of controversy in Nicaragua, and the nation's constituent assembly promptly adopted a charter expressly prohibiting such arrangements as the customshouse clause; under pressure from Washington, Estrada dissolved the assembly and called for new elections. Virulent protests forced Estrada to resign in favor of Adolfo Díaz. To keep Díaz in office, the United States responded by dispatching a warship.

By June 1911 a new bilateral agreement specified terms for authorization of $15 million in loans to Nicaragua, reaffirming U.S. control of customs. Nicaragua also pledged not to alter customs duties without U.S. approval. The first loan under this accord was floated in September, by J. and W. Seligman and by Brown Brothers; 51 percent of customs receipts would go to themselves, for service on the debt, and 49 percent would go to the government of Nicaragua. In December 1911 Colonel Clifford D. Ham arrived to take charge of customs, in violation of the constitution, and in May 1912 the American bankers assumed all liabilities for debts owed to a syndicate in London. In exchange for this favor the New York financiers insisted on their right to "apply to the United States for protection against violation of the provisions of this agreement and for aid in the enforcement thereof."

Liberals continued to reject Conservative rule. An uprising in July 1912 brought the arrival of U.S. troops under the colorful Smedley Butler and then led to a full-scale intervention. United States marines crushed the Liberal insurrection, established order, and oversaw elections—which were won, not surprisingly, by the congenial Adolfo Díaz. For twenty out of the next twenty-one years, U.S. marines would remain on Nicaraguan soil.

Combining concerns over debts and the canal route, the Bryan-Chamorro treaty in February 1916 called for a $3 million payment by the United States to Nicaragua in return for three concessions: (1) the exclusive right to construct a transisthmian canal, (2) a ninety-nine-year lease on the Great Corn and Little Corn Islands and on a naval base in the Gulf of Fonseca, and (3) a U.S. option to renew the naval base lease for an additional ninety-nine years. The $3 million would enable Nicaragua to pay off a large share of current debt. And for the United States, according to Colonel Ham, the Bryan-Chamorro agreement would forever eliminate "the danger of a foreign power seeking and obtaining those concessions," while it also forged "an important link in the chain . . . of preparedness and national defense, and the protection of our investment in the Panama Canal." In 1918 the two countries established a high commission on finances—with two Americans and one Nicaraguan. In effect, the United States created a protectorate in Nicaragua.

United States military occupation of Nicaragua led to conflict and tension. In February 1921 a group of U.S. marines wrecked the offices of a prominent newspaper. A clash in January 1922 resulted in the death of four Nicaraguan civilians. After payments to U.S. bankers were completed in 1924, Washington proceeded the next year to withdraw its troops, which were replaced by a constabulary—a force that was created, trained, and officered by Americans.

Dollar Diplomacy III: Haiti (1915–34)

As the crusading Wilson struggled with problems in Mexico, the Dominican Republic, and Nicaragua, he came to launch a long-term occupation in Haiti. The country was in disarray. With plantations long ago destroyed, wild coffee was the only export crop. The government had no money and was borrowing from anyone that would lend. Between 1908 and 1915 there were seven presidents and about twenty uprisings and insurrections. When President Vilbrun Guillaume Sam was torn limb from limb by a mob in Port-au-Prince in mid-1915, the U.S. marines invaded.

There were three reasons for the intervention. One had to do with loans from the ubiquitous National City Bank of New York. The fiscal agent for the Haitian government was Banque Nationale de la Republique d'Haiti, owned by the Banque de l'Union Parisienne, but the National City Bank itself possessed a 5 percent share in a new loan of 1910—and served as agent for a number of German and French bondholders as well. National City thus had considerable influence within the Haitian national bank. When the local government showed signs of defaulting on payments, National City representatives persuaded the Banque Nationale to withhold payments to the Haitian government—in hopes of provoking U.S. intervention. After Haitian authorities responded by issuing paper currency, they tried to retrieve a $2 million deposit at the Banque Nationale. Bankers requested assistance from Washington, and U.S. marines aboard the cruiser *Machias* seized $500,000 and transported it for safe-keeping to the National City Bank in New York.

A second motivation concerned foreign influence. France held the largest share of Haitian debt and therefore possessed a clear incentive to invade. At this point in World War I there was, as well, concern that Germany might attempt to take over Haiti. As Secretary of State Robert Lansing explained to Congress, the U.S. action was "designed to prevent the Germans from using Haiti as a submarine base." In the event, of course, both France and Germany were much too preoccupied with the European theater to devote much time or attention to Haiti.

A third concern focused on the Panama Canal, the protection of which was a national security interest. As in Nicaragua, U.S. authorities took action in Haiti with an eye toward Panama.

Thus the U.S.S. *Washington* steamed into Port-au-Prince, oversaw elections, and assured the victory of the obsequious Philip Sudre Dartiguenave. By August 1915 the State Department pressed by-now-familiar treaty terms on the new government: U.S. control of the customshouse, U.S. appointment of a financial adviser, a gendarmerie manned by Haitians but commanded by U.S. officers, and U.S. control over sanitation and public works. Haiti further agreed not to sell or surrender any territory "to any foreign government or power, not to enter into any treaty or contract with any foreign power or powers that will impair or tend to impair the independence of Haiti." And "should the necessity occur," according to the document, "the United States will lend an efficient aid for the preservation of Haitian independence and the maintenance of a government adequate for the protection of life, property and individual liberty." The treaty was to be in force for ten years, renewable for a second term "if, for specific reasons presented by either of the high contracting parties, the purpose of the Treaty has not been fully accomplished." Within a year of its ratification it was extended to 1936.

Acting through the gendarmerie, the so-called Garde d'Haiti, the United States erected an indirect form of military rule. In the midst of constitutional debates, American officers of the gendarmerie dissolved the national assembly in 1916 and arranged for new elections in 1917. When the resulting assembly refused to ratify a U.S.–sponsored constitution, reportedly drafted by the assistant secretary of the navy, Franklin Delano Roosevelt, the Garde dissolved the congress for a second time. To gain approval for the constitution, U.S. authorities then arranged for a national plebiscite in June 1918—an utterly farcical exercise that resulted in the charter's approbation by a vote of 98,294 to 769.

There were puppet presidents, Dartiguenave (1915–22) and Louis Borno (1922–30). But the real source of power came from the U.S. marines. In the words of Paul Douglas, later a distinguished U.S. senator from Illinois,

> The American powers over Haiti are in reality almost complete. American approval is needed for the enactment of laws, the revenues of the country are collected under the supervision of Americans, and the budget is drawn up by the American financial adviser. The financial adviser scrutinizes all vouchers and withholds payments that he believes to be not in conformity with the principles of the budget or with efficient administration. The control over the gendarmerie is in American hands, as are also the services of Health and Public Works, and Agriculture. Only Justice and Education are outside of American control.

Under the terms of additional loans, it became apparent that the United States might retain control of the Haitian customshouse well into the 1940s.

Indirect rule by American forces promoted precious little progress. United States–supported governments acquiesced in the imposition of Jim Crow–style segregation rules and reinstituted the long-hated *corvée* law, under which peasants could be drafted for road building. While accumulating a surplus on government accounts, thanks to careful management of customs receipts, U.S. authorities concentrated all their energies on debt repayment, rather than investments in infrastructure and education. The United States failed to train a civil service, improve agriculture, or change the political culture. "In fact," as historian Robert Rotberg has observed, "the marine occupation simply prepared Haiti for a renewal of dictatorship and instability."[2]

One justification for extension of the military occupation, and also for the inattention to democracy, came from racist doctrine. In 1921 a U.S.

diplomat carefully explained to his superiors key differences between Haiti and the Dominican Republic, which American marines would evacuate in several years:

> It is well to distinguish at once between the Dominicans and the Haitians. The former, while in many ways not advanced far enough for the highest type of self-government, yet have a preponderance of white blood and culture. The Haitians on the other hand are negro for the most part, and, barring a very few highly educated politicians, are almost in a state of savagery and complete ignorance. The two situations thus demand different treatment. In Haiti it is necessary to have as complete a rule within a rule by Americans as possible. This sort of control will be required for a long period of time, until the general average of education and enlightenment is raised. In the Dominican Republic, on the other hand, I believe we should endeavour to counsel rather than control.

The political difficulty posed by such racist contentions was that they offered no prospect for a gracious exit by U.S. troops. Here again was the principal conundrum of contemporary imperialism: how to exert effective control with minimal administrative and military costs.

Ultimately, the United States would welcome the chance to withdraw from Haiti. In 1930 Herbert Hoover appointed a joint U.S.–Haitian commission that recommended Borno's resignation and new elections, won by Stenio Vincent (1930–36). A relieved Hoover then began to expedite withdrawal, and in 1934 Franklin Delano Roosevelt ordered the complete evacuation of U.S. forces. The financial mission nonetheless stayed until 1941.

Promoting Democracy?

From the 1830s to the 1930s, despite high-minded rhetoric and ostensible nobility of purpose, not a single U.S. intervention led to installation of democracy in Latin America. For Mexico, the political consequence of military conquest and territorial dismemberment in the 1840s was the ill-starred importation of a European emperor. (The country would subsequently endure civil war and decades of dictatorship, but largely as a result of internal factors rather than American interference. Similarly, U.S. intrusions in the 1910s had relatively minor impact on the political course of the Mexican Revolution.) Fate was no kinder to the islands of the Caribbean. Under the vigilant eye of the Platt Amendment, Cuba oscillated between episodes of social protest and cosmetic pseudodemocracy that, in the 1930s, would be followed by long-term authoritarian rule. Nicaragua and the Dominican Republic would suffer comparable fates. And Haiti, perhaps the most desperate instance of all, would embark on a seemingly endless course of dictatorship when U.S. forces finally departed after nineteen years of military occupation.

There were several explanations for this dismal record. One dealt with the goals of U.S. policy. Stripped of rhetoric, Washington's actions had geopolitical and economic motivations. A primary purpose was to assert U.S. influence throughout the greater Caribbean Basin and, in so doing, to reduce if not eliminate the European presence. An additional and related purpose was to protect the business investments, especially the banking interests, that had become vital instruments of imperial expansion. A remarkably virulent condemnation of these unlovely motivations came in 1933 from none other than Smedley Darlington Butler, the flamboyant U.S. marine who reflected back on his career:

> I spent thirty-three years . . . being a high-class muscle man for Big Business, for Wall Street and the bankers. In short, I was a racketeer for capitalism. . . . I helped purify Nicaragua for the international banking house of Brown Brothers in 1909–1912. I helped make Mexico and especially Tampico safe for American oil interests in 1916. I helped make Haiti and Cuba a decent place for the National City [Bank] boys to collect revenue in. I helped in the rape of half a dozen Central American republics for the benefit of Wall Street.

Butler was said to be embittered by his failure to become commandant of the U.S. Marine Corps. He may also have felt that, in the absence of an ennobling mission, he and his troops had been abused and deceived.

A second explanation for the failure to achieve democracy derived from the methods employed by the United States. In keeping with the political myopia of the era, U.S. occupation forces made little effort to construct, strengthen, or bolster democratic practices or institutions. From time to time they oversaw elections, sometimes patently fraudulent ones, as much for the purpose of extricating themselves from unpleasant situations as for the goal of promoting pluralistic competition. And in each of the three countries with the longest U.S. occupations—Nicaragua, the Dominican Republic, and Haiti—Washington supervised the creation of local constabularies that would eventually become the agents of dictatorial repression. Not only did the United States fail to promote democratic development in Latin America; it could even be argued, with considerable reason, that U.S. military interventions tended to retard the prospects for political democracy.

The paucity of U.S. efforts in this area stemmed partly from ambivalence. While Woodrow Wilson and his cohorts espoused the universal applicability of democracy, policymakers in Washington—and U.S. citizens in general—had severe reservations about the political suitability, capability, and desirability of Latin American peoples. As a result of history, religion, and race, many Americans believed, Latin America was incapable of sustaining true democracy. Rather than waste time and effort on illusory hopes, analysts commonly argued, it made more sense to concentrate on law and order. The goal of stability thus came to replace the ideal of democracy. And if stability required an iron hand, that was neither the fault nor the responsibility of the United States.

From the early nineteenth century to the 1930s, in summary, the United States routinely deployed military power in the name of political democracy. From the formulation of "manifest destiny" to the adoption of Wilson's democratic crusade, American policymakers, legislators, scholars, and journalists justified the application of power as a means of propagating the gospel of democracy. It was Herbert Hoover, of all people, who would articulate the fundamental contradiction underlying these efforts. During a goodwill tour of South America in 1928, the then-popular president-elect promised that the United States would be respectful of national sensibilities and would endeavor to promote democracy in Latin America by example rather than by force. In fact, he said somewhat disingenuously, suppression of neighboring nations would be foreign to America's political tradition. "True democracy is not and cannot be imperialistic."

3

Mr. Roosevelt's Neighborhood

*That is a new approach that I am talking about to these South
American things. Give them a share. They think they are just as good as
we are and many of them are.*
Franklin Delano Roosevelt (1940)

*A new era of colonial ambitions, determined more by economic factors
than strictly political ones, is going to take charge of universal destinies.*
Oswaldo Aranha (1935)

The decade of the 1930s stands out as a golden era of U.S. relations with
Latin America. President Franklin Delano Roosevelt's proclamation of a
"Good Neighbor" policy marked an abrupt change in U.S. policy toward
the region. Washington withdrew military troops, refrained from intervention, and initiated a process of consultation and cooperation. The United
States began treating Latin American nations as sovereign entities, rather
than subordinates, as equal partners engaged in the collective promotion of
hemispheric interests. This new stance promoted goodwill and mutual
respect among countries of the Americas, according to conventional accounts, and its practical consequence was the achievement of nearly unanimous support for the United States throughout World War II. Being a
Good Neighbor turned out to be good policy.[1]

There is another way of viewing these events. Within the context of
the Imperial Era, the Good Neighbor policy can be seen not as a departure
from past practices but as the *culmination* of trends in U.S. policy toward
the region. In effect, FDR's stance reflected a hardheaded sense of *realpolitik* that promoted and protected the long-standing U.S. quest for hegemony throughout the hemisphere. In the name of nonintervention, the

Good Neighbor policy constituted yet another attempt to achieve, impose, and consolidate American supremacy.

The Good Neighbor concept recognized that political intervention and democratic proselytization à la Woodrow Wilson were ineffective, that the costs were greater than the benefits. At a time when most European powers were reducing their involvement in the Americas, it was no longer necessary or advantageous for the United States to engage in heavy-handed intervention. And to an increasing extent, the United States could apply economic leverage over countries in the hemisphere. As a result, Washington could now extract voluntary cooperation from Latin American governments through diplomatic and economic means. Instead of seizing territory or creating colonies or nurturing protectorates, the United States was using new instruments in behalf of time-honored goals. In essence, the Good Neighbor policy would amount to a declaration of triumph in the imperial contest.

The significance of the Good Neighbor policy derived from changes in the global arena. As a result of World War I, which severely interrupted commercial flows between Latin America and Europe, the economic influence of European powers was in marked decline. The United States seized the opportunity to accentuate links to the region: between 1919 and 1929 direct U.S. investments in Latin America climbed from $1.987 billion to $3.519 billion, while portfolio investments (bonds and securities) increased from $419 million to $1.725 billion. The Depression intensified this pattern. Latin American trade with Europe dropped sharply in the early 1930s, and despite the crisis in its own economy, the United States moved in to fill the gap.

Another major factor was the imminence of war. The rise of Adolf Hitler in Germany and his alliance with Benito Mussolini of Italy confronted Europe with the specter of fascism. Similarly, the emergence of a military-led government in Japan posed a looming threat to all of Asia. In this setting, extrahemispheric powers were hardly in a position to expand their influence in the Western Hemisphere—with the exception of the Nazis, who made vigorous efforts to establish footholds in South America. Most European nations had to concentrate their energies on grave and immediate challenges, including Hitler's military aggressions. This left the United States with a relatively free hand in its dealings with the hemisphere.

As a result of these developments, inter-American relations assumed primary importance for the United States. In the language of a State Department document of 1933, "among the foreign relations of the United States as they fall into categories, the Pan American policy takes first place in our diplomacy." Contrary to historical stereotype, the United States did not adopt an isolationist stance toward all world regions throughout the 1930s. While Washington refrained from major involvement in the European theater and strident voices in support of "America First" called for strict isolationism, the United States steadily increased its level of commitment and concern with regard to Latin America. In other words, the United States was consolidating its own sphere of influence.

Crucibles: Nicaragua and Cuba

As often occurs, the inception of a new U.S. policy emerged from the self-evident failure of a prior policy. During the 1920s, as explained in chapter 2, the United States dispatched troops frequently to Central America and the Caribbean, with long-term occupations in Haiti and the Dominican Republic—for the ostensible purpose of promoting democracy and (especially) imposing economic order. None of these episodes proved to be an unqualified success. It was the outcome of two other adventures, however, that marked a turning point in Washington's views away from military intervention. The first, and more important, took place in Nicaragua.

Nicaragua, 1927–33

During the 1920s Washington was casting wary eyes on Mexico, still emerging from its "Bolshevist" revolution of 1910. In 1923 the administration of Warren Harding agreed to provide diplomatic recognition to Mexico only in exchange for assurances to U.S. investors, especially petroleum companies. Shortly afterward the Calvin Coolidge administration expressed concern over prospects for large-scale land reform, while American Catholics expressed vehement opposition to anticlerical tendencies within the revolution and the constitution of 1917. A source of manifold dangers, Mexico also sought to take advantage of instability in Nicaragua. Costa Rican officials reported to Washington that "Mexico is attempting to develop a sphere of influence in Central America," while a State Department analysis argued that the government of Plutarco Elías Calles was making "an unmistakable attempt . . . to extend Mexican influence over Central America with the unquestionable aim of ultimately achieving a Mexican primacy over the Central American countries." The United States and Mexico thus found themselves on a collision course.

Within Nicaragua, the United States continued to support the Conservatives against the Liberals. Coolidge had withdrawn U.S. marines in 1925 only after the patently fraudulent election of 1924 extended Conservative rule. With Americans gone the Liberals, who probably enjoyed the majority of popular support, staged a rebellion in 1926. To promote stability Washington persuaded Emiliano Chamorro to step down in favor of Adolfo Díaz, who was then elected president by a pliant legislature. The United States extended recognition to the trusty Díaz almost immediately; Mexico continued to recognize the would-be Liberal government of archrival Juan Sacasa. In response, a State Department spokesman publicly charged that Mexico "was seeking to establish a Bolshevist authority in Nicaragua in order to drive a 'hostile wedge' between the United States and the Panama Canal."

As Díaz' grasp on power weakened, President Coolidge dispatched a contingent of U.S. marines in December 1926. Explaining his action to Congress, Coolidge argued that conditions in Nicaragua "seriously threaten American lives and property, endanger the stability of all Central America, and put in jeopardy the rights granted by Nicaragua to the United States for the construction of a canal." Denouncing Sacasa's "Mexican allies," Coolidge surmised that the Díaz government was unable to protect foreigners "solely because of the aid given by Mexico to the revolutionists." Concluded the president: "The United States can not, therefore, fail to view with deep concern any serious threat to stability and constitutional government in Nicaragua tending toward anarchy and jeopardizing American interests, especially if such state of affairs is contributed to or brought about by outside influences or by any foreign power."

European observers quickly denounced the U.S. intervention as "frankly imperialist." Responded the *New York Times,* with an air of sanctimonious defiance: "All that we do has at least the motive of aiding and protecting the weaker republics on this continent, rather than of overriding or despoiling them. If this be Imperialism, make the most of it."

A decision to arbitrate land and petroleum rights led to an easing of U.S. bilateral tensions with Mexico. In Nicaragua, however, Liberal forces continued their relentless advance on Managua. Faced with difficult choices, Coolidge eventually assigned Henry L. Stimson to negotiate a settlement that would permit a face-saving exit. Having no prior experience in Nicaragua—"So far as ignorance would free it from prejudices or commitments," he would later recall, "my mind was a clean slate"— Stimson chose to supervise elections in hopes of bringing order to the country. He also convinced Conservatives and Liberals to accept a power-sharing arrangement. There were 5,500 U.S. marines on hand for the election in 1928 of José María Moncada, a Liberal who had consented to the Stimson compromise.

Governmental authority proved tenuous, however, so U.S. troops remained in Nicaragua. César Augusto Sandino denounced the Liberal-Conservative bargain and took to the mountains, where he led an armed rebellion. By April 1931 Stimson was forced to proclaim that the United States was unable to assure "general protection of Americans" in Nicaragua. Attempts to capture Sandino merely made him a national hero. United States troops supervised yet another presidential election in 1932, but instability continued to mount. In recognition of this fact the United States helped develop the Guardia Nacional, which promptly fell under the leadership of Anastasio Somoza.

Armed intervention was not achieving its goals. As one American coffee planter in Nicaragua wrote to Stimson: "Today we are hated and despised and in danger of massacre any time the Marines are withdrawn. This feeling has been created by employing the American Marines to hunt down and kill Nicaraguans in their own territory. This was a fatal mistake. The intervention of the U.S. government in the internal affairs of Nicaragua has proved a calamity for the American coffee planters doing business in this Republic."

Appointed by Herbert Hoover as secretary of state, Stimson decided to withdraw the marines after the election of 1932. Asked if he would advocate the dispatch of American troops elsewhere in Latin America, Stimson replied: "Not on your life. . . . If we landed a single soldier among those South Americans now, it would undo all the labor of three years, and it would put me in absolutely wrong in China, where Japan has done all of this monstrous work under the guise of protecting her nationals with a landing force."

In short, the seven-year episode in Nicaragua conveyed sobering lessons for Washington. Its costs were painfully clear: 21 marines were killed during 1927–28, and over 100 U.S. soldiers had lost their lives by the end of 1931. Financial costs were mounting as well: it took $1.5 million dollars to mount the operation in 1927–28 alone (about $15 million in 1994 dollars), and by 1932 neither the White House nor Congress was prepared to authorize the $750,000 required to sustain the U.S. presence. American troops withdrew in January 1933. Somoza had Sandino murdered in February 1934. Two years later Somoza would take power for himself.

Cuba, 1929–33

Cuba presented a different kind of challenge. From 1925 Gerardo Machado y Morales had kept himself in power through an astute combination of bribery and repression. Reelected for a six-year term in 1929, he reacted harshly to social agitation caused by the economic Depression. In February 1931 Machado suspended constitutional guarantees, also shutting down the University of Havana.

Washington found itself obliged to respond to these developments. Ironically enough, these policy deliberations were greatly complicated by the fact that the Platt Amendment specifically authorized precisely the kind of U.S. intervention that Stimson had come to oppose. Besides, Machado had achieved for foreign investors the political and economic stability that the amendment was designed to assure. Eventually, Washington decided that the amendment guaranteed "the protection of life, property, and individual liberty" of *foreigners only,* especially Americans, and not of anti-Machado Cuban nationals.

Consequently there would be no intervention. As Stimson would later explain:

> The attitude taken by these people in Cuba is similar to the attitude which is almost constantly taken by factions in other Latin American countries when the tension between them and their Government become acute. . . . If we complied with all these requests, our hands would be full indeed and, however much these factions might like it, we should make ourselves extremely unpopular with every country in Latin America if we adopted such a course of action.

Contending that a request for Machado to resign would be "a very serious intervention," Stimson pondered the possibility of supervising an election:

> that would be even more of an intervention on our part. We have done it in Nicaragua in order to bring to a termination a long period of civil war and anarchy and, in that case, we only did it upon the request of all parties and factions in Nicaragua. Even then, we found the expense and difficulty involved in such an operation, even in such a small country as Nicaragua, a very serious burden. Under present conditions, it would be quite out of the question in Cuba.

It was the precedent of Nicaragua, as much as the reality of Cuba, that argued against direct U.S. action.

By the early 1930s, in summary, the practice of military intervention appeared to have failed. There was need and opportunity to forge a new approach. It was at this moment, and in this context, that Franklin Delano Roosevelt swept to victory in the presidential election of 1932.

The Good Neighbor Policy: Political Dimensions

Antecedents for a shift in U.S. policy date from the late 1920s. During his 1928 tour of South America, President-elect Herbert Hoover expressed hope that countries of the hemisphere could learn to treat each other as "good neighbors." In a campaign article that same year in *Foreign Affairs,* Franklin Roosevelt attacked the Republican Party for placing "money leadership ahead of moral leadership." Turning to the Americas—"in many ways, most important of all"—FDR expressed skepticism about U.S. actions in Haiti and the Dominican Republic and appealed for multilateral approaches. "Single-handed intervention by us in the internal affairs of other nations must end; with the cooperation of others we shall have more order in this hemisphere and less dislike." One practical consequence of increased goodwill, FDR surmised, would be increased trade with countries of the region.

In his inaugural address of 1933 Roosevelt coined the phrase that would define the lines of policy. "I would dedicate this nation to the policy of the Good Neighbor," he said, "—the neighbor who respects his obligations and respects the sanctity of his agreements in and with a world of neighbors." Though vague in content, this formulation directly challenged isolationist sentiments that would continue to gain strength during the course of the Depression. And while the idea was initially intended for the world as a whole, it would acquire its most specific meaning in relation to Latin America.

The cornerstone of the Good Neighbor policy was nonintervention. This began to take shape at the inter-American meeting of 1933 at Montevideo, where delegates concurred in a resolution firmly asserting that "No state has the right to intervene in the internal or external affairs of another." United States secretary of state Cordell Hull not only assented to this language, but further explained that "the United States government is as much opposed as any other government to interference with the freedom, the sovereignty, or other internal affairs or processes of the governments of other nations." As a result, Hull pledged, "no government need fear any intervention on the part of the United States under the Roosevelt administration."

This commitment became even more explicit at the Buenos Aires conference of 1936, with the adoption of a formal protocol: "The High Contracting Parties declare inadmissible the intervention of any one of them, directly or indirectly, and for whatever reason, in the internal or external affairs of any other of the Parties." The condemnation of intervention as "inadmissible" was strongly promoted by the Mexican delegation, still apprehensive over differences with Washington in regard to Central America. Understandably enough, Latin American representatives continued to fear the possibility of U.S. military action.

Nonintervention sharply modified the Monroe Doctrine. More particularly, it amounted to a rejection of the 1904 Roosevelt Corollary, which had proclaimed that the United States possessed not only a right to intervene—but also a moral duty (in cases of "impotence" or "chronic wrongdoing"). According to the Buenos Aires protocol, military intervention was henceforth prohibited "for whatever reason." At least on this one issue, Franklin Roosevelt repudiated the legacy of cousin Theodore.[2]

By upholding the principle of national sovereignty, the doctrine of nonintervention supported the juridical equality of states. Under Good Neighbor precepts, large countries were supposed to respect the integrity of smaller countries. As Latins came to say with pride: "Now there are no little nations." Moreover, nonintervention meant that force should no longer be used for the protection of property or citizens abroad. It thus overthrew Calvin Coolidge's dictum that the U.S. government was obliged to protect the property rights of U.S. citizens in foreign lands. In effect, the Good Neighbor position held that U.S. citizens and investments overseas must obey the sovereign laws of host societies. In addition, the policy called for consultation among the states of the Americas. At the 1936 meeting in Buenos Aires, delegates concurred in a resolution that hemispheric states "shall consult together for the purposes of finding and adopting methods of peaceful cooperation." In translation, this meant that the United States would no longer act in unilateral fashion. And as a result, it was imagined, the hemisphere would become a cooperative community of states.

A final component was the principle of noninterference. Going much further than the idea of nonintervention, which held that countries should refrain from the deployment of military force, noninterference meant that nations should abstain from *any* form of meddling in the internal affairs of sovereign states—through coercion, enticement, manipulation, or other means that might range from unsought advice to economic pressure to the threat or show of force.

Cuba, 1933–36

The concept of noninterference evolved not from presidential declaration but from the passage of events, especially in Cuba. Taking office as FDR's secretary of state, Cordell Hull immediately initiated diplomatic negotiations that led to abrogation of the Platt Amendment by May 1934. The United States thus forfeited its long-standing right to intervention within Cuba. But this did not imply total disengagement. On the contrary, Hull replaced the threat of outright intervention with more subtle efforts to direct the course of Cuban affairs.

The principal agent of this new approach was Sumner Welles, who arrived as U.S. ambassador to Havana in May 1933. As opposition mounted against the relentless rule of Machado, Welles took it upon himself to present the ruler with a five-point plan that included his taking a leave of absence from office. Machado dissented but lost the support of his army and departed Cuba in August. Subsequent conditions under Carlos Manuel de Céspedes rapidly deteriorated, however, and Welles responded with a plan for new elections. And then, in September 1934, rank-and-file army elements under Sergeant Fulgencio Batista imposed a junta that included five civilians. Apoplectic as his plans unraveled, Welles denounced the ruling leadership as representing "a group of the most extreme radicals of the student organization and three university professors whose theories are frankly communistic." This was perhaps the first occasion, but by no means the last, that U.S. officials would denounce the threat of communism in the Western Hemisphere.

Welles pursued several courses of action. First, he urged Washington to intervene. The cautious Hull rejected this advice, warning that "if we have to go in there again, we will never be able to come out and we will have on our hands the trouble of thirty years ago." Second, Welles persuaded the State Department to withhold recognition of the new government, eventually led by Ramón Grau San Martín, a university professor, on the grounds that the regime was incapable of maintaining law and order. In the meantime, Welles continued to denounce the Grau San Martín administration as "an undisciplined group of individuals of divergent tendencies representing the most irresponsible elements in the city of Havana with practically no support whatsoever outside the capital." Despite FDR's claim that the U.S. decision on nonrecognition was wholly impartial, it was, of course, a highly partisan act—yet it failed to topple the government. Third, Welles courted and supported domestic opposition to the new regime, proclaiming in September 1934 that "a social revolution" was in progress against the government. His successor as ambassador, Jefferson Caffery, openly encouraged Batista to overthrow Grau. Shortly thereafter Grau resigned and was replaced by Carlos Mendieta. Greatly relieved by this turn of events, the United States followed with swift diplomatic recognition. From that point onward, nonrecognition was abandoned as a diplomatic weapon.

No longer meddling outright in Cuban affairs, the United States continued to express its interests and its preferences. When Mendieta suspended constitutional guarantees in mid-January 1935, Caffery interpreted the move as strictly anticommunist: "The Mendieta government has been fighting for its life against the communistic elements, and, although it has strengthened its position in the country by its recent firm attitude, the communists have by no means given up hope and will continue to be a menace for some time to come." After presidential elections in 1936, won by Miguel Mariano Gómez, the U.S. government continued its close communications with Fulgencio Batista, inviting him to Washington in 1938 for high-level discussions with FDR as well as Cordell Hull and others. Such displays of tacit support no doubt influenced Batista's decision to run for the presidency in 1940.

From 1933 to 1936, in other words, U.S. diplomats made persistent attempts to interfere in Cuban politics—and eventually chose to desist. This does not quite mean that all their efforts met with failure. As one Mexican diplomat recalled, the succession of threats and enticements during this period was "one of the most effective and skillful interventions ever carried out by the American government." But from Welles' blustering to Caffery's persuasion, the methods for exerting U.S. pressure underwent visible change. Open interference was no longer part of the diplomatic arsenal.

By the end of the 1930s, much of Latin America fell under the sway of long-lived dictatorships: Maximiliano Hernández Martínez in El Salvador, Jorge Ubico in Guatemala, Rafael Trujillo in the Dominican Republic, Fulgencio Batista in Cuba, and Anastasio Somoza in Nicaragua. Somewhat conspicuously, these regimes emerged precisely in those countries where the United States had intervened or intermeddled to the greatest degree. As FDR is alleged to have said of Somoza during a visit to Washington in 1940: "He's a son of a bitch, but at least he's our son of a bitch." More serious, and more damning, was the comment of Víctor Raúl Haya de la Torre, the aspiring young reformist from Peru, who proclaimed in 1938 that FDR had made himself "the Good Neighbor of tyrants."

The Good Neighbor Policy: Economic Dimensions

Roosevelt's policy toward Latin America entailed not only political accommodation but also economic influence. During the 1930s Washington reached the conclusion that military intervention—even political intermeddling—was costly, ineffective, and counterproductive. Economic leverage was something else again. The first inkling of this strategy came in the form of reciprocity, which called for straightforward exchange: the United States would grant political benefits to Latin America in anticipation of favors to come, particularly economic benefits. Washington expressed continuing concern about the treatment of U.S. nationals and their property, especially $5 billion in investments ($1.5 billion in portfolios,

$3.5 billion in direct investments). From the U.S. perspective, active defense of economic interests of U.S. nationals abroad "would not constitute intervention in the internal affairs of another state. It would be simply a matter of protection." Such claims were, of course, utterly inconsistent with nonintervention principles.

Promoting Trade

Upon taking office the Roosevelt administration promptly started to fashion instruments for stimulating economic recovery and, in the Americas, extending economic influence. In 1933 FDR maintained that the stimulation of trade was "the most important item in our country's foreign policy," and as secretary of state he appointed Cordell Hull, a zealous proponent of trade liberalization. Hull believed that commercial opening would not only expand U.S. exports and stimulate production, but that, as a general principle, it would diminish tendencies toward conflict and strengthen prospects for world peace. He also detected geopolitical advantage in the consolidation of commercial ties: the political lineup followed the economic lineup, according to his oft-quoted homily, and Washington could greatly enhance its international position through the artful pursuit of trade policy.

After a hesitant start, the Roosevelt administration began to implement Hull's approach. In 1934 the government established an Export-Import Bank to extend commercial loans to U.S. exporters. That same year Congress approved the Reciprocal Trade Agreements Act (as FDR affixed his signature to the bill, Hull would recall that "each stroke of the pen seemed to write a message of gladness on my heart"). In effect, the legislation authorized the negotiation of bilateral agreements for trade liberalization, which Hull interpreted as the mutual reduction of tariffs and, if possible, the unconditional extension of most-favored-nation status. Paradoxically, the Smoot-Hawley Tariff Act of 1930 strengthened Washington's bargaining position, since the reduction or elimination of its protectionist barriers offered major incentives to U.S. trading partners.

Latin America became a starting point and testing ground for U.S. commercial strategy. The region offered a strong potential market. Between 1929 and 1932 American exports to Latin America declined by 78 percent; recuperation of these sales would help promote U.S. recovery. Moreover, imports from Latin America—which dropped by 68 percent between 1929 and 1932—would not displace American goods. On the contrary, over 80 percent of these goods were raw materials used in manufacturing (for industrial production) or noncompetitive foodstuffs (such as coffee, cocoa, and bananas). Under these conditions customs duties and excise taxes were mutually disadvantageous. And for Hull, especially, successful agreements to liberalize trade with Latin America could set a precedent for negotiations with Europe and other parts of the world. "In carrying out our policies toward Latin America," he later recalled, "it was never my wish to make them exclusively Pan-American."

True to his convictions, Hull went to the Montevideo conference of 1933 with the avowed intention to "introduce a comprehensive economic resolution calling for lower tariffs and the abolition of trade restrictions." The administration simultaneously initiated bilateral trade discussions with Argentina, Brazil, and Colombia. In view of Colombia's dependence on the U.S. coffee market, one-sided negotiations with Bogotá promptly led to the signing of an advantageous treaty for the United States; "it actually costs us nothing," in the revealing judgment of a State Department memorandum. Passage of the Trade Agreements Act in 1934 required subsequent revisions that led to considerable tension, and it was not until 1936 that the two governments exchanged ratification. Ever gracious, Colombia's exhausted foreign minister expressed appreciation for the Good Neighbor policy with its "new criterion in the diplomatic sphere, and commercial relations based on liberal principles which consecrate the operation of the most-favored-nation clause."

With its tariff legislation in place, Washington next turned to Cuba. As a result of the Depression, the island's sugar income in 1933 had declined to 30 percent of its 1929 level (and merely 12 percent of the 1924 level). Cuba badly needed secure access to the U.S. market; for its part, the United States sought protection for its $1.5 billion in investments. Once the "communistic" Grau San Martín was out of power, Washington promptly reached a trade agreement with the Mendieta administration. The final compact was a purely bilateral affair, with no mention of most-favored nation provisions, but it effectively lowered reciprocal duties. Also in 1934 Congress fixed quotas among domestic and foreign suppliers for the U.S. sugar market, granting Cuba a 28 percent share.

Soon afterward Washington reached a series of commercial agreements with nations of Central America: Honduras in 1935, Guatemala and Costa Rica in 1936, El Salvador in 1937. As with Colombia and Cuba, these negotiations revealed a common pattern: the United States managed to reach trade agreements only with countries that were heavily dependent on U.S. markets for agricultural (usually monocultural) exports. During the course of the decade Washington was unable to conclude agreements with Argentina, Chile, Uruguay, Peru, Bolivia, Paraguay, and Mexico.

By far the most dramatic trade negotiations focused on Brazil, the world's fifth-largest supplier to the United States and the source of 60 to 65 percent of its coffee imports. Even more significantly, Brazil was a cornerstone for Adolf Hitler's attempts to augment Germany's political and economic presence throughout Latin America. During the 1930s Germany launched an economic offensive in the Americas, aggressively promoting the sale of German industrial products in exchange for raw materials from Latin America. Under bilateral arrangements, Germany would often arrange to pay handsome prices for imports with "compensation marks," a special currency that could only be used to purchase German goods in return (this was, fumed Cordell Hull, "a cut throat double-dealing method of trade"). From 1936 to 1939 imports from Latin America came to 7 percent of Germany's total, while German exports to Latin America climbed to over 14 percent of the regional total. Ominously, too, Germany held military instructorships in over half the countries of Latin America. As one U.S. chargé reported back to Washington, Nazi Germany was "conducting a well organized and astute campaign . . . to discredit in every way possible American efforts on this continent."

Because of its size, location, and importance, Brazil became a central object of this U.S.–German rivalry. For Germany it represented not only a substantial market but also an important source of raw materials, especially cotton (which could be used in the manufacture of explosives). Moreover, the country had a sizable Germanic community, consisting of around 100,000 German nationals and 800,000 German-Brazilians or *teuto-brasileiros*. Seeking to maximize its own commercial exports and its political room for maneuver, the Brazilian government managed to steer an artful middle course. In 1935 the Getúlio Vargas administration announced a Reciprocal Trade Agreement with the United States, which placed over 90 percent of Brazilian imports on its duty-free list; the following year it reached a secret "gentlemen's agreement" with Nazi Germany. Between 1933 and 1938 the German share of Brazilian imports climbed from 12 percent to 25 percent, while the German share of Brazilian exports jumped from just over 8 percent to nearly 20 percent.

United States politicians took notice of the Third Reich's campaign. In the spring of 1938 New York Mayor Fiorello La Guardia sounded a public alarm:

> For the maintenance of our economic well-being, for the preservation of peace, it is vital that we take immediate steps to eliminate this new growing sore on the soil of the Western Hemisphere. In this way, we may lay the foundation of peace and security for our world of the future. A united people in the Western Hemisphere, without invasion of the sovereign rights of any government. The Americas for the Americans.

Shortly afterward an experienced U.S. businessman speculated about the commercial implications of German penetration of the Western Hemisphere: "Markets would be closed to our exporters. Political, naval and aviation concessions would be linked to commerce. We should soon find a European 'sphere of influence' creeping up toward us from the south, and outposts of the Empire appearing closer and closer to the Panama Canal." President Roosevelt added his own commentary on the possibility of Axis influence in Latin America: "Do you think that the United States could stand idly by and have this European menace right on our own borders? Of course not. You could not stand for it."

As a result of governmental policy, the United States steadily improved its commercial position in the hemisphere. By 1938 the United States had become the leading overall trade partner for every major country of Latin America—with the sole exception of Argentina, which continued to sell large quantities of high-quality beef in the British market, and with the partial exception of Chile (Table A2). Germany was making substantial headway, especially in the ABC countries, but it was nowhere predominant. In South America, as well as in the Caribbean Basin, the United States was gaining the upper hand.

In the end, it was neither diplomatic pressure nor neighborly sentiment that blunted the German offensive in South America. It was the eruption of World War II and, more particularly, the British naval blockade against Hitler's vessels. Commerce with Germany ground to a virtual halt. "What the commercial policy of the United States failed to achieve with its relentless opposition to the expansion of our compensation trade," one Rio de Janeiro newspaper remarked in 1940, "the war brutally realized from one moment to the next."

Applying Leverage

In its promotion of U.S. economic interests, the Roosevelt administration encountered serious challenges from Latin American governments against American oil companies. The first conflict erupted in Bolivia, where the government in March 1937 annulled its concession to the Standard Oil Company and confiscated its properties. The decree alleged that the company had defrauded the government by failure to pay taxes and by the illegal exportation of oil to Argentina in 1925–26. Technically speaking the governmental decision was not an expropriation, for which compensation might have been offered, but an outright cancellation, which would not entail any compensation at all.

The announcement immediately led to wrangling in the Bolivian courts. By February 1938 Sumner Welles, now assistant secretary of state, decided to advocate some form of arbitration, explaining to a Bolivian representative that "the only way in which public opinion in this country was going to support the 'Good Neighbor' policy as a permanent part of our foreign policy would be for the policy to be recognized throughout the continent as a completely reciprocal policy and not one of a purely unilateral character." In March 1938 Standard Oil filed a suit under protest after consultation with the Department of State, which promised to support a claim for arbitration once legal remedies were exhausted in Bolivia. A year later the Bolivian Supreme Court decided unanimously that Standard Oil did not possess a legal status in Bolivia which entitled it to sue the government.

As the U.S. Department of State pondered its next steps, Cordell Hull issued a blunt warning that:

> in this dangerous, chaotic world situation there was never such a ripe plum dangled before a hungry person than Latin America appears to be

to . . . lawless nations, hungry as wolves for vast territory with rich unde-
veloped natural resources such as South America possesses; that it is all-
important for the American nations to pursue a lawful, friendly and reasonable
course with each other; and that the dollars and cents involved in the oil
seizure were small compared to the great injury that would result to Bolivia, as
well as to my own and other countries, if that sort of an act should go
uncorrected and the friendship between the two countries should be seriously
impaired.

The allusion to Germany was as transparent as the threat to Bolivia itself.
The petroleum dispute was being drawn into the worldwide arena.

In June 1939 the Department of State offered to act as intermediator.
Subsequent news leaks from Bolivia scuttled this idea, and the United
States retaliated by applying two forms of economic pressure: first, the
United States tried to prevent Bolivia from obtaining help from immediate
neighbors (an effort that was partly successful with Paraguay but less so
with respect to Argentina, which continued to purchase Bolivian oil);
second, and more important, the United States blocked loans and technical
assistance. To emphasize this point, heads of the Reconstruction Finance
Corporation and the Export-Import Bank told the U.S. Senate that they
would refuse to make loans to "a country that is confiscating our property."

Affected by this economic pressure, Bolivian officials began seeking a
way out of the impasse by August 1940. And as World War II approached,
U.S. diplomats began to fear inroads by Germany—implicated in a plot to
overthrow the Bolivian government in July 1941—and soon began drawing up plans for a resumption of economic assistance. Under these changed
circumstances, Bolivia and Standard Oil eventually agreed upon a settlement in January 1942: a payment of $1.5 million (plus 3 percent interest)
for sale of the company to the Bolivian state under conditions "freely
entered into." A check arrived on April 22. Washington achieved its goal.

The second challenge came in Mexico. Disputes over wages and working conditions in the foreign-owned oil industry led to a strike in May
1937. Unions found support for their position from the federal Board of
Conciliation and Arbitration, a mixed-member body on which the Mexican government held the balance of power between workers and management, and in March 1938 the Mexican Supreme Court upheld the board
ruling. Foreign companies refused to comply, however, rejecting the offer
of a guarantee from President Lázaro Cárdenas against further tax or wage
demands. On March 18, 1938, a frustrated Cárdenas announced expropriation of Dutch, British, and U.S. companies. Delirious crowds
throughout Mexico expressed jubilant support for the government action,
and the newspaper *El Nacional* captured the popular mood: "First, political
independence, then internal emancipation, today the inexorable rupture of
this umbilical cord which ties us to imperialism. . . . The country writes
its history with its own blood."

The stakes in this conflict were high. The total value of oil lands came
to approximately $500 million. The U.S.–held concession was worth

about $200 million, and U.S. direct investments amounted to $60 million. Given interests of this magnitude, the Mexican crisis was bound to set a precedent for U.S. policy.

The American position took time to evolve. Shortly after Cárdenas' announcement, Cordell Hull issued an ultimatum, demanding to know "what specific action with respect to payment for the properties in question is contemplated by the Mexican government, what assurance will be given that payment will be made, and when such payment may be expected." Apprehensive about the tone of this missive, U.S. ambassador Josephus Daniels exceeded customary bounds of diplomatic discretion and urged the Mexicans to consider the note as "not received." He also reported to Washington that Mexico would be willing to pay compensation. Daniels' bold action endangered his career and cost him the confidence of Hull and Welles, but it managed to prevent a damaging break in U.S.–Mexican relations.

The United States renounced the use of force but was quick to apply economic pressure. Barely one week after the expropriation the Department of Treasury terminated a 1936 agreement for the purchase of 5 million ounces of silver each month from Mexico at slightly above the world price. This was an important blow to Mexico: exports of silver were almost as large as for oil, and the purchase arrangement represented a significant source of revenue for the Mexican government. After a three-month hiatus, Treasury resumed the purchase of Mexican silver on a day-to-day basis at the world level. On balance, suspension of the silver deal had more symbolic than practical impact.

More significant were efforts by the oil companies to prevent the export of Mexican oil. In open collusion, the companies sought to obstruct the acquisition of tankers and the purchase of drilling equipment. The result was a highly effective boycott on Mexican petroleum in major markets, including the United States. In May 1939 the U.S. State Department endorsed the boycott on Mexican oil, issuing a statement that it would be "undesirable" for U.S. government agencies to purchase Mexican oil and encouraging Latin American governments to take a similar stand. (For its part, Mexico responded by making deals with Axis powers: as war approached, Mexico was earning about $1.2 million per month from petroleum exports, over half from Germany and Italy.) United States government lending agencies also refrained from making loans to Mexico between August 1937 and November 1941.

The Dutch and British governments and all the oil companies—with the exception of Sinclair, which was breaking ranks to negotiate its own agreement—called for arbitration by an international tribunal. In 1939 FDR, too, wrote directly to Cárdenas with a proposal for international arbitration. After Mexico rejected this overture, favoring instead a two-person bilateral commission, Welles proposed arbitration again. It was the fall of France in mid-1940 that ultimately led the United States to accept the Mexican position. Under pressure from the War Department, in fact, the State Department consented to the idea of a two-person commission in late 1941. "In the event the United States is attacked and must enter the war," one U.S. official noted, "Mexico's oil resources might be of importance from the point of view of national and even hemispheric defense." For the United States it thus became urgent not only to settle the controversy but also to maintain Mexico's capacity for production. The decision came in April 1942, just after the creation of a joint U.S.–Mexico defense commission: Mexico would pay to U.S. companies compensation of $24 million plus 3 percent interest since the date of expropriation, for a total of $29 million.

The third instance of petroleum politics occurred in Venezuela, where the United States applied lessons that it may have learned in Bolivia and Mexico. After the death of long-time dictator Juan Vicente Gómez in 1935, the Venezuelan labor movement began to assert its independence and power—achieving an eight-hour day, rights to collective bargaining, and the imposition of export taxes on petroleum—steps that the oil companies would normally oppose. At the same time, the government of Eleazar López Contreras granted new concessions to Socony and Standard Oil of New Jersey. In view of the Mexican crisis there was no effective threat of governmental expropriation. On the contrary, the Venezuelan goal was to capture market share—thus taking advantage of the boycott on Mexican oil.

In an effort to prevent recurrence of the Bolivian or Mexican scenario, the Department of State in 1940 decided to consult with U.S. oil companies on strategies for negotiation and representation. Discussions followed from December 1942 through March 1943 on provisions of a new Venezuelan law that raised the royalty on petroleum from a range of 7.5–11 percent to a uniform $16^2/_3$ percent, established a new base for calculation of taxes, and reduced customs exemptions. In this the oil companies freely concurred. Washington thus secured another wartime goal: maintaining the flow of petroleum to allied forces.

Extending Assistance

The Roosevelt administration began to shift its policy on economic assistance toward Latin America in 1939. Prior to that time the United States had used economic assistance as a carrot-and-stick, withholding loans from Bolivia and Mexico in order to protect American investments in petroleum. As war loomed on the international horizon, however, Washington started to emphasize hemispheric security instead of economic interests.

In the absence of centralized coordination, changes in U.S. foreign economic policy faced substantial inertia and resistance. Harry Dexter White, a monetary expert in the Treasury Department, encouraged Roosevelt to "use our great financial strength to help safeguard future peace for the United States, and to make your 'Good Neighbor' policy really effective." Unless the United States were to embark on "a program of assistance to Latin-American countries on a scale appropriate to the problem with which we are faced," White continued, "Latin America will gradually succumb to the organized economic and ideological campaign now being waged by aggressor nations." Eventually the president concurred, indicating in a speech to the Board of Governors of the Pan American Union in April 1939 that the United States would "give economic support, so that no American nation need surrender any fraction of its sovereign freedom to maintain its economic welfare." Implicitly contradicting then-current U.S. policy toward Mexico, a State Department memorandum contended in June 1939: "Our national interests as a whole far outweigh those of the petroleum companies." Economic assistance would be used to keep Latin American nations on the U.S. side in case of war.

In 1939 the State Department began laying plans for a commercial cartel that would handle Latin American exports and take up slack caused by the closing of European markets. The idea met resistance in Latin America, but Washington eventually backed off for reasons of its own: it feared a backlash in Asia, since Japan would be likely to demand comparable commercial hegemony over China, and it came to the conclusion that the scheme was unworkable. As U.S. trade official Will Clayton noted: "Cartels must be world cartels—not Hemisphere cartels." The United States decided to continue its reliance on bilateral arrangements.

Also in 1939 the Export-Import Bank initiated transactions with governments, thus greatly enlarging its role. By late 1940 the bank was making substantial loans for broad-based development projects. Especially significant was support for construction of the Volta Redonda steel mill in Brazil. Bernard Baruch, ever the businessman, expressed skepticism about the wisdom of this venture: "After the property is developed," he wondered aloud, "will they pull a Mexican stunt on us?" But Washington went ahead with the loan, and the Eximbank embarked on an ambitious lending program throughout the war: $45 million to Brazil, $5 million to Chile, $5 million to Uruguay, $2 million to Nicaragua, $400,000 to Paraguay. William Culbertson, former ambassador to Chile, observed the appearance of a new kind of diplomacy: "to use Federal funds in order to conserve and develop the economic life of the Latin American countries, I presume with the idea in mind that we are to keep them lined up politically for the purpose of economic defense of the hemisphere. You are really witnessing the entrance of the American Government into the field of political loans."

While flows of aid increased at this time, the U.S. government displayed considerable uncertainty over the proposed creation of an Inter-American Bank. At the Panama Conference of 1939, without a firm U.S. commitment, Sumner Welles could state only that "the United States Government wishes to cooperate with all other American Republics in the efforts of each to develop the resources of its country *along sound economic and non-competitive lines* and when desired to assist them through the services and facilities of its privately owned banking system as well as its Government-owned agencies when the latter have funds available for such purposes." Latin American delegates called for multilateral approaches, in contrast to the bilateral methods of the Eximbank, and Mexican diplomats espoused the "creation of an inter-American financial institution of a permanent character."

Plans for a bank proceeded, but without provisions for enabling Latin American governments to repay any loans they might acquire. What the Latins wanted was access to U.S. commercial markets. Without enhanced trade, said Dr. Pedro Larránaga of Peru, the result would be counterproductive: "Why obscure the meaning of this solution, which instead of giving the Americas a new independent and neutral credit structure is merely going to increase our indebtedness to the United States?" Latin American representatives objected to a February 1940 draft proposal that insisted on government guarantees for loans to Latin American private citizens, gave a veto power to the United States in voting rules, and provided no assurance about commercial access to the U.S. market. At the same time, U.S. bankers and financiers expressed skepticism about the creation of an official, governmentally sponsored agency. "I hope," said Bernard Baruch, that "our Latin-American efforts will not have too much government action, but rather more by individuals." The proposal then died in committee. In 1947 President Harry S. Truman finally withdrew the convention from the U.S. Senate.

The Good Neighbor Policy: Cultural Dimensions

The Good Neighbor policy rested on ideological foundations, as the Roosevelt administration continually emphasized the mythical unity of the New World and its differences from the Old World. While Europe was falling prey to totalitarian dictatorship, according to this litany, nations of the Americas stood for justice and democracy. "We and the other American Republics have distinguishing ideals and beliefs which bind us together in contrast with other non-American powers," insisted a State Department memorandum of 1939; among these were "faith in republican institutions, loyalty to democracy as an ideal, reverence for liberty, acceptance of the dignity of the individual and his inviolable personal rights, belief in peaceable adjustment of disputes . . ." Invoking what historian Arthur P. Whitaker has described as "the Western Hemisphere idea," U.S. officials maintained that the New World was culturally unified, ideologically unique, and politically superior to other realms of the globe.[3] It stood apart from Europe—and, by implication, was under the leadership and guidance of the United States.

United States representatives pressed this argument in forum after forum. At the Pan-American gathering in Montevideo in 1933, the American delegation supported a series of resolutions designed to advance "mutual knowledge and understanding of the peoples of the Americas." At Buenos Aires in 1936, U.S. delegates supported the Declaration of Principles of Inter-American Solidarity and Cooperation, which proclaimed that

American republics shared a "common likeness in their form of democratic government." And at Panama in 1939, the United States sponsored a resolution recommending that "in view of the democratic ideal which prevails in the American hemisphere," it was necessary "to eradicate from the Americas the spread of doctrines that tend to place in jeopardy the common inter-American democratic ideal." Alien doctrines were unwelcome. In keeping with the Monroe Doctrine, Washington must lead the fight against extrahemispheric ideologies.[4]

In this diplomatic effort, cultural connections received high-level attention. The assumption was that mutual respect arising from a sympathetic understanding of history, literature, and the arts would not only bind together countries of the hemisphere but would also promote trade and commercial cooperation. For such reasons the Roosevelt administration established a cultural division in the Department of State "to promote mutual progress and understanding in the Americas." And it was to counteract the growing Axis menace that FDR created, in August 1940, the Office of the Coordinator of Inter-American Affairs (OCIAA) and placed it under the leadership of the youthful Nelson Rockefeller. Invested with a broad mandate, OCIAA oversaw economic cooperation, cultural exchange, and public information; its primary purpose was to counter "subversive, insidious, destructive Nazi propaganda." The budget for the OCIAA's first year of operation was $3.5 million; by the end of the war it was $45 million. As Rockefeller reflected in 1945: "The United States came in with a program of truth in answer to enemy lies."

From the outset, the OCIAA worked with a broad range of media. It distributed articles to magazines and newspapers throughout the hemisphere. OCIAA produced and distributed the magazine *En Guardia* in Spanish and Portuguese, on sale at newsstands and sent without charge to about 40,000 prominent Latin Americans each month. OCIAA sponsored art exhibitions, musical concerts, and literary translations (but not of John Steinbeck's *The Grapes of Wrath,* which it deemed inappropriate). The office cooperated with major radio networks, enticing the industry through tax benefits to increase its number of short-wave broadcasts and to improve the quality of programs aired to Latin America. By 1941 U.S. news broadcasts expanded from a handful of shortwave programs a week, mostly in English, to eighteen reports in Spanish and eight in Portuguese. OCIAA purchased advertising space in pro-U.S. newspapers announcing the time, wavelength, and call letters of American broadcasts, and blacklisted Latin American radio stations that carried pro-Axis programs.

It was in the motion picture industry that OCIAA had its most remarkable influence. As explained by the director of the agency's film department, John Hay ("Jock") Whitney:

> The Office of the Coordinator of Inter-American Affairs has a share in the task of imparting the full force of the meaning of freedom and sovereignty to a quarter of a billion people in the Americas. The menace of Nazism and its allied doctrines, its techniques and tactics, must be understood from Hudson

Bay to Punto Arenas. Wherever the motion picture can do a basic job of spreading the gospel of the Americas' common stake in this struggle, there that job must and shall be done.

To pursue this goal OCIAA installed in Hollywood a consultant to the Motion Picture Association who could offer advice on scripts, censor films, and encourage distribution of movies that would display "the truth about the American way." In effect, OCIAA became the clearinghouse and censor for all films sent to Latin America.

The OCIAA was highly effective. It successfully opposed distribution in Latin America of a film entitled *Mr. Smith Goes to Washington,* starring Jimmy Stewart, because of its adverse commentary on the U.S. political establishment. It persuaded Twentieth Century Fox to spend $40,000 to remove potentially offensive scenes from *Down Argentine Way* (1940), which featured one Argentine character as a gigolo, depicted another with a Mexican accent, and revolved around an allegedly crooked horse race at the Buenos Aires Jockey Club. And it urged the producers of *Juarez* (1939), a cinematic classic comparing Mexico's Benito Juárez with Abraham Lincoln, to eliminate a scene in which an American diplomat notified Napoleon III that France must get out of Mexico because of the Monroe Doctrine, thus minimizing the role of Mexican resistance. In a variety of ways, Rockefeller and Whitney urged Hollywood to reiterate the messages of hemispheric solidarity.

The industry responded with alacrity. During 1941 alone Twentieth Century Fox produced *The Road to Rio,* RKO came out with *They Met in Argentina,* MGM released *Simon Bolivar.* Twentieth Century Fox would go on to film a whole series of Charlie Chan adventures in South America. Perhaps the biggest hit came from the Disney Studio, which created an animated feature film, *Saludos Amigos* (1943), in which a baby Chilean airplane gallantly brought mail across the Andes and a dapper Brazilian parrot, José Carioca, continually got the best of a bewildered Donald Duck.

There were several reasons for Hollywood's cooperation. One was political: leading movie producers, many of them Jewish, strongly opposed Nazism and objected to U.S. calls for isolationism. Another was creative, particularly musical: in the words of one executive, swing music of the big-band era was on the way out and "the rhumba stuff is jumping into the number one position in American taste." Third, and perhaps most critical, was the need for a new export market. As World War II closed off commercial access to Europe and Japan, there was no alternative to Latin America. Political imperatives and economic calculations thus neatly converged, creating a powerful partnership between Hollywood and Washington.

As reported by historian Allen Woll, "Hollywood's attitude toward the Latin countries suddenly bordered on reverence."[5] No longer did U.S. films depict Latins as uncouth greasers or ignorant peasants. The picture *Juarez,* with Paul Muni, presented the Mexican leader as a hero of epic proportions. There were lighthearted forms of approval as well. In *They Met in Argentina* (1941), for example, gauchos on the pampas sang the same song as had the American hero as a youth in Texas. And in *That Night in Rio* (1941), Don Ameche warbled a tune called "Chica Chica Boom Chic" with touchingly ludicrous lyrics:

> My friends, I extend felicitations,
> To our South American relations.
> May we never leave behind us
> All the common ties that bind us.
> One hundred and thirty million people
> Send regards to you. . . . [6]

It sounded more like a speech at the Pan American Union than a Hollywood song, but it seemed to accomplish its purpose.

Rockefeller's OCIAA was not reluctant to propose specific themes. "Right now," its oversight committee urged at one point, "we need to create 'Pan-Americana,' a noble female figure, bearing a torch and cross, subtly suggesting both the Virgin Mary and the Goddess of Liberty." What they got instead was pulsating music and throbbing sensuality, from the song-and-dance routines of Brazil's Carmen Miranda to the passionate outbursts of Lupe Vélez, who gained renown as "the Mexican spitfire." Throughout U.S. popular culture, Latin America came to be seen as provocative, thrilling, cooperative—and desirable. Hollywood films drew mixed reactions in Latin America, even after OCIAA-sponsored amendments, but on balance they strengthened popular support for U.S. foreign policy. According to a State Department memorandum on OCIAA's overall activity as of 1942: "It was the greatest outpouring of propagandistic material by a state ever."

Sizing Up the Neighborhood

The crowning achievement of Roosevelt's Good Neighbor policy was hemispheric solidarity during World War II. During the quest for this goal, however, the precepts of nonintervention and noninterference posed dilemmas for U.S. policymakers. Assistant Secretary Welles expressed opposition to the idea of open intervention against pro-Fascist governments in Latin America. But after the defeat of Poland and Hitler's assault on the Netherlands, Ambassador Hugh Wilson took note of the problem:

> We have assumed defense of the hemisphere and at the same time we have nothing south of the Caribbean Sea which will aid us in making such an assumption definitive. We have neither landing fields nor sea bases, nor have we any such control of policy of the individual states which would prevent them from inviting trouble. Our underwriting of the defense of the hemisphere, while, I think, an indispensable step in the defense of this nation, is nevertheless a blank check for bad behavior or irresponsible action on the part of the States of South America.

Then Wilson posed the key question: "How can we find an answer to this difficulty which is compatible with the Good Neighbor Policy?" In other words, how could the United States forestall Axis influence on the basis of noninterference?

The fall of France in mid-1940 led to intense concern over the fate of overseas territories in the Americas, such as Guadeloupe and French Guiana, now in danger of Nazi takeover. The State Department promptly drafted a no-transfer resolution that passed unanimously in the Senate and by an overwhelming vote (380–8) in the House. Cordell Hull also notified Berlin that "the United States would not recognize any transfer, and would not acquiesce in any attempt to transfer, any geographic region of the Western Hemisphere from one non-American power to another non-American power." German foreign minister Ribbentrop replied with an appeal for equal treatment, noting that England and France still had colonies within the Western Hemisphere, but Hull retorted that the Monroe Doctrine proscribed not the *possession* of historic colonies but their *transfer* from one European power to another.

The Japanese attack on Pearl Harbor in December 1941 raised immediate questions about the hemispheric response. During World War I only eight Latin American states, most U.S. protectorates, declared war on Germany; the majority assumed neutrality. Within days of Pearl Harbor, however, all nine Central American and Caribbean republics (as before, virtual U.S. protectorates) declared war on Japan. Colombia, Venezuela, and Mexico promptly severed relations with the Axis. Shortly thereafter the 1942 Meeting of Ministers of Foreign Affairs of the American Republics sought to reinforce solidarity in the war effort. Two countries were decidedly unenthusiastic: Chile, which feared Japanese hit-and-run attacks along its coastline, and Argentina, which harbored strong pro-Axis sympathies. Delegates nonetheless supported a resolution asserting that "The American Republics . . . recommend the rupture of their diplomatic relations with Japan, Germany, and Italy, since the first of these states has attacked and the other two have declared war upon an American country." Peru, Uruguay, Bolivia, and Paraguay quickly complied, and Oswaldo Aranha of Brazil announced his country's adhesion in a dramatic closing session. Looking back on the Rio meeting, a U.S. observer opined that "It was excellent statesmanship—and damned fine showmanship, too."

Chile and Argentina struggled to maintain neutrality—a position which had the disadvantage, however, of providing diplomatic haven for Nazi agents. Chile eventually succumbed to U.S. threats to cut off economic assistance and broke relations with the Axis in January 1943. Argentina's insistence on neutrality eventually prompted the United States to withdraw the U.S. ambassador, withhold diplomatic recognition, and threaten economic sanctions—which failed to gain support from the British, who relied heavily on imports of beef and wheat. On the eve of Allied victory, in March 1945, Argentina finally agreed to declare war on Germany and Japan. Hemispheric solidarity was at last complete.

In retrospect, Franklin Roosevelt's Good Neighbor policy was not so much a departure from past practice as an adaptation and extension of it. The United States continued to pursue hegemony within the Western Hemisphere, in keeping with the imperialist codes of the international system, but now employed new tactics in response to changing circumstances. Instead of relying on Teddy Roosevelt's "big stick," on military force and intervention, the United States could now rely on economic strength and diplomatic persuasion. The policy was not an exercise in charity. After undoing the Platt Amendment and withdrawing troops from Nicaragua and Haiti and the Dominican Republic, for instance, Washington continued to interfere in Cuban and Nicaraguan politics and to retain control over customshouses on Hispaniola to protect returns on American investments. "In actuality," one scholar has written, "the United States abrogated what was obsolete and retained what it considered vital to the national interest."[7] Tactics had changed, but goals were much the same.

With its emphasis on hemispheric unity—and on consolidation of a U.S. sphere of influence—the Good Neighbor policy came to be seen as a cloak for isolationism during the 1930s. Its ideological emphasis on the uniqueness of the Americas, and on differences with Europe and Asia, appeared to justify indifference to world affairs. As Congressman Joe Henricks (D-Florida) proclaimed in late 1939: "The future of the United States lies to the south, and if we bend our efforts to effecting closer relationships with Latin America we will never worry about getting entangled with the petty quarrels of old Europe." But if the United States was relatively passive in Asia and Europe, it was highly activist with regard to Latin America. Hemispheric affairs assumed topmost priority in U.S. foreign policy, and leading figures in U.S. diplomatic circles—from Cordell Hull to Sumner Welles and Adolf Berle—devoted great energy and attention to relations with Latin America. It is only in European (or Asian) perspective that U.S. policy during this period might be construed as isolationist; in the perspective of the Americas, it most decidedly was not.

To be sure, the "Western Hemisphere idea" declined sharply after World War II. United States policy took on a global cast, with strong commitments to European affairs, and the postwar world witnessed new kinds of division—between communist and noncommunist, North and South. In this context the notion of hemispheric solidarity became irrelevant and obsolete. As will be shown in chapters 9–12, it is only now, in the 1990s, that the concept is regaining significance and currency.

An epitaph for the Good Neighbor era came from Philip Jessup, a professor at Columbia University who made a tour of Latin America in 1941. "A decade of the good neighbor policy has helped enormously to overcome the results of mistaken policies of the past," Jessup reported, "but the postwar situation will be a great challenge to our intelligent self-restraint. We shall meet that challenge successfully because the government and people of the U.S. are irrevocably committed to the sound conclusion that the old stupid type of imperialist policy can never be used again."

4

Latin America: Responses
to Imperialism

*I have lived inside the monster and know its entrails—and my weapon is
only the slingshot of David.*
José Martí (1895)

*Each day the United States advances farther in its imperialistic preten-
sions against Latin America. We cannot stand by with folded arms. We
must devise our own master plan for resisting United States aggression.*
Joaquín Walker Martínez (1906)

I will not sell myself, nor will I surrender. *I must be conquered.*
Augusto César Sandino (1927)

Participation by the United States in the global imperial contest had serious implications for Latin America. As political and intellectual leaders
throughout the region attempted to forge strategies for national development, they needed to take explicit account of the inexorable expansion of
U.S. power. Around the turn of the nineteenth century, from the American Revolution through the Wars of Independence, there existed a genuine
sense of confraternal solidarity between statesmen of North America and
Latin America, bound by their common cause against European rule. Yet
the subsequent U.S. quest for hemispheric hegemony, increasingly successful from the 1830s to the 1930s, presented Latin America with a
challenging combination of incentives, restrictions, and opportunities.
This new situation seemed a bitter pill: having cast off colonial bonds to

Spain and Portugal, at considerable cost, Latin America now had to confront a rising imperial power within the Western Hemisphere.

What could Latin America do in response? What strategic options were available to countries of the continent? What was *possible* and *plausible* to do? The range of feasible alternatives for Latin America embraced not only diplomacy, geopolitics, and foreign policy. It also included schemes for economic development, political change, and intraregional cooperation. Not surprisingly, the breadth of these programs often provoked substantial internal disagreement, and for this reason the struggle over Latin America's destiny reached far into the domestic political arena. The continental predicament also provoked intellectual discourse and ideological debate, entering realms of popular culture. This is not to exaggerate the role of the United States: a great deal of conflict and contention in Latin America reflected purely domestic interests, forces, and purposes, especially as peoples of the region struggled to establish national and collective identities in the wake of independence. The century-long extension of U.S. power would nonetheless have fundamental ramifications for countries of the region.

Capitulation offered one expedient solution. Latin Americans could align themselves with U.S. power and/or succumb to U.S. pressure in hopes of salvaging as much as possible; this option was especially tempting for social oligarchies and political elites needing external support in order to survive. This reaction became especially commonplace in countries around the Caribbean Basin, where the United States established neo-colonial protectorates in the wake of military intervention. Tomás Estrada Palma in Cuba and Adolfo Díaz in Nicaragua, among others, realized that their political fortunes depended directly on U.S. sponsorship. The extension of U.S. economic influence, through trade and investment, provided additional incentives for collaboration. Juan Vicente Gómez in Venezuela and a host of lesser-known executives in Central America made personal fortunes by consenting to lucrative contracts with U.S. petroleum, banana, and mining companies. Corruption could help pave the way for empire. A tacit rule thus emerged: the more informal the U.S. penetration, the greater the likelihood of local collaboration.

Yet most Latin American leaders made efforts to resist, or at least deflect, the rise of U.S. power. With the exception of extremely small minorities (and occasional secessionist movements), virtually all sectors of Latin American society opposed the forcible seizure and incorporation of territory throughout the nineteenth century; even Mexico's faithless Santa Anna claimed to have succumbed to U.S. pressure only under duress, and only scattered voices in turn-of-the-century Cuba called for outright annexation by the United States. Similarly, military intervention and the imposition of protectorates between 1898 and 1934 provoked widespread condemnation and denunciation. The expansion of economic influence created a more equivocal circumstance, allowing local elites to benefit from complicity with the United States without explicit endangerment to political sovereignty, but it also met with apprehension and concern throughout the region. In all its various forms, U.S. imperialism confronted Latin America with a real and rising threat.

Over time, Latin American leaders developed a range of responses to the realities of U.S. power. Ultimately, they faced distinct choices:

- They could attempt to unify themselves, thus creating a continental counterweight to the United States.
- They could attempt to strengthen ties with (and seek protection from) European powers.
- They could attempt to establish subregional hegemony, thus challenging the United States or sharing power with it.
- They could fashion doctrines of international law that would impose constraints on the United States.

And in addition, more as an expression of feeling than as a strategy, they could formulate nationalistic cultures of resistance. These options were not all mutually exclusive, and they would appear in a variety of combinations, settings, and times. They reflected realistic appraisals of and reactions to the changing configurations of power throughout the Imperial Era. As such, they revealed an underlying, systematic logic in the conduct of U.S.–Latin American relations.

Option 1: The Bolivarian Dream

The ideal of Latin American unity captured the continental imagination from the outset of independence. It was none other than Simón Bolívar, *El Libertador,* who first gave expression to this hope. In his famous "letter from Jamaica," written in 1815 at the height of the struggle for independence from Spain, Bolívar expounded on the possibility of forging Spanish America into a single new nation:

> It is a grandiose idea to think of consolidating the New World into a single nation, united by pacts into a single bond. It is reasoned that, as these parts have a common origin, language, customs, and religion, they ought to have a single government to permit the newly formed states to unite in a confederation. But this is not possible. America is separated by climatic differences, geographic diversity, conflicting interests, and dissimilar characteristics. How beautiful it would be if the Isthmus of Panama could be for us what the Isthmus of Corinth was for the Greeks!

"Surely," he continued,

> unity is what we need to complete our work of regeneration. . . . I shall tell you with what we must provide ourselves in order to expel the Spaniards and to found a free government. It is *union,* obviously; but such union will come about through sensible planning and well-directed actions rather than by divine magic.

In practical terms, Bolívar at this point envisaged the formation of three Spanish American federations: Mexico plus Central America; northern Spanish South America, including Peru and Bolivia; and southern South America. But the ultimate goal, what became known as the "Bolivarian dream," was the unification of all Spanish America.[1]

External pressure provided motivation for the movement. Throughout the 1820s there persisted the fear that Spain, with help from the Holy Alliance, would attempt to regain its empire in America. In December 1824 the government of Colombia, led by Bolívar, extended formal invitations to a conference to be held in Panama (then a Colombian province) for the purpose of establishing a Spanish American union. As preparations continued, Bolívar exulted that the upcoming congress "seems destined to form a league more extensive, more remarkable, and more powerful than any that has ever existed on the face of the earth." Delegates finally convened in mid-1826, but with representation from only four states: Mexico, Colombia, Peru, and the Central American federation. (Brazil and the United States were invited, over Bolívar's own objections, but to his relief Brazil declined the invitation and the U.S. delegates never attended the meeting.) The congress reached agreement on a treaty "to uphold in common, defensively and offensively, if necessary, the sovereignty and independence of all and every one of the confederated powers of America against all foreign domination." But the threat from Spain was subsiding, a spirit of nationalism within Spanish America was increasing, and the United States was not yet challenging Mexico. Only Bolívar's Colombia actually ratified the document.

The first attempt at unity thus ended in failure. It was perhaps this outcome, as much as the dissolution of Gran Colombia (a confederation of Colombia, Ecuador, and Venezuela), that led Bolívar to sketch out "a few sure conclusions" while en route to exile in November 1830: "first, America is ungovernable for us; second, he who serves a revolution ploughs the sea. . . . [and] the Europeans will not deign to conquer us." Yet the Panama Congress managed to bring together official representatives from a geographical area stretching from Mexico to Peru, it reached agreement on a compact for mutual defense, and, most of all, it placed the question of unification on the continental agenda. By giving credence to the dream, Bolívar ignited aspirations that would long endure.

The spread of U.S. power provoked additional appeals for Spanish American unity. Expressing fear of the United States and opposition to the Monroe Doctrine, Juan Bautista Alberdi, later president of Argentina, wrote in 1844 a *Memoria sobre . . . un Congreso General Americano* that called for an "American union" for the peaceful settlement of disputes, creation of a common coinage, and the elimination of trade barriers throughout Latin America. A few years later the U.S.–Mexican war added a sense of urgency to such demands. North Americans are the "Islamites" of the nineteenth century, fumed Mexico City's *El Universal* in 1853, and they can be stopped only by "an alliance of all peoples of Hispanic origin."

A second Latin American conference took place in Lima in 1847–48. The gathering came in response to two threats: renewed Spanish designs upon the west coast of South America, and U.S. incursions into Mexico. Official delegates took part on behalf of Bolivia, Chile, Ecuador, Colombia, Peru; Venezuela, Argentina, Brazil, and the United States all declined. (Mexico, then under military siege, was unable to dispatch a delegation.) The conference agreed on a mutual defense treaty, as had the Panama Congress more than twenty years before, but it was never ratified by the signatories. The only practical achievement was approval of a consular convention among those countries in attendance.

Largely in reaction to William Walker's infamous filibustering in Nicaragua, there followed a third meeting in 1856 that was attended by Chile, Ecuador, and Peru. Delegates approved a continental treaty—later adhered to by Bolivia, Costa Rica, Nicaragua, Honduras, Mexico, and Paraguay—to respect the integrity of national territories, to refrain from hostile acts, and to adopt uniform procedures for trade and commercial law.

A fourth gathering, in Lima again, took place in 1864–65. By this time Latin America was facing multiple pressures from abroad: in 1861 Spain had retaken Santo Domingo; having occupied the Chincha islands (off Peru) in 1864, Spain was at war with both Chile and Peru; and France was supporting a European monarchy in Mexico. In response Chilean patriots formed a Sociedad de la Unión Americana de Santiago, published a two-volume set of documents on the movement for unification, and depicted the United States as a major source of danger. Warned Francisco Bilbao: "The United States extends more each day the predatory hunt which it has already undertaken. We see fragments of America falling into the Saxon jaws of the voracious serpent. Yesterday, Texas. Soon, northern Mexico will accept a new sovereign," and, eventually, all of Spanish America could be reduced to a U.S. protectorate. Representatives came from Bolivia, Chile, Colombia, Ecuador, El Salvador, Guatemala, Peru, and Venezuela; reflecting their desires to maintain close ties with Europe, Argentina and Brazil declined to attend. Peru explored the possibility of inviting the United States but met with disapproval. Delegates approved a resolution denouncing Spain's seizure of the Chincha islands, but produced no treaties of any kind.

The Lima conference was perhaps the last institutional embodiment of Bolívar's exalted dream. Subsequent efforts would founder on the lack of complete consensus among countries of the region, and, in particular, on the historic rivalry between Chile and Argentina. Ambivalence about Brazil posed yet another obstacle, since it was unclear whether the project should embrace a Luso-American nation or focus only on Spanish America. Nonetheless the idea of regional unification would appear, time and again, throughout the twentieth century. It would remain a fundamental aspiration of the region.

Option 2: External Powers

Complications in the quest for unity encouraged a search for alternatives. One of the most straightforward options for confronting the United States was to seek protection from one of its major rivals. This tactic was entirely consistent with rules of the prevailing imperial contest, and it offered weaker states (in Latin America) the opportunity of aligning themselves with stronger nations (in Europe) to counter the influence of the United States. As shown in chapter 1, several European states were pressing for advantage in the Western Hemisphere throughout the nineteenth century. The task was persuading them to embrace the Latin American cause.

Pax Britannica?

Simón Bolívar recognized the opportunity. In his conception there was one nation that presented itself as an exceptionally desirable ally, patron, and protector—a nation with colonial possessions in the Caribbean, territorial holdings in Central and South America, and extensive commercial and financial interests throughout the region: Great Britain, which offered the additional advantage of being the preeminent power in the nineteenth-century world. From the outset, Bolívar's plans for continental unification included the explicit hope that Great Britain would join the confederation. As he wrote to General Santander in March 1825, while preparing for the upcoming Panama congress: "Believe me, my dear General, we shall save the New World if we come to an agreement with England in *political and military matters*. This simple sentence ought to tell you more than two whole volumes." And as time for the congress approached, Bolívar emphasized his hopes: "Should Great Britain agree to join it as a constituent member, the Holy Alliance will be less powerful than this confederation. Mankind will a thousand times bless this league for promoting its general welfare, and America, as well as Great Britain, will reap from it untold benefits." Bolívar's reasoning was crystal-clear: a British protectorate over Spanish America would discourage attempts at reconquest by the Holy Alliance, it would protect the newly independent region from the expansionist United States, and it would utterly demolish the Monroe Doctrine.

The Liberator's scheme was not as farfetched as it might in hindsight seem. English statesmen were acutely concerned about the prospect of U.S. hegemony within the Western Hemisphere. In December 1824 the prime minister, the 2nd Earl of Liverpool, wrote one of his colleagues: "I am conscientiously convinced that if we allow these new states to consolidate their system and their policy with the United States of America, it will in a very few years prove fatal to our greatness, if not endanger our safety." The foreign minister, George Canning, expressed particular unease over U.S. ambitions toward Cuba: "The possession by the United States of both shores of the channel through which our Jamaica trade must pass . . . would amount to a suspension of that trade, and to consequent total ruin." Latin America was thus of considerable interest to the British and their imperial policy. Congratulating himself on his master stroke of gaining British recognition for the newly independent countries of Spanish America, Canning summarized the outlook succinctly: "The fight has been hard," he wrote in 1826, "but it is won. The deed is done. Spanish America is free; and if we do not mismanage our matters sadly, she is English, and *Novus saeclorum nascitur ordo.*"

Canning nonetheless resisted Bolívar's overtures, dispatching only a British observer (rather than conference delegate) to the Panama congress. For the remainder of the century Britain chose to protect its growing economic interests in Latin America through diplomatic pressure and, on occasion, military operations. Indeed, British vessels blockaded the port of Buenos Aires in 1846–47 and the port of Rio de Janeiro in 1894; British troops entered Venezuela and Nicaragua in the 1890s; and British authorities maintained tight hold on valued colonial possessions throughout the Caribbean. On mainland Latin America, however, Britain relied upon commercial and financial prowess to consolidate an "informal empire." By the mid-1890s the British foreign office consented to Washington's resolution of the Venezuelan crisis, tacitly accepting America's claim to hemispheric hegemony, and a few years later Britain took refuge behind Teddy Roosevelt's corollary to the Monroe Doctrine. In the end, Latin America was simply not important enough to tempt Britain into open alliance with countries of the region. At least as envisioned by Bolívar, the *pax britannica* would never come to pass.

Opposition to Pan Americanism

The U.S. promotion of Pan Americanism in the 1880s met stiff resistance throughout the hemisphere. In literary journals and diplomatic forums, in private and public arenas, spokesmen for Latin America developed three related reasons for opposition to Washington's plan: apprehension about the rise of U.S. power, resentment of the Monroe Doctrine, and insistence on retaining ties to Europe.

As preparations were under way for the first Pan American conference in Washington, the Cuban writer and patriot José Martí in 1889 urged Latin America to proceed with caution:

> Never in America, from its independence to the present, has there been a matter requiring more good judgment or more vigilance, or demanding a clearer and more thorough examination, than the invitation which the powerful United States (glutted with its unsaleable merchandise and determined to extend its dominion in America) is sending to the less powerful American nations (bound by free and useful commerce to the European nations) for purposes of arranging an alliance against Europe and cutting off transactions with the rest of the world. Spanish America learned how to save itself from the tyranny of Spain; and now, after viewing with judicious eyes the antecedents,

motives, and ingredients of the invitation, it is essential to say, for it is true, that the time has come for Spanish America to declare its second independence.

The congress, Martí warned, was meant to usher in "the frank and forthright achievement of an era of United States dominion over the nations of America."

During the conference itself, delegates from Latin America sought ways to resist demands by the United States. They fought successfully against James G. Blaine's pet proposal for a customs union, which, in the words of one assessment, entailed "the proposition of excluding Europe from the advantages accorded to its commerce. . . . The present convocation has as its object the erection of an American Zollverein." Moreover, they maintained, the setting of tariffs was a prerogative of national sovereignty. Insistence on self-determination was thus identified with maintenance of commercial ties to Europe. The plan for a customs union met an early death in a conference committee, which came out with a lukewarm recommendation in favor of bilateral or reciprocity treaties—signed by the United States, Mexico, Brazil, Nicaragua, Colombia, and Venezuela, over a minority dissenting report from Chile and Argentina. And as the conference was preparing to adjourn, in April 1890, Argentine representative Roque Saenz Peña (later his country's president) uttered an elegant demurral to demands for hemispheric solidarity. "What I lack is not love for America," declared the future president, "but suspicion and ingratitude towards Europe. I cannot forget that in Europe are Spain, our mother; Italy, our friend; and France, our elder sister." Instead of "America for the Americans," he proclaimed, the congress should uphold the principle of "America for all humanity."

Condemnation of the Monroe Doctrine went hand-in-hand with celebration of the European connection. As early as the mid-1820s, Diego Portales of Chile issued a stern admonition about Monroe's pronouncement: "Be careful," he wrote, "of escaping one domination at the price of falling under another. We must distrust those who take advantage of the work of our champions of freedom, without having helped us in any way." Alberdi of Argentina would later urge Spanish American states to forge commercial links to Europe, "so as to defend themselves against Brazil and the United States. Their peril is in America; their safeguard in Europe." And at a 1916 financial conference, Chilean representative Armando Quesada Acharán emphasized the value of the European connection: "Closer economic ties between the United States and Latin America must not, in any way, interfere with the maintaining and increasing of economic relations with Europe." Reformers and nationalists would continue to denounce the Monroe Doctrine, its corollaries, and its applications well into the twentieth century.

The Pan American movement and the Monroe Doctrine thus became twin symbols of U.S. preponderance. In the 1920s the Argentine sociologist José Ingenieros neatly summarized the challenge for Latin America:

> We are not, we do not want to be any longer, we could not be Pan American-
> ists. The United States is to be feared because it is great, rich, and enterprising.
> What concerns us to is find out whether there is a possibility of balancing its
> power to the extent necessary to save our political independence and the
> sovereignty of our countries.

For Washington, keeping Europe out of the hemisphere meant keeping Latin America under U.S. control; for Latin America, the protection of national sovereignty required the maintenance of ties with Europe.

Hispanidad and Francophilia

A frequent corollary of this general position stressed the importance of Latin America's cultural, social, and intellectual connections with Europe, rather than the United States. During the nineteenth century the quest for self-identity meant not *indigenismo,* a movement that would emerge later in the twentieth century, but appreciation of European ancestries. In practice this pattern took two forms: *hispanidad,* or glorification of things Spanish, and unabashed Francophilia.

Veneration for Spain implied a celebration of Catholic, conservative values that placed dignity, status, and manners above talent and tangible accomplishment, religious faith above mundane achievement, dogma above curiosity, the traditional over the novel, the graceful and artistic over the functional and practical. In 1845 former president Joaquín Pinto of Chile stressed the Hispanic legacy in declaring that "we will never utilize the methods of democracy as practiced in the United States of America, but rather the political principles of Spain." And in the wake of Mexico's calamitous mid-nineteenth-century war with the United States, conserva-tive writer-politician Lucas Alamán spoke disdainfully of a conflict that had resulted from the ambitions "not of an absolute monarchy, but of a repub-lic which claimed to be in the vanguard of nineteenth-century civilization." Alamán went on to condemn U.S. culture as derivative, a place where religion was mixed with commercial spirit, where the cult of individualism led to systematic disregard for morality, order, and good customs. By contrast, he wrote,

> We are not a people of merchants and adventurers, scum and refuse *(hez y
> desecho)* of all countries, whose only mission is to usurp the property of the
> miserable Indians, and later to rob the fertile lands opened to civilization by
> the Spanish race. . . . We are a nation formed three centuries ago, not an
> aggregation of peoples of differing customs.

In due course Alamán and his conservative associates would turn for salva-tion toward France, importing ill-starred Emperor Maximilian from the House of Hapsburg.

Democracy and capitalism came under attack as vehicles for the promotion of alien and materialistic values. Uruguayan writer José Enrique Rodó penned a consummate statement of this position in *Ariel y Calibán,* a turn-of-the-century essay that extolled the virtuous morality of Spanish America and denounced the grasping materialism of the United States, depicted as Calíban. Invocation of Hispanic virtue intensified during and after the Spanish-American War, which provoked widespread fear of U.S. imperial ambitions. Although the motherland might suffer defeat, one Chilean proclaimed, "Spanish valor was still worth more than all the gold of the United States." United States materialism came in for particular scorn. If Argentina were never to be anything more than a colossal *estancia,* crisscrossed by railroads and bursting with wealth, said Juan Agustín García, "I would rather live in the most miserable corner of the earth where there still lives a feeling for beauty, goodness, and truth."

For these generations, France represented the center of civilization and *haute couture.* Boulevards in bustling capitals, from Mexico City to Buenos Aires, were copies of the Champs Elysées. Stately mansions were erected in imitation of Parisian models. Opera houses, even in such removed locations as the Amazonian city of Manáus, were carbon copies of L'Opera. Oligarchs took vacations in France and sent their sons to study at the Sorbonne. When Victor Hugo died in 1885, *Sud América* in Buenos Aires devoted its entire front page to recapitulating his career.

Such insistent evocation of European legacies had several implications for Latin America's ruling elites. One was to stress their cultural superiority over the United States. Another was to deemphasize the importance of the economic realm, where the United States was rapidly increasing its advantage. Third was to demonstrate the continuing affinity between Latin America and Europe and, by so doing, to affirm the foundation for joint political collaboration.

Option 3: Rivalry and Subregional Hegemony

A third strategic option was for individual countries of Latin America to achieve subregional hegemony and compete on a more or less equal basis with the United States.[2] Nationalism thrived on visions of grandeur. This aspiration was in fact unavailable to small nations around the Caribbean Basin, where the United States was steadily gaining the upper hand over Europe, or to Mexico, humiliated and dismembered by the war of 1847–48. By virtue of geographical location, size, and resources, only two nations could seriously entertain such an ambition: Argentina and Brazil.

Argentina's Manifest Destiny

During the late nineteenth century, Argentina saw itself as similar to the United States and therefore its natural rival. The winning of the American West had its counterpart in Argentina's Conquest of the Desert and settlement of the pampa, routinely referred to in presidential statements as *nuestro "Far West"* (with deliberate employment of the English phrase). Both countries received mass waves of immigrants from Europe between 1870 and 1910. In keeping with racist assumptions of the day, Argentine leaders took pride in the Caucasian composition of its ethnic stock, which made it feel comparable to the United States and vastly superior to neighbors with large indigenous or black populations. Geopolitically, too, many Argentines believed that location in the southern cone of South America placed the country in a natural position to impose subregional hegemony.

It was in this sense that Domingo Sarmiento, the great reformer of the nineteenth century, evolved his own view of the United States. Initially a Francophile, he became disenchanted with Europe and at one point embraced the Monroe Doctrine. While serving as minister to Washington, from 1865 to 1868, he even appeared to accept U.S. claims to manifest destiny: "It is the province of the United States," he once told an American audience, "the highest mission intrusted by Providence to a great people, that of conducting others through the new paths opened by mankind to advance firmly to their great destinies." As Argentina gained political stability and enjoyed rapid economic growth, however, Sarmiento's attitude changed from awe to rivalry. His final written words, in 1888, presented his compatriots with a prediction and a challenge: "We shall reach the level of the United States. We shall be America as the sea is the ocean. We shall be the United States."

Many of Sarmiento's colleagues were supremely confident. The Buenos Aires newspaper *La Prensa* anticipated that Argentina could achieve both political democracy and economic prosperity. "The Argentine Republic ought to aspire to grow like the United States," declared its editors in 1886, "and not in the manner, and with the elements, of France, England, and Germany." Thus appeared the elements of a national strategy, or at least of a national aspiration: Argentina would be to South America what the United States had become in North America. Each would enjoy continental hegemony; in tandem, they would dominate the hemisphere.

For Argentina this project did not imply alliance or collaboration with the United States. On the contrary, Argentine leaders intended to maintain extremely close ties to European powers, especially to England. These European connections would assert and emphasize Argentina's distance and independence from Washington. As rivals of the United States, both Europe and Argentina would have a natural interest in diplomatic and economic partnership.

Foreign observers gave further credence to the dream. After a brief visit, journalist William Eleroy Curtis predicted in 1888 that "the Argentine Republic will some day become a formidable rival of the United States." A French economic geographer, M. E. Vavasseur, wrote in 1890: "The Argentine Republic, which occupies in the temperate zone of South America a position analogous to that of the United States in North America, may dream, if not of equal power, at least of a similar future." To complete the picture, some Argentine commentators even developed a vision of "manifest destiny," analogous to pretentious claims made on behalf of the United States. As the only white, prosperous, and democratic nation on the continent, Argentina would have an obligation to spread the gospels of development through South America: according to *La Prensa* in 1893, Argentina has "a great civilizing mission in the New World."

Predictably enough, Argentine leaders looked upon Brazil with a mixture of fear and contempt. According to one nationalist just after the turn of the century: "The natural enemy of all the Hispanic-American nations is Brazil. It is our born enemy. . . . Speaking a different language, differently oriented in culture and politics, entirely different because of the mixture with the Negro race . . . Brazil forms a foreign element within our body." Racist criteria thus assured Argentina of social superiority over its principal rival on the continent.

By the early twentieth century Argentina seemed to be heading for its predestined greatness. In the late 1920s it was ranked as the seventh richest country in the world. It was also one of the world's most democratic nations, having institutionalized a system of genuinely competitive elections in 1912. Ably, and energetically, Argentina successfully resisted the U.S. drive toward regional hegemony in a variety of diplomatic settings. Political and economic setbacks during the 1930s began to unravel the dream, however, and it would later come apart at the seams. The notion of Argentina's manifest destiny may look, in retrospect, like a quaint historic artifact; but for generations of *argentinos*, from the 1860s to the 1930s, it offered a vision of national greatness.

God Is a Brazilian

The other country aspiring to emulate the United States was Brazil. Even during the colonial period, love of land and a sense of natural majesty had inspired a feeling of greatness, as suggested by the titles of such books as Ambrósio Fernandes Brandão's *Diálogos das Grandezas do Brasil* (1618) and André João Antonil's *Cultura e Opulência do Brasil* (1711). Indeed, the beauty and vastness of the land gave rise to the not-always tongue-in-cheek assertion that "God is a Brazilian." In 1838, with an independent monarchy in place, the Visconde de São Leopoldo, president of the recently founded Brazilian Geographical and Historical Institute, offered an optimistic prediction: "Everything points to the fact that Brazil is destined to be not accidentally, but by necessity, a center of enlightenment and civilization and an arbiter of the politics of the New World." Sargento Albuquerque echoed this theme in 1917: "The historic and political superiority of Brazil is manifest: united, colossal, irreducible. . . . It is destined to occupy in South America within a century the same preponderant place that the United States occupies in North America."

Noting with asperity the condescension expressed by Argentines, Brazilians responded with their own contempt. "Whether the [Argentines] like it or not," in the words of one Brazilian, "we have already proved the superiority of our organizational talents by systematizing juridic, economic, and intellectual forces, while the Hispanic inferiority becomes obvious in the fragmentation of states all more or less weak, all more or less turbulent." The Baron of Rio Branco, Brazil's legendary diplomat, likewise condemned "those political evils which so greatly hurt the South American nations. There is nothing more ridiculous and extravagant than the manifestations of dictators, the pronouncements, the revolutions for possession of power, the military demagoguery."

In contrast to Argentina, which sought alliances in Europe, Brazil cultivated close connections with the United States. Rio Branco once explained that Brazil "prides itself on the spontaneous and affirmed friendship of that American nation and its great president [Cleveland]. There is no friendship more coveted in the world." And in 1906, just before the third Pan American conference, he expressed public support for the Monroe Doctrine and the Roosevelt Corollary. These principles guaranteed that the Americas "cannot be touched by any European greed or conquest," in his words, "because the Monroe Doctrine is not an abstraction. It has for its base the prodigious ascendancy of the United States." Rio Branco continued:

> Latin America has nothing to fear from Anglo-Saxon America. The United States is a nation of English origin and principles and therefore beneficial for the civilization of other people because the sentiment of individualism is so much a part of their race that English or North American imperialism, if it should manifest itself, never would be of the same type as German or Latin imperialism which seeks to destroy and annihilate everything, contorting everything, in order to create from the incompatibilities and irreconcilables the same kind of country in all the regions of the world. Nothing, absolutely nothing, in the policies of the United States would be able to cause uneasiness to the national sensitivity of the other American countries. Just the opposite, these nations find in the preponderance of the first nation of the continent support for their causes and aspirations.

United States power was a benefit for Latin America, not a threat to sovereignty. In a world of major-power rivalries, Washington would shield the region from continental Europe.

Thus the Brazilian strategy took shape. Brazil would gain ascendancy in South America, following the U.S. model, and would forge a partnership with the United States. In effect, the two countries would establish a joint condominium over the Western Hemisphere. They would sustain their greatness and subregional superiority through mutual collaboration.

For Brazil, and especially for Rio Branco, emulation of the United States had practical meaning as well. Like its partner to the north, Brazil was busily engaged in expanding its territorial reach, usually at the expense of increasingly resentful neighbors. Under Rio Branco's leadership, Brazil proclaimed the doctrine of *uti possidetis* and triumphed in successive territorial disputes over Argentina, France, Bolivia, and Peru. All in all, Rio

Branco managed to delineate 9,000 miles of frontier and to add nearly 115,000 square miles to the national domain. It seemed only fitting that, as expansionist powers, Brazil and the United States should give support to one another.

Dreams of Brazilian *grandeza* have since foundered on hard times. Political instability, economic stagnation, and persistent poverty have created uncertainty and apprehension about the nation's future. Because of its vast natural and human resources, however, there still lingers the idea that Brazil is a great power of the future, a sleeping giant, a nation destined for fulfillment. Coequal partnership (or rivalry) with the United States may seem like an unlikely prospect, at least within the next generation, but it remains a vital part of national mythology.

Option 4: Doctrines and Diplomacy

A fourth alternative for Latin America took the form of a quest for protection under international law. Legal codes represented a positive asset for weaker nations in their dealings with stronger powers. Theoretically, international law obliged all countries to abide by universal principles of conduct. Since the rules applied to all members of the international community, great and small, the rules imposed constraints upon the powerful. Within the context of inter-American relations, therefore, international law came to be seen as a means of curtailing the United States.

International jurisprudence was undergoing intense development during this era. In practice, the expansion of imperial holdings and pursuit of major-power rivalries reflected raw demonstrations of power; in response, idealists sought to strengthen the corpus and meaning of international law. The Permanent Court of International Arbitration was established at The Hague in 1899. And nearly thirty years later, in 1928, U.S. secretary of state Frank P. Kellogg and his French counterpart, Aristide Briand, would announce their own grand faith in legal principles: through the Pact of Paris, they proposed to outlaw the use of war as an instrument of national policy. It was a touching declaration, overwhelmingly naive in retrospect, but a fitting expression of the hopes and contradictions prevailing in the world arena at this time.

A principal contribution of Latin American jurists was the doctrine of sovereign immunity from external intervention. First formulated in the mid-nineteenth century by Andrés Bello of Chile and by Carlos Calvo of Argentina, the basic idea insisted upon the absolute equality of sovereign states—regardless of size, position, or power. As a logical result, courts of one country should not be subject to appeal in cases involving rights of foreign nationals. Out of this emerged what came to be known as the Calvo clause, typically applied to foreign (especially U.S.) companies with investments in Latin America: the foreign party would agree to the settlement of disputes by courts of the host country and forswear any right of appeal for special assistance from its own government.

In support of this principle, Venezuela offered a proposal at the first Pan American conference denouncing diplomatic representation for economic claims by foreign nationals. As reported out of committee—with the support of Argentina, Chile, Ecuador, and Guatemala—the resolution stipulated that foreigners were "entitled to enjoy all the civil rights enjoyed by natives," but no more than that: "A nation has not, nor recognizes in favor of foreigners, any other obligations or responsibilities than those which in favor of the natives are established, in like cases, by the constitution and by the laws." The conference adopted the majority report by a vote of 15–1, with the United States alone in opposition. Equally revealing were the terms of debate, where the U.S. representative sharply criticized the concept of an "American" or hemispheric international law. Stressing the differences between Europe and the Americas, Latin American delegates were attempting to fashion a special body of international law for the Western Hemisphere; the United States insisted that there could only be a single and universal code of conduct.[3]

Another central issue at the 1889–90 conference concerned a U.S. proposal for compulsory arbitration of legal disputes. Latin American delegates regarded the plan with suspicion, as an effort to circumvent national courts through international tribunals or panels that would inevitably reflect the interests of the United States. In particular, Chileans feared that such a mechanism would deprive them of hard-won spoils from the War of the Pacific (1879–83). More generally, José Martí condemned the project as a transparent scheme to create a hemispheric institution under Washington's control. Manuel Quintana offered an eloquent statement of the Latin American view:

> In the eyes of international American law there are neither great nor small nations. All are equally sovereign and independent, all equally worthy of consideration and respect. The arbitration proposed is not, consequently, a compact of abdication, of vassalage, or of submission. Before as well as after its conclusion, all and each of the nations of the Americas will preserve the absolute direction of their political destinies, absolutely without interference by the others.

At this point the proposal for final arbitration included a "point of independence," allowing any country to exclude from arbitration any matter appearing to endanger its own vital interests, but even this watered-down version did not gain the approval of the conference. Latin America thus upheld the principles of sovereignty and equality of nations.

The question of international arbitration resisted resolution. Essentially, Latin America upheld the sovereignty and integrity of national courts; the United States held out for international arbitration in cases of dispute. The two sides reached a compromise at the 1902 Pan American conference, in Mexico City, accepting the idea of voluntary arbitration through the international court at The Hague. Latins agreed because adherence would be voluntary; Americans consented because the world court would apply principles of universal law, not a regional or hemispheric doctrine. Also at the Mexico conference, Brazil proposed creation of a legal panel to begin work on a specifically regional or inter-American system of arbitration, on private international law, and on a code of public international law "to govern the relations between American republics." Essentially, Latin Americans were attempting to find a way to enshrine the principles of national sovereignty and nonintervention; the United States wanted to preserve the rights of intervention, then recognized under some circumstances by international law. The impasse continued for years.

Another key development in legal circles emerged from the Venezuelan crisis of 1902–3 (during which Great Britain, Germany, and Italy began taking military action in order to collect outstanding debts). As reported in chapter 1, the foreign minister of Argentina, Luis María Drago, dispatched a note to U.S. secretary of state John Hay proposing "that the public debt gives no place for armed intervention, and less still to the material occupation of the soil of American nations by a European power." Revealingly, Drago invoked both the Monroe Doctrine and the principle of national sovereignty, concepts that would soon be at odds with each other. Hay responded noncommittally and the Europeans soon consented to arbitration in their dispute with Venezuela. There the matter rested until 1904, when Teddy Roosevelt laid bare the implicit contradiction in Drago's proposition by announcing his "corollary" to the Monroe Doctrine, proclaiming that the United States would act as hemispheric policeman in cases of "chronic wrong-doing or impotence." Quickly sensing the danger, *La Prensa* denounced Roosevelt's proclamation as "the most serious and menacing declaration against South American integrity which has come out of Washington."

After William Howard Taft's election as president, however, the United States decided to support a diluted version of Drago's proposal at a 1907 conference on international law at The Hague. United States delegates agreed that the use of force should be in principle prohibited for the collection of "contract debts claimed from the government of one country by another," but insisted that force could be admissible if countries refused to abide by the results of arbitration. Latin Americans greeted the Hague protocol with justifiable skepticism. Not a single South American country agreed to it. Several countries ratified it—Mexico, Panama, Guatemala, Nicaragua, Haiti, and El Salvador—and only Panama (a U.S. protectorate) and Mexico (under Porfirio Díaz) without reservation. Years later, in 1931, postrevolutionary Mexico denounced the convention and gave notice of its intent to withdraw.

World War I interrupted these legal and diplomatic maneuvers. At a 1923 Pan American conference in Santiago, Alejandro Álvarez, a distinguished Chilean jurist, renewed the debate by taking a clear position on the existence of a unique body of inter-American law. "The States of America," Álvarez proposed, even before reaching a mutual agreement, have proclaimed certain regulations or principles different and even contradictory to those ruling in European countries, and which these latter are compelled to respect in our Continent, for instance, nonintervention and the nonoccupation of territories of the States of America by ultra-continental countries.

Firmly supporting the doctrine of nonintervention, the American Institute of International Law, a private organization, drafted a resolution for a 1925 meeting which stipulated: "No Nation has the right to interfere in the internal or foreign affairs of an American Republic against the will of that Republic. The sole lawful intervention is friendly and conciliatory action without any character of coercion." With U.S. troops still stationed in Haiti and poised for a return to Nicaragua, Washington was cool to these proposals.

The minuet continued. In 1927 a legal conference at Rio discussed a resolution that "No State has the right to interfere in the internal affairs of another." The next year, at a Pan American conference in Havana, chief U.S. delegate Charles Evans Hughes disputed this idea:

> What are we going to do when government breaks down and American citizens are in danger of their lives? Are we to stand by and see them killed because a government in circumstances which it cannot control and for which it may not be responsible can no longer afford reasonable protection? . . . now it is a principle of international law that in such a case a government is fully justified in taking action—I would call it interposition of a temporary character—for the purpose of protecting the lives and property of its nationals.

In effect, Hughes was recasting the Roosevelt Corollary, justifying "interposition of a temporary character" as a principle of international law.

In the early 1930s Argentina launched an aggressive diplomatic offensive against the U.S. position. Under its flamboyant foreign minister, Carlos Saavedra Lamas, Argentina pressed repeatedly for an absolute statement of prohibition against intervention. Seeking to mediate the Chaco War (between Bolivia and Paraguay), Saavedra Lamas in September 1932 unveiled a proposal for an Anti-War Treaty condemning "wars of aggression," denying territorial acquisitions or occupations by force, and prohibiting all forms of intervention, "either diplomatic or armed." The key clause was, of course, the absolute stricture against intervention.

On the eve of the 1933 Pan American conference, in Montevideo, Saavedra Lamas induced six Latin American nations to accede to his proposal. It now had the standing of an actual treaty, backed by multilateral calls for accession. The newly inaugurated administration of Franklin Delano Roosevelt, about to embark on its Good Neighbor policy, agreed not only to support the Anti-War Treaty but also to approve a resolution that "No State has the right to intervene in the internal or external affairs of another." Thus triumphant, Saavedra Lamas presided over the commission—technically associated with the League of Nations—that brought an end to the Chaco War. For this accomplishment, and for his Anti-War Treaty, he received the Nobel Peace Prize in 1936.

Cultures of Resistance

An additional development in Latin America during this period was the formulation of cultural and rhetorical codes for resisting U.S. power in the hemisphere. This was not a strategic option or policy guideline so much as an expression of popular feeling, the adoption of a general stance, and the construction of a national and regional discourse. Yet these "cultures of resistance" grew in complexity and intensity from the mid-nineteenth century through the early twentieth century. They would have considerable impact on the tenor and tone of inter-American relations. In time, they would also provide both a basis and a resource for populist and nationalist movements throughout the region.

The creeds of resistance contained a series of interlocking assumptions. To uphold the sovereignty of young and fragile republics in Latin America was to be a nationalist. To be a nationalist was to be anti-imperialist. To be anti-imperialist, as U.S. power grew, was to become anti-American, anti-*gringo,* and anti-*yanqui.* Paradoxically, however, nationalism also implied solidarity with other countries of Latin America: victims of a common enemy, according to this view, they must band together for the sake of mutual support. In one form or another this outlook appeared in virtually every part of the region, finding particularly acute expression in countries most directly affected by the application of U.S. power: Mexico, Cuba, and Nicaragua. Not coincidentally, each of these countries eventually underwent social revolution.

Mexico: War and Invasion

Mexico felt the presence of its neighbor in frequent, profound, and often painful ways. Most deeply etched in the national memory are recollections of the "war of the North American invasion," the mid-nineteenth century military conflicts that resulted in the loss of nearly half the country's territory. For Mexicans this episode began in the 1820s, when the newly independent republic granted permission for colonists under Moses and Stephen Austin to settle in what was then the northern province of Texas. When Texans began demanding self-government, the U.S. government lent moral support to the rebels by dispatching a military expedition into Mexican territory. This itself was cause for war; but when Mexico desisted, the United States responded by recognizing Texan independence and then, in the mid-1840s, by approving its annexation as a state. This was not, in the Mexican outlook, an accidental series of spontaneous events, but the expression of long-held expansionist ambitions. As José Vasconcelos would write in his *Breve Historia de México,* "the Texas colonists were the advance guard for yankee imperialism."

As recounted in chapter 1, boundary disputes persisted in the 1840s. Under Mexican rule the western frontier of Texas had stretched to the Nueces River, well north of the Rio Grande, but U.S. authorities began disputing this fact. In 1846 troops under General Zachary Taylor moved across the Nueces, in defiance of Mexican sovereignty, and a U.S. naval force moved near the coast of Veracruz. Mexico's embattled president José Joaquín Herrera agreed to talks about the Texas question, but U.S. emissary John Slidell scuttled the negotiations by proclaiming his intent to discuss not only Texas but also the purchase of New Mexico and California. In frustration General Mariano Paredes overthrew Herrera and canceled the Slidell negotiations. One thoughtful Mexican observer left this record of the affair:

> While the United States seemed to be animated by a sincere desire not to break the peace, their acts of hostility manifested very evidently what were their true intentions. Their ships infested our coasts; their troops continued advancing upon our territory, situated at places which under no aspect could be disputed. Thus violence and insult were united: thus at the very time they usurped part of our territory, they offered us the hand of treachery, to have soon the audacity to say that our obstinacy and arrogance were the real causes of the war.

In May 1846 Polk went on to declare war against Mexico, and U.S. troops swiftly overwhelmed Mexican forces. In 1847 General Winfield Scott invaded Mexico City, where young cadets fought to the death in defense of their country and, in an act of heroic bravado, hurled themselves off a parapet in Chapultepec rather than surrender the national flag. The *niños héroes* came to symbolize the noble struggle of Mexico against impossible odds, obtaining a place of mythic honor in the pantheon of Mexican patriots. The disastrous defeat at the hand of the United States carved a deep scar on Mexico's national soul.

Additional traumas came through the Mexican Revolution, when the United States would intervene in a variety of ways. Even as Francisco Madero was in the process of ousting Porfirio Díaz, U.S. representatives reported widespread anti-Americanism. Consul Samuel E. Magill at Guadalajara reported to Secretary of State Philander Knox in 1911 that "the anti-American sentiment is almost universal among rich and poor alike." Consul Charles M. Freeman at Durango wrote that "this district is 95% anti-American, and that is a most conservative estimate for I have yet to meet a Mexican who has any love for the people of the United States as a whole." M. S. Largey, a banking and mining operator, returned to the United States in 1913 with a report that "the great masses of the population hate Americans with an intensity that is awful to contemplate." The logic was ineluctable: virtually by definition, a nationalist movement in quest of social justice would have to be anti-American.

There existed a constant, understandable fear that the United States would take advantage of rising unrest in Mexico. As Madero mounted his drive against Díaz, commentators expressed apprehension about U.S. troop movements along the northern border and naval operations off the coast. Posters and billboards summoned compatriots to resist: "Death to the Yankees!" "Down with Gringos!" "Kill Díaz and his Yankee friends."

Once in office, the mild-mannered Madero dismissed U.S. workers from the Mexican railroad system out of fear that they might comprise a fifth column. Anticipating a U.S. invasion, in April 1912 the newspaper *El Tiempo* called for the Mexican people to rise up, repel the aliens, and make sure that "each bullet fired goes to strike the heart or the forehead of the profaner of our soil."

Conservatives joined in this chorus as well. After Woodrow Wilson refused to recognize the administration of Victoriano Huerta (following the assassination of Madero), a pro-Huerta spokesman claimed that a resistance movement in Sonora was in fact the first step in a plan formulated by Teddy Roosevelt and "Yankee bankers" to partition Mexico into small republics that would then be at the mercy of the United States. In 1914 Wilson authorized a naval occupation of the port of Veracruz, after Mexico had refused to fire a twenty-one-gun salute of respect; bloody confrontations led to at least 200 Mexican dead and 300 wounded, compared with 19 American deaths and 71 additional casualties.

Later in the revolution, as the Wilson administration began to favor the forces of Venustiano Carranza, an outraged Pancho Villa massacred fifteen American citizens at Santa Ysabel in January 1916. Two months later he conducted a daring cross-border raid on the town of Columbus, New Mexico, resulting in the death of eighteen Americans. As noted in chapter 2, Wilson responded by mobilizing 150,000 militia along the southern frontier and dispatching 12,000 troops under General John Pershing to pursue and punish Villa. Pershing never came close to capturing Villa in the mountains of Chihuahua, U.S. troops were routed in a battle at Carrizal, and after ten months of frustration the expedition returned to the United States. For his successful defiance of the *gringos,* Villa would become a national hero.

Thus did Mexico develop its culture of resistance, a fierce pride in *lo mexicano* and resentment of U.S. depredations. In 1924 a Catholic priest, José Cantú Corro, spoke of underlying strength in the national character. Because of its Indian and Spanish strains, he wrote in *Patria y raza,* "there throbs in our heart the spirit of El Cid and of Cuauhtémoc." Continued Cantú Corro: "Mexico must not be for foreigners; no, a thousand times no. . . . Mexico, idolized Motherland, nest of affections, mansion of happiness, noble Republic; Mexico, my Motherland, let the Saxons never assault your soil, nor implant their false religion, nor tarnish your flag."

Cuba: Inside the Monster

One of the most revered patriots in Cuban history is José Martí. A passionate advocate of Cuban independence from Spain, a writer, publicist, and essayist, Martí went into exile in the United States from 1880 to 1895. While acknowledging respect for the United States, he expressed continual apprehension about its annexationist tendencies and its long-standing designs upon Cuba. In a reference to Francis Cutting, one of the most noted

militants in the American Annexationist League, Martí once observed that
"We love the land of Lincoln just as we fear the land of Cutting." What he
condemned most was *ultraguilismo,* as he called it, the policy of "extending
over much of the earth the wings of the American eagle."

In Martí's view, the U.S. drive toward empire had an economic basis.
American producers were in desperate need of new markets:

> The manufacturers of North America . . . have come to produce more arti-
> cles than the country needs, but are unable, as a result of the cost of produc-
> tion . . . to place their excess production in foreign markets, [and] today
> they urgently and actually need to display and sell their surplus at low cost
> in the nearby American markets; and with their additional production, in
> the absence of a corresponding demand to absorb it, the surplus will con-
> tinue to accumulate on top of the current surplus. People here, thus, need
> someone to display their products. People there need someone to explain and
> point out to them the appropriateness and advantages of their purchases. *La
> América* is a timely answer to both needs.

Here was precisely the problem. For Martí, U.S. imperialism was not a
whimsical impulse or a partisan cause. It was a fundamental requirement
for continued development of the North American economy.

Equally hazardous, in Martí's eyes, was the power and presence of pro-
annexationist forces in Cuba. As he explained in 1882:

> There is still a greater danger, perhaps greater than all others. In Cuba there
> has always been an important group of cautious men, quite bold in their
> rejection of Spanish domination, but yet quite reserved in endangering their
> own personal comfort to combat it. This kind of man, aided by those who
> would enjoy the benefits of freedom without paying its high price, vehemently
> favors the annexation of Cuba to the United States. All these shy, irresolute
> men, all these shallow observers, so attached to their possessions, are tempted
> to support this solution, which they believe to be cheap and easy. In this way
> they satisfy their patriotic conscience and appease their fears of real patriotism.
> But, since this is human nature, we must not look upon their temptations with
> stoic contempt, we must stop them.

Martí thus formulated an enduring element in Latin America's emergent
political culture: the detection and identification of turncoats, of pro-U.S.
traitors ready to forswear national dignity for the sake of personal and
private gain. This would be a persistent theme in the continental culture of
resistance.

In a fashion reminiscent of Bolívar, Martí summoned progressive elements throughout the region to the dream of unification. It was essential,
he wrote in a famous essay entitled "Nuestra América," for Latin American
nations to acknowledge their common cause with Cuba: "The urgent task
for our America is to reveal itself for what it is, united in purpose and soul,
rapidly triumphant over its suffocating past, its hands stained only by
blood spent in the struggle against [colonial] ruins, blood from the veins
pricked by our masters. The disdain of a powerful and unknowing neigh-

bor is the greatest danger for our America . . . because this ignorance could inspire greed." Regional unification faced an intimidating array of internal obstacles and external threats, mainly from the United States; all the more reason to realize Bolívar's noble dream.

Martí expressed continuous fear that, once the Spaniards were ousted, the United States would attempt to annex Cuba. "Every day," he wrote in 1895,

> my life is in danger. I am in danger of giving up my life for my country, for my duty—as I understand it and must execute it—so that Cuba's independence will prevent the expansion of the United States throughout the Antilles, allowing that nation to fall, ever more powerfully, upon our American lands. Everything I have done, everything I will do, is toward this end. It has been a silent and indirect process, for there are things which must be kept hidden if they are to take place. . . . I have lived inside the monster and know its entrails—and my weapon is only the slingshot of David.

The independence of Cuba, he insisted once again, was essential to the sovereignty and integrity of the remainder of Latin America.

Once back in Cuba, Martí met an early death upon the battlefield. The "pearl of the Antilles" lost one of its most devoted and capable leaders, and Latin America gained a martyr for the continental cause.

Nicaragua: Origins of Sandinismo

Nicaragua was long the object of imperial intrigue. As early as the seventeenth century, European powers began to contemplate the possibility of constructing a transisthmian canal through Nicaragua, thus connecting the Atlantic with the Pacific; in the mid-nineteenth century the United States and Britain agreed to keep the project to themselves. After a filibustering expedition in the 1850s William Walker, an American citizen, proclaimed himself to be the president of Nicaragua. In response to an insult (and an outstanding debt) the United States occupied the country from 1909 to 1925, controlling national politics through local minions. In 1926, after a fraudulent election, the United States invaded again. This time a young guerrilla leader named Augusto César Sandino took to the hills in order, in his words, "to fight the Yankee piracy." He organized an effective military unit, which he called the Army in Defense of the Sovereignty of Nicaragua, and he adopted a powerful slogan: *Patria y Libertad.*

In letters and testimonials, Sandino described American soldiers and leaders in scathing terms. His prose dripping with vituperation, he referred in April 1927 to "drug-dependent Yankees." Months later he wrote of "Yankee cowards and criminals," and went on to denounce "the adventurous Yankees, who are trampling Nicaragua's sovereignty under foot." In December 1927 he railed against "Yankee imperialism" once again, openly decrying "the monstrousness of the crimes committed by the *patricides and Nordic punitive army* upon the Nicaraguan people." On occasion he ridiculed the "blond beasts" and "blond pirates" from the north; at times he criticized "Wall Street magnates" and "North American piratical assassins." Sandino aimed his scorn not only at the U.S. government and military. Though he welcomed support from some groups in the United States, such as the All-America Anti-Imperialist League, he concluded by January 1930 that "the North American people support and will always support the expansionist policies of their unprincipled governments." "The North American people," he observed in another communiqué, "are as imperialistic as their own leaders."

Sandino reserved his sharpest criticism, however, for traitorous groups within Nicaragua. Shortly after initiating his campaign, Sandino claimed that partisan divisions had divided national society into three groups: "Puritanical and honorable Liberals," meaning himself and his followers; "Chicken Liberals (or eunuchs)," meaning José María Moncada and others who agreed to abide by the U.S.–sponsored election pact of 1928; and "Sell-outs of their country, in other words, Conservatives." Time and again he heaped scorn on the political leaders who collaborated with U.S. occupation forces: Moncada, Adolfo Díaz, and Emiliano Chamorro, "the unholy trinity of miserable sell-outs of their country." And against these forces, the guerrilla leader vowed unending resistance: *We swear before the symbol of the fatherland to die rather than to sell ourselves or to surrender to the offers of the invaders, oligarchs, and traitors who for so many years have trafficked with the Nation's honor.*

His avowed mission was the achievement of national sovereignty. "My obsession," Sandino said in September 1927, "is to repel with the dignity and pride of our race every imposition that, with the cynicism derived from strength, the assassins of weak nations are imposing upon our country, and you may be firmly convinced that as long as I possess bullets, I will make them understand that their audacity will cost them dearly." In view of the strength of the opposition, victory could come only through force. Antedating Mao Zedong's later dictums in China, Sandino proclaimed in October 1927: "Freedom is not won with flowers! It is with bullets that we must drive the enemy from power! The revolution is synonymous with purification!"

As did Martí for Cuba, Sandino asserted that the cause of Nicaragua was the cause of all Latin America. Invoking the struggles "of all the Latin American peoples against the imperialist policies of the Anglo-Saxon colossus" in May 1928, he maintained that his cause "is also the cause of Latin America." Later in the year he warned leaders of Latin America about U.S. ambitions to reduce the entire region to the status of "an Anglo-Saxon colony." And like Martí, he sought to reawaken the Bolivarian dream. In March 1929, after drafting a proposal for a continental congress to "assure the sovereignty and independence of our twenty-one Indo-Hispanic republics and friendship between the America of our race and the United States of America, upon a basis of equality," Sandino developed a multipoint "plan for the realization of Bolívar's highest dream":

Profoundly convinced, as we are, that North American capitalism has arrived at its last stage of development, transforming itself as a result into imperialism; and that it no longer has any respect for theories of right and justice, ignoring the inexorable principles of independence of the divisions of the Latin American nationality, we view as indispensable, and even more so, undelayable, the Alliance of our Latin American states as a way to maintain that independence before the designs of U.S. imperialism, or before that of any other power that may wish to subject us to its interests.

"There is nothing more logical, nothing more decisive or vital," Sandino asserted, "than the fusion of our twenty-one states of our America into one unique Latin American nationality." Calling for the abolition of the Monroe Doctrine, establishment of a Latin American court, organization of a continental army, regional control of the Panama Canal, and other collaborative measures, Sandino addressed his appeal to heads of government throughout the region. "We are proposing an alliance," he assured them, "and not a confederation." He was also seeking a gesture of continental solidarity in his struggle against the U.S. marines.

Despite his radical-sounding appeals to the working classes and furious condemnations of imperialism, Sandino was not a Marxist. (Indeed, he stoutly resisted attempts at socialist indoctrination.) He displayed, instead, a mystical faith in religion and in God. But there would be, he predicted, no messianic arrival during the twentieth century. Instead:

> What will happen is the following: the oppressed people will break the chains of humiliation, with which the imperialists of the earth have sought to keep them in backwardness. The trumpets that will be heard will be the bugles of war, intoning the hymns of the freedom of the oppressed peoples against the injustice of the oppressors. The only thing that will be submerged for all time is injustice, and Love, king of Perfection, will remain, with his favorite daughter, Divine Justice.

Partly in recognition of Sandino's political and military strength, Franklin Delano Roosevelt withdrew U.S. forces from Nicaragua in 1933. The next year Anastasio Somoza masterminded the assassination of Sandino, and then proceeded to install a dictatorial regime conspicuous for its brutality, venality, and nepotism. It was hardly surprising that, decades later, youthful leaders of a guerrilla movement against the Somoza dynasty would christen themselves as Sandinistas.

Continental Solidarity

Calls for pan-Latin American solidarity steadily mounted in response to U.S. power. Despite the unattainability (and perhaps implausibility) of the Bolivarian dream, writers and essayists took frequent note of common cause against the United States. Even in Brazil, perhaps the most pro-American country in the region, Eduardo Prado attacked "the absorbent, imperialist, and tyrannical policies of North American diplomacy" as early as 1893, concluding bitterly: "There is no Latin American nation that has not suffered in its relations with the United States." José Enrique Rodó (of Uruguay) and Rubén Darío (of Nicaragua) would sound anti-American themes around the turn of the century, a tradition soon followed by Manuel Pesqueira (of Mexico).

In 1912 an articulate and irascible Argentine, Manuel Ugarte, wrote a letter congratulating Woodrow Wilson on his election to the presidency and enumerating a long list of grievances that Latin Americans held in common. "We desire," he lectured the president-elect,

> that Cuba be freed from the painful weight of the Platt Amendment; we desire that there should be granted to Nicaragua the ability to dispose of their soil, *leaving to the people to depose those who govern them with the aid of a foreign army, if they deem it necessary;* we desire that the status of Porto Rico [*sic*] be settled in accordance with the rights of humanity; we desire that the abominable injustice committed against Colombia be repaired so far as possible; we desire that Panama which today suffers the consequences of a temporary displacement be ceded the dignity of a nation; we desire that the pressure being exerted on the port of Guayaquil shall cease; we desire that the archipelago of the Galápagos be respected; we desire that liberty be conceded to the heroic Filipinos; we desire that Mexico shall not always see suspended above her flag Damocles's sword of intervention; we desire that the disorders of Putumayo shall not serve as a pretext for diplomatic dexterities; we desire that the companies which go beyond their authority shall not be supported in their unjust demands; we desire that the Republic of Santo Domingo be not suffocated by unjust oppression; we desire that the United States abstain from officiously intervening in the domestic politics of our countries and that they discontinue the acquisition of ports and bays on this continent; we desire that measures of sanitation shall not serve to diminish the sovereignty of nations of the Pacific; we ask, in short, that the star spangled banner cease to be a symbol of oppression in the New World.

It was a stirring challenge, more effective in rallying Latin America than in deterring the United States. During his first term in office Woodrow Wilson, the professorial idealist, would send U.S. troops headlong into Cuba, Mexico, Haiti, and the Dominican Republic.

Dollar-diplomacy gave further impetus to the drive for cultural and political unity in Latin America. In 1925 a prominent Mexican philosopher, José Vasconcelos, would proclaim that the *mestizo* combination, or "cosmic race," provided Latin America with a social identity, a legacy different from North America, and an inherently virtuous ethnic stock. And from an entirely different quarter, outgoing president Arturo Alessandri of Chile would in 1926 express frustration with U.S. diplomacy: "During my five years in office, I worked to give true life to Pan-Americanism," he reflected bitterly. "But now I will devote all the energies that remain to me in preaching that. . . . We [Latin American republics] must arise, and together, in union, proclaim: Latin America for the Latin Americans."

During the 1920s and 1930s, anti-U.S. argumentation began to acquire a sharp analytical edge. A young Peruvian reformer, Víctor Raúl Haya de la Torre, would sound a clarion call for the continental solidarity of "indo-America" in its "international struggle against Yankee imperialism in Latin America" as he launched his program for the Alianza Popular Revolucionaria Americana (APRA), the keystone for the *Aprista* party in his native country. Around the same time his brilliant compatriot, José Carlos Mariátegui, developed an explicitly Marxist analysis of social and racial inequities in a famous tract, *Siete tesis de interpretación de la realidad peruana* (1928). Spreading out from intellectual circles, Marxism would eventually become a major component of the continental cultures of resistance.

In Retrospect

Notwithstanding constancy of effort, Latin America had relatively little success in curtailing the rise of U.S. imperial power. Conspicuously ineffective were attempts to establish subregional hegemony, as on the part of Argentina and Brazil, which simply lacked the necessary capabilities for such an enterprise. Equally ineffective were efforts to induce extra-hemispheric powers to step into the hemisphere and provide protection for nations of Latin America. European policymakers gradually relaxed their resistance to U.S. advances during the course of the nineteenth century, and by the early twentieth century most became willing to allow Washington to guarantee their loans, investments, and commerce. As major powers accepted U.S. participation in the worldwide imperial contest, in other words, they became increasingly prepared to regard Latin America as Washington's backyard.

The Bolivarian pursuit of continental unification produced ambiguous results. In one sense, the ideal proved a quixotic failure: despite several attempts, leaders of the region were unable to create any kind of meaningful organization. But in another sense, the notion had significant impact: it drew upon beliefs in common origins, it defined a sense of collective purpose, and on occasion it played a crucial political role. Its diplomatic significance was especially apparent in the decades-long promotion of hemispheric international law, most notably in regard to doctrines of sovereignty and nonintervention. To a considerable extent, inculcation of these provisions in FDR's Good Neighbor policy represented a triumph for Latin America and a vindication of its quest for solidarity. Of course this outcome was only as meaningful as international law itself, but at the time it represented a remarkable achievement.

Ultimately it was the formulation of cultures of resistance that left the most enduring legacy. Throughout this historical era Latin America's search for self-identity became profoundly, inextricably, and necessarily entwined with its relationship to the United States. The rise of U.S. power, and its application to the region, left no other choice for Latin Americans. They could embrace the U.S. claim to hegemony, as many of them did, they could tolerate the U.S. role, as more of them did, or they could resist advances by the Colossus of the North, as most of them did. The unavoidable reality of U.S. power led some *pensadores* to denigrate American culture and to celebrate Latin America's lofty appreciation for faith, beauty, and nobility; it prompted others to issue urgent appeals for support and solidarity; it led still others to compose trenchant critiques of U.S. imperialism and its underlying purposes. Resistance to the United States became an integral part of national and continental self-assertion. This connection would persist in times to come.

II

THE COLD WAR

Soviet Communism is not only the gravest threat that ever faced the United States, but the gravest threat that has ever faced what we call western civilization or, indeed, any civilization that was dominated by a spiritual faith.

John Foster Dulles (1953)

5

Closing Ranks

*Conditions in Latin America are somewhat comparable to conditions as
they were in the mid-thirties when the communist movement was getting
started. . . . Well, if we don't look out, we will wake up some morning
and read in the newspapers that there happened in South America the
same kind of thing that happened in China in 1949.*
  John Foster Dulles (1953)

Foreign affairs! That's for people who don't have to work for a living.
  American blue-collar worker (ca. 1954)

The Cold War altered the logic of inter-American relations, elevating the
protection of "national security" to the top of the U.S. foreign policy
agenda and turning Latin America (and other Third World areas) into
both a battleground and prize in the conflict between communism and
capitalism, East and West, the USSR and the United States. In response to
Soviet challenges, the United States sought to extend and consolidate its
political supremacy throughout the hemisphere. Launching an anti-communist crusade, the United States institutionalized military and political
alliances with nations of the region; offered to collaborate with authoritarian regimes so long as they were anticommunist; encouraged (or compelled) friendly governments to crush leftist labor movements and to outlaw communist parties; and orchestrated the military overthrow of an
elected government on the ground that it was "soft" on communism. Fear
of a "Soviet menace" in the Americas was greatly exaggerated, but it nonetheless had crucial implications for U.S. policy. By the mid-1950s Washington laid down policy lines that would continue through the 1980s.

117

United States as Superpower

World War II transformed global arrangements and elevated the United States to the status of a superpower. By the late 1930s the United States had a very small military establishment, with only 185,000 combat-ready troops; no military alliances at all; and, after the withdrawals from Haiti and Nicaragua, no troops on foreign soil. The centerpiece of U.S. foreign policy was Roosevelt's Good Neighbor stance toward Latin America and cultivation of a "sphere of influence" within the Western Hemisphere, but not in other parts of the world. In the Atlantic and Pacific theaters, the United States was a relatively unimportant actor.

This would suddenly change. One consequence of World War II was to weaken classic European powers—not only the defeated Axis countries, but triumphant Allies as well. Overall, the fighting and associated devastation took the lives of approximately 55 million people, at least 35 million in Europe. The Soviet Union alone lost more than 21 million soldiers and civilians. Poland and Germany (including Austria) suffered 6 million deaths each; Yugoslavia, 1.6 million; France about 600,000; Britain around 400,000. Whole cities were destroyed and thousands of villages reduced to rubble. With England a partial exception, economic production on the European Continent (outside of coal mining and agriculture) had ground to a virtual halt.

At the same time World War II greatly strengthened the United States. Despite the sacrifice of servicemen, there were no bombings of U.S. cities, no occupations of U.S. territory. Economic production climbed to unprecedented levels: it was wartime mobilization, in fact, that lifted the United States out of the Depression of the 1930s. At war's end the United States enjoyed a position of extraordinary economic preponderance. By 1947 the United States accounted for one-third of the world's total exports and nearly one-half of the world's industrial output. The Roosevelt and Truman administrations applied this leverage to establish foundations for a postwar economic order, one that would avoid repetition of the Depression by promoting trade and stabilizing monetary exchange. As Harry Truman explained, "A large volume of soundly based international trade is essential if we are to achieve prosperity in the United States, build a durable structure of world economy and attain our goal of world peace and prosperity."

Moreover, the war altered international alignments and the structure of relative power. The United States did not enter the war until December 1941, nearly a year and a half after the Nazi conquest of France, and did not cross the English Channel until June 1944. Until that time the Soviet Union bore the brunt of the land war with Germany, and, as the Red Army pushed toward Berlin, the USSR slowly gained control of Eastern Europe. Joseph Stalin succinctly summarized the political implications of these military developments: "Whoever occupies a territory," he once proclaimed, "also imposes on it his own social system."

In the Pacific theater, as well, the United States did not have troops on the most important land masses—China, Korea, and Japan. Atomic bombs at Hiroshima and Nagasaki cut the campaigns short in August 1945, leading to Tokyo's unconditional surrender. Allied forces under U.S. leadership promptly occupied Japan and South Korea, but not China or North Korea. In keeping with Stalin's dictum, this would have profound results on politics.

In addition to its economic and military power, the United States possessed a monopoly on a new instrument of warfare—the atomic bomb. To consolidate its advantage, Washington built a stockpile of these deadly weapons, each capable of destroying a city at a time. The U.S. arsenal contained 7 atomic bombs in 1946, 13 in 1947, 50 in 1948, nearly 300 by 1950, and around 1,000 in 1953. In 1950 the government initiated development of the even more powerful hydrogen bomb, carrying out the first test in 1952. Nuclear capacity gave the postwar United States an enormous sense of power. First, it appeared to offer an efficient and inexpensive key to military security without the need for military mobilization. Second, it was thought, the bomb conferred on the United States both the right and the duty to control processes of change throughout the world. Naively, and hopefully, the United States thus entered the nuclear age.

The United States retained its military dominance in years to come. By the late 1960s the United States had 2 million soldiers in the armed forces, forty-eight military alliances with other countries, and 1.5 million troops stationed in 119 countries of the world. It was, beyond doubt, the strongest power on earth.

Cold War: The Rules of the Game

Unilateral triumph soon gave way to bilateral tension. Stalin tightened his grip on Poland. In March 1946 Winston Churchill denounced the lowering of an "iron curtain" in the midst of continental Europe and called for liberation from communist rule. In 1948 there came a Soviet-sponsored coup in Czechoslovakia; later in the year Stalin sought to cordon off the occupied city of Berlin, which required a months-long airlift of food and supplies by the Allies. In 1949 the USSR announced successful detonation of its own atomic bomb, thus shattering America's postwar monopoly. On front after front, the Soviet Union appeared to provoke confrontation with the United States.

What would Washington do? The answer came in 1947, when President Harry S. Truman decided to support the government of Greece in its struggle with a leftist insurgency. As heir to the anti-Nazi partisan movement, it should be noted, this insurrection reflected political realities evident throughout the Continent. During the war, centrist and monarchist leaders generally fled their countries for the relative safety of Great Britain; those who remained to lead the resistance—fabled as *la resistance* in France—tended to come from the political left. And not surprisingly, in view of their heroic sacrifices, they strongly resisted claims by conservative exile leaders to reclaim power at war's end.

In response to the crises in Turkey and Greece, the American president launched what became known as the Truman Doctrine in a momentous address to Congress: "I believe it must be the policy of the United States to support free peoples who are resisting attempted subjugation by armed minorities or by outside pressures." This phrasing implied a remarkably capacious mandate. It committed the United States to assist "free peoples" (however defined) in struggles against external *or internal* foes. This called for both defense against outside threats and intervention against domestic challenges. In effect, the Truman Doctrine proclaimed that the United States would assume the role of global policeman.

In fact the doctrine —and the policy that it defined—rested on a series of crucial assumptions. One was that the Soviet Union was seeking to conquer the world in the name of international communism. A second was that these Soviet ambitions would produce a long and continuous struggle with the capitalist world, not a military conflagration but a "cold war." And this conflict, as George F. Kennan wrote in 1947, would require from the United States "the adroit and vigilant application of counter-force at a series of constantly shifting geographical and political points, corresponding to the shifts of Soviet policy." Washington's principal goal, in other words, would be to halt the spread of communism. The policy thus came to be known as one of *containment*.

This strategy initially focused on Europe. One key component was a massive program of economic assistance, launched as the Marshall Plan in 1947. Since communism thrived amid despair and poverty, in Washington's official view, economic recovery would bolster the forces of capitalism and democracy. In support of this belief the United States provided $19 billion in foreign aid to Western Europe in 1945–50. A second pillar of the policy was the North Atlantic Treaty Organization (NATO), a military pact established in 1949. Its principal effect was to commit U.S. military forces to the defense of Western Europe. In the phrase of Senator Tom Connally, "The Atlantic Pact is but the logical extension of the principle of the Monroe Doctrine." United States power now stretched far beyond the limits of the Western Hemisphere.

During the 1950s the doctrine of containment extended to Asia as well. American occupation forces quickly built up Japan as a pro-U.S. bulwark in the fight against international communism. Concern mounted rapidly after the "loss" of China in 1949 to revolutionaries under Mao Zedong, an event that gave rise to Senator Joseph McCarthy's infamous accusations against "traitors" in the U.S. State Department. The invasion of South Korea by North Korea in 1950 provoked a three-year conflict ending in a virtual stalemate, reestablishing the line of demarcation between North and South at the 38th parallel.

Developments in Asia had several fundamental implications for U.S. policy. One was abandonment of the idea of "liberation." First in Korea and later in Europe, the United States came to acknowledge the practical limits of containment—tacitly accepting the existence of a Soviet sphere of influence in 1956, when Western powers failed to provide support for an anti-Soviet uprising in Hungary. Second was a conviction within U.S. society and government that the communist movement was worldwide, coherent, and monolithic—led by Moscow, in close collaboration with Beijing. Third was a perception of the entire world as a single theater; events in Europe and Asia were inextricably linked together by the fact of global struggle. Fourth was unremitting hostility toward the Soviet Union, the People's Republic of China, and all their "stooges" or "puppets" (whether or not they were consciously acting on behalf of communist goals). Finally, the invasion of South Korea supported the view that communist tactics would consist not only of internal subversion, as in Greece, but also of outright military aggression. This led to the formation in 1954 of the Southeast Asia Treaty Organization (SEATO), in principle (if not in practice) a Pacific counterpart to NATO, and it also prompted an intensive rearmament campaign that lasted throughout the 1950s.

In paradoxical ways, the waging of the Cold War led to a series of tacit understandings or rules of the game. Each side strove mightily to establish military superiority over the other, yet there existed no plausible chance of military victory. In view of the potential for nuclear retaliation, neither side could take the risk of attacking the other. The United States and the USSR thus found themselves locked in a nuclear standoff, accumulating arsenals they could never use. Instead they could merely resort to threats, saber-rattling, and ever-larger military budgets. In a conventional sense, the Cold War promised neither victory nor peace.

Each side defined its purpose in the name of high and principled causes. The Soviet Union sought to extend communist influence in support of social solidarity and economic justice. The United States positioned itself as leader of the "free" and democratic world. Despite the grandeur and intensity of this ideological conflict, however, both powers tended to accept each other's established sphere of influence.

There could be constant conflict—but always on the periphery, not in the central arena. The principal contenders never fought among themselves; they assigned that task to clients and/or surrogates. In the 1950s hostilities thus erupted in Korea, Iran, and Lebanon. Such struggles were assumed to represent a "zero-sum" game, in which one side's gain would be another's loss. Even more worrisome was the U.S. notion of a "domino theory," in which the loss of one country would immediately and automatically endanger its neighbors. Conflicts within or among small countries were therefore resistant to negotiation; because they entailed symbolic contests between the superpowers, neither side had much interest in accommodation.

By the 1960s Washington explicitly extended the doctrine of containment to what became known as the Third World. As President John F. Kennedy would say: "The great battleground for the defense and expansion of freedom today is the southern half of the globe . . . the lands of the rising peoples." The United States and the Soviet Union thus engaged in competition for political allegiance among the poorer regions of the world. The principal target for U.S. policy would be so-called wars of liberation, a diagnosis that eventually led to a decade-long involvement in Vietnam. Around this same time, as we shall see, U.S. policy sharpened its focus on Latin America as well.

The Cold War bore some resemblance to traditional balance-of-power politics and spheres of influence, but there were important differences as well. One defining feature of the post–World War II era was the bipolar structure of world power, whereas the historic quest for a balance of power relied upon a multipolar system. The Cold War was utterly dominated by two superpowers, the United States and the Soviet Union. "Not since Rome and Carthage," U.S. Secretary of State Dean Acheson once claimed, "had there been such a polarization of power on this earth."

A second key characteristic was the emphasis on ideological factors. To be sure, traditional powers justified the subjugation of other peoples in the name of religious conversion or cultural mission or some other uplifting purpose. But the *intensity* of East–West ideological competition, of the contest between Karl Marx and Adam Smith, provided a special ingredient to the Cold War. In a world of modern communications, this was not only an academic contest for intellectual superiority. It became a bitter debate over the meaning of social order, the direction of historical change, and the future of the world community; ultimately, and fundamentally, it was a struggle for the allegiance of society at large. Ideology magnified the stakes of competition.

Third was its worldwide scope. While the principal actors never challenged each other in direct military fashion, their frequent use of surrogates—and their constant invocation of ideology—extended their rivalry to all corners of the globe. There was a brief moment after World War II, as historian Thomas Paterson has pointed out, when Washington contemplated the possibility of creating explicit spheres of influence for the United States and the USSR.[1] By the late 1940s and early 1950s, however, policymakers saw the entire world as consisting of a single theater; no countries or regions were exempt from participation. Unlike classic big-power contests, this was not confined to a specific area or based upon territorial acquisition. It was a geopolitical and ideological contest that covered the world as a whole.

Partly because of its breadth, the Cold War provoked systematic tension between the superpowers and their allies (or client states). Often haughtily, policymakers in both Moscow and Washington presumed and asserted that only they, not their allies, could truly understand the nature of the global conflict under way; only they could comprehend the challenges and stakes. To the undisguised irritation of the British and French, especially, this conviction fostered the idea that only the United States could accurately ascertain genuine threats to the West. And within the Western

Hemisphere, it implied that Washington possessed an inherently superior perspective on international matters; U.S. policymakers could identify, analyze, and eradicate communist threats more effectively than local leaders. Such presumptuousness not only offended Latin Americans, including reformers and dedicated anticommunists; it could also result in grievous miscalculations by the U.S. government.

Policymaking during the Cold War became a special prerogative of political and bureaucratic elites. The U.S. Congress quickly reached a bipartisan consensus on foreign policy that prevailed from the late 1940s through the 1980s. Encouraged by the Red-baiting tactics of Joseph McCarthy and alarmed by the realities of Soviet power, the American public fervently supported anticommunist positions. Partly in response to this unanimity, governmental elites—political appointees (usually from the East Coast establishment), career foreign service officers, and longtime legislators—assumed control of the policy-making apparatus. The business community played occasional but supportive roles, displaying neither the initiative nor the power wielded during the foregone era of "dollar diplomacy." Organized labor entered the international arena, also in staunch support of official policy, as did other interest groups from time to time. Throughout this era, however, responsibility for and control of U.S. foreign policy rested almost exclusively within the political and bureaucratic apparatus.[2] The center of decision making was neither in corporate boardrooms nor on the electoral hustings, it was in the nation's capital—and the name of the city, "Washington," became synonymous with the sinews of power.

Ultimately, the waging of the Cold War was bound to result in frustration. The doctrine of containment called for vigilance, persistence, and sacrifice, but it could not bring victory in any classic sense of the term. From the late 1940s through the 1980s it was nonetheless the Cold War, with its curious logic, that defined and enforced the rules of the game for international competition.

The Cold War in Latin America

Latin America commanded significant attention from U.S. policymakers during and just after World War II. In December 1943 the Joint Army and Navy Advisory Board established its Western Hemisphere Defense Program. The State Department pressed Latin countries to join the Allied cause throughout the course of the war. At the founding of the United Nations, in 1946, U.S. diplomats accorded special attention to the region—which at that time controlled nearly two-fifths of the votes in the General Assembly (twenty out of fifty-one). Latin America also offered U.S. producers a major export market and site for direct investment. In 1946–47 one-quarter of U.S. exports flowed to Latin America; in 1950 U.S. investments in the region amounted to more than one-third the country's global total of $12 billion overseas.

As World War II drew to a close, Washington seems to have envisioned a continuation of (or reversion to) the Good Neighbor policy—including its assertion of hemispheric hegemony. "I think that it's not asking too much to have our little region over here which never has bothered anybody," Secretary of War Henry L. Stimson once remarked. His assistant John J. McCloy agreed, casting an eye across the Atlantic and insisting that "we ought to have our cake and eat it too; that we ought to be free to operate under this regional arrangement in South America, [and] at the same time intervene promptly in Europe."

In 1945 a top State Department official, Charles Bohlen, offered both a reinterpretation and reassertion of the doctrine of nonintervention. "While we do claim the right . . . to have a guiding voice in a certain limited sphere of the foreign relations of Latin America," the diplomat explained, "we do not attempt on the basis of that right to dictate their internal national life or to restrict their intercourse with foreign nations, except in that limited sphere"—that is, "the politico-strategic aspect of their foreign relations." At this point, Washington assumed the right to place constraints on the foreign policy of Latin American countries but not upon their domestic politics.

In this spirit the United States endorsed Latin America's push for an endorsement of regional security organizations at the founding conference of the United Nations in 1946. Article 51 of the UN charter thus provided a juridical basis for the Rio Pact of 1947, a mutual defense treaty between Latin American nations and the United States. There would be differing views on the significance of this development. Secretary of War Stimson interpreted Article 51 as a preservation of "the unilateral character of the Monroe Doctrine," since the United States could take action in Latin America without being "at the mercy of getting the assent of the Security Council." Latin Americans, by contrast, imagined that Article 51 would encourage the formation of a regional security agreement that could provide protection for existing governments and, at the same time, place constraints on the United States. In essence, their hope was that international organization could accomplish the goals they had earlier pursued through international law.

The principle of nonintervention found further expression at the founding meeting of the Organization of American States in Bogotá in 1948. Seeking to bolster their autonomy, Latin American delegates won approval of key language in Chapter 15: "No state or group of states has the right to intervene, directly or indirectly, for any reason whatever, in the internal or external affairs of any other state." This stipulation expressly prohibited not only armed intervention, so common in the prewar period, but also "any other form of interference or attempted threat." Thus the United States continued to forswear the use of force in its relations with Latin America and to cultivate cooperation in the name of hemispheric unity. As historian Steven Rabe has remarked, both the Rio Treaty and the OAS "reflected the spirit of the Good Neighbor policy."[3]

Global crises turned U.S. official attention away from Latin America. From Greece to Berlin, events in Europe came to dominate the Washington agenda; the fall of China and hostilities in Korea focused concern on Asia as well. One of the most experienced Latin American specialists at the State Department, Adolf A. Berle, noted growing lack of interest in the region with dismay. "Men [in high office] who know the hemisphere and love it are few," he said in 1945, "and those who are known by the hemisphere and loved by it are fewer still." By 1949 the situation had grown still worse: complaining about "sheer neglect and ignorance," Berle declared that "we have simply forgotten about Latin America."

Gradually, however, the Cold War came to the Americas, and the United States braced itself to contend with communist threats. At first the Truman administration made a relatively calm and realistic assessment of the situation. A national security memorandum observed that "communism in the Americas is a potential danger, but that, with a few possible exceptions, it is not seriously dangerous at the present time." Under these conditions, the document warned, the United States should be concerned about counterproductive consequences of authoritarian rule. Anticommunist compacts ran the risk of legitimizing repression "against all political opposition, Communist or otherwise, by dictatorial governments, with the inevitable result of driving leftist elements into the hands of the Communist organization." Fearing such a backlash, the Truman administration even took steps to defeat a proposal at the founding conference of the OAS in 1948 to create "a multilateral inter-American anti-Communist agreement."

Another level-headed evaluation of Latin America appeared in a 1950 article in the well-known journal *Foreign Affairs* by State Department specialist Louis Halle, writing under the pseudonym "Y." Seeking to explain the persistence of dictatorship within the region, Halle asserted—with considerable condescension—that Latin American nations had not yet come to maturity. "Democracy is not an absolute condition, to be assumed by a people as one puts on an overcoat. It is political maturity. Like all maturity, it is various in its degrees and manifestations, and it is produced by the slow process of maturation. You cannot impose it by force, you cannot acquire it by decree or legislative enactment, you cannot produce it out of a hat by exhortation. It must be cultivated lovingly, tirelessly over the generations." The historical record showed a long-term trend toward democracy, in Halle's estimation, and the United States should contribute to this process by cultivating partnership with Latin American nations, by according them respect, and by providing economic assistance. "The very fact that these nations are, in so many respects, younger than we, and much weaker, should persuade us to maintain an attitude of *noblesse oblige.*" Most remarkable is Halle's exposition of obstacles to democratic development, a list that included poverty, illiteracy, social insecurity, and, in somewhat circular fashion, "a tradition of political behavior marked by intemperance, intransigeance [*sic*], flamboyance and the worship of strong men." Conspicuous by its absence was any reference to foreign agitation, Marxist influence, Soviet pretension, or communism as a whole.

But 1950 also marked a turning point in American attitudes toward the region. In May President Truman approved a National Security Council memorandum on "Inter-American Military Collaboration" insisting that "the cold war is in fact a real war in which the survival of the free world is at stake." (The following year Congress voted $38.2 million for direct military assistance to Latin America; in 1952 the figure climbed to $51.7 million.) In late 1950 an official statement declared that "U.S. security is the objective of our world-wide foreign policy today," and "U.S. security is synonymous with hemisphere security."

Cold War calculations also provoked reinterpretation of nonintervention. In an extraordinary display of intellectual acrobatics, Assistant Secretary of State Edward Miller explained the U.S. position in 1950. Early interventions by the United States might be regrettable, he said, but they were justified by the Monroe Doctrine. Under the terms of the Rio Pact and the OAS there could now be only collective, not unilateral, action: "The fact is that the doctrine of nonintervention [under the Good Neighbor policy] never did proscribe the assumption by the organized community of a legitimate concern with any circumstances that threatened the common welfare. On the contrary it made the possibility of such action imperative. Such a collective undertaking, far from representing intervention, is the alternative to intervention. *It is the corollary of nonintervention*" (emphasis added). Warning about the prospects of "communist political aggression," Miller went on to call the Rio Pact "a Monroe Doctrine of our inter-American community." Thus did the United States begin to stake its claim: members of the Rio Pact and/or the OAS could, as collective bodies, legitimately decide to intervene within the affairs of a member state. This would not violate the doctrine of nonintervention. A prime justification for such action would be "communist political aggression."

Around this same time George Kennan, chief architect of the containment policy, offered his conception of the goals of U.S. policy in Latin America:

1. The protection of our [*sic!*] raw materials,
2. The prevention of military exploitation of Latin America by the enemy, and
3. The prevention of the psychological mobilization of Latin America against us.

Communists "represent our most serious problem in the area," Kennan insisted, and they "have progressed to the point where they must be regarded as an urgent, major problem." Under no circumstances could they be allowed to take power. "The final answer might be an unpleasant one," Kennan conceded, "but . . . we should not hesitate before police repression by the local government. This is not shameful since the Communists are essentially traitors. . . . It is better to have a strong regime in power than a liberal one if it is indulgent and relaxed and penetrated by Communists." Danger to U.S. security came not only from declared Marxists but also from their unwitting accomplices. Eternal vigilance must be extended to the Americas.

Electoral politics intensified public concern about communist threats within the hemisphere. During the 1952 presidential campaign Dwight D. Eisenhower, the Republican candidate, accused the Truman administration of disregarding Latin America and creating "terrible disillusionment" throughout the region. Economic distress was "followed by popular unrest, skillfully exploited by Communist agents there." "Through drift and neglect," Eisenhower charged, the Truman administration had turned a Good Neighbor policy into "a poor neighbor policy."

At his congressional confirmation hearings John Foster Dulles, soon to be Eisenhower's secretary of state, claimed that communists in Latin America were determined "to destroy the influence of the so-called Colossus of the North in Central and South America." The president's brother, Milton S. Eisenhower, echoed this sentiment in a November 1953 report on conditions in the region:

> The possible conquest of a Latin American nation today would not be, so far as anyone can foresee, by direct assault. It would come, rather, through the insidious process of infiltration, conspiracy, spreading of lies, and the undermining of free institutions, one by one. Highly disciplined groups of communists are busy, night and day, illegally or openly, in the American republics, as they are in every nation of the world. While many persons may now think of Latin America as not being in the line of attack in the modern world struggle, success by the communists in these nations could quickly change all the maps which strategists use in calculating the probabilities of the future.

Himself a university president, Milton offered a philosophic rumination on the incompatibility of East and West: "The greater the differences in the cultures of nations, the more arduous cooperation becomes. This is the basal difficulty between the communist countries of the East, with their rejection of God and their adherence to a militant dialectic materialism, and the West with its long adherence to the cardinal principles of the Judeo-Christian philosophy." There could be no dealing with communists. They would have to be purged, hounded, driven, and excluded from the hemisphere.

Early in his administration President Eisenhower endorsed a policy statement in favor of "orderly political and economic development" in the region. Stressing the importance of international support to eliminate the "menace of internal Communist or other anti-U.S. subversion," NSC 144/1 conveyed considerable disdain for Latin leaders and their inability to comprehend the nature of the threat. The implication, of course, was that the United States might have to go it alone.

Courting Dictators

A central goal of U.S. policy was to foster and strengthen anticommunist regimes in Latin America. This often led to acquiescence in dictatorship. Just after World War II, in fact, Latin America experienced a broad surge of democratic rule. Civilian governments gained strength in Chile, Costa Rica, and Colombia. Relatively free elections took place in Ecuador, where José María Velasco Ibarra won the presidency in the wake of a popular uprising; in Cuba, where Ramón Grau San Martín (once again) emerged triumphant; in Peru, where José Luis Bustamante y Rivero was victorious; and, perhaps most important, in Venezuela, where the Acción Democrática party finally managed to win the presidential election of 1947. In the meantime dictatorships abandoned power in Guatemala, where Juan José Arévalo took over from a military junta; in Brazil, where elections took place in December 1945; and in Argentina, where a sharp increase in popular participation characterized the presidential elections of 1946. While these shifts toward democracy were for the most part incomplete, they represented significant departures from the blatant repressions of the past.

There were several key features in these political transitions. One was the appearance of "progressive" political parties or movements dedicated to social reform (the Auténticos in Cuba, the Apristas in Peru, Acción Democrática in Venezuela, even Peronistas in Argentina). A second was participation of the political left, including the communist left. During the war Latin America's communist parties joined in antifascist activities, and at war's end they benefited from the temporary prestige of the Soviet Union; because they increasingly tended to act as integral parts of national popular movements, rather than as members of an international network, communist parties were legalized or at least tolerated in virtually every country. Their total membership, less than 100,000 in 1939, reached close to 400,000 by 1947. A third feature was the political mobilization of organized labor; by the war's end about 3.5–4.0 million workers were unionized throughout the region. Fourth was a shift in ideological discourse, with a notable emphasis on the virtues and superiority of Western-style "democracy" as a result of the Allied triumph over Nazism.

As this process of democratization began, the United States found itself in an awkward position. During the course of the war, as historian Leslie Bethell has pointed out, "Washington actively cooperated with *all* stable, cooperative regimes in Latin America, dictatorships and democracies, that opposed the Axis powers."[4] A 1944 cable from U.S. ambassador Walter Thurston captured the dilemma as it applied to El Salvador, still under the authoritarian grip of Maximiliano Hernández Martínez:

> Our pronouncements such as the Atlantic Charter and the Declaration of Four Freedoms (the latter blazoned by us throughout El Salvador in the form of posters) are accepted literally by the Salvadorans as endorsement of the basic democratic principles we desire to have prevail currently and universally. . . . It is difficult for them to reconcile these pronouncements with the fact that the United States tolerates and apparently is gratified to enter into association with governments in America which cannot be described as other than totalitarian. . . .

The principal defect of a policy of nonintervention accompanied by propaganda on behalf of democratic regimes is that it simultaneously stimulates dictatorships and popular opposition to them. Moreover, by according dictators who seize or retain power unconstitutionally the same consideration extended to honestly elected presidents we not only impair our moral leadership but foment the belief that our democratic professions are empty propaganda and that we are in fact simply guided by expediency.

It is of course unthinkable that we should revert to the folly of intervention—but it seems to be evident that our present policy is not satisfactory, especially in the Caribbean and Central American areas.

World War II was fought in the name of democracy, of course, but the exigencies of military security required (or seemed to require) collaboration with nondemocratic regimes.

Faced with this contradiction, Washington began a subtle shift in policy. In 1944 Norman Armour, acting director of the Office of American Republic Affairs, wrote to U.S. ambassador Boaz Long in Guatemala, when General Ubico's successors seemed disinclined to proceed with elections:

This problem of support for democratic processes is not an easy one and was discussed at some length in the staff meeting this morning. The idea was advanced that we might have President Roosevelt or the Secretary include in an early address a statement more or less along the following lines: "We wish to cultivate friendly relations with every government in the world and do not feel ourselves entitled to dictate to any country what form of government best suits its national aspirations. We nevertheless must naturally feel a greater affinity, a deeper sympathy and a warmer friendship for governments which effectively represent the practical application of democratic processes."

Dictatorships would get cool recognition, but democracies would receive warm approval. By treading this fine line, U.S. policy could reconcile support for democracy with respect for nonintervention.

Preference for democracy gained momentum the following year. At the Chapultepec conference of February–March 1945, the U.S. delegation led Latin America in declaring "fervent adherence to democratic principles." In May 1945 an official document prepared by prominent diplomat Spruille Braden recommended "aloof formality" toward dictatorships, including termination of financial assistance and military aid. In October 1945 Eduardo Rodríguez Larreta, the foreign minister of Uruguay, proposed that Pan American nations consider taking multilateral action against any member states violating elementary human rights; within a month James F. Byrnes, the U.S. secretary of state, gave his endorsement to this doctrine.

In the immediate postwar environment it was fascism, not communism, that was seen as the principal challenge to democracy in Latin America—and to U.S. interests. Accordingly the United States focused attention on South American countries with pro-Axis tendencies. Argentina, which joined the Allied cause only at the last minute, came in for special criticism. United States diplomats were especially exercised over the emergence of a nationalist, populist, working-class movement in that country and spared no efforts to derail Juan Perón's bid for the presidency in 1946. Briefly appointed as ambassador to Argentina, Spruille Braden campaigned openly and avidly against Perón. According to *peronista* publicists, the ambassador's antics offered Argentine voters with a clear-cut choice: "Braden or Perón!" By a stunning 54 percent majority, the electorate favored Perón.

Abruptly, the political cycle then turned from democracy toward authoritarian rule. Military coups took place in Peru, where Manuel Odría seized power (and repressed the APRA party) in October 1948; in Venezuela, where Marcos Pérez Jiménez overturned a democratic government in November 1948; and in Cuba, where Fulgencio Batista reasserted control in 1952. In Nicaragua, Anastasio Somoza took steps to perpetuate his one-man rule. In Colombia, meanwhile, a state of siege in November 1949 led to a decade-long closure of congress. By the end of 1954 there were only four democracies remaining in Latin America, even by generous standards for classification: Uruguay, Costa Rica, Chile, and Brazil.

The turn toward dictatorship primarily reflected political reactions by Latin America's dominant classes (and their military forces) against progressive movements for social reform. Changing U.S. policy appeared to support this turn toward the right, however, especially as Washington began to mount its assault on communist influence. In 1947 the United States renewed licenses for arms sales to the ruthless regime of Rafael Leonidas Trujillo Molina in the Dominican Republic; refused to provide support (moral or otherwise) to a fledgling "Caribbean Legion" of exiled democrats; and finally came to terms with Peronist Argentina. As James Reston of the *New York Times* aptly noted that same year, "The administration is concentrating not on catching fascists but on stopping communists." The wheel had come full circle.

Continuing its accommodation with right-wing authoritarians, the State Department in 1948 granted prompt diplomatic recognition to coupmasters Odría of Peru and Pérez Jiménez of Venezuela (and, after some hesitation, to Somoza of Nicaragua). A few years later, as though to rub salt in the wounds of democratic opponents, the United States bestowed the Legion of Merit on both dictators, who had proclaimed themselves firm anticommunists. The bemedaling of Pérez Jiménez took place in a particularly ostentatious ceremony in Caracas in October 1954. It was an occasion that Venezuelans would not forget.

As Cold War perceptions hardened in Washington, the United States placed increasing emphasis on ties with Latin American military establishments. As President Eisenhower argued, apparently with reference to a potential conventional war (rather than a nuclear exchange), it was important to strengthen armed forces throughout the region because "we can't defend South America if this Communist war starts." By mid-1954 Congress approved $105 million in military aid for Latin America. In fact the strategic benefits were slight, notwithstanding Eisenhower's military judgment, but the anticipated political benefits were substantial. As U.S. Army Chief of Staff J. Lawton Collins explained, "The Latin American officers who work with us and some of whom come to this country and see what we have and what we can do are frequently our most useful friends in those countries."

As was so often the case, Secretary of State John Foster Dulles had the last word on this issue. "Do nothing to offend the dictators," he instructed U.S. diplomats throughout the region; "they are the only people we can depend on." In the cause of anticommunism, the Eisenhower administration nurtured exceptionally close relations with Pérez Jiménez, Batista, and Trujillo. The consummate expression of this policy came in 1955, when Vice President Richard M. Nixon offered a toast to Batista and compared him with Abraham Lincoln.

Cleaning House

The U.S. embrace of dictatorship in Latin America did not reflect a value judgment in favor of authoritarianism over democracy. It represented, instead, a cold-blooded calculation: that dictatorial regimes would be more predictably and efficiently anticommunist than other types of governance, including democratic systems. This analysis went far beyond Charles Bohlen's 1945 expression of U.S. concern only with the "politico-strategic" aspect of Latin America's foreign policy, and plunged Washington deep into the internal affairs of hemispheric states. As the Cold War unfolded, the United States and military rulers in Latin America joined together in a three-part crusade to stanch the influence of communists through: (1) virtual elimination of Latin American communist parties, (2) assertion (or reassertion) of state control over labor movements, and (3) diplomatic exclusion of the Soviet Union from the Western Hemisphere.

The first assault declared the existence of communist parties to be against the law. Throughout Latin America support for communist parties peaked in 1944–47, partly as a result of euphoria over the Allied victory and partly as a result of democratization. Overall membership climbed to 375,000—some say as high as half a million—while many citizens and voters cast ballots for communist candidates in local and national elections. In Chile, for instance, Gabriel González Videla of the Radical Party won the presidency in 1946 with the support of the Communist Party, which took 17 percent of the total vote in the next year's municipal elections; in Brazil, as well, the Partido Comunista Brasileiro (PCB) won 10 percent of the vote in elections of 1945 and 1947. Communist parties polled an aggregate of well over a million votes to elect their candidates to local, state, or national offices in more than half of the twenty republics. In Cuba, Ecuador, and later in Chile, communists received cabinet positions and took active part in the formulation of national policies.

Upper-class strata and conservative groups in Latin America regarded this trend with fear and distaste. In democratic and pseudodemocratic political arenas, they mounted challenges against communist parties for leadership of labor and student organizations and for electoral support. Most effective were two movements with working-class foundations of their own: the Partido Revolucionario Institucional (PRI) in Mexico and the Partido Laborista (later Peronista) in Argentina. In campaigns and contests throughout the region, centrist and rightist groups denounced communist parties for their identification with Stalin, their allegiance to an international movement, and their abstract ideology. And with the advent of the Cold War, reactionary forces throughout the region found a strong and willing ally in their confrontation with the left: the United States.

As a result of this collaboration, there began a concerted campaign to outlaw communist parties (many of which had been previously outlawed in the 1920s and 1930s as well). In one country after another—in Brazil in May 1947, in Chile in April 1948, and in Costa Rica in July 1948—communist parties were declared to be against the law even though they had played by the rules of the democratic game. Elected party members were removed from the cabinet and from congress in Chile in 1947 and from congress (as well as state and municipal assemblies) in Brazil in 1948. Before the end of 1948 the communist movement had again been outlawed in eight nations of the region, including Nicaragua and Peru; in Mexico the party was technically legal but unable to register for elections. "By 1956," as one historian has noted, "most Communists had been removed from public office, the party had been stricken from the electoral lists, and Communist propaganda outlets had been closed or restricted in fourteen of the twenty countries."[5]

In the face of this onslaught, communist party membership underwent a sharp decline. Between 1947 and 1952 total enrollment fell by nearly half—from nearly 400,000 to less than 200,000—and stayed around that level for the remainder of the 1950s. This pattern was particularly evident in Brazil, Chile, Cuba, and Peru. The only major country to show an increase in party membership was Argentina, where Communist Party stalwarts helped lead the fight against the Peronist dictatorship—only to find themselves under the grip of a military regime in 1955–58 (Table A3). For all practical purposes, communist parties had ceased to exist in much of Latin America.

Emasculation of communist parties represented a clear triumph for the United States. It also offered an opportunity for dictators in Latin America: outlawing communist parties was a quick and certain way to curry favor from Washington. By one count, there were a dozen authoritarian regimes in Latin America by 1954—and all but one (Perón's Argentina) had banned communist parties. Prosecution of the Cold War thus entailed not so much protection from extrahemispheric threats as penetration into the domestic realm of national politics.

The crackdown extended to labor unions as well as to political parties. The industrial working class was presumably more receptive to leftist appeals than other sectors of Latin American society (as Marx himself would have predicted), and communist organizers sought to establish their institutional base among the labor movement. Postwar governments took stern measures in response: in Brazil, the Dutra administration introduced new legislation to bring labor under state control in 1946; in Chile, the government helped break a crucial strike by coal miners in 1947; in Mexico, the ruling PRI crushed independent labor leaders and installed pliant collaborators in the so-called *charrazo* of 1948. Similar events took place in Cuba, Costa Rica, and elsewhere. Throughout the region labor confederations in the postwar period were intervened, marginalized, disbanded, or placed under state control.

The United States joined this campaign directly, through the appointment of labor attachés to embassy staffs, and indirectly, through the anticommunist efforts of the American Federation of Labor. Under the leadership of George Meany and the remarkable Serafino Romualdi—the gregarious, rotund, Italian-born deputy in charge of Latin American operations—the AFL launched a militant campaign against the World Federation of Trade Unions, regarded as a "communist front organization," and its regional affiliate, the Confederación de Trabajadores de América Latina (CTAL), established in 1938 under the leadership of Mexican labor leader Vicente Lombardo Toledano, whom Romualdi denounced in 1943 as a "well-known follower of the Communist Party line." The CTAL represented a broad front of democratic forces throughout the region, especially during the war, and it accordingly accepted the participation of communist groups. Bitterly denouncing the whole idea of collaboration with communists, Romualdi firmly declared the CTAL to be "the Communist front designed to control the Latin American labor movement."

In close collaboration with the U.S. government, and with the active support of the State Department, Romualdi set out to organize an anticommunist movement that could challenge both the WFTU and the CTAL. His tireless efforts came to fruition in January 1948 with the creation of the Confederación Interamericana de Trabajadores (CIT). Under the presidency of Bernardo Ibáñez of Chile, himself a Christian Democrat, the CIT affiliated itself with the International Conference of Free Trade Unions (ICFTU) in 1949 and changed its own name in 1950 to the Organización Regional Interamericana de Trabajadores (ORIT).

Drawing on strong international support, plus fervent backing from Washington, ORIT and its local affiliates steadily took over the labor movement in Latin America. In his memoirs, Romualdi narrates a tale of unceasing struggle against communist influence among working-class syndicates in Bolivia, El Salvador, Colombia, Guatemala, Chile, Brazil, and Venezuela (Peru was out of danger, he reported, only because of the

anticommunist APRA party and the charismatic leadership of Víctor Raúl
Haya de la Torre). By the mid-1960s ORIT had reached 28 million
workers grouped in fifty-two affiliated organizations located in thirty-nine
republics, territories, and possessions of the hemisphere.

Training of labor leaders became a high priority. The early 1960s
witnessed the creation of the American Institute of Free Labor Development (AIFLD), which Romualdi directed from 1962 to 1965. Within a
few short years over 40,000 men and women attended AIFLD field program courses. In 1966 ORIT and the ICFTU also founded the Inter-
American Labor Institute in Cuernavaca, Mexico, under the presidency of
Bernardo Ibáñez. The goal, of course, was to assure that future generations
of labor leaders would resist the blandishments of communist publicists
and agitators.

Yet another component of hemispheric Cold War strategy was diplomatic isolation of the USSR. The idea was to seal the Americas off from
Soviet influence and thus to prevent its contamination by Marxist thought
or Leninist agents. In a sense, a diplomatic cordon around Latin America
would amount to reassertion of the Monroe Doctrine.

Prior to World War II, in fact, only three Latin American nations
granted de jure recognition to Soviet Union: Mexico (1924), which then
severed relations again in 1930; Uruguay (1926), which ruptured relations in 1935 partly at the behest of Brazil; and Colombia (1935), with
Bogotá the only host to a Soviet diplomatic mission anywhere in the
region until 1942. At the wartime urging of the United States, however,
thirteen nations recognized the USSR between 1942 and 1945. By 1946
the Soviet Union enjoyed diplomatic relations with fifteen out of twenty
Latin American republics, with resident missions in eight countries of the
region.

Then came the Cold War. By the mid-1950s all but three of the fifteen
governments that had recognized the Soviet government severed relations
with the USSR. "In each case," as analyst Rollie Poppino has said, "a
specific grievance was cited as justification for the action taken. In most
instances, however, the decision to cut formal ties with the Communist
power reflected broad anti-communist policies being adopted by the Latin
American governments, at least in part to win favor with the United
States."[6] Brazil and Chile broke relations in 1947; Colombia followed suit
in 1948; Venezuela (under Pérez Jiménez) and Cuba (under Batista) did
the same in 1952. Guatemala became a special case in 1954.

Economic ties with the Soviet bloc were no stronger than political
links. Latin America's trade with communist countries surpassed the paltry
sum of $200 million (out of a total of $15 billion) for the first time in
1954; by 1962 the value of trade had risen to $1 billion, still only 5 percent
of the total of $20 billion. In commerce, as well as in diplomacy, the
United States for the most part succeeded in keeping the Soviet Union out
of the Western Hemisphere. Cold War policies insulated the Americas
from alien, dangerous, subversive Soviet influence.

Intervention in Guatemala

United States tactics of supporting anticommunist regimes, suppressing leftist parties, containing labor movements, and restricting diplomatic relations were remarkably successful. During the post–World War II period Latin America was, for the most part, safely and securely aligned with the United States. Still to be determined, however, was the U.S. reaction to installation of an allegedly "communist" government within the Western Hemisphere. How would Washington react?

The answer unfolded in the otherwise unlikely context of Guatemala, where Colonel Jacobo Arbenz Guzmán won the presidency through free elections in 1950. A center-left reformist, Arbenz proclaimed three objectives for his administration: "to convert our country from a dependent nation with a semi-colonial economy to an economically independent country; to convert Guatemala from a backward country with a predominantly feudal economy into a modern capitalist state; and to make this transformation in a way that will raise the standard of living of the great mass of our people to the highest level." Key to this program was agrarian reform. Enacted in June 1952, the bill empowered the government to expropriate only uncultivated portions of large plantations. All lands taken were to be paid for in twenty-five-year bonds bearing a 3 percent interest rate, and the valuation of land was to be determined according to its taxable worth as of May 1952. During its eighteen months of operation the agrarian reform distributed 1.5 million acres to some 100,000 families. The expropriations included 1,700 acres owned by Arbenz himself, who had become a landowner through the dowry of his wife.

Almost immediately, Arbenz and the agrarian reform ran into implacable opposition from the United Fruit Company and from the U.S. government. For its banana production *La frutera* held enormous tracts of land in Guatemala, 85 percent of which was unused—or, as the company maintained, held in reserve against natural catastrophes. And in calculating tax obligations, UFCO consistently undervalued its holdings. On the basis of tax declarations, the Guatemalan government in 1953 offered UFCO $627,572 in bonds in compensation for a seized portion of property; on behalf of the company, the U.S. State Department countered with a demand for $15,854,849!

Washington was deeply involved. Some of the ties were personal. Secretary of State John Foster Dulles and his brother, CIA director Allen Dulles, both came from a New York law firm with close links to United Fruit. The company's Washington lobbyist was Thomas Corcoran, prominent lawyer who was on close terms with President Eisenhower's trusted aide and undersecretary of state, Walter Bedell Smith, himself once interested in a management position with UFCO.

More important than personal ties, however, was the anticommunist crusade. UFCO publicists and the Dulles brothers accused the Arbenz regime of being "soft" on communism, branding it a threat to U.S. security and to the free world at large. They cultivated fears that defeat in Guatemala might lead to a Soviet takeover of the Panama Canal. They warned that if Guatemala fell, then the rest of Central America might go as well. But the principal issue was agrarian reform. Such writers as Daniel James in *The New Leader* warned that communists would use the program as a stepping-stone to gain control of Guatemala. ("The battle of the Western Hemisphere has begun," he wrote at one point. "We enter upon a new era in our history. We face, for the first time, the prospect of continuous struggle against Communism on a hemispheric scale. . . . Such is the ultimate meaning of Moscow's first attempt to conquer an American country, Guatemala.") Whatever Arbenz may have intended, from the U.S. viewpoint he was merely a "stooge" for the Russians.

Calls for action quickly mounted. In March 1953, just two months after Eisenhower's inauguration, now-retired diplomat Spruille Braden challenged the new administration to take decisive action. In a blunt defiance of logic he insisted that the suppression of communism, "even by force, in an American country, by one or more of the other republics, would not constitute an intervention in the internal affairs of the former." Concluded Braden: "It is necessary to fight fire with fire!"

United States policy soon began to take shape. President Eisenhower warned Guatemalan foreign minister Guillermo Toriello that because the United States was "determined to block the international communist conspiracy," he "couldn't help a government which was openly playing ball with communists." The newly dispatched U.S. ambassador, John Peurifoy, offered a succinct impression of his first meeting with Arbenz: "If the president is not a Communist he will certainly do until one comes along."

At an OAS meeting at Caracas in March 1954 John Foster Dulles pressed delegates to support a resolution that "the domination or control of the political institutions of any American state by the international communist movement . . . would constitute a threat" to the entire hemisphere and would require "appropriate action in accordance with existing treaties." His reference was to the Rio Treaty of 1947, which permitted collective action if two-thirds of OAS members concurred that the political independence of any member state was threatened by "an aggression which was not an armed attack." As Dulles explained, the United States wanted to extend "the Monroe Doctrine to include the concept of outlawing foreign ideologies in the American Republics." And as Assistant Secretary John Moors Cabot observed, there was no need to demonstrate conscious intent to serve the Soviet cause: "It is our position that anyone traveling in the interests of communism is in fact part of the whole subversive program of international communism."

Latin American diplomats immediately realized that the U.S. resolution sought to establish a pretext for action against Guatemala. After two weeks of intense debate, the resolution carried by a vote of 17–1–2 (only Guatemala was opposed; Mexico and Argentina abstained). Its impact was greatly softened by an amendment that called for OAS consultations instead of immediate action. Thus the resolution lost its teeth. In summary, opined long-time diplomat Louis Halle, the message of Caracas was "that there was more fear of U.S. interventionism than of Guatemalan communism."

Even so, the Arbenz government concluded that the United States was preparing to intervene. The regime cracked down on domestic opposition and turned to Eastern Europe for small arms, which were en route by May. Meanwhile the U.S. government was demanding, in increasingly blunt language, compensation for U.S. property in Guatemala, meaning, of course, United Fruit.

Unable to obtain OAS sponsorship for direct intervention, the Eisenhower administration turned to covert action. The CIA organized an exile force under an obscure renegade Guatemalan colonel named Carlos Castillo Armas. A rebel column of several hundred men was assembled across the border in neighboring Honduras. They were equipped and directed by the CIA, which set up and operated a rebel radio station and provided a few World War II fighter planes to strafe Guatemala City. Under attack by these planes and convinced that a large army was approaching the capital, Arbenz lost his nerve and gave up. Upon leaving office, however, he delivered a blistering resignation speech: "The United Fruit Company, in collaboration with the governing circles of the United States," Arbenz proclaimed, "is responsible for what is happening to us. . . ."

> In whose name have they carried out these barbaric acts? What is their banner? We know very well. They have used the pretext of anticommunism. The truth is very different. The truth is to be found in the financial interests of the fruit company and the other U.S. monopolies which have invested great amounts of money in Latin America and fear that the example of Guatemala would be followed by other Latin American countries.

The president disappeared behind the walls of the Mexican embassy, and the Castillo Armas rebels rolled into the capital virtually unopposed.

The Eisenhower administration exulted in its Guatemalan triumph. In July the White House held a reception for top CIA officials, to whom the president offered his gratitude: "Thanks to all of you. You've averted a Soviet beachhead in our hemisphere." The redoubtable George Meany, ever the anticommunist, expressed satisfaction in similar language: "The American Federation of Labor rejoices over the downfall of the Communist-controlled regime in Guatemala, brought about by the refusal of the Army to serve any longer a Government that had betrayed the democratic aspirations of the people and had transformed the country into a beachhead of Soviet Russia in the Western Hemisphere."

In Latin America, however, the U.S. action sparked dozens of protests. In Mexico, students and workers marched against the United States at rallies in marketplaces and the university. In Honduras, students held a demonstration to denounce "Wall St. interests." In Panama, students staged a twenty-four-hour strike. In Cuba, demonstrators hurled stones at offices of United Press International and the North American Electric Company. In Argentina, the national congress passed a resolution backing Arbenz; in Uruguay, the congress enacted a resolution condemning the U.S. "aggression"; and in Chile, the Chamber of Deputies voted 34–15 to denounce the U.S. operation. While the Guatemalan intervention provoked nationalist and antiimperialist outcries throughout the region, the U.S. mainstream weekly *Life* magazine offered its own interpretation of the protests: "World communism was efficiently using the Guatemalan show to strike a blow at the U.S. . . . in the form of Red-run anti-U.S. demonstrations which loudly supported Guatemala and waved the bloody shirt of Yankee imperialism from Mexico City to Santiago."

Under a temporary military junta, the new government of Guatemala reversed the expropriation of United Fruit lands and, even more brazenly, wiped out the banana workers' union. Summoned to help reorganize the Guatemalan labor movement, even the hard-line Serafino Romualdi could barely contain his consternation, reporting that "it is generally accepted that the decree dissolving the banana workers' union and the railway workers' union . . . was issued at the insistent request of the American companies," United Fruit and its subsidiary International Railways of Central America. Within a year, union membership dropped from 100,000 to 27,000.

In addition the regime established a National Committee of Defense Against Communism, followed by a Preventive Penal Law Against Communism—establishing the death penalty for "crimes" that could be construed as "sabotage," including union activities. The National Committee had the right to place citizens under arrest without charges for up to six months; those under suspicion could not hold public office or own radios. By November 1954, only months after the coup, the National Committee had the names of 72,000 persons on file; its professed goal was 200,000. And as part of its ideological crusade, the Guatemalan junta commanded the banning and burning of such "subversive" books as *Les Misérables,* by the same Victor Hugo whose death had caused such mourning among intellectuals in fin de siècle Buenos Aires, as well as novels by the Nobel Prize-winning author Miguel Angel Asturias.

On September 1, 1954 the junta stepped down and Castillo Armas assumed power alone. To legitimize his authority he staged a mock plebiscite the following month: 485,531 favored his continuation as president, 393 were opposed, 655 had no answer. He then reestablished ties with the Catholic Church, brought Guatemala back into the OAS, and lifted prohibitions on foreign oil concessions. Eventually assassinated in 1957, Castillo Armas left a dolorous legacy. As later described by one of the CIA operatives who took part in the Arbenz overthrow, "Castillo Armas was a bad president, tolerating corruption throughout his government and kowtowing to the United Fruit Company more than to his own people. The United States could have prevented this with the vigorous exercise of diplomatic pressure on Castillo Armas to assure that he pursued social reform for the many rather than venal satisfaction for a few. Instead, Washington breathed a collective sigh of relief and turned to other problems."

The Nixon Trip

Through the mid-1950s the Eisenhower administration continued to regard its Latin American policy with self-satisfaction. In late 1957 John Foster Dulles assured a group of journalists that "we see no likelihood at the present time of communism getting into control of the political institutions of any of the American Republics." And in February 1958 Allen Dulles of the CIA admitted to Congress that there might be "soft points" within the region, but nonetheless concluded that communism in Latin America was not "a situation to be frightened of as an overall problem."

It was with confidence, then, that Vice President Nixon undertook a tour through South America in May 1958. Originally planned as a courtesy call at the inauguration of newly elected Arturo Frondizi in Argentina, the trip gradually expanded into a two-and-a-half-week tour of eight countries. On "a bleak and drizzly day," Nixon later recalled, he and Patricia Nixon left Washington's National Airport on what was shaping up as a tedious and time-consuming exercise in diplomatic protocol.

To his evident surprise, Nixon met an unruly reception. In Uruguay, the first stop on his tour, the vice president noticed a mild demonstration against U.S. imperialism. A defiant Nixon then went straight to the university, the hotbed of leftist ideology, and engaged a crowd of students in spirited but friendly debate. In Argentina, too, Nixon spoke to labor groups and to university students—engaging in a confrontation with Gregorio Selser, "a well-known Communist newspaper writer" (actually, Selser was a widely respected social scientist)—and emphasizing the danger of communist threats to the region. In neighboring Paraguay, still in the iron grip of General Alfredo Stroessner, Nixon saluted the government for its "strong opposition . . . to Communism." So far so good.

In Peru things started to change. The night before a scheduled visit to the University of San Marcos, in Lima, Nixon received warnings of possible violence. "It was apparent that the Communists, after the failure of their efforts to disrupt my tour in Uruguay, Argentina, or Bolivia, had decided to make an all-out effort to embarrass me and the United States at San Marcos University, an institution so well known throughout Latin America that whatever happened there would be front-page news everywhere." As Nixon decided whether to keep his appointment, a crowd kept up a steady chant outside his hotel: *Fuera Nixon, Fuera Nixon, Fuera Nixon*. Approaching the students at San Marcos, Nixon claimed to pick out the leaders—"the usual case-hardened, cold-eyed Communist operatives"—and then retreated when the crowd began throwing stones. Back at his hotel he encountered another angry mob, and "one of the most notorious Communist agitators in Lima" spit directly in his face. Having directly challenged the demonstrators, Nixon would look back upon the visit to Lima as a personal triumph.

Ecuador and Colombia provided pleasant interludes, and then Nixon headed for Caracas. Only five months before, the detested right-wing dictator of Venezuela, Marcos Pérez Jiménez—recipient of the Legion of Merit from the Eisenhower administration for his anticommunist efforts— had fled the country and, together with his notorious chief of secret police, found exile in the United States. En route to Caracas Nixon heard rumors of plans for huge anti-American manifestations and even an assassination plot: as Nixon would later remember, "the Communist high command in South America had made a high-level decision to regain the ground they had lost in Lima by mounting a massive pay-off demonstration in Caracas."

Venezuelans lost no time in expressing their anger over U.S. policy. A taunting, jeering crowd greeted the Nixons at the airport. The motorcade to the city ran into a blockade, and a mob surged toward the Nixons' automobile. Rocks filled the air, and, as Nixon graphically recalled, "The spit was flying so fast that the driver turned on his windshield wipers." The crowd rocked the car, threatening to turn it over, but then the driver managed to escape. Heading for the U.S. embassy, Nixon remembered, "I felt as though I had come as close as anyone could get, and still remain alive, to a firsthand demonstration of the ruthlessness, fanaticism and determination of the enemy we face in the world struggle."

Astonished by these expressions of popular hostility, Washington immediately denounced the anti-Nixon demonstrations as the result of communist agitation. Nixon himself expressed "no doubt that the riots were Communist-planned, Communist-led, and Communist-controlled." Senator Homer Capehart, Republican of Indiana, proclaimed that the vice president's reception was "a 100 percent Russian penetration." Bourke Hickenlooper, Republican senator from Iowa, said that it revealed a "world-wide pattern of Communist stimulus." Concurred Serafino Romualdi, leader of the anticommunist ORIT: the anti-Nixon demonstrations "clearly indicated a prearranged plan of unquestionable Communist organization and direction."

Parameters for Policy

The Nixon tour prompted an immediate (but incomplete) reassessment of U.S. policy toward Latin America. Nixon himself suggested that Washington distance itself from authoritarian rulers, explicitly recommending a "formal handshake for dictators; an *embraso* [*sic!*] for leaders in freedom." By February 1959 Eisenhower appeared to accept the spirit of this idea, despite resistance from John Foster Dulles, approving gestures of "special encouragement" toward representative governments. The following year

Eisenhower even endorsed a plan to persuade the ruthless Rafael Trujillo to step down from the presidency of the Dominican Republic.

Opposition to dictatorship was, however, equivocal at most. In the midst of a discussion about military assistance, for which the United States sent approximately $400 million during the 1950s, Christian Herter, Dulles' successor as secretary of state, framed the key rhetorical question: "Is the country on our side?" In view of communist threats, he asserted, "a more urgent value—security and survival—must take precedence over an absolute commitment to the promotion of democracy." Unless they were becoming fragile, unpopular, or inconvenient, anticommunist dictators could expect continuing support from Washington.

A second reassessment concerned economic assistance. In the wake of his South American tour, Nixon declared: "We must develop an economic program for Latin America which is distinctively its own. . . . There must be a new program for economic progress for the hemisphere." The proposal met with time-honored skepticism throughout the U.S. government. As one frustrated embassy official blurted out in 1959, looking back on the $129 million in economic assistance that Washington had granted to Bolivia since 1953: "We don't have a damn thing to show for it. We're wasting money. The only solution to Bolivia's problems is to abolish Bolivia."

With cautious hesitation, Eisenhower moved ahead. In 1959 the United States supported the creation of an Inter-American Development Bank (IDB), thus realizing one of the early visions for a Pan American community. And in July 1960 the government announced in Bogotá a Social Progress Trust Fund with $500 million earmarked for health, education, housing, and land reform throughout the region, to be administered through the new IDB. By the end of his term, observers noted, Eisenhower had forged a two-pronged policy toward Latin America: the 1954 Declaration of Caracas, with its renunciation of Marxism, and the 1960 Act of Bogotá, with its assault on poverty and underdevelopment. At long last, the United States was seeking to eradicate what it took to be the underlying causes as well as the political expressions of communism in the hemisphere.

Even so, the Eisenhower policy left deep scars on the inter-American relationship. In Guatemala, the Cold War had prompted the United States to launch its first military intervention in the region since the 1920s. Most Latin American democrats regarded the Arbenz overthrow as ill-considered, intrusive, and counterproductive. "As you know," a saddened President José Figueres of Costa Rica wrote to Adolf A. Berle in 1954, "reaction throughout Latin America has been bad. Intervention is considered a worse evil than communism, especially since intervention is never applied to foster a democratic cause."

6

Making Friends

The U.S. can win wars, but the question is can we win revolutions.
Henry Cabot Lodge (1959)

There are three possibilities in descending order of preference: a decent democratic regime, a continuation of the Trujillo regime, or a Castro regime. We ought to aim at the first but we really cannot renounce the second until we are sure that we can avoid the third.
John F. Kennedy (1961)

The Cold War precipitated an incessant search by the United States for allies in Latin America. Geopolitical dimensions of the U.S.–Soviet competition obliged both of the superpowers to seek allies, friends, and clients throughout the world, especially in unaligned parts of the globe. Enlistment of new partners not only increased the relative strength of each side, but, if the inscription could be portrayed as voluntary, it also testified to the presumed superiority of the rival social systems. The extension of economic assistance by Washington offered an excellent means for making friends, through the dispensation of material benefits, and a promising method for weakening foes, since the alleviation of poverty would presumably undercut the social base of communist movements. From the 1960s through the 1980s Washington threw its support behind anticommunist regimes in other ways, welcoming the advent of military regimes in Brazil and Argentina and aligning itself with right-wing dictatorships throughout the hemisphere.

The 1960s marked the explicit extension and adaptation of the U.S. strategy of "containment" to the Third World. (According to this hierarchical lexicon, the "first" world contained industrialized capitalist democracies, principally Western Europe and the United States; the "second" world comprised the communist bloc, especially the USSR and Eastern Europe; the "third" world was a residual category, embracing all countries not included in the first or second worlds.)[1] Despite this subjective (and rather presumptuous) clarification, it was apparent that Third World countries shared common characteristics. In economic terms, they were poor, disadvantaged, and dependent; many, with small populations, lacked both the consumer market and the human resource bases vital for self-sustaining development. In political terms, especially in Asia and Africa, many had been European colonies or protectorates prior to World War II, and they earned their independence through a variety of means: often through peaceful negotiation, but in some cases, like India, after decades of resistance, and in others, like Vietnam, after armed struggle. Consequently they were profoundly suspicious of the Western "first" world, they were fiercely proud of their sovereignty, and they were intent on improving their socioeconomic circumstance. During the Cold War, with its struggle for geopolitical and ideological supremacy, these countries also marked a critical arena for U.S.–Soviet rivalry.

Countries of the Third World began to seek common political cause in the mid-1950s, with the foundation of the Non-Aligned Movement, and soon found strength in numbers: in time, more than 100 members of the movement could dominate international forums like the UN General Assembly. In the 1960s they joined together in a quest for economic development, with the establishment of the United Nations Conference on Trade and Development (UNCTAD) and the creation of the Group of 77 (G-77). In the 1970s a few of its members, partners in the Organization of Petroleum Exporting Countries (OPEC), managed to use their control over strategic commodities to extract major economic concessions from the industrialized world. From the viewpoint of the United States, such assertions of power were made all the more dangerous by the prevalence of political instability, which appeared to invite left-wing subversion. As Secretary of State George Shultz would say in 1983: "The fault line of global instability runs strongly across the continents of the Third World. This instability is inimical to our security."

Despite sharp contrasts with Asia and Africa, Latin America clearly belonged to this emergent Third World. With the conspicuous exception of small island nations in the Caribbean, most of Latin America had achieved political independence in the 1820s. With the painful exception of Haiti, most countries of the region were considerably more prosperous—or less poor—than sub-Saharan Africa and South Asia. And as a result of their proximity to the United States, leaders of Latin America would find it difficult to claim neutrality in the Cold War and/or to play the two superpowers off against each other. Nonetheless Latin America pertained to this heterogeneous category—if only through a process of elimination, since it could not be regarded as part of the first or second worlds—and regional spokesmen would frequently assert solidarity with other "less developed" areas around the globe. By the outbreak of the Cold War, Latin America had already endured a long and instructive relationship with the United States; as a result of lessons learned from this experience, Latin America could claim leadership among newly independent nations in the developing areas.

The rise of the Third World presented the United States with a pressing challenge. What kind of policy should Washington use for dealing with these emergent areas? And how should it apply to Latin America? The need was urgent and, in light of the Cold War, the stakes seemed very high. What was needed was a doctrine, a general strategy for the promotion of U.S. interests in the face of communist threats.

Social Science, Ideology, and Foreign Policy

The formulation of a long-term strategy emerged from an unusual convergence of academic talent and political purpose. Drawing heavily on a group of "action intellectuals" based primarily at Harvard and MIT, the Kennedy administration developed and implemented a doctrine for U.S. policy toward the Third World. Eventually known as "modernization theory," the argument rested on complex logic and dubious premises. From time to time it also revealed overtly partisan purposes (one of its charter documents, Walt Rostow's famous essay on "The Stages of Economic Growth," carried the subtitle "An Anti-Communist Manifesto"). Espoused by some of the nation's most prominent social scientists, including Gabriel Almond, Max Millikan, Lucian Pye, and Samuel P. Huntington, modernization theory provided a programmatic basis and intellectual rationale for U.S. actions throughout the 1960s and much of the 1970s.

An underlying assumption was that the diffusion of political democracy throughout the developing world would serve and protect U.S. national interests. If governments were freely elected, it was believed, they would support the United States in its titanic struggle with the Soviet Union. Given an opportunity to express an opinion, in other words, citizens around the world would necessarily and inevitably choose to join and support the "free world." The idea that people might voluntarily choose socialist or communist rule seemed utterly preposterous. Communism, everyone knew, could spread only by conquest, conspiracy, or subversion. Democratic elections would lead to democratic governments that would support the U.S. side in the Cold War.

The operative question then became: how to promote political democracy? Modernization theory found ready and congenial answers in processes of economic and social development. In its most essential form, the argument posited simple causal connections. Economic development would create middle-class sectors that would in turn espouse political democracy, either as a tactical means of gaining power or as an expression of enlightened values (this distinction did not seem to matter at the time).

Rather than provoking class struggle between the proletariat and bour-geoisie, as Marxists held, industrial development would lead to reform, transformation, and social harmony. The greater the level of economic modernization, in other words, the greater the likelihood of democratic politics. According to David E. Bell, head of the U.S. Agency for Interna-tional Development (USAID) in the 1960s, there existed an "over-whelmingly" positive historical relationship between economic growth and political democracy, a correlation that bore optimistic implications for the Third World: "while there is no guarantee that improved political institutions will follow in any automatic way," Bell asserted, "it seems clear that without economic progress the chances for strengthening democratic processes in the less developed countries would be greatly diminished." Even in this understated formulation, economic development was a *neces-sary* if not sufficient condition for the emergence of democracy.

Economic development was therefore extremely desirable, in Wash-ington's eyes, and it could be promoted by U.S. foreign aid. During the 1940s and 1950s the Marshall Plan had comprised a crucial element in U.S. efforts to contain communist advances in post–World War II Europe. In the 1960s, analysts thought, foreign assistance could perform a similar function throughout the Third World. Of course there was a world of difference between stimulating a *recovery* of formerly advanced European economies and achieving the *development* of never-industrialized societies, but this discrepancy seemed trivial at the time. Central to the prevailing model of structural change was the idea, associated with Walt Rostow, of an economic "take-off." Countries underwent uniform stages of economic growth, according to this theory, and fulfillment of sufficient conditions propelled countries through a "take-off" phase into self-sustaining growth and continuing development. Foreign aid would not have to go on for-ever. Its task was to help countries reach the moment of take-off. Once that was done, the process of development would become more or less auto-matic, and Washington could apply its resources to other needy causes or nations.

Unlike classical economists (and conservatives in the Eisenhower ad-ministration), Kennedy's "new frontiersmen" insisted that governmental planning was essential to achieve self-sustaining development. Unfettered forces of the market could lead to economic distortions and social imbal-ances. Instead, governments would have to design and implement policies to ensure that economic modernization would alleviate social inequities and benefit popular masses. Thus modernization called for comprehensive country programming, not just blueprints for capital projects or injections of private capital. The state, as well as the market, would play a central role in the promotion of development. As a result, U.S. foreign aid came to rely on government-to-government agreements.

As formulated by "the best and the brightest" recruits in Kennedy's administration, the modernization paradigm quickly seized Washington. It enjoyed academic respectability, it offered bright hopes for the future, and it established clear guidelines for policy. Intellectually, it issued a rebuttal to Leninist notions about imperialism as the highest stage of capitalism; politically, it envisioned a convergence of interests between the United States and the Third World. Promote economic development and you promote democracy—which, by definition, would advance U.S. interests in the struggle with the Soviets.

Modernization theory was fraught with ambiguity. Perhaps the most telling failure, evident in academic writings as well as official declarations, was its inadequate definition of political "progress" or "development" or "modernization." At times the concept referred to democratization—that is, to the progressive expansion of meaningful participation in the quest for political power by growing sectors of the population. At other times, and with frequency, it referred to stability—that is, to the continued preservation of political regimes and the imposition of law and order. These were not only differing notions. They could also be in direct conflict with each other.

As appropriated by the U.S. government, modernization theory was at bottom an antirevolutionary doctrine. It stressed the benefits of guided, gradual, evolutionary change. It emphasized the need for peaceful reform, rather than violent upheaval. It called upon Third World governments to accept and promote change to assure their own survival. As John F. Kennedy declared on one occasion: "Those who make peaceful revolution impossible make violent revolution inevitable." According to rigorous definition the idea of "peaceful revolution" represented a contradiction in terms, but Kennedy nonetheless made his point: gradual reform would provide the antidote to radical revolution. "If the only alternatives for the people of Latin America are the status quo and communism," Kennedy once insisted, "then they will inevitably choose communism."

Revolution itself was held to be a bad thing. It would upset the social order, destroy political institutions, unleash nationalist sentiments, and invite left-wing takeovers. These concerns gave rise to a widespread conviction, virtually an article of faith by the 1960s, that Latin America stood on the brink of massive revolution (it was "one minute to midnight," in the hackneyed language of the time). The prospect of social upheaval contained two forms of political danger. One was that revolutionary leaders would turn out to be Marxists, dedicated agents or pliant "puppets" of the Soviet Union who would align their governments with the communist bloc. Another was that revolutionaries might be well-meaning idealists but they would provoke political instability, thus opening their movements and their governments to communist subversion. Either way, uprisings by the "have-nots" seemed threatening to the United States.

In addition to opposing revolution, U.S. strategy made strenuous efforts to prevent the rise of any leftist movements. Under Kennedy, Washington tended to favor reformist governments of the political center (or center-left); under Nixon, Washington tended to favor status quo governments of the political center-right (or extreme right). But Kennedy and

Nixon agreed on one thing: implacable opposition to the left and to radical tendencies. Prevention of revolution and suppression of the left would provide time and opportunity for processes of socioeconomic modernization to unfold, for countries to attain the stage of economic take-off and self-sustaining change. Thus it was Kennedy who urged the development of counterinsurgency strategies within the Pentagon, and it was Kennedy, as well, who established the antiguerrilla unit known as the Green Berets.

The ultimate application of modernization theory, in conjunction with the doctrine of containment, came in Vietnam. As Vice President Lyndon B. Johnson reported after a trip to the region in 1961: "The basic decision in Southeast Asia is here. We must decide whether to help these countries to the best of our ability or throw in the towel in the area and pull back our defenses to San Francisco and a 'Fortress America' concept." Proclaimed presidential adviser Eugene Rostow in 1964, as the U.S. Congress approved the fateful Gulf of Tonkin resolution: "It is on this spot that we have to break the liberation war—Chinese type. It we don't break it here we shall have to face it again in Thailand, Venezuela, elsewhere. Vietnam is a clear testing ground for our policy in the world." The Third World, analysts claimed time and again, was like a row of dominoes; if Vietnam fell, according to elementary laws of physics, others would necessarily collapse. The U.S. commitment in Vietnam swelled from 1,400 advisers in 1961 to 541,500 troops in 1969. By 1967 there had been more bombardments in Vietnam than in the European theater during World War II; by 1970, more conventional bombs had been dropped over Vietnam than in the prior history of humankind. Over 58,000 U.S. soldiers were killed, and millions of Vietnamese were killed or maimed. In 1975 the United States finally withdrew the last of its troops in defeat. Ho Chi Minh, nationalist and communist, had achieved his nation's liberation.

Elsewhere in the developing world, U.S. policy evolved according to a two-track strategy: strict opposition to leftist movements, with paramilitary or even military means, and long-term promotion of socioeconomic development and of centrist reform. The idea was relatively clear: foreign aid would lead to economic development, which led to political stability, which led to eventual democracy. The anticipated results were uniformly benign: more democracy, less communism, greater national independence and greater political stability. All these outcomes would be good for the United States.

Foundations for Development: The Alliance for Progress

Latin America's economic relations with the United States turned disadvantageous in years just after World War II. As wartime suppliers of price-controlled commodities to the Allied cause, Latin countries accumulated $3.4 billion of credits—only to discover that the United States would promptly raise prices on its capital-goods exports. "In effect," as historian

Steven Rabe has written, "Latin America made a $3-billion non-interest bearing loan to the United States and could not collect on the principal."[2] Nor was there much assistance in the offing for the region. Quashing any hopes for a Pan American "Marshall Plan," Secretary of State George Marshall told delegates at the 1948 founding meeting of the Organization of American States that "it is beyond the capacity of the United States government itself to finance more than a small portion of the vast development needed. The capital required through the years must come from private sources, both domestic and foreign. . . . As the experience of the United States has shown, progress can be achieved best through individual effort and the use of private resources." A year later his successor, Dean Acheson, lectured to Latin Americans that the United States "has been built by private initiative, and it remains a land of private initiative." Industrialization, continued Acheson, was not necessarily a sign of positive development, and countries should not look to Washington for support: "I cannot stress too strongly that progress will come most rapidly in countries that help themselves vigorously." The emphasis should be on trade, not aid, and on the benefits of direct foreign investment.

In exchange for its solidarity with the United States in World War II, Latin America obtained scant material recognition. Between 1945 and 1952, the era of the Marshall Plan, the entire region received less economic aid from the United States than did Belgium and Luxembourg. The Mutual Defense Assistance Act of 1949 authorized expenditures of $1.3 billion; not a penny went to Latin America. Between 1948 and 1958, under Truman and Eisenhower, Latin America received only 2.4 percent of U.S. foreign economic aid. Asked why Washington was paying such short shrift to the region, veteran diplomat Louis Halle responded with customary candor: "The United States no longer desperately needs Latin America."

The fallout from Richard Nixon's 1958 tour of South America began a shift in priorities. In January 1956 Juscelino Kubitschek, the new president of Brazil, had attempted to persuade Eisenhower that the "way to defeat leftist totalitarianism" was "to combat poverty wherever it may be encountered." Two weeks after the Caracas episode, in 1958, Kubitschek followed up with a letter to Eisenhower, later explaining to U.S. officials that "the problem of underdevelopment will have to be solved if Latin American nations are to be able more effectively to resist subversion and serve the Western cause." For these reasons, the Brazilian proposed a twenty-year development program with $40 billion in economic assistance, to be known as Operation Pan America. Nixon himself advocated "a new program for economic progress in the hemisphere" after his tour of South America, but Eisenhower took only halting steps.

The 1959 triumph of the Fidelista movement in Cuba created a new sense of urgency. From the outset, long before Fidel Castro declared himself to be a Marxist-Leninist, the United States regarded his regime with apprehension and disdain. Castro's nationalist rhetoric, his confiscation of

U.S.–held companies, and program for land reform—reminiscent of the Arbenz plan in Guatemala—provoked a predictably negative response in U.S. policy circles. Compounded by fears of the "communist threat," the Cuban Revolution became utterly intolerable. To Washington, it was both an insult and a challenge.

Forming the Alliance

It was in response to the Cuban Revolution that newly elected President John F. Kennedy, an ardent and eloquent Cold Warrior, would launch a bold and new initiative. At a glittering White House reception in March 1961, less than two months after his inauguration, Kennedy observed to Latin American diplomats that "we confront the same forces which have imperiled America throughout its history—the alien forces which once again seek to impose the despotisms of the Old World on the people of the New." To meet this challenge Kennedy proposed a ten-year effort, an Alliance for Progress or *Alianza para [el] Progreso*,[3] that would promote economic growth, social development, and political democracy. "We propose to complete the revolution of the Americas," Kennedy proclaimed,

> to build a hemisphere where all men can hope for a suitable standard of living, and all can live out their lives in freedom and dignity. To achieve this goal political freedom must accompany material progress. . . . Let us once again transform the American continent into a vast crucible of revolutionary ideas and efforts—a tribute to the power of the creative energies of free men and women, an example to all the world that liberty and progress walk hand in hand. Let us once again awaken our American revolution until it guides the struggle of people everywhere—not with an imperialism of force or fear, but the rule of courage and freedom and hope for the future of man.

It was a stirring address, appearing to mark a dramatic and fundamental reorientation of Washington's policy toward Latin America.

At a historic meeting in August 1961 at Punta del Este, Uruguay, representatives from the United States and Latin America (minus Cuba) gathered to put Kennedy's sweeping vision into practice. A charter established a series of goals for the decade of the sixties:

- Raising per capita income "to attain, at the earliest possible date, levels of income capable of assuring self-sustaining development"—with minimum growth rate targets of 2.5 percent per capita per year.
- Social reform, especially focused upon "unjust structures of land tenure and use."
- Diversification of trade—by broadening the range of export products and overseas markets.
- Industrialization and increased employment.
- Enhanced education, including the elimination of adult illiteracy by 1970.
- Price stability, so as to avoid either inflation or deflation.

By accelerating development through the 1960s, the Alliance for Progress would bring Latin America through its "take-off" stage for economic growth. This would yield social and political benefits both for the region and for the United States.

Delegates at Punta del Este also designed a series of measures for achieving these lofty goals. First was a requirement for participating countries to draw up comprehensive plans for national development. These plans were, moreover, to be submitted for approval or amendment by an inter-American board of experts ("the nine wise men," as they promptly came to be known, Walt Rostow among them). This procedure represented a major step for state activism in economic affairs. Said Felipe Pazos, director of the United Nations Economic Commission for Latin America (ECLA/CEPAL): "Planning represented a break with the mentality of an earlier generation which accepted Latin American poverty as a natural consequence of Latin inferiority."

The second measure was an insistence on redistributive reform. Changes in tax codes should demand "more from those who have most." Even more important was a call for land reform. This proved to be a crucial issue. In the early 1960s nearly half the population of Latin America lived in the countryside; as a general rule, 5 to 10 percent of the people owned 70 to 90 percent of the land. Imbued with symbolic and cultural value, land represented a key to subsistence, prosperity, and stability; a significant change in ownership patterns would necessarily entail a major social transformation. As political scientist Tony Smith has pointed out, the United States attempted comparable changes only in postwar Germany and in Japan. "Only in countries occupied after World War II had the United States tried anything so bold."[4]

Third was a U.S. commitment for sustained and large-scale economic assistance. The ambitions of the alliance were to channel $20 billion in foreign assistance within a single decade to Latin America, "with priority to the relatively less developed countries." Of this amount $10 billion was to come from official sources and $10 billion from private sources; the expectation was that this infusion would trigger additional investments by Latin American governments and businesspeople. In the August 1961 declaration from Punta del Este, Washington agreed to shoulder its responsibility, promising to provide "a major part of the minimum of $20 billion, principally in public funds, which Latin America will require . . . in order to supplement its own efforts." The Kennedy administration was committing the United States to a multiyear, multibillion-dollar effort in the Americas. This was utterly unprecedented.

From Washington's point of view the ultimate purpose of the Alliance for Progress was explicitly political. As stated in the *Declaration to the Peoples of America,* which accompanied the Charter of Punta del Este, a principal goal of the alliance was "to improve and strengthen democratic institutions through application of the principle of self-determination by the people." It was furthermore a "basic principle" that "free men working through the institutions of representative democracy can best satisfy man's aspirations, including those for work, home and land, health and schools. No system can guarantee true progress unless it affirms the dignity of the individual which is the foundation of our civilization." In keeping with the tenets of modernization theory, socioeconomic development in Latin America would improve and strengthen political democracy.

As was so often the case, President Kennedy offered the most clear-cut explanation of U.S. motivations. "Latin America is seething with discontent and unrest," he observed. "We must act to relieve large-scale distress immediately if free institutions are to be given a chance to work out long-term solutions." The point, in other words, was to bolster reformist democratic regimes and to forestall revolutionary threats. Such centrist parties as Acción Democrática in Venezuela and Christian Democracy in Chile offered desirable models for political reform and leadership. Support for the center would prevent the rise of the left.

The Alliance for Progress led to an immediate and substantial increase in U.S. aid to Latin America. Bilateral economic assistance nearly tripled between FY 1960 and FY 1961, thereafter climbing to well over $1 billion in the mid-1960s (Figure 3). Under Kennedy and Johnson, Latin America received nearly 18 percent of total U.S. aid, compared with just 3 percent under Truman and 9 percent under Eisenhower. According to one U.S. official, the United States supplied $1.4 billion per year to Latin America from June 1962 through June 1967; when private investments and other international sources are included, the total for new investments rose to $3.3 billion per year.[5] United States bilateral aid dropped sharply in the late 1960s, especially after Richard Nixon won the presidential election of 1968, but the cumulative amount of assistance was nonetheless substantial.

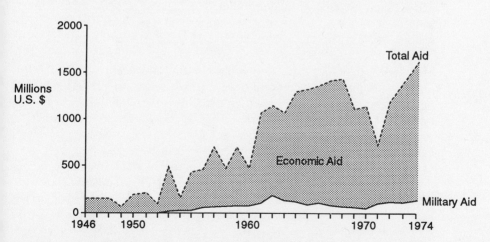

Figure 3. U.S. bilateral aid to Latin America, 1946–1974. [*Source:* Data in Samuel L. Baily, *The United States and the Development of South America, 1945–1975* (New York: Franklin Watts, 1976), p. 74.]

According to another calculation, the total amount of economic aid during the decade of the alliance came to $22.3 billion.[6]

Yet these impressive increases in gross transfers did not necessarily mean that Latin America was receiving major *net* transfers of resources for investment and development. During the 1960s Latin American countries had to pay significant amounts to first world countries, especially to the United States, for service on accumulated debt. In addition, foreign enterprises in Latin America tended to repatriate profits back to their home country—especially, again, the United States—and profit remittances frequently exceeded quantities of new investment. As William T. Dentzer, deputy U.S. ambassador to the OAS, explained to the House Committee on Foreign Affairs in March 1969: "High gross official capital flows to Latin America under the Alliance have been necessary to help Latin America deal with the problems she had accumulated previously. When you look at net capital flows and their economic effect, and after all due credit is given to the U.S. effort to step up support to Latin America, one sees that not that much money has been put into Latin America after all."[7]

Accomplishments and Limitations

Nonetheless, the 1960s witnessed a marked acceleration in economic growth for Latin America. Regional output expanded by 2.4 percent per capita per annum during the 1960s, nearly matching the alliance goal of 2.5 percent, and per capita growth was on a steady rise—reaching 2.7 percent in the latter half of the decade, and climbing to 3.8 percent in 1970–74. Compared with 2.1 percent in the 1950s, this growth was a major achievement. It stemmed from several factors: the successful implementation of strategies for "import-substitution industrialization," the continuing strength of major trading markets (especially in the United States), and the stimulation of private investments. Expansion of the industrial sector, especially in Argentina, Brazil, and Mexico, proved to be the driving force behind the region's growth. Economic performance varied widely across nations: Mexico made strong and steady progress, Brazil and Colombia made significant gains during the second half of the 1960s, Argentina and Venezuela held their ground, while Chile and Peru slipped downward; comparable variation took place within Central America, where Costa Rica moved upward and El Salvador and Nicaragua, after a very promising start, slumped toward the end of the decade (Table A4). Overall, seven countries actually reached the target of 2.5 percent per capita per year, twelve nations fell short of the goal, and two countries, Haiti and Uruguay, actually suffered declines in GDP per capita. Foreign assistance under the Alliance for Progress played a relatively minor part in this picture. But with regard to regional rates of per capita growth, according to its own criteria, the alliance nonetheless proclaimed the near-fulfillment of a central goal.

Social reform presented a more discouraging picture. It proved impossible to eliminate adult illiteracy within the decade, as alliance planners projected, but access to secondary and higher levels of education showed a notable increase; in some countries, the number of people going on to higher education doubled or even tripled. Housing projects expanded but could not keep up with population growth, and overcrowding continued to proliferate in urban slums. Provision of potable water and sewage systems became the focus of major efforts, especially in urban areas, but with modest impacts on general welfare. Perhaps the most poignant indicator of public health concerned infant mortality, which the alliance vowed to reduce by one-half within five years. Infant mortality rates declined nearly everywhere (with the exception of Guatemala), but not a single country was able to reach its target under the alliance (Table A5).

The most intractable issue was, predictably, agrarian reform. As former OAS official Ronald Scheman has written, "The agricultural sector was the problem child of the Alliance."[8] Of more than 15 million peasant families living in Latin America at the beginning of the 1960s, fewer than 1 million benefited from any kind of land reform policy. Determined to maintain their base of power, traditional elites mounted effective resistance to land-reform programs. The ideal of social reform also came into conflict with another of the alliance's declared goals, the increasing of production. When push came to shove, efficiency triumphed over justice.

Requiem for Failed Expectations

The Alliance for Progress represented an earnest and high-minded attempt by the United States to make friends in Latin America—quite literally, in the sense of creating the friends, as well as forming the friendships. There were several basic reasons for its eventual failure. First, perhaps, was the modesty in levels of economic aid. A ten-year injection of $20 billion in a single world region sounded like a massive enterprise, which it was in many respects, but it also amounted to approximately $10 per capita per year. There were limits to what this could achieve.

Second, planners misread social facts of the region. They confidently assumed that Latin America's emerging middle classes would uphold democracy as a matter of moral principle and idealistic conviction. This presumption turned out to be wrong. For in Latin America, the so-called middle classes—those whose lifestyle bore essential resemblance to that of middle classes in the United States—belonged to the upper strata of society. They found very little in common with workers in the cities or peasants in the countryside. Lacking in ideological conviction, opportunist at times, Latin America's middle sectors tended to identify their interests with the upper classes. Revealingly enough, it was the middle classes that provided moral and political support for military rulers in Brazil, Argentina, and elsewhere. They did not comply with the prescriptions of the Alliance for Progress.

Third, designers of the alliance misunderstood the relationship between social change and political conflict. It was their anticipation that transformation of Latin American society could come about within a context of political stability (it was their idea, as one analyst has noted, that "all good things go together"). The reality, in contrast, was that upper-class sectors would fight to maintain their privilege and power. This determination was especially evident with regard to land reform, which explicitly called for a redistribution of resources from top to bottom. Ultimately, Washington lost its nerve and backed off from its promises. Agrarian reform, the U.S. government believed, might stir up radical sentiments and play into the hands of communist subversives. Better to leave things as they were.

Finally, alliance planners assumed that social and political change would enhance the strength of a reformist center. This expectation was mistaken for at least two reasons. First, Washington overestimated the significance and ubiquity of reformist forces in Latin America. Acción Democrática in Venezuela and Christian Democracy in Chile were viewed as attractive models, but these types were relatively rare; there was nothing quite comparable in Argentina, Brazil, Ecuador, or most other countries of the region. Second, social change and conflict did not usually benefit moderate reformist tendencies. These processes often led to a political polarization that fortified extremes of left and right, rather than the center, thus weakening the prospects for gradual reform. They also undermined a central conviction, especially apparent during the Kennedy era, that the United States would have clear and simple political choices: Washington could circumscribe the left, contain the right, and nurture an enlightened center. Unhappily, this option turned out not always to be available.

Holding the Line: Dictators as Friends

The most striking failure of the Alliance for Progress occurred within the political realm. Instead of promoting and consolidating reformist civilian rule, the 1960s witnessed a rash of military coups throughout the region. There were six *golpes* in 1962–63 alone, within the early years of the alliance: in Argentina (March 1962), Peru (July 1962), Guatemala (March 1963), Ecuador (July 1963), the Dominican Republic (September 1963), and Honduras (October 1963). Subsequent overthrows led to the installation of new styles and longer-term dictatorial regimes that sought to bring about fundamental transformations in society rather than mediation of disputes through short-term periods of intervention. Military coups in Brazil (April 1964) and Argentina (June 1966) imposed repressive and far-reaching machineries that became archetypes for what came to be known as "bureaucratic-authoritarian" regimes; another coup in Peru (October 1968) installed military leadership with a nationalist outlook and a reformist social agenda. By the end of 1968 dictators were holding sway in Argentina, Brazil, Peru, Paraguay, and most of Central America; Bolivia and Ecuador were controlled by the military; and Mexico remained under the rule of its unique, dominant-party, civilian-led, but unmistakably authoritarian regime.

United States reaction to these developments evolved over time. John F. Kennedy took particular and somewhat personal umbrage at the overthrow of centrist reformers, precisely the type of leadership that he hoped to nurture and support with alliance programs. Washington accordingly mounted a strong diplomatic offensive in response to the 1962 coup in Peru, where the military intervened to prevent an electoral victory by Víctor Raúl Haya de la Torre and his Aprista party. Kennedy suspended diplomatic relations, cut off economic aid, ordered technical personnel not to go on their jobs—and considered suspension of the Peruvian sugar quota. As the president announced in a news conference: "We are anxious to see a return to constitutional forms in Peru. . . . We feel that this hemisphere can only be secure with free and democratic governments." Washington received precious little support for its position from Latin American governments—Argentina, Brazil, and Mexico protested against the "intervention," while the Chilean foreign minister warned the United States against being "more royalist than the king"—but the Peruvian junta departed from power after supervising another election in 1963. This time, however, the Apristas were not permitted to win.

Similarly, Kennedy expressed considerable displeasure with the overthrow of Ramón Villeda Morales, a moderate civilian who was elected to the presidency of Honduras in 1957. In keeping with the mandate of the Alliance for Progress (and, ironically, with the legacy of Guatemala's Jacobo Arbenz), Villeda Morales designed and promoted a project for land reform. His proposal inspired the wrath of traditional aristocrats as well as the armed forces, of course, and they ousted him from office in October 1963. Kennedy had sharp words for the new ruling junta, but took no meaningful action.

In reaction to this rash of coups, the U.S. State Department began to soften its opposition to military rule in Latin America. On this subject Assistant Secretary of State for Inter-American Affairs Edward M. Martin composed a key policy statement in October 1963: "We all have respect for motherhood and abhor sin. We may observe, however, that while motherhood has prospered, so has sin. In an increasingly nationalistic world of sovereign states, a U.S. frown doesn't deter others from committing what we consider to be political sins." Military coups had serious negative consequences. In Martin's assessment, they "thwart the will of the people, destroy political stability and the growth of the tradition of respect for democratic constitutions, and nurture communist opposition to their tyranny." Yet the United States could not prevent them from occurring. Under these circumstances, he continued, the U.S. government should engage resulting regimes in positive ways and encourage the military "to assume the more constructive peacetime role of maintaining internal security and working on civic action programs."

> We must use our leverage to keep these new regimes as liberal and considerate of the welfare of the people as possible. We must support and strengthen the civilian components against military influences and press for new elections as soon as possible so that these countries once again may experience the benefits of democratic legitimacy.

"I fear," he wrote in conclusion,

> there are some who will accuse me of having written an apologia for coups. I have not. They are to be fought with all the means we have available. Rather . . . I am insisting . . . that democracy is a living thing which must have time and soil and sunlight in which to grow. We must do all we can to create these favorable conditions, and we can and have done much. But we cannot simply create the plant and give it to them; it must spring from seeds planted in indigenous soil.

Seeking middle ground between "impatient idealists" and "defeatist cynics," Martin attempted to define a realistic and pragmatic approach for U.S. policy. Within two and a half years after its lofty proclamation, the Alliance for Progress was obliged to tolerate military dictatorship as a persisting fact of political life in Latin America.

The U.S. stance took a sharp turn toward the right after Kennedy's assassination in November 1963. From his own personal experiences in Mexico and Texas, Lyndon B. Johnson concluded that JFK's policy toward Latin America was "a thorough-going mess." Skeptical about prospects for social reform and disdainful of political idealists, Johnson was adamant about the need to avoid a "second Cuba" in the hemisphere. A victory for communism in Brazil, he thought, would confront the United States with "another China." It was time for the United States to get tough.

Abruptly dismissing Martin and Teodoro Moscoso, chief administrator of the Alliance for Progress, Johnson united both State Department and AID functions in the person of Thomas C. Mann, assistant secretary of state for economic affairs in the last years of the Eisenhower administration and ambassador to Mexico. A self-styled "country lawyer" from southwest Texas, Mann embodied Johnson's approach toward the region. ("I know my Latinos," Mann was once reported to have said. "They understand only two things—a buck in the pocket and a kick in the ass.") In March 1964 he convoked a three-day meeting of U.S. ambassadors to Latin America and, in an off-the-record statement, announced the administration's new line. What subsequently became known as the Mann Doctrine propounded four basic objectives: (1) promotion of economic growth with absolute neutrality on questions of social reform, (2) protection of U.S. private investments, (3) display of no preference, through aid or other means, for representative democratic institutions, and (4) opposition to communism. In effect, Mann discarded cherished ideas of the Alliance for Progress, especially its insistence on social reform and political democracy. Indeed, Mann expressed no political or moral reservations about cooperation with military governments. In his view, so long as a government was not communist-controlled, or in danger of becoming so, it would be acceptable to the United States.[9]

The Mann Doctrine found virtually immediate application in Brazil, where military officers overthrew the center-left government of João Goulart on April 1, 1964. Concerned about the possibility of a sharp leftward turn by the wavering Goulart, the U.S. government was fully aware of the military conspiracy and even offered assistance (which was never needed). Within hours of the coup, President Johnson dispatched a congratulatory telegram expressing "warmest good wishes" to the titular president of the new regime, stating that "the American people have watched with anxiety the political and economic difficulties through which your great nation has been passing, and have admired the resolute will of the Brazilian community to resolve these difficulties within a framework of constitutional democracy and without civil strife." Johnson's message thus adopted the transparently specious argument that Goulart had voluntarily "vacated" the presidency of Brazil, so the constitutional requirements for succession were maintained. Plainly enough, the U.S. government was establishing a rationale to justify the coup.

Even after the regime began to reveal its brutal side, U.S. Ambassador Lincoln Gordon continued to extoll its political virtues. In a speech on May 5, at the Higher War College of Rio de Janeiro, Gordon proclaimed that the Brazilian change of government "can indeed be included along with the Marshall Plan proposal, the Berlin Blockade, the defeat of Communist aggression in Korea, and the resolution of the missile crisis in Cuba as one of the major turning points in world history in the middle of the twentieth century." As Brazil adopted a strongly pro-U.S. foreign policy, Washington showed its appreciation in tangible ways. Between 1964 and 1968 Brazil received more than $1.5 billion in military and economic aid, nearly 25 percent of the U.S. total for Latin America.

Encouraged by the denouement in Brazil, Mann offered a public description of the new U.S. policy in a commencement address at Notre Dame in June 1964. The United States sought to strengthen democratic government and to discourage military intervention, he said, and Washington would promote the return to democracy in cases where coups occurred. But the practice of democracy, Mann continued, was not just a question of civilian rule. It also entailed respect for rights of expression and organization. As a result, Mann contended, the United States should:

> encourage democracy in a quiet, unpublicized way and on . . . [a] day-to-day basis; broaden the scope of collective action in the hemisphere; [make] a careful evaluation of each case of the use of force to overthrow a government; if as a result of this evaluation it is decided not to recognize a regime, it should be made clear that nonrecognition is tied to a breach in established international conduct; and if it is decided to recognize a government, it should be made clear that recognition in no way constitutes approval.

In translation: the United States would offer diplomatic recognition to military regimes that were not in flagrant defiance of minimal standards of international conduct. Washington would henceforth deal with dictators on a practical, pragmatic, and realistic basis.

Mann stipulated one key exception to this policy of nonintervention. "The question of our relations with Communist regimes in this hemisphere is, of course, a separate subject. . . . It raises separate questions, such as our inherent right of self-defense and measures, under existing treaties, to deal with situations which threaten the peace and security of the hemisphere." While the United States would not take action against dictatorships of the right, it reserved the option of deposing left-wing regimes. Intervention would thus be allowable in order to forestall communist rule.

The U.S. posture toward military regimes thenceforth oscillated between passive acceptance and outright endorsement. Washington saw little convincing reason to denounce or oppose authoritarian rule. In June 1966, perhaps emboldened by the Brazilian example, the Argentine armed forces ousted Arturo Illia, installed a general in the presidency, abolished legislative bodies, outlawed political parties, expressed abhorrence for international communism, and embarked on a conservative economic program; the Johnson administration warmly welcomed the new government. In the meantime the United States approved loans to the tyrannical government of François ("Papa Doc") Duvalier in Haiti, continued to support the Somoza dynasty in Nicaragua, and cooperated with the autocratic Stroessner regime in Paraguay.

Washington's acceptance of dictatorship became even more explicit under Richard M. Nixon, one of whose first acts as president after the 1968 election was to commission political rival Nelson Rockefeller to conduct a study of U.S.–Latin American relations. Rockefeller's expansive entourage made four trips through the region, conferred with more than 3,000 leaders, endured frequent anti-U.S. demonstrations, and submitted its final report in August 1969. "The United States has allowed the special relationship it has historically maintained with the other nations of the Western Hemisphere to deteriorate badly," stated the report. This deterioration stemmed from several causes, in the commission's view, including "narrow special interests," competing foreign-policy priorities, "well-intentioned but unrealistic rhetoric," and a "paternalistic attitude. . . . The United States has talked about partnership," in the view of the commission, "but it has not truly practiced it." Partly as a consequence, Latin America presented a disturbing picture. Expectations were rising but population growth, urbanization, unemployment, nationalism, radicalism, and anti-U.S. sentiment were commonplace: "The seeds of nihilism and anarchy are spreading throughout the hemisphere." Emerging forces for social change included women ("by and large, a middle-of-the-road influence") and the Roman Catholic Church, although, like young people in general, the idealistic priesthood was "vulnerable to subversive penetration." Indeed, the potential for Castroite and Marxist infiltration was powerful: "Clearly, the opinion in the United States that communism is no longer a serious factor in the Western Hemisphere is thoroughly wrong."

In the face of these challenges, the Rockefeller group found one strong and positive influence: the Latin American military. As the commission proclaimed, "a new type of military man is coming to the fore and often becoming a major force for constructive social change in the American republics. Motivated by increasing impatience with corruption, inefficiency, and a stagnant political order, the new military man is prepared to adapt his authoritarian tradition to the goals of social and economic progress." Implicitly referring to the maverick regime in Peru, the report went on to observe that military governments "have an intrinsic ideological unreliability and a vulnerability to extreme nationalism. They can go in almost any doctrinal direction." The question, therefore, was whether they would favor the United States—"Or will they become radicalized, statist, and anti-U.S.?" To prevent this undesirable outcome, the commission called for more training of Latin American officers in U.S.-sponsored programs, more contact and cooperation, and more types of military assistance. As a general proposition, the commission opined, it made much more sense to collaborate with Latin American military rulers "than to abandon or insult them because we are conditioned by arbitrary ideological stereotypes."

In sum, the Rockefeller commission argued that the United States should be willing to cooperate with authoritarian regimes throughout the region. Despite the virtues of democracy, the commission said, Washington should engage in pragmatic partnership: "We must recognize that the specific forms or processes by which each nation moves toward a pluralistic system will vary with its own traditions and situation. We know that we, in the United States, cannot determine the internal political structure of any other nation, except by example." Even more to the point: "The United States cannot allow disagreements with the form or the domestic policies of other American governments to jeopardize its basic objective of working with and for their people to our mutual benefit."

Cooperation with dictators would therefore continue to be a basic element in U.S. policy toward Latin America in years to come. The Nixon administration formed close relations with the ruling generals in Brazil, and in 1973, as will be recounted in chapter 7, Nixon warmly welcomed a military takeover in Chile. In 1976 President Gerald Ford granted prompt recognition to an antidemocratic junta in Argentina. In the meantime Washington worked together with dictatorial regimes throughout most of Central America.

A partial exception to this rule came under Jimmy Carter, the only Democrat to occupy the White House during the remainder of the Cold War. Driven by the president's moral convictions and spurred by an activist Congress, the U.S. government launched a major campaign on behalf of human rights that led to the denial of economic and military assistance to regimes in Guatemala, Chile, and Argentina that were flagrantly abusing their citizens. And in 1979, as a Sandinista rebellion spread throughout Nicaragua, the Carter administration withdrew its support from Anastasio Somoza and allowed his tyrannical regime to come to an end. It is to be observed, however, that Carter was willing to overlook human-rights violations in countries outside the hemisphere that were viewed as crucial to U.S. security, mostly notably Iran under the shah and the Philippines under the Marcos family. To this degree, even the Carter administration ratified a long-standing principle in U.S. Cold War policy: to oppose dictators in Latin America only if they (1) became a serious embarrassment to Washington, (2) ran a risk of being overthrown by radical or "communist" movements, or (3) both. In such cases the United States would typically seek to persuade the ruler to cede power to a trusted centrist, who (with support from Washington) could prevent a victory by communists. The idea was not so much that dictatorship was inherently bad; it was fear that the alternative would be much worse.

Carter's policy on human rights, cautious as it was, came in for critical excoriation. In a well-known essay entitled "Dictatorships and Double Standards," first published in 1979, neoliberal analyst Jeane Kirkpatrick denounced the Carter administration for withdrawing support from the shah of Iran and Somoza in the face of popular challenges. Because of a naive belief in the feasibility of democratic politics, Kirkpatrick charged, the Carter team allowed both countries to fall under the grip of hostile, totalitarian movements. In her own words:

> The rise of violent opposition in Iran and Nicaragua set in motion a succession of events which bore a suggestive resemblance to one another and a suggestive similarity to our behavior in China before the fall of Chiang Kai-shek, in Cuba before the triumph of Castro, in certain crucial periods of the Vietnam War, and more recently, in Angola. In each of these periods, the American effort to impose liberalization and democratization on a government confronted with violent internal opposition not only failed, but actually assisted the coming to power of new regimes in which ordinary people enjoy fewer freedoms and less personal security than under the previous autocracy—regimes, moreover, hostile to American interests and policies.[10]

In both contexts, misconceived American policies had brought about precisely the situations they sought to avoid.

The practical implication of Kirkpatrick's argument was clear: the United States should support traditional authoritarian regimes so long as they promote the cause of anticommunism. The consequence of Carter's high-minded mistakes was, she proclaimed in yet another essay, a serious threat to U.S. security: "The deterioration of the U.S. position in the hemisphere has already created serious vulnerabilities where none previously existed, and threatens now to confront this country with the unprecedented need to defend itself against a ring of Soviet bases on its southern flanks from Cuba to Central America." Once again, eternal vigilance would be the price of liberty. In the name of national security, Washington should back its friends and challenge its true foes.

The Search for Political Allies

During the Cold War, the cultivation of ideological allegiance was an essential part of the geopolitical calculus between the rival superpowers. In its quest for advantage, the United States repeatedly stressed the claim that its alliances were based on voluntary preference, in contrast to the forced "captivity" imposed by the Soviet Union. This led Washington to entice prospective allies with material and other incentives, especially economic aid. And in consideration of hard-headed *realpolitik,* it seemed essential for the United States to assure itself of support from Latin American governments. Not only did the region pose a potential security threat because of geographical proximity. Historically, too, it had become a U.S. sphere of influence, a putative "backyard" for the United States. If Washington proved unable to maintain friendly relations within its own neighborhood, according to this perspective, it would have difficulty keeping partners in other parts of the world.

As a result, the United States showed a tendency to vacillate in its dealings with dictatorial regimes in Latin America. For a brief time around the end of World War II, Washington expressed strong opposition to authoritarian rule in the Americas. In the late 1940s and throughout the 1950s Presidents Truman and (especially) Eisenhower showed conspicuous willingness to consort with dictatorial governments so long as they were anticommunist. In the early 1960s President Kennedy and his cadre of academic advisers attempted to nurture, and even to create, reformist alternatives to dictatorship and (especially) leftist revolution; in the 1970s President Carter took a similar though less activist stance. In the late 1960s, and then again by the 1980s, Washington ceased its quest for democratic alternatives and supported dictatorial rulers who (1) expressed anticommunist beliefs and (2) backed U.S. foreign policy. Throughout this entire period, the overriding consideration in Washington's outlook was the strengthening of its position vis-à-vis the Soviet Union. Whatever their qualities as statesmen, rulers of Latin America were needed as allies and friends.

As construed by the Kennedy brain trusters, the Alliance for Progress represented an extremely ambitious attempt by the United States to cultivate democracy and to nurture democratic leaders in Latin America. The governing assumption, fortified by prevailing social science theory, was that economic development would lead to social change that would result in political democratization—and foreign aid could set the whole process in motion. The envisioned result would be moderate, reformist, elected politicians who, by their action and example, would discredit the temptations of socialist revolution and strengthen the legitimacy of U.S. leadership throughout the hemisphere.

Throughout the 1960s and 1970s, world events took their toll on U.S. policy. The U.S.–Soviet rivalry intruded directly (but briefly) in the hemisphere in October 1962, when the Kennedy administration faced down the Khrushchev regime during the Cuban missile crisis. And the Cold War expanded and intensified during the course of the 1960s and 1970s, most notably in Vietnam. Latin America lost relative importance for the United States. The lofty goals of the Alliance for Progress seemed less urgent as well as unattainable.

Eventually, the United States came to embrace, or at least to accept, dictatorial governments throughout the region. In keeping with the time-honored maxim of international politics—an enemy of my enemy is my friend—the United States worked closely with authoritarian rulers who proclaimed themselves to be anticommunist. In the long run it was the perceived exigency of global issues, rather than a concern with Latin America, that gave shape to U.S. policy.

7

Crushing Enemies

*I don't see why we should have to stand by and let a country go
communist due to the irresponsibility of its own people.*
  Henry Kissinger (1970)

*The enduring test for Americans is not whether we have the will to use
[our] power but the skill to avoid having to.*
  New York Times (1983)

*If the Soviet Union can aid and abet subversion in our hemisphere, then
the United States has a legal right and a moral duty to help resist it.
This is not only in our strategic interest; it is morally right.*
  Ronald Reagan (1984)

Throughout the Cold War the United States considered the installation in
Latin America of radical regimes—socialist, Marxist-Leninist, or "leftist"
in any way—to be utterly intolerable. Any such development would represent an advance for the communist cause and, in the zero-sum calculus of
the time, a vital loss for the West. In view of Soviet strategy, with its
presumed domination of clients and puppets, the presence of a socialist
government would represent an intrusion of extrahemispheric power
within the Americas—and violate the Monroe Doctrine. Acceptance of
this outcome could weaken the credibility of the United States as the leader
of the West and as a rival for the USSR. In the eyes of Cold Warriors, the
consolidation of any left-wing regime in the Western Hemisphere would
have dire and dangerous implications for U.S. national security and for the
global distribution of power.
    It was therefore essential to resist this possibility. As shown in chapters

163

5 and 6, the United States developed strategies in the 1950s and 1960s to prevent such unfavorable denouements. On occasion, however, Washington found itself face-to-face with what it regarded as an unacceptably "leftist" regime within the hemisphere. In such cases U.S. policymakers felt obliged to take action—which meant overthrowing the government in question. Exigencies of the Cold War thus led the United States to adopt a tacit but consistent policy of political intervention in Latin America. American officials routinely attempted to justify each episode as singular, exceptional, and nonprecedential, as in the case of Guatemala in 1954, but U.S. interventions occurred with relentless regularity—from Cuba in 1961 to the Dominican Republic in 1965 to Chile in 1973 to Grenada in 1983 and to Central America throughout the 1980s.

Cuba, Castro, and the Bay of Pigs

The Cuban Revolution confronted the United States with the gravest— and most enduring—challenge of the Cold War period. Its economy dependent on sugar exports, its society controlled by a narrow-minded elite, its politics governed by disorder and venality, its history marked by U.S. interference and intervention, Cuba was preparing for upheaval. In March 1952 Fulgencio Batista seized power in order to stave off likely electoral defeat, an action that prompted Fidel Castro, a would-be candidate for a congressional seat, to launch a paramilitary assault against the dictatorship on July 26, 1953. Captured and imprisoned, Castro delivered his famous "History Will Absolve Me" speech, and was released as part of a general amnesty in 1955. Exiled to Mexico, he organized an invasion of Cuba; routed in his abortive December 1956 landing, Castro withdrew to the hills and developed a guerrilla force (the 26th of July Movement, named in commemoration of the 1953 attack). In July 1957 Castro released his "Sierra Maestra Manifesto," focusing largely on questions of political reform, and his movement steadily gained popular support. Through 1958 the Batista government came apart at the seams; on January 1, 1959 Fidel Castro and his M-26 took the reins of power.

Washington had greeted early signs of unrest against the Batista dictatorship with proclamations of support for the ruler. Arthur Gardner, Eisenhower's first ambassador to the island, expressed his opinion that "I don't think we ever had a better friend [than Fulgencio Batista] . . . he was doing an amazing job." And Gardner's successor, Earl E. T. Smith, explained solidarity with Batista in classic Cold War terms: "Our two nations I feel will always be the closest of friends and allies in the common fight against communism."

As the Batista regime began to weaken, Washington opted in the late 1950s for an alternative course: *batistianismo sin Batista*—keeping the regime intact but changing topmost personnel. William Wieland, head of the Caribbean desk at the State Department, later explained the U.S. predicament:

Our problem . . . was a desire to see an effective solution to Cuba's political strife that would ensure a democratic transition and the support of the bulk of the Cuban people [and] that would have eliminated any major threat from the violence which was at that time being waged by the Castro forces. . . . Castro was at that time still a small figure in the east. . . . We were not thinking of dictating on the type of government.

The principal goal was prevention of a Fidelista triumph. As Wieland would recall: "Fidel Castro is surrounded by commies. I don't know whether he himself is a communist. . . . [But] I am certain he is subject to communist influences."

United States analysts were busy hatching conspiracies right up to the collapse of the Batista regime. William Pawley, a tough-minded business-man and ex-ambassador, remembered a meeting in Miami in November 1958: "What do you do about this Cuba problem? . . . Everything we were doing was wrong. I told them that we should now try to save the peace, see if we can go down there and get Batista to capitulate to a caretaker unfriendly to him but satisfactory to us, whom we could imme-diately recognize and give military assistance to in order that Fidel Castro should not come to power." The following month a policy group at the Pentagon concluded that Castro was "not the right man" for Cuba—or for the United States—but failed to produce any clear alternatives. Soon it would be too late.

After Fidel Castro made his triumphant entrance into Havana, Wash-ington greeted his government with undisguised hostility. As anti-Castro emigrés flocked to Florida and other destinations, the American media provided negative coverage to "popular" trials and executions of *batistiano* collaborators. When Castro visited the United States in April 1959, Eisenhower refused to meet with him—and delegated Vice President Nixon to be an intentionally uncongenial host. Government officials railed loudly against Cuba's agrarian reform, which entailed the confiscation (albeit with compensation) of U.S.–owned sugar estates. As hostility mounted in Washington, Castro turned toward the Soviet Union. In early 1960 Cuba signed an economic agreement with the USSR, which prom-ised to purchase 450,000 tons of sugar in 1960 and a million tons per year for the following four years—and to lend 100 million pounds sterling to the struggling young government.

Eisenhower promptly reacted. In March 1960 the president endorsed a CIA recommendation for "A Program of Covert Action against the Castro Regime." The plan included four points: strengthening the political opposition outside Cuba, launching "a powerful propaganda offensive," conducting espionage within Cuba, and promoting "the development of a paramilitary force outside of Cuba for future guerrilla action." By October 1960 the CIA was training 400–500 Cubans (in Guatemala) for the pur-pose of overthrowing Castro's government. Shortly thereafter the Eisenhower administration decided to prepare for an outright invasion, instead of merely supporting a guerrilla underground, and in November

1960 the program began training a paramilitary force of about 1,000 attackers. Estimates that an invasion force of this size would be sufficient rested on either (or both) of two assumptions: first, the arrival of rebels would draw instant and widespread support from the Cuban populace; second, an amphibious landing would establish an opportunity for U.S. armed forces to intervene.

The U.S. presidential campaign of 1960 further intensified America's resolve, as candidates Nixon and Kennedy both sought to demonstrate anti-Castro credentials. (In this Kennedy had the upper hand, since Vice President Nixon was unable to reveal government plans then under way.) Activity continued through the November election, with a new training program for guerrillas undertaken in Louisiana. The Cuban exile organization was broadened to include moderate opponents of Castro as well as the prestigious figure of José Miró Cardona, who had served as Fidel's first premier in 1959–60. In January 1961, just as JFK was about to assume the presidency, Eisenhower severed diplomatic relations with Cuba. In March 1961 Kennedy launched the Alliance for Progress, as described in chapter 6, and on April 3, as part of the same overall strategy, the White House published a white paper asserting that: "The present situation in Cuba confronts the western hemisphere and the Inter-American System with a grave and urgent challenge . . . [and] offers a clear and present danger to the authentic and autonomous revolution of the Americas." Among the Washington elite, only Senator William J. Fulbright had the courage to counsel caution: "The Castro regime is a thorn in the flesh," the lawmaker pointed out, "not a dagger in the heart."

Plans for an invasion went ahead. The CIA placed sixteen B-26 planes at the disposal of the rebel force. The detachments moved from Guatemala (then under Miguel Ydígoras Fuentes) to Nicaragua (under the Somoza dynasty). On April 14 they embarked on ships for Cuba—after receiving a final word of encouragement from Luis Somoza, who challenged them to bring back hairs from Castro's beard. Throughout this operation, the United States was not only undertaking an intervention against a revolutionary regime in the Caribbean; it was also tightening links to right-wing dictatorships in Central America.[1]

Early on the morning of April 15 a detachment of B-26 planes based in Nicaragua (painted with Cuban markings by the CIA) made a brief sortie against key airfields in Cuba. Military damage was slight, but the attack prompted Castro to crack down on dissidents, real and imagined. Over the next couple of days, Castro arrested approximately 100,000 suspects, including all bishops, many journalists, and the vast majority of the CIA's 2,500 agents and their 20,000 sympathizers. In effect, the air raid smashed all chances that an opposition underground might rise up to assist the invasion. At a mass rally in Havana on April 16, Castro referred for the first time to his revolution as socialist and concluded with a vow: *Patria o muerte, venceremos.*

At 3:15 A.M. on the morning of April 17, Castro received news that an invasion force was attempting to land at the Bay of Pigs, on the south-central coast of the island. (The choice of this site for disembarkation seemed curious, since it was a hotbed of pro-Fidelista sentiment: as chronicler Hugh Thomas has remarked, "It would have been hard indeed to have found a region in Cuba in which a rebellion could have been less easily inspired among the local people.")[2] Moving quickly to the invasion site, Cuban forces reacted with power and efficiency. At dawn two T-33 jet trainers and a Cuban B-26 began to attack landing craft and ships, sinking the *Houston* and causing the *Rio Escondido* to explode. As Cuba's air force chased away supply ships, the hapless invaders awaited help from the United States. An indecisive Kennedy hesitated to authorize air strikes from the U.S. carrier *Essex* lying off Cuba, instead permitting only six unmarked jets to provide cover for a B-26 attack from Nicaragua (in actual fact, the jets never left the *Essex* at all). Eventually Cuban forces took 1,180 prisoners—out of the 1,297 who had landed—and held them for a year and a half, to the great embarrassment of the United States. Castro eventually agreed to release the prisoners in exchange for medical supplies.

The Bay of Pigs would have far-reaching implications. At a cost of $45 million, it represented a humiliating failure for U.S. strategy. It boosted Castro's political stature in Cuba, Latin America, and the developing world. And it helped drive him and his revolution toward the Soviet Union; it was in December 1961, not before, that Castro declared his lifelong allegiance to Marxist-Leninism.

The Bay of Pigs would also affect the Cold War as a whole. In October 1962 the Soviet Union began to install medium-range missiles in Cuba, apparently to deter yet another U.S. attack. Kennedy responded with a naval blockade, and after several days of nuclear confrontation Nikita Khrushchev consented to withdraw the missiles—in exchange, it appears, for a U.S. commitment to desist from further invasions. The Cuban Revolution, U.S.–Cuban relations, and the U.S.–Soviet rivalry thus brought the world to the brink of nuclear holocaust. Paradoxically enough, this episode encouraged both superpowers to pursue eventual détente—and to restrain their rivalries in the Third World.

None of this would prevent the United States from its unrelenting opposition to Cuba's maximum leader. The CIA steadfastly pursued a variety of efforts to eliminate Castro, including premeditated assassination. According to the 1975 report of the Senate Select Committee on Governmental Operations, there came to light

> concrete evidence of at least eight plots involving the CIA to assassinate Fidel Castro from 1960 to 1965. Although some of the assassination plots did not advance beyond the stage of planning and preparation, one plot, involving the use of underworld figures, reportedly twice progressed to the point of sending poison pills to Cuba and dispatching weapons to commit the deed. Another plot involved furnishing weapons and other assassination devices to a Cuban dissident. The proposed assassination devices ran the gamut from high-

powered rifles to poison pills, poison pens, deadly bacterial powders, and
other devices which strain the imagination.[3]

These plots took place under three successive presidents: Eisenhower,
Kennedy, and Johnson. Despite their comic-opera quality, these were serious attempts to eliminate a head of state through deliberate acts of murder. They also represented an exceedingly primitive form of political
analysis. According to this view, the problem with Cuba was neither social
injustice nor *batistiano* brutality nor the tortured history of U.S.–Cuban
relations. The problem was Fidel Castro: eliminate *El Líder* and all would
be well. This was hardly a constructive approach to the reality of social
revolution.

The Dominican Invasion

Fidel Castro, the Cuban Revolution, and the Bay of Pigs made profound
impressions on Washington's assessment of political tendencies in Latin
America. The United States became grimly determined to prevent
"another Cuba" in the Western Hemisphere—an obsession that fastened
itself, in particular, on the Dominican Republic. Superficial parallels between the situations seemed intriguing. Both Cuba and the Dominican
Republic had suffered long bouts of political interference by the United
States and could therefore be expected to harbor anti-*Yanqui* sympathies.
Both economies were dependent on the cultivation of sugar (largely for
export to the U.S. market) on large-scale plantations whose oppressed and
downtrodden work forces could be susceptible to clamors against social
injustice. And, perhaps most telling, both countries had long been under
the heel of brutal dictators, Batista in Cuba and Trujillo in the Dominican
Republic. After Castro's triumph, in fact, Washington became deeply concerned that the Trujillo regime would provoke a left-wing opposition and
ultimately a communist takeover, a fear that prompted the stoutly anticommunist Eisenhower administration to withdraw support from the dictator and to explore means of removing him through assassination.[4]

After Trujillo fell victim to a gunshot assault (by a Dominican) on May
30, 1961, the Kennedy administration was quick to take action. Washington immediately dispatched a naval task force to the vicinity of Santo
Domingo to discourage (or prevent) leftists from moving into the political
vacuum, and it kept a close eye on subsequent events. The United States
was especially supportive of the Council of State which governed the
country in 1962–63, bolstering the regime with substantial amounts of
economic aid, assistance to the national police, development of a "public
safety corps" for riot control, and building a counterinsurgency capacity
within the national army. As U.S. ambassador John Bartlow Martin would
later recall, the preoccupation with a leftist threat in the Dominican Republic was pervasive: "A Castro-Communist takeover was the one thing the
United States government, and the American people, would not tolerate."

The Council of State oversaw general elections in December 1962 that gave the presidency to Juan Bosch of the Dominican Revolutionary Party (PDR). Inaugurated in February 1963, Bosch was a respected journalist and intellectual who was committed to social reform and political change. Bosch was not, however, an especially gifted politician, and he proceeded to alienate most key sectors of Dominican society—including the military, the business community, and out-of-office politicians. By September 1963, these groups came together in support of a military coup. Offering little resistance, Bosch went off to Puerto Rico.

The Dominican *golpe* led to installation of a fragile, civilian triumvirate that sought to impose order on the polarized nation. In late 1963 the presidency passed to Donald Reid Cabral, the relatively moderate foreign minister. On April 24, 1965 a group of younger, disgruntled military officers in league with elements of Bosch's PDR rose up against the government of Reid Cabral. As his position weakened, a desperate Reid inquired if the U.S. government might come to his aid through military intervention. Washington declined the invitation, and a political split within the Dominican armed forces came to dominate the scene: calling themselves "constitutionalists," one group demanded the reinstatement of Bosch and a return to constitutional government; calling themselves "loyalists," another faction of pro-Trujillistas sought to reconstitute some kind of military-dominated junta. The two groups set up rival governments and prepared for serious battle.

The United States government defined its position with care. First, the Johnson administration never gave any serious consideration to the prospect of returning Bosch to the presidency, since he was regarded as being leftist, weak, and unreliable. Second, Washington was disinclined to uphold the cause of Reid Cabral and his unpopular junta. By a process of elimination, the United States thus arrived at its policy preference: installation of a provisional junta that would hold a new round of elections (to be won by someone other than Bosch).

Initially, the U.S. embassy and State Department believed that Dominicans would reach this same conclusion on their own. As "constitutionalist" prospects improved, however, Washington threw its support to the right-wing "loyalist" side. United States authorities expressed pious concern about law and order and the protection of American lives. More important, they were worried about the presence of leftists and suspected communists in the pro-Bosch camp. Within days the U.S. ambassador reported that radio broadcasts from the rebel side were exhibiting a "definite Castro flavor" and that communist groups, well-armed and organized, were poised to take advantage of the chaos.

As pro-Bosch forces gained ground, the loyalists formed a new junta under Colonel Pedro Benoit—but failed to stem the tide. By 3:00 P.M. on Wednesday, April 28 a besieged Benoit telephoned the U.S. embassy to request a detachment of 1,200 U.S. marines "to help restore peace." An hour later Benoit submitted a formal written request (in English) emphasizing that the pro-Bosch movement "is directed by Communists and is of authentic Communist stamp, as shown by the excesses committed against the population, mass assassinations, sacking of private property, and constant incitations to fight [that are] broadcast by Radio Havana." The document failed even to mention the need for protection of U.S. citizens.

Events then moved with lightning speed. Lyndon Johnson huddled with his advisers and instantly approved the landing of 500 marines. By 6:00 P.M., when the president signed his formal authorization, U.S. forces had already occupied parts of Santo Domingo. By 8:00 P.M. William Raborn, sworn in that same day as new director of the CIA, was warning congressional leaders about the communist threat and explaining that President Johnson had taken action against a "Moscow-financed, Havana-directed plot to take over the Dominican Republic."

The United States undertook an extraordinary buildup of military capacity. For six days after the initial invasion an average of 243 flights landed at the San Isidro airport—an average of one every six minutes around the clock. Within ten days there were nearly 23,000 American troops on Dominican soil, almost half as many as were then serving in Vietnam. Almost 10,000 additional troops stood ready just off the Dominican coast and thousands more were on alert at U.S. military bases. (Once again, the specter of Cuba deeply affected Washington: believing that the inadequate use of military force led to failure at the Bay of Pigs, Johnson's advisers were determined to avoid this same mistake.) The goal was to prevent a leftist takeover. As General Earl Wheeler stated to Lt. General Bruce Palmer, Jr., who would take command of American troops on the ground: "Your announced mission is to save American lives. Your unstated mission is to prevent the Dominican Republic from going Communist. The President has stated that he will not allow another Cuba. . . . You are to take all necessary measures . . . to accomplish this mission." And as Secretary of State Dean Rusk would publicly say, "What began in the Dominican Republic as a democratic revolution was taken over by Communist conspirators who had been trained for and had carefully planned that operation. Had they succeeded in establishing a government, the Communist seizure of power would, in all likelihood, have been irreversible." Assistant Secretary of State Thomas C. Mann echoed this claim, asserting that a large U.S. military presence was necessary "in view of the clear and present danger of the forcible seizure of power by the Communists."

The factual basis for the U.S. government's allegations proved to be exceedingly weak. At one point the State Department released a list of fifty-eight so-called communist conspirators within the pro-Bosch movement. The criteria for designating "communists" were unstated and ambiguous, and inspection showed that the roster contained only fifty-five names, not fifty-eight, due to double listing; that several other individuals were ill, out of the country, or in jail; and that still others could not have been available for revolutionary activity. On another occasion, too, the CIA reported that

Francisco Caamaño Deñó, military leader of the pro-Bosch uprising, had been seen in the company of two Europeans—who, the CIA intimated, might be communist agents from afar. Of course they could just as well have been Swedish tourists, but that was beside the point: in Washington's view, Reds were lurking everywhere.

Ever the politician, Johnson sought to prevent diplomatic isolation of the United States by engaging the Organization of American States in the Dominican operation. On April 29, the day after the landing, the council of the OAS met in special session at the request of the United States and asked the papal nuncio in Santo Domingo to keep them informed of developments. That same night the OAS asked all parties to accept a cease-fire. By May 6, a meeting of foreign ministers endorsed a U.S. proposal to request governments of member states to take part in the formation of what became euphemistically known as the Inter-American Peace Force. Although seven nations eventually sent modest contingents, the peace-keeping operation was totally under U.S. control. Throughout the summer of 1965, as in an earlier era, the Dominican Republic was governed through military occupation by the United States.

The OAS played an instrumental role in supporting U.S. policy, and lost credibility throughout the hemisphere as a result. One OAS study group confirmed the claim that communists were active within the Dominican Republic. An ad hoc committee of the OAS also helped persuade constitutionalists and loyalists to agree to the Act of Santo Domingo, which formalized a cease-fire and established a security zone within the city. And while a three-person commission dispatched by the Inter-American Commission on Human Rights was able to document at least forty-two cases of political executions by the loyalist forces, the OAS included a provision for total amnesty as part of an overall Act of Reconciliation. On September 3 the OAS oversaw the installation as president of the unobtrusively moderate Héctor García Godoy. Within a year he would be succeeded by Joaquín Balaguer, a longtime collaborator of none other than Rafael Leonidas Trujillo Molina, and Bosch was removed from the political scene. The United States got what it wanted.

Chile: Allende Overthrown

Several years later, electoral politics in Chile would confront the United States with yet another undesirable outcome. Results of a three-way presidential race in 1970 bore considerable resemblance to previous national patterns—with left, right, and center each earning about one-third of the votes—but on this occasion the center and right failed to join forces to assure victory in the election. In consequence a modest plurality of 36.6 percent went to Salvador Allende, leader of the Unidad Popular movement with backing from both socialists and communists. Jorge Alessandri, of the right-wing National Party, won 34.9 percent; Radomiro Tomic, of the centrist Christian Democrats, garnered only 27.8 percent. The Chilean constitution stipulated that in cases of elections without majority winners there was to be a runoff in a joint session of both houses in the national congress. And according to long-standing civic tradition, the legislature would decide in favor of the candidate with the most votes.

Even more clearly than with Bosch in the Dominican Republic, the prospect of an Allende presidency in Chile presented Washington with its worst-case scenario—a free and fair election that gave power to the left. Cold War ideology construed this as a logical impossibility: communists could come to power only through force of one kind or another, either conquest or subversion; given the opportunity, free-thinking citizens— especially within the Western Hemisphere—would *always* cast their ballots against left-wing radicals. Even worse, from Washington's standpoint, electoral processes in Chile were so notoriously efficient that there was no point in claiming that Allende had triumphed through fraud.

Henry Kissinger, then head of the National Security Council under Richard M. Nixon, sprang quickly to action. Bringing together the Forty Committee (with representatives from the CIA, the State Department, the Joint Chiefs of Staff, and the Department of Defense), Kissinger excoriated the people of Chile for their political "irresponsibility" and oversaw the formation of a two-part strategy to prevent the Chilean congress from ratifying the Allende electoral victory. Track I, as it came to be known, involved maneuvers to reinstate Eduardo Frei, the outgoing Christian Democrat who was constitutionally prevented from direct reelection. According to one variation on this scheme, Frei would resign in favor of a military government, which would promptly call new elections—in which Frei could become the candidate of a center-right coalition. According to another, more promising version of the "Frei gambit," the congress would vote in favor of Jorge Alessandri, not Allende, and soon after his inauguration Alessandri would call for the new elections to be won by Frei. All that was needed was influence over the Chilean legislature. Toward this end the Forty Committee established a bribery fund of $250,000.

Track II entailed outright promotion of a military coup. A right-wing group in Chile called Patria y Libertad began pressing for a *golpe* right after the election, promptly receiving $38,500 from the CIA on behalf of its efforts. Over the opposition of the U.S. ambassador, Edward Korry, President Nixon threw his support behind Track II. In mid-September 1970 the president demanded measures to "make the economy scream" in order to provoke a coup. As Richard Helms, director of the CIA, would later recall: "The President came down hard. He wanted something done and he didn't much care how. . . . If I ever carried a marshal's baton out of the Oval Office, it was that day."[5] Proclaimed a subsequent CIA cable: "It is firm and continuing policy that Allende be overthrown by a coup. We are to continue to generate maximum pressure toward this end utilizing every appropriate resource."

Seeking to protect its investments in Chile, International Telephone and Telegraph offered $1 million in support of the CIA's attempts to prevent Allende from taking office. The Council of the Americas, a business organization, volunteered another $500,000. By the time the CIA responded to these offers ITT had decided to withdraw because it could not muster sufficient backing from other U.S. companies, most of which felt they could continue to operate under an Allende government.

The CIA continued on its own. In a confidential assessment, an agency memorandum sized up the situation: "(1) The U.S. has no vital national interests within Chile. There would however be tangible economic losses. (2) The world military balance of power would not be significantly altered by an Allende government. (3) An Allende victory would, however, create considerable political and psychological costs," including a threat to "hemispheric cohesion" and "a definite psychological advance for the Marxist idea." In its efforts to reduce these "psychological and political costs"—and to control the direction of Chilean politics—the agency would spend no less than $8 million between 1970 and 1973.

One persistent obstacle to Track II was the resolute opposition of General René Schneider, the Chilean army commander-in-chief who stoutly adhered to constitutional principles. For a successful coup, said Ambassador Korry, Schneider "would have to be neutralized, by displacement, if necessary." Apparently in response to this assessment, the CIA began to contemplate means of removing Schneider through assassination. It also made contact with a group that planned to kidnap the general, take him to Argentina, and demand that Frei resign and dissolve the congress before it could designate Allende as president-elect. The U.S. military attaché in Santiago promised $50,000 in cash and delivered a supply of submachine guns in support of this effort.

As things turned out it was a different group that actually kidnapped Schneider. The commander-in-chief was gravely wounded while resisting his abduction, however, an event that sent shock waves throughout the country. In deference to popular will and Chilean traditions, a horrified Alessandri urged his congressional supporters to cast their ballots for Unidad Popular, and in late October the legislature ratified Allende's presidential victory. Schneider died the next day and received a hero's funeral.

Undaunted by this development, the United States mounted a bitter campaign against the Allende government. One reason, perhaps, was protection of U.S. business interests. American corporations had more than $1 billion invested in Chile; ITT plus Anaconda and Kennecott, two copper companies, had especially sizable holdings. Corporate executives were fearful of nationalization. Despite the protection of the Hickenlooper Amendment, providing for the automatic termination of economic assistance to countries that failed to take "appropriate steps" toward compensation of expropriated firms, mining companies were feeling especially vulnerable. Unlike other investors, they could not pick up their assets and move them someplace else.

There were political interests as well. Of minor importance were two clandestine intelligence stations in Chile that had been monitoring the

Soviet submarine fleet in the South Pacific. More significant, from the viewpoint of the Nixon White House, was anticipation of a domino effect. As Kissinger declared at one point, "I have yet to meet somebody who firmly believes that if Allende wins there is likely to be another free election in Chile." And on another occasion, he ruminated on the consequences of an Allende regime:

> In a major Latin American country you would have a Communist govern-
> ment, joining, for example, Argentina, which is already deeply divided, along a
> long frontier, joining Peru, which has already been heading in directions that
> have been difficult to deal with, and joining Bolivia, which has also gone in a
> more leftist, anti-U.S. direction. . . . So I do not think we should delude
> ourselves that an Allende takeover in Chile would not present massive prob-
> lems for us, and for democratic forces in Latin America, and indeed to the
> whole Western Hemisphere.

An Allende "takeover," in Kissinger's words, would thus lead to the long-term installation of a Marxist regime that would conspire to spread its influence throughout the Americas.

Kissinger harbored yet another fear. According to Roger Morris, a policy aide at the NSC, Kissinger held a complex view of Chile. "I don't think," Morris later recalled, that

> anyone in the government understood how ideological Kissinger was about
> Chile. I don't think anybody ever fully grasped that Henry saw Allende as
> being far more serious a threat than Castro. If Latin America ever became
> unraveled, it would never happen with Castro. Allende was a living example of
> democratic social reform in Latin America. All kinds of cataclysmic events
> rolled around, but Chile scared him. He talked about Eurocommunism [in
> subsequent years] the same way he talked about Chile early on. Chile scared
> him.

The real problem, in other words, was not that Allende would establish dictatorial control; it was that he would hold free and fair elections in 1976, thus confirming the proposition that socialism could rise and govern through democratic means. It was this, the essence of the *via chilena,* that posed such a threat to Kissinger and to the United States. And it was for precisely this reason that Washington could not permit Allende to succeed.

Once Allende took office, the Nixon administration developed a multi-faceted campaign to destabilize politics in Chile. One component consisted of what Allende himself would label an "invisible financial and economic blockade." On November 9, shortly after Allende's inauguration, a national security memorandum outlined the U.S. intent: "Within the context of a publicly cool and correct posture toward Chile," the United States would undertake to "maximize pressure on the Allende government to prevent its consolidation and limit its ability to implement policies contrary to U.S. and hemisphere interests." This involved a shutdown of U.S. economic assistance ($70 million per year in the late 1960s, under the Alliance for Progress), opposition to international credits, discouragement of private investment, and examination of means to disrupt the world copper market. The document also proposed the application of diplomatic pressure "to assure that other governments in Latin America understand fully that the United States opposes consolidation of a Communist state in Chile hostile to the interests of the United States and other hemisphere nations, and to the extent possible encourages them to adopt a similar posture."

A second part of the U.S. campaign entailed covert support for electoral opposition to the Unidad Popular government. In January 1971 the Forty Committee approved the expenditure of $1.2 million by the CIA to finance opposition parties in the April municipal elections (which turned out to be a triumph for Allende). The committee also authorized $500,000 for Christian Democrats and, later in the year, another $150,000 for opposition candidates in various electoral runoffs.

Through the rest of 1971 and 1972 the CIA continued to finance anti-Allende elements, including the well-known conservative newspaper *El Mercurio*. In May 1972 break-ins occurred at the Chilean embassy in Washington and at three residences of Chilean officials in New York—perpetrated by those who would later gain fame as the Watergate plumbers! United States funds may also have supported a strike by independent truckers in October 1972, a protest activity that began as a complaint by private drivers against a government announcement that it would set up a state-run trucking firm. Especially devastating in an economy so dependent on road transportation, the truckers' strike drew support from a broad cross-section of workers and employees. Another truckers' strike, in mid-1973, appears to have received at least indirect funding from the CIA.

For the March 1973 midterm elections the Forty Committee approved expenditures of more than $1.4 million in support of opposition candidates and parties. The result was inconclusive. Buffeted by declining foreign exchange and runaway inflation, Unidad Popular took just 44 percent of the vote—higher than its 1970 percentage, in fact, but lower than its 1971 performance. By contrast, combined forces of the opposition won 56 percent—and claimed an outright victory. As polarization intensified, the absence of a clear electoral mandate tended to paralyze the Unidad Popular government.

The military was in the meantime moving over to the opposition. In June 1973 a detachment from the Second Armored Regiment attempted to rescue a captain imprisoned for plotting against the government along with Patria y Libertad; ostentatiously driving tanks through downtown Santiago (and politely stopping for red lights en route!) the rebels eventually withdrew their demands but made their political point. In August 1973 the moderate army commander stepped down, making way for the ascendancy of Augusto Pinochet. On August 22 the congress adopted a partisan resolution denouncing the Allende government for "habitually" violating the constitution and national laws, and called upon the armed forces to "put an immediate end to all the de facto situations . . . which violate the constitution and the law."

Finally, on September 11, naval units seized the port city of Valparaíso at 7:00 A.M. The city of Concepción fell by 8:15. In Santiago, air force planes began bombing the presidential palace by 11:55 A.M. Most defenders of the palace surrendered by 1:30 P.M. At 4:00 P.M., the armed forces announced that Salvador Allende had committed suicide.

A brutal crackdown followed. The day after the coup the head of the air force proclaimed the need for Chile to extirpate "the cancer of Marxism." Members of the Allende government were rounded up and placed under detention; thousands of alleged leftists were detained, questioned, and tortured in the national soccer stadium; sweeps were conducted through working-class districts of Santiago and other cities. At least 3,000 Chileans were killed or disappeared in the aftermath of the *golpe*—and this by a conservative count. Soldiers ransacked the headquarters of socialist and communist parties, imposed a strict curfew, dissolved labor unions, and took over once-proud universities.

In retrospect, it appears that the overthrow of Allende was due more to the escalation of political and social conflict within Chile than to the efforts of the United States. It is undeniably true, however, that the United States was making strenuous efforts to undermine and overthrow the Allende regime. It is also true that the U.S. government greeted Allende's overthrow with gleeful enthusiasm. Kissinger and Nixon were ecstatic. Jimmy Carter, with his concerns about human rights, expressed reserve toward Pinochet, but the Reagan administration quickly abandoned this position and embraced the anticommunist regime. Assistant Secretary of State for Inter-American Affairs Langhorne Motley would proclaim in early 1985: "The democracies of the western world have a debt of gratitude to the people and government of Chile for what they did in 1973 . . . the destiny of Chile is in good hands, Chilean hands."

The Seizure of Grenada

The triumph of Ronald Reagan over Jimmy Carter in the 1980 election campaign brought a marked change in the tone and style of U.S. foreign policy. Reagan lost little time in announcing a hard line toward what he perceived as the communist threat. "I know of no leader of the Soviet Union," he said shortly after his inauguration in 1981, "since the revolution and including the present leadership, that has not more than once repeated in the various Communist Congresses they hold, their determination that their goal must be the promotion of world revolution and a one world Socialist or Communist state—whichever word you want to use." Denouncing the Soviet bloc as an "evil empire," Reagan would later consign socialism to the "ash can of history" in a speech to the British parliament in mid-1982. Shortly afterward the Reagan administration announced the initiation of its "Star Wars" project, a fanciful effort to construct an impermeable shield in outer space that would completely protect the United States from the threat of nuclear attack—thus overturning the long-standing anticipation of "mutual assured destruction" that was the military underpinning of superpower détente. One way or another, Reagan made clear his intention of challenging Soviet and socialist authority throughout the world.

The new president and his associates quickly sought to demonstrate this resolve within the Western Hemisphere. Justifying U.S. assistance to a military government in El Salvador (about which more below), Secretary of State Alexander Haig explained that guerrilla opposition to the ruling junta in that tiny country did not merely represent demands for social justice and political democracy. Instead it was, he said in February 1981, a "well-orchestrated international Communist campaign designed to transform the Salvadoran crisis from the internal conflict to an increasingly internationalized confrontation. . . . This effort involves close coordination by Moscow, satellite capitals and Havana, with the cooperation of Hanoi and Managua. It is a repetition of the pattern we have already seen in Angola and Ethiopia, and, I may add, elsewhere. It is a threat, in our view, not just to the United States but to the West at large."

An opportunity for action finally came in 1983 in a most unlikely place—the English-speaking nation of Grenada, with a total population of 90,000 scattered over three small islands in the Caribbean Sea. Established as a British crown colony in 1877, Grenada acquired "associate statehood" in 1967 and full independence in 1974. In legal terms Grenada nominally remained a monarchy, with a resident governor general representing Her Majesty Queen Elizabeth II in her capacity as queen of Grenada, but in practice it was a sovereign nation.

Political life in the 1950s and 1960s fell under the spell of Eric Matthew Gairy—"Hurricane Gairy," an energetic, charismatic, volatile, and ultimately megalomaniac leader with personal interests in self-aggrandizement and unidentified flying objects. As Grenada's first prime minister, Gairy promptly set out to repress his rivals, to enhance his wealth, and to pursue his quixotic fascination with the occult. Opposition appeared with the foundation in 1972 of a movement called JEWEL (Joint Endeavour for the Welfare, Education and Liberation of the People). A year later this group joined forces with the Movement for the Assemblies of the People to create the "New Jewel Movement." Led by Maurice Bishop and Bernard Coard, the NJM began to espouse a vaguely Marxist-Leninist ideology in the mid-1970s. And in March 1979, while Gairy was in New York attempting to persuade the United Nations to establish an agency for the investigation of UFOs, the New Jewel Movement seized power in a near-bloodless coup. A celebrating populace happily chanted a sardonic refrain:

> Freedom come, Gairy go,
> Gairy gone with UFO.

The gregarious and popular Bishop became prime minister in what soon came to be known as the People's Revolutionary Government (PRG); the intense and taciturn Coard became minister of finance.

Despite its rhetorical flourishes, the PRG pursued a moderate path. It sought to increase tourism. A labor code established the legality of unions and led to a sharp rise in union membership. To diversify the economy, dependent on the export of agricultural goods (principally nutmeg), the PRG sought to develop the country's infrastructure—improving roads and cultivation techniques—and to explore new methods of marketing and packaging. While Bishop and his advisers expanded the role of the state within a mixed economy, they did not impose a socialist regime. They never confronted the question of land reform, for instance, the issue that had toppled Jacobo Arbenz in Guatemala in 1954. Their only radical stance came in the realm of foreign policy, where they proclaimed an alliance with Cuba and other socialist states. At bottom, the PRG under Bishop was national-democratic, reformist, and anti-imperialist.

It was this moderation, in fact, that led to the implosion of the PRG. Bernard Coard and his wife, Phyllis (both educated in the United States), became increasingly critical of Bishop for his willingness to compromise. In September 1983 a split within the PRG yielded a proposal for joint leadership by Bishop and Coard. After some equivocation Bishop denounced the plan; Coard and his supporters then placed Bishop under house arrest. A crowd of citizens released Bishop from confinement, but in a display of stupidity and cruelty, the Coard faction executed Bishop on October 19. Within hours, the People's Revolutionary Government was replaced by a Revolutionary Military Council.

The Reagan administration watched these events with mounting interest. On October 19, the day of Bishop's murder, the U.S. ambassador recommended that Washington consider plans for the possible evacuation of American citizens from Grenada. State Department officials argued that an evacuation would in itself be insufficient; instead, the entire main island would have to be seized "to save American lives and to serve broader goals."

Conservative leaders in surrounding microstates began calling for U.S. action. On October 20 Tom Adams of Barbados asked the American ambassador to propose an outright invasion of Grenada. On October 21 the Organization of Eastern Caribbean States (which included Antigua, Dominica, Grenada, Montserrat, St. Kitts-Nevis, St. Lucia, and St. Vincent) met without Grenada in Barbados (a non-OECS country) and announced what was, in view of their military capability, a ludicrous decision to intervene in Grenada—more to the point, they invited friendly governments to lend assistance. This meant the United States. On Saturday, October 22 the Caribbean Community (CARICOM) voted to suspend Grenada from its roster and to impose economic and diplomatic sanctions; that same day Reagan "gave the go-ahead to proceed with invasion plans."

It proved to be a fateful weekend. On Sunday, October 23 a suicide attack by an Islamic fundamentalist led to the massacre of 241 U.S. marines in faraway Beirut. This provoked intense concern within the White

House about the possible taking of American hostages in Grenada, a central fear in the Middle East, and it greatly raised the political stakes. As one participant in the planning sessions recalled: "The overriding principle was not to allow something to happen worse than what we were proposing to do. The purpose was to deny the Russians/Cubans a feeling of potency in grabbing small vulnerable states in the region. It had to be nipped in the bud before it developed into another Cuba." The next day Reagan signed an executive order approving an invasion.

At 5:00 A.M. on the morning of October 25, 1983, a detachment of 1,900 U.S. marines and army airborne troops (plus token contingents from a handful of Caribbean countries) launched an assault on Grenada. Resistance was spotty at most. All significant military objectives were achieved in a couple of days. The death toll included forty-five Grenadians (twenty-four of whom were civilians), twenty-four Cubans, and nineteen U.S. servicemen. Reagan justified the operation as an effort to protect 800–1,000 U.S. citizens whose safety was threatened because "a brutal gang of leftist thugs" had seized power, "to forestall further chaos," and to assist in the restoration of democracy. In an address to the nation he also stressed construction of an airport facility in Grenada "which looks suspiciously suitable for military aircraft including Soviet-built long-range bombers." As a matter of fact, the president contended, this otherwise lovely tropical nation actually "was a Soviet-Cuban colony being readied as a major military bastion to export terror and undermine democracy." He breathlessly concluded, "We got there just in time."

Reagan's invocation of a global communist threat in this tiny island country seemed patently absurd. The airport runway to which he referred was intended for the tourist trade. It was to be 9,000 feet long—shorter than similar runways in Barbados, Guadeloupe, and Martinique. Financing came from Venezuela and the European Community as well as from Cuba. A U.S. firm from Miami did the necessary dredging of an inlet; a British firm had been contracted to install navigation and communication equipment (after the invasion a company representative flatly denied that the equipment could have been used for military purposes, citing the absence of no less than eleven key items such as underground fuel tanks). Washington nonetheless persisted in its grandiose interpretations. One official drew an explicit connection between events in Lebanon and Grenada: "Not only has Moscow assisted and encouraged the violence in both countries, but it provides direct support through a network of surrogates and terrorists." Another commented on broad implications for foreign policy:

> Think of the precedent it would set. . . . Throughout the region, there are little-bitty leftist groups with power ambitions. If we improved relations with Grenada at no cost to the [allegedly pro-Cuban] government, imagine what it would say to other putative authorities in the eastern Caribbean. They would say, "We can pull off a coup and then, after three or four years of trouble with Uncle Sam, he'll come around."

Said yet another spokesperson: "We obviously don't like being put in the position of the heavy. We want to act like a mature, responsible world power. But here's a little country saying insolent things, and we're forced to reply."

The rest of the world did not quite agree. At the UN Security Council, Mexico's ambassador Porfirio Muñoz Ledo denounced the invasion as "a clear violation of the rules of international law . . . totally lacking in justification." A council resolution which "deeply deplored the armed intervention in Grenada" received a favorable vote of 11–1–3—with support from France and the Netherlands, and an abstention from Britain—and was vetoed by the United States. An identical resolution passed the General Assembly by a vote of 108–9. Perhaps most stunning to Ronald Reagan was the vociferous criticism of Margaret Thatcher, his ideological soul mate, who pointedly observed that the U.S. government had engaged in the military invasion of a British Commonwealth nation.

Order returned to Grenada. First, the U.S. occupation force swelled to more than 6,000 troops. Second, political authority was invested—in name, at least—in the governor general, Paul Scoon, who oversaw a new round of elections in 1984. Victory went to a moderate group, the National Party, and peace came back to Grenada. By his own standards, Ronald Reagan had achieved a decisive success.

Central America: The Contra War

While Grenada appeared to lend itself to a quick-fix solution, Central America would preoccupy the Reagan administration during its entire eight-year period in office. Convolutions in El Salvador and Nicaragua threatened to change the political order, to spread to neighboring countries, and to pose new challenges to the United States. Reagan's analysts seized upon the opportunity to stress the global implications of this otherwise local imbroglio, identifying the isthmus as a fundamental testing-ground of national resolve in a worldwide struggle against the forces of communism. As early as 1981 this would lead Jeane J. Kirkpatrick, Jimmy Carter's acerbic critic and Ronald Reagan's ambassador to the United Nations, to make the absolutely remarkable statement that "Central America is the most important place in the world for the United States today."

El Salvador

Part of the story began in El Salvador, a mountainous coffee-growing country of 5 million citizens ruled by an unholy alliance of large-scale landowners and military officers. Acceleration of agricultural exports during the 1960s led to increased concentration of rural holdings and the rapid displacement of *campesinos*—by the mid-1970s about 40 percent of peasants had no land at all, compared with 12 percent in 1960. A reformist challenge to the status quo came through the Christian Democratic Party, under the leadership of José Napoleón Duarte. As mayor of San Salvador (1964–70), the dynamic and articulate Duarte built a strong following among intellectuals, professionals, and other middle-class groups. As presidential candidate he may well have won the election of 1972, but the military intervened and imposed dictatorial rule. Fraudulent elections in 1977 led to the installation as president of General Carlos Humberto Romero, who promptly imposed a "law to defend and guarantee public order." Duarte himself was imprisoned, tortured, and exiled—but he did not take to the hills.

Others took a revolutionary path. A movement called the Farabundo Martí Liberation Front (FMLN)—named for the leader of a popular uprising in 1932—came to pose a major challenge to El Salvador's right-wing regime. A complex organization, including a political wing as well as a military capacity, the FMLN developed considerable support among the peasants of the countryside. It would soon expand to the cities as well.

In October 1979 a group of junior officers ousted Romero and attempted to implement long-needed reforms. The junta sought support from "popular organizations" and invited Christian Democrats to join the government. Official repression persisted, however, and killings continued at the astonishing rate of nearly 1,000 per month. On March 24, 1980 Archbishop Oscar Arnulfo Romero, an outspoken critic of the violence, was assassinated in the national cathedral; on December 3 four U.S. churchwomen were murdered on a country road. Civilians protested and the liberal wing of the PDC defected from the ruling coalition. Now looking undeniably conservative, a beleaguered Duarte took over as titular head of the government. For most of the 1980s, official forces and the FMLN would carry on the struggle in a political stalemate.

While the Carter administration withdrew assistance to the Salvadoran regime because of its human rights abuses, the Reagan White House devoted unequivocal support to the government in its fight against the rebels. Though the uprising had fully indigenous roots, Washington saw the conflict as a sign of alien communist agitation. As explained by Secretary of State Haig, "Our problem with El Salvador is external intervention in the internal affairs of a sovereign nation in this hemisphere—nothing more, nothing less." In February 1981 the State Department released a white paper purporting to offer "definitive evidence of the clandestine military support given by the Soviet Union, Cuba, and their Communist allies to Marxist-Leninist guerrillas now fighting to overthrow the established government of El Salvador." According to this analysis, the Salvadoran insurgency represented a "textbook case" of communist interference within the hemisphere. Not surprisingly, Washington did not look kindly upon a joint Mexican-French declaration in August 1981 recognizing the FMLN as a "representative political force."

The logical corollary for U.S. policy was to terminate this external intrusion in El Salvador. With much bravado, the swaggering Haig de-

clared that the United States would have to go to "the source"—by which
he meant Cuba. Others focused their attention on nearby Nicaragua. It
was this accusation that would provide the rationale for a renewal of U.S.
activity within that troubled country.

Nicaragua

The Somoza dynasty contained the seeds of its own destruction. Coming
to power in the wake of the U.S. occupations of 1916–33, the Somoza
family drew support from several sources: the Guardia Nacional, the
landed elite, and, of course, the United States. Anastasio Sr., it will be
remembered, supported the U.S. conspiracy against Arbenz in Guatemala
in 1954; and it was Luis, the elder son, who encouraged the anti-Fidelista
brigade as it set sail for Cuba in 1961. Yet the regime began to weaken in
the 1970s. Self-seeking and corrupt, Anastasio Jr. ("Tachito") clamped an
iron rule over the country but offended thoughtful Nicaraguans by his
excesses, most notably his extraction of windfall profits from the reconstruction of Managua after a devastating earthquake in 1972. He also
made the mistake of excluding the country's traditional elite from his
entrepreneurial activities.

Unlike El Salvador, where the existence of legal institutions encouraged a reformist option, the near-complete absence of representative institutions in Nicaragua meant that opposition to Somoza could take only one
form: armed resistance. In the 1960s there emerged a guerrilla movement
known as the Sandinista National Liberation Front (FSLN), which took
its name from nationalist hero Augusto César Sandino. After years of
fighting, the Somoza regime suddenly collapsed in 1979, just as Batista
had given way in Cuba two decades before. The triumph exacted an enormous toll. Approximately 45,000 lives were lost during the insurrection;
economic output declined by 6 percent in 1978 and 24 percent in 1979.

Once in power, the youthful Sandinistas proclaimed two broad policy
goals. One called for the creation of a "mixed economy" in order to achieve
social justice. The other espoused an "independent and nonaligned" foreign policy. In pursuit of these objectives the FSLN sought economic
assistance from other countries of Latin America, from West Europe, from
the United States—and from the Soviet bloc. Between 1979 and 1982
communist countries supplied about 20 percent of Nicaragua's credit;
Latin America provided 32 percent, and Mexico alone gave almost twice as
much economic aid as the Soviets. As late as 1984, the communist bloc
accounted for less than 20 percent of Nicaragua's international trade.

The Reagan administration viewed the Sandinista government with
fervent hostility. The 1980 Republican Party platform openly denounced
"the Marxist Sandinista takeover of Nicaragua and the Marxist attempts to
destabilize El Salvador, Guatemala, and Honduras. . . . We [Republi-
cans] will support the efforts of the Nicaraguan people to establish a free
and independent government"—in other words, to overthrow the San-

dinistas. In early 1981, just after taking office, Reagan formally ended economic aid to Nicaragua. In March 1981 Reagan signed a "presidential finding" authorizing the CIA to undertake covert actions in Central America to interdict arms trafficking by Marxist guerrillas.

True to form, the CIA began to organize a paramilitary opposition—as before, in right-wing Guatemala. This was the origin of a counterrevolutionary movement whose adherents were known as *contrarevolucionarios* in Spanish, "Contras" for short. From the start it included disaffected Nicaraguans of various political persuasions, but its heart and soul—and its military capability—rested with former members of the Guardia Nacional. Heartened by early developments, Reagan signed an order on November 17, 1981 authorizing $19 million for a 500-man Nicaraguan force aimed primarily at the "Cuban infrastructure in Nicaragua that was training and supplying arms to the Salvadoran guerrillas."

In early 1982 a group of pro-Somoza former guardsmen, trained by the CIA, destroyed two bridges in northern Nicaragua. Encouraged by this tangible success, the Reagan administration then made a firm commitment to the Contra cause—and expanded its policy goals. The purpose of U.S. activity was no longer just interdiction of arms shipments to neighboring El Salvador. It became, first and foremost, an attempt to topple the Sandinista government. As the deputy director of the CIA would claim in March 1982, this was necessary because Nicaragua was turning into a "Soviet bastion."

Reagan's policy encountered serious obstacles. One was the U.S. Congress, which, in reflection of public opinion, was reluctant to endorse outright intervention in Central America. In December 1982 the House approved an amendment sponsored by Edward Boland of Massachusetts (later known as Boland I), prohibiting the use of U.S. funds to overthrow the government of Nicaragua. The other obstacle loomed in January 1983, when representatives of four countries—Mexico, Venezuela, Colombia, and Panama—met on the island of Contadora in order to devise a plan for peaceful negotiations among contending parties on the isthmus. This diplomatic initiative would continue for years and would prove to be a constant thorn in Reagan's side.

Seeking to muster popular support, the president addressed a joint session of the U.S. Congress in April 1983. "The government of Nicaragua," he solemnly proclaimed, "has treated us as an enemy. It has rejected our repeated peace efforts. It has broken its promises to the Organization of American States, and most important of all, the people of Nicaragua. . . . The national security of all the Americas is at stake in Central America." Moreover, Reagan insisted, the stalemate in Central America threatened to damage the credibility of U.S. commitments elsewhere around the globe: "If the United States cannot respond to a threat near our own borders," the president asked, "why should Europeans or Asians believe we are seriously concerned about threats to them?"

Buildups meantime continued. By 1983 the Contra forces comprised

12,000–15,000 troops and by 1985, according to some estimates, they may have grown to 20,000 fighters. In response the Sandinista government expanded the Nicaraguan military from around 5,000 troops in 1979 to 31,000 in 1981 to 119,000 in 1985. And not surprisingly, the October 1983 action in Grenada had a profound impact on the Sandinista leadership: it signaled that Nicaragua would have to prepare not only for the Contras but for a U.S. invasion as well.

Reagan continued his relentless campaign. In September 1983 he skirted Boland I through a presidential finding that authorized "material support and guidance to the Nicaraguan resistance groups" not for overthrowing the FSLN government, but for two other reasons: pressuring the Sandinistas into negotiations with neighboring countries, and forcing them to terminate support for the FMLN in El Salvador. A month later the Sandinista government accepted this second condition, offering to pledge that Nicaragua "will not permit [its] territory to be utilized to affect or threaten the security of the United States or to attack any other state." The White House ignored the proposal.

Amid continuing skepticism, Reagan resorted to yet another means of quieting his critics: appointment of a bipartisan, blue-ribbon panel to study the problem and produce policy recommendations. Chaired by Henry Kissinger, the commission consisted largely of pliant Republicans and conservative Democrats. Its explicit purpose was to build a national consensus around a single policy. As its January 1984 report insisted at the outset, there was to be "no room for partisanship. . . . The crisis is nonpartisan, and it calls for a nonpartisan response." The Kissinger commission produced a meandering report that advocated a large-scale program of economic assistance to Central America, conditional support of the military forces in El Salvador, and—in rather opaque prose—continued support for the Contras.[6] To justify this conclusion, the commission engaged in fanciful speculation:

> A fully militarized and equipped Nicaragua, with excellent intelligence and command and control operations, would weigh heavily on the neighboring countries of the region. This threat would be particularly acute for democratic, unarmed Costa Rica. It would have especially serious implications for vital U.S. interests in the Panama Canal. We would then face the prospect, over time, of the collapse of the other countries of Central America, bringing with it the spectre of Marxist domination of the entire region and thus the danger of a larger war.

Here again was the domino theory, now applied to Central America, with Mexico the largest domino of all. Given this analysis, the United States had no choice but to stand firm.

The Reagan White House interpreted the Kissinger report as an endorsement of its policy. The CIA, in the meantime, was off on a path of its own. In September 1983 CIA-backed planes bombed the airport in Managua—just at the time that U.S. Senators William Cohen (R-Maine) and Gary Hart (D-Colorado) were landing!—an episode that heightened congressional criticism. In early 1984, just after submission of the Kissinger report, CIA-trained operatives planted mines in three of Nicaragua's harbors, and the explosives inflicted damage on a British ship. Congress had never been told about these plans, as required by statute, and a furious Barry Goldwater sent a famous letter to CIA director William Casey summing up his feelings: "I am pissed off!" The Senate followed up with a resolution denouncing and prohibiting the mining of the harbors by a lopsided vote of 84–12. (In a 1986 judgment the World Court would join this chorus of condemnation, finding the United States in breach of international law for "training, arming, equipping, financing, and supplying the contra forces" as well as for mining the harbors and attacking various facilities in Nicaragua; characteristically enough, the Reagan administration chose to ignore the decision.) And in mid-1984 the CIA was revealed to have circulated in Nicaragua a manual on psychological war that included advice on how to hire professional criminals for "selective jobs" that might help "neutralize" officials, especially judges and the police.

Congressional support collapsed under the weight of these disclosures. Despite an impassioned speech by Reagan in May 1984, the legislature passed another amendment (Boland II) stipulating a termination of all lethal aid to the Contras by October 1. This brought an end to congressionally sanctioned support for the Nicaraguan insurgency.

Undaunted by this turn of events, the White House continued with its policy. Casey's CIA trained speedboat teams that conducted a predawn raid at the port of Corinto in October 1984, causing the evacuation of 20,000 residents. In May 1985, after his reelection as president, Reagan used his executive authority to impose a trade embargo on Nicaragua in light of a national emergency deriving from "an unusual and extraordinary threat to the national security and foreign policy of the United States." The UN General Assembly condemned this application of economic sanctions on a small, impoverished country by a vote of 91–6, but Washington persisted nonetheless.

The administration's most problematic response to the shutoff of congressional aid was the initiation of a covert war. Under the direction of Lt. Col. Oliver North, the National Security Council (NSC) secretly continued and expanded operations in Central America. Unable to turn to Congress, U.S. officials requested funds in support of the Contras from, among others, Saudi Arabia ($32 million), the Sultan of Brunei ($10 million), Taiwan ($2 million), and possibly Israel. (In 1991 a Colombian drug kingpin told a Florida court that his cartel had given $10 million to the Contras during the 1980s.) The operation began to unravel in October 1986, when Sandinista troops captured a CIA agent named Eugene Hasenfus after shooting down his plane over Nicaraguan territory. Under interrogation, Hasenfus revealed that Washington was supporting the Contras with funds diverted from the (equally covert) sale of arms to allegedly moderate groups in fundamentalist Iran. It was only a matter of days before the Iran-Contra scandal was out in the open.

The White House faced withering accusations that it had violated U.S. law and flouted its own policies in order to continue supporting the Contra cause. As the furor mounted, Reagan was forced to accept the resignations of John Poindexter, head of the NSC, and of Oliver North. In an unusually friendly telephone call the president described North as a "national hero," then issued his ultimate compliment: "Your work," he told North, "will make a great movie one day."

With participants weakened by exhaustion, after eight years of warfare and 43,000 Nicaraguan casualties, the conflict finally wound to a close. In 1987 President Oscar Arias of Costa Rica proposed a new peace plan calling on all sides to agree to an immediate cease-fire, negotiation with the opposition, and termination of outside aid. Implementation of these provisions was to be followed by reductions in armed forces and by free elections. In August 1987, as the world watched in amazement, leaders of all five countries signed the document. Reagan and his advisers could barely contain their fury. The Nobel Peace Prize Committee rubbed salt in Reagan's wound by granting the 1987 award to Arias.

In February 1989 the Sandinista leadership announced plans to hold an election the following year. The country was in a state of devastation. Because of the continuous fighting, defense had been soaking up 40 percent of the national budget. Economic production had been sliced in half since the late 1970s. In 1978 Nicaragua had exported $660 million worth of goods; a decade later the figure was around $200 million and still declining. Inflation was running at 14,000 percent in 1988, and at 800 percent in 1989. A compulsory draft plus the imprisonment of political dissidents (a fairly standard wartime measure) further alienated many Nicaraguans. It should have come as no surprise, then, when the opposition movement under Violeta Barrios de Chamorro won the 1990 election with 55 percent of the vote. At last, in roundabout fashion, Reagan thus achieved what he had sought: ouster of the Sandinistas.

On U.S. Interventions

As interpreted by Washington, the imperatives of the Cold War led to recurrent U.S. interference in the internal affairs of Latin American states. One of the most telling features of these interventions was political consistency. Under the leadership of both political parties, Democrats and Republicans, the United States attempted the forceful overthrow of *each and every* socialist (or allegedly socialist) government in the Americas.[7] The only conceivable exceptions actually prove the rule: they occurred in Bolivia, where a hybrid government taking power after the revolution of 1952 soon joined the U.S. anticommunist campaign, and Peru, where a nationalist military regime from 1968 to 1975 attempted major reforms but was neither Marxist in dedication nor pro-Soviet in foreign policy. The pattern of U.S. action was impressively consistent.

Washington's perception of "communist" dangers and tendencies rested upon exceedingly broad, loose, and often irresponsible criteria. Neither Bosch in the Dominican Republic nor Allende in Chile nor Bishop in Grenada represented sinister threats to American society or to national security; they were civilian reformers, more akin to European social democrats than to Soviet KGB operatives. Moreover, even those who declared opposition to the United States and accepted support from the USSR— the Fidelistas in Cuba and the Sandinistas in Nicaragua—turned toward the Soviet bloc only after Washington adopted blatantly hostile policies. Much of what happened was the result of exaggeration, misperception, and misunderstanding. History did not always have to be the way it was.

Once decided on a course of action, the United States was usually able to achieve its goals. Only the Cuban invasion of 1961 proved unsuccessful. All the other campaigns, through either covert support for opposition groups or the overt application of military force, from the Dominican action of 1965 to the Contra wars of the 1980s, led to the ouster of allegedly socialist regimes. Of course they engendered political backlash in Latin America. But by the narrowest of Cold War criteria, intervention worked.

8

Latin America: Fighting the Cold War

We are all Bolsheviks! I don't know what socialism is; but I am a Bolshevik, like all patriotic Mexicans. . . . The Yankees do not like the Bolsheviks; the Yankees are our enemies; therefore the Bolsheviks must be our friends, and we must be their friends. We are all Bolsheviks!
  Mexican general (early 1920s)

Before our eyes were these two models—Puerto Rico and Cuba. Surely there was another path, a third path. . . . we were to spend the next years in our periphery exploring that third path.
  Caribbean leader (late 1970s)

The Cold War placed Latin America in a difficult predicament. The United States emerged from World War II as a preeminent superpower and it was intent, moreover, on asserting its historic claim to hegemony throughout the Western Hemisphere. In the meantime Latin America, as part of the developing world, became a principal battleground in the conflict between East and West. Mindful of protecting its global position, the United States took decisive and extraordinary steps to counter threats of communist intrusion, real and imagined, anywhere in the Americas; from the late 1940s through the late 1980s Washington applied diplomatic pressure, offered economic incentives, engaged in covert operations, and on several conspicuous occasions resorted to military intervention. Leaders from Latin America—intellectuals, politicians, and unionists among them—looked upon these developments with apprehension, alarm, and disdain.

They also had to face unpleasant realities of power: the Colossus of the North was stronger than ever before. What could Latin America do?

The Cold War closed off several previously available policy alternatives. It was no longer possible to seek protection from a rival European power, as Bolívar and others had done during the nineteenth century. It was implausible to pursue subregional hegemony, as Brazilians and Argentines had once imagined. It was useless to formulate high-minded doctrines of diplomacy or international law, as Bello and Calvo and Drago had attempted, since the United States simply refused to recognize adverse decisions by the World Court; nor could international organizations impose meaningful restraints on American power, as shown by Washington's domination and emasculation of the OAS. Essentially, Latin American leaders had only three options for confronting the Cold War: (1) they could defy the United States and pursue socialist paths of political change, (2) they could seek support from the United States on the basis of anticommunist solidarity, or (3) they could attempt to forge an intermediate or "third" strategy, hoping to avoid alignment with both East and West and thus to secure economic, political, and cultural independence.

Option 1: The Socialist Path

Marxist ideology achieved substantial appeal in Latin America. Its diagnosis of class conflict applied directly to social inequities throughout the region. Its summons to revolutionary action offered hope to downtrodden workers and peasants. Its identification of imperialism as "the highest form of capitalism," in the language of V. I. Lenin, offered both a coherent explanation of big-power politics and a foundation for asserting national sovereignty. Moreover, Marxist internationalists and Latin American nationalists had one enemy in common: the United States, leader of the capitalist world and dominant power in the Western Hemisphere. More important than its doctrinaire principles, however, was an underlying attraction of Marxist-Leninist thought: as an ideology of the oppressed, it struck a deep and resonant chord with the cultures of resistance welling up in Latin America ever since the acquisition of independence. For all these reasons, socialism seemed to offer a promising pathway for Latin America.

Parties and Elections

Initial efforts in the name of Marxism focused on political parties and electoral competition. In the wake of the Russian Revolution, old-school communist parties appeared in a number of Latin American countries during the 1920s. Usually based in the cities, led by intellectuals and politicians, they tended to espouse "the peaceful road to power" rather than insurrectionary action. During the 1930s and 1940s they developed close, often servile relations to the Soviet Union. As the Cold War erupted Latin America's communist parties became seriously divided, weakened, or divorced from their traditional or potential constituencies. As recounted in chapter 5, governments of Brazil, Chile, Mexico, and other countries declared them to be illegal in 1947 and 1948; papers were seized, leaders jailed, and followers harassed, repressed, or exiled. During most of the 1950s parties sought Soviet protection by defending the USSR in the context of the Cold War, thus becoming "tribunal" organizations that were more devoted to the advocacy of Soviet interests than to the struggle for power. Their true "vocation," according to French theoretician Régis Debray, "was not to promote an assault on power, but rather to resist assaults from power." By the 1960s and 1970s communist parties had become passive observers of national politics in most countries of the region.

It was perhaps in Guatemala, during the Arbenz administration in the early 1950s, that local communists (through the Partido Guatemalteco de Trabajadores) exercised their most significant influence on national policy. As coalition partners, communists performed only marginal roles in elected governments in Brazil (1961–64), Chile (1970–73), and to a lesser degree in Uruguay (1973–74). Nor were they major factors in revolutionary situations. In Cuba the Partido Socialista Popular achieved an eventual rapprochement with the Fidelista movement but was never a center of power. In Nicaragua, Sandinista revolutionaries quickly abandoned their efforts to accommodate the Partido Socialista Nicaraguense. And in other contexts, from El Salvador to Bolivia, communist party apparatchiks stoutly opposed the activities and aspirations of armed guerrilla groups.

Ultimately, communist parties in Latin America were victims of the Cold War. Despite their advocacy of the "peaceful road" and their cautionary policies, their alignment with the Soviet Union opened them to charges of repressiveness and wickedness. "On the one hand," as Mexican commentator Jorge Castañeda has written, the communist party "no matter how often or vigorously it stressed its moderation and pragmatism, could not shake the image of Communist rule as it existed elsewhere. It was a victim of its own reputation and former policies." Forces of the political right could not trust the party's avowal of moderate positions; but because of its conservatism, the party could not reach agreements with the extremist left. "The Communist parties of Latin America never overcame this contradiction, this powerful paradox that haunted them from their conception to their slow and silent passing toward the end of the 1980s."[1] As formal entities, communist parties never posed much of a threat.

Socialist parties, on the other hand, sometimes managed to play a major role in the postwar politics of Latin America. These were groupings that, for the most part, blended Marxist analysis of class struggle with nationalist insistence on the sanctity of sovereignty; while denouncing U.S. "imperialism" they did not, however, follow Soviet dictates in the international arena. More flexible than the communists, more attuned to local realities, socialist parties (in a variety of forms) gave substantial credibility to the political left. Their most conspicuous successes came in Guatemala, under Jacobo Arbenz, and in Chile, under Salvador Allende.

But the fate of those same governments demonstrated the impossibility of the "peaceful road" toward socialism. In collaboration with local allies, the United States worked to overthrow Arbenz in 1954 and Allende in 1973. And for good measure, Washington helped displace the moderately left-of-center administration of Juan Bosch in the Dominican Republic in 1965. No matter how free or fair the ballot, electoral politics could not offer a meaningful route to socialist reform; Washington would always block the path. It did not take long for Latin American leftists to see the handwriting on the wall: their only alternative was armed revolution.

Guerrilla Movements

Nearly thirty separate guerrilla movements emerged in Latin America from the early 1950s to the 1980s. Virtually all proclaimed Marxist ideologies, of one sort or another, though they tended to espouse nationalist and populist causes as well. First and foremost among them was the Fidelista vanguard in Cuba, where Castro's rise to power, as Debray recalled, "descended like a clap of thunder on skepticism and legalism." Universally emboldened by the Fidelista example and sometimes instigated by Cuban conspiracy, guerrilla movements sprang up in a variety of countries. In Guatemala, reformist military officers challenged the post-Arbenz dictatorship in 1960 by forming the MR-13 guerrilla movement (Movimiento Revolucionario 13 de Noviembre) and later still the Rebel Armed Forces (FAR). In Venezuela, social opposition to the economic austerity program of elected president Rómulo Betancourt erupted in violence and the appearance of guerrilla bands in 1962, followed a year later by the organization of the Armed Forces of National Liberation (FALN), sponsored by the communists, and the Movement of the Revolutionary Left (MIR), led by a splinter group from Betancourt's own party. In Colombia, decades of fratricidal conflict between Liberals and Conservatives (known as *La Violencia*) gave way in the mid-1960s to the formation of multiple guerrilla groups: the Colombian Revolutionary Armed Forces (FARC), allied to the communist party (PCC); the Army of National Liberation (ELN), inspired directly by the Cuban example; and a Maoist group, the Popular Army of Liberation (EPL). Two guerrilla groups made brief, if unsuccessful, appearances in the Peruvian Andes. And in the Bolivian highlands, Ernesto "Ché" Guevara organized a Cuban-led *foco* in late 1966. Opposed by local communists and unsupported by the peasantry, Guevara's guerrillas were destroyed in October 1967; Ché himself was killed after his capture.

For all practical intents and purposes, Guevara's death marked the beginning of the end to what sociologist Timothy Wickham-Crowley has called the "first wave" of guerrilla movements in contemporary Latin America.[2] Despite this ignominious defeat, the Cuban Revolution continued to fire the imagination of the continental left. Through the 1960s and into the 1970s, the Fidelista triumph showed that it was possible for a radical movement to embrace Marxist-Leninism and to seize power; to oppose the United States but to nonetheless endure; and to promote the cause of social revolution throughout Latin America, partly as an act of solidarity and partly in the interests of self-defense. In emulating Cuba regional revolutionaries moved away from the ideology and experience of the Fidelista movement of 1956–58, when Castro was stressing populist issues and political reform, including restoration of the 1940 constitution, and closer to the radical tactics espoused by Guevara and others in the 1960s.

A second wave of guerrilla movements crested in the 1970s and 1980s. In Guatemala, offshoots of the FAR came to include the Guerrilla Army of the Poor (EGP), the FAR (again), and the Organization of People in Arms (ORPA); by 1982, according to some estimates, the total number of guerrillas came to 6,000 combatants. In Colombia, the 19th of April Movement emerged in protest against allegedly fraudulent elections of 1970; making its first public appearance in 1974, M-19 stole the sword of Simón Bolívar from its hallowed place in a national museum and proclaimed: "Bolívar, your sword returns to the struggle." Pragmatic in its ideology, M-19 cultivated connections with *narcotraficante* chieftains and maintained close communication with the Cubans. In Peru, professors and students at the University of Huamanga organized a Maoist guerrilla group, Sendero Luminoso, or "Shining Path" (originally known as "The Communist Party of Peru—Along the Shining Path of José Carlos Mariátegui," in deference to the country's great Marxist intellectual of the 1920s). Never pro-Castro, its leaders regarded the Cuban Revolution as "revisionist" and unduly pro-Soviet. Launching armed struggle in April 1980, Sendero succeeded in forming a "popular guerrilla army" by 1983. It thereafter expanded operations into urban areas, especially in the shanty-towns around Lima, where it posed a major threat to governmental rule.

But the most important movements in this second wave of armed resistance, especially the ones that riveted attention from the United States, erupted in Central America. In El Salvador, a long-standing alliance between the local oligarchy and the military rule showed signs of decay in the early 1970s. A number of guerrilla groups took up irregular warfare: the Popular Forces of Liberation—Farabundo Martí (FPL), born of a 1970 split within the communist party; the Revolutionary Army of the People (ERP), formed of Christians and communists in 1971; and the Armed Forces of National Resistance (FARN), which split from the ERP in 1975. Popular opposition to military rule mounted against patent electoral fraud in 1972 and 1977 and against the undisguised brutality of the General Carlos Humberto Romero regime (1977–79). Guerrilla groups gradually reached a modus vivendi and merged to form the Farabundo Martí National Liberation Front (FMLN), later establishing an alliance with the civilian-led Democratic Revolutionary Front (FDR). Resistance accelerated after a "reformist" civilian-military junta took power in late

1979 but failed to deliver on its promises of social and political change. A "final offensive" by the guerrillas in early 1981 was unable to oust the government, however, and armed revolutionaries retreated to the country-side. As described in chapter 7, stalemate continued through the 1980s. Finally, after years of conflict and the loss of more than 80,000 lives, El Salvador reached an uneasy truce under the auspices of the United Nations.

In Nicaragua, resistance to the thirty-year-old dynasty of the Somoza family foundered in the 1960s despite sporadic efforts by the Sandinista National Liberation Front (FSLN). In the early 1970s the movement broke into three separate factions: one, known as Prolonged Popular War (GPP), gathered strength among peasants in the mountainous north-central region; a second, the Proletarios, splintered from the GPP in 1973 to carry the movement to workers and intellectuals in cities; third were the Terceristas, a politically moderate and non-Marxist grouping. Throughout the 1970s elements from the middle classes and the business sector began to express dissatisfaction with Somoza, and in 1978 it was widely assumed that he masterminded the assassination of his conservative opponent, newspaper editor Pedro Joaquín Chamorro. Civil and guerrilla opposition to Somoza thereafter coalesced into a semblance of unity. Insurrection continued, pressure mounted, and Somoza left for exile in July 1979. As Castro had done in Cuba twenty years before, the Sandinistas entered their capital city amidst an atmosphere of popular euphoria.

Of all the guerrilla movements emerging in Latin America during the course of the Cold War, only two managed to seize political power: the Fidelistas and the Sandinistas. The reasons are not far to seek: the success of revolutionary movements depended not only upon their own resources but also upon the social support and military strength of incumbent governments.[3] Especially noticeable is the fact that Fidelistas and Sandinistas were both challenging corrupt and patrimonial dictatorships that had lost support from their natural constituencies, landowners and businessmen, and that in the end received only lukewarm backing from the United States. Throughout the Cold War as a whole, El Salvador was more the rule than Nicaragua: wherever feasible, Washington scurried to the aid of governments under siege from Marxist revolutionists.

Revolutionary States

As a matter of *realpolitik,* it should have been perfectly possible for revolutionary governments to reach practical accommodations with the United States. The new regimes in Cuba and Nicaragua posed little if any direct threat to the security of the United States; on their own, they were incapable of mounting any significant challenge to U.S. power. They also had much to gain from positive commercial and economic relations with the United States. From Washington's point of view, a modus vivendi with these revolutionary states could reduce the likelihood of Soviet meddling in the hemisphere and, in the bargain, help identify the United States with popular forces for change throughout the world.

What seemed possible in principle proved unattainable in practice. To the extent that revolutionary movements in Latin America had a nationalist and anti-imperialist purpose, they were necessarily opposed to the United States; this was especially true in Cuba and Nicaragua, which had suffered long and painful experiences of U.S. domination. (In fact, the Sandinista party anthem proudly proclaimed its determination to struggle against *"el yanqui, enemigo de la humanidad."*) Opposition to the United States had deep historical roots. And to the extent that revolutionary movements in Latin America followed Marxist ideology, they were bound to seek support and solidarity within the communist bloc. Almost inevitably, anti-Americanism and pro-Marxism translated into approval for the Soviet Union. Under the pressure of the Cold War, Fidelistas and Sandinistas had shared incentives to befriend the enemy of their enemy.

Nor did Washington greet revolutionary governments with open arms. In the case of Cuba, as detailed in chapter 7, the Eisenhower administration first sought to keep Batista in power, and then attempted to sustain *batistianismo sin Batista.* And after Fidel's triumph, U.S. officials treated his government with undisguised hostility. In early 1960 Eisenhower authorized the CIA to undertake a series of covert actions, including the arming and training of exiles, and in January 1961 Washington severed diplomatic relations with Cuba. Soon after taking office, President John F. Kennedy approved the fateful Bay of Pigs invasion of April 1961. All this took place before Castro declared his revolution to be "socialist," in April and May 1961, and months before he proclaimed himself to have been a lifelong Marxist-Leninist. In the meantime, U.S. operatives continued to plot assassination attempts. It is little wonder, in retrospect, that Castro turned to the Soviet Union for help: his country and his revolution were under constant siege from the United States.

A similar pattern emerged in Nicaragua. Once in power, the Sandinistas attempted to create a mixed economy and to pursue an independent foreign policy. Following Cuba's example, the Nicaraguan government achieved prompt and tangible progress through social programs for literacy, public health, and education. In the political realm, however, the FSLN decided to preserve a monopoly on power rather than share it with late-arriving bourgeois supporters. This proved a fateful step. "Once they did," as Castañeda has said, "the die was cast. In particular, the role that Cuba would play was all but predestined: To make a revolution, as opposed to a power-sharing scheme of deep reforms, meant building a new state, without the trusted cadres to do it with: those could only be borrowed, like the funds to reconstruct a nation torn apart by years of civil war."[4] Toward these ends the Sandinistas welcomed approximately 2,500 Cubans (the count was carefully monitored by the CIA and the State

Department)—doctors, nurses, schoolteachers, sanitary engineers—as well as Cuban military, police, and intelligence personnel. And in order to seek allies elsewhere in Central America, the Sandinistas began distributing arms and aid to FSLN comrades fighting in El Salvador.

In both Cuba and Nicaragua, the United States deliberately pursued courses of action that ended up by pushing revolutionary states more and more toward the left and into the arms of the Soviet Union. Of course it is impossible to know what might have happened if the United States had made genuine efforts at accommodation. Yet the basic trend was apparent. By attempting to isolate, intimidate, and harass revolutionary governments in Latin America, Washington succeeded in provoking, promoting, and strengthening their reliance upon the Soviet Union. Approaching these regimes within a rigid Cold War framework, the United States thus managed to accomplish precisely what it sought to avoid: revolutionary entanglements with the USSR that could lead to Soviet intrusions in the Americas.

Option 2: The Anticommunist Crusade

If the Cold War helped galvanize the radical left in Latin America, it proved to be a godsend for the authoritarian right. In the immediate aftermath of World War II, flushed with triumph over totalitarian forces, the United States embarked on a short-lived effort to promote democracy in the Western Hemisphere. Acknowledging the legacy of FDR's Good Neighbor policy, Harry Truman's secretary of state, James F. Byrnes, insisted in October 1945 that "nonintervention in internal affairs does not mean the approval of local tyranny" and soon endorsed a call from Uruguay for multilateral action against autocratic regimes. Spruille Braden, as U.S. ambassador to Argentina, openly denounced authoritarian and protofascist tendencies in the surging Peronist movement. Also in 1945 a State Department report expressed displeasure over the perpetuation of dictatorship within the region and expressed the view, repeated frequently and publicly in ensuing years, that "the United States cannot but feel a closer friendship and a warmer sympathy for those governments which rest upon the periodically and freely-expressed consent of the governed."

Against this background, the outbreak of the Cold War suddenly offered right-wing forces a new lease on life: enlistment in the anticommunist crusade. For elites in Latin America, ideological and political commitment to the anti-Marxist cause could earn goodwill and material benefits from the world's preeminent power. It also had the inestimable benefit of enabling autocrats to denounce domestic opponents as "communists," "socialists," and/or "servants of Soviet imperialism." The dynamics of East-West conflict in the global arena thus led to redefinition of political struggle within the local arena, a formulation that depicted opposition to pro-

U.S. rulers as alien, disloyal, atheistic, unpatriotic, and totalitarian. Given this twist in terms of debate, the central issue was no longer dictatorship versus democracy; it was anticommunism versus communism.

Deliverance for Dictatorship

First to benefit from this fortuitous turn of events was Anastasio Somoza, Sr., of Nicaragua. As World War II came to an end, the U.S. State Department earnestly attempted to persuade the dictator to step down from power. As an "elder statesman," Spruille Braden contended, General Somoza could promote the ideals of democracy "and thus write his name large on the pages of history." Reluctantly, Somoza allowed one of his longtime cronies, Leonardo Argüello, to assume the presidency in May 1947—but when Arguello started acting on his own, Somoza threw him out of office after just twenty-six days. Outraged by this betrayal, the Truman administration decided to withhold diplomatic recognition of the new Somoza regime.

The impasse lasted for nearly a year. Unfazed by Washington's denunciations, the wily Somoza maintained close working relations with the U.S. military mission, thus exploiting a breach between the State Department and the War Department. And once the Cold War erupted in Europe, Somoza took a strident anticommunist stand. Washington retreated to a policy of de facto recognition and soon resumed diplomatic relations. Somoza responded with vigorous efforts to please U.S. officials. By 1950 he confidently explained to an American military attaché that he had successfully met leftist threats to his government and "put his foot firmly on the spark of Communism." On countless occasions he declaimed communism as a great danger to the hemisphere, a result of Soviet infiltration and "a cancerous growth which had to be cut away." Pledging his government's allegiance to the United States, Somoza instructed his diplomats to vote invariably with Washington at the United Nations and the Organization of American States.

The culmination of Somoza's efforts came in 1954, when he actively supported the U.S.-sponsored coup against the Arbenz government in Guatemala. As a dictator, Somoza had long regarded the existence of elected governments in Costa Rica and Guatemala as implicit challenges to his authority. (He often liked to claim that Nicaragua occupied an unusually difficult geopolitical position because of its location between the "leftist" governments of José Figueres and Juan José Arévalo, whom he had attempted to overthrow in 1949.) The U.S. campaign against Arbenz thus came as a heaven-sent opportunity. Somoza eagerly promoted a diplomatic resolution declaring communism as a danger to the region and a proposal for the formation of a Central American military force to eradicate the menace from the isthmus. As the CIA prepared for action against Arbenz, the United States and Nicaragua signed a bilateral military assistance agreement that opened the way for an enlarged military mission and the resumption of arms sales. And once the coup had taken effect, Somoza loudly applauded Eisenhower's decisiveness. Patiently, and cleverly, Somoza had worked his way back into the good graces of Washington.

Others followed the anticommunist tide. Seizing power in Cuba in 1952, Fulgencio Batista immediately gave Washington private assurances that he would respect U.S. interests, especially business interests, and he promised not to renew his old ties to the communists. He depicted his overthrow of Carlos Prío Socorrás as an anticommunist action:

> The Caribbean Legion, composed of Leftists, demogogues, adventurers, and Communist agitators whose mission was to carry out international assignments for the Soviet Union, had the enthusiastic support of President Prío. The Russian Embassy in Havana was the propaganda center for the entire Caribbean region and the Gulf of Mexico. Russian agents came and went carrying printed material from Mexico to Cuba, and vice versa. With the blessings of the President and his Administration, Communist travelers and Havana University students met in the Embassy to conspire against Western democracy.

Once in office Batista promptly met a long-standing U.S. desire by breaking relations with the USSR—which he had himself established in 1942—and went on to outlaw Cuba's communist party. In 1953 Batista denounced Fidel Castro's July 26 attack on the Moncada barracks as "Communist," "anti-American," and "anti-democratic." In 1954 Batista promulgated a decree stipulating that communist activity of any kind was sufficient cause for dismissal from the civil service, from universities, or from labor unions. At the suggestion of U.S. ambassador Arthur Gardner, Batista established a special office in the Ministry of War to "fight" the communists, the Buró de Represión a las Actividades Comunistas (BRAC). In recognition of these services, Batista earned the gratitude of U.S. leaders: after a visit to the island in 1955, Vice President Nixon reported that Batista was "a remarkable man" who "seems desirous of doing a job more for Cuba than a job of [*sic*] Batista and is also concerned about the social progress of his country."

Equally audacious was Rafael Leonidas Trujillo Molina, who ruled the Dominican Republic with an iron hand from 1930 to 1961. Like Somoza, Trujillo initially felt U.S. pressure to liberalize his regime at the end of World War II. In 1947 the enterprising Trujillo claimed 92 percent of the popular vote in presidential elections, however, and with the outbreak of the Cold War he quickly suppressed the political opposition. Proclaiming himself to be "the foremost anti-Communist of the hemisphere," he released a *White Book of Communism in the Dominican Republic* that specifically criticized unwitting servants of communism who were falsely working in the name of democracy: foreign journalists, domestic politicians, a growing number of exiles—all were branded as "communist." One of the first Latin Americans to reach agreement with the United States under the Mutual Security Act of 1951, Trujillo would receive over $6 million in military assistance from 1952 through 1961. In exchange for his loyalty,

Trujillo earned extravagant accolades in the United States: Senator Olin D. Johnson (D-South Carolina) proclaimed in 1957 that "the Dominican Republic has rendered a greater force [*sic*] in deterring the spread of communism in Latin America than any other country in the Caribbean area." And during a visit to the Dominican Republic in 1959, Representative Gardner R. Withrow (R-Wisconsin) made the astonishing declaration that had Trujillo been born on U.S. soil, he would have become president of the United States!

For these dictators, and many others like them, the Cold War provided a transparent political script. To ensure their perpetuation in power, autocrats were encouraged to take several steps:

- Declare fervent opposition to communism in all its forms and expressions.
- Provide support for the United States in international forums, especially the United Nations (where the costs of compliance were virtually zero).
- Endorse the Monroe Doctrine.
- Denounce all domestic opponents as communists, as communist-inspired, or as unwitting dupes of communist conspiracies; outlaw the local communist party.
- Subscribe to the domino theory, which meant that domestic subversion presented a threat to neighboring countries as well as to their own governments.
- Open the economy to U.S. investments and commercial interests.
- Express support for U.S. military, paramilitary, and covert actions against "communist threats" throughout the hemisphere.
- Maintain close relations with the U.S. military establishment (Somoza Sr. went so far as to send Somoza Jr. to West Point).
- Curry friendships with members of the U.S. Congress (Somoza Jr. had perhaps the closest friend of all in Representative John Murphy, D-New York).
- Cultivate close personal relations with U.S. ambassadors.

The courting of U.S. ambassadors was routinely facilitated by their intellectual mediocrity. Appointments to small Latin American countries did not receive the highest priority within the U.S. government; in the 1940s and 1950s ambassadorships often went to stalled-out career diplomats or to wealthy businessmen, some of whom could not speak Spanish. Thus Somoza Sr. managed to captivate Thomas Whelan, Somoza Jr. did the same with Turner Shelton, Batista had his Arthur Gardner, and Trujillo had William T. Pheiffer. All were severely afflicted by what diplomats called "clientitis." All were unswerving spokesmen for their autocrats.

Just as the Cuban Revolution came to inspire the left, it hardened the resolve of the political right. After 1959 (or 1961) the threat of a "communist takeover" no longer seemed distant, abstract, unlikely. If it could happen in Cuba—where the United States had maintained a virtual protectorate until 1933, only ninety miles off the coast of Florida—it could happen anywhere. Moreover, the prorevolutionary activism of the Castro regime allowed the autocrats to identify Cuba as the geographical and political source of their problems. As Anastasio Somoza, Jr., recalled, he had for years "been advising the appropriate people in Washington that my real enemy was Fidel Castro and Cuba." And as late as November 1978 he pointedly insisted to a U.S. diplomat: "The real FSLN is in Cuba. They left from Havana, and some went from Panama to Cuba." In other words, there was no genuine domestic opposition to the Somocista dynasty; it was all the result of international conspiracy.

It is ironic, perhaps, that the United States withdrew support from its dictatorial allies at crucial political moments. In Cuba, Washington attempted to persuade Batista to step down from office in the late 1950s and halted military assistance to his regime. In the Dominican Republic, Washington tried to convince Trujillo to leave power (and when he refused, the CIA took active part in plots on his life).[5] And in Nicaragua, twenty years later, U.S. diplomats eased Somoza Jr. into exile. Yet these reversals (or betrayals) did not contradict Cold War ideology. In each and every case, U.S. policymakers reached the conclusion that the perpetuation of dictatorship would increase the chances of a communist takeover, and that removal of the autocrats would keep the communists at bay. Even while abandoning its dictatorial allies, Washington remained faithful to its anticommunist convictions.

National Security Doctrines

In contrast to the personalistic satrapies of the Somoza-Trujillo category, political developments in South America produced a spate of "bureaucratic authoritarian" regimes from the 1960s to the 1980s. Initiated and usually dominated by professional armed forces, these governments typically represented an alliance of multinational business, local capital, and state interests. With cold-blooded instruments of repression they challenged, intimidated, undermined, and emasculated peasant movements and organizations of the working class. To justify such policies they formulated doctrines of "national security" that drew heavily upon anticommunist litanies of the Cold War, tailoring the dogma to their own realities and purposes. While American theoreticians of national security stressed total war and nuclear weapons strategy, and the French, well into the Algerian war, focused on the use of limited warfare in response to the communist movements, their South American counterparts emphasized the threats of internal subversion and revolutionary warfare.

The prototypical version of national security doctrine appeared in Brazil, where the armed forces ousted left-leaning president João Goulart from office in 1964. In collaboration with colleagues at the Escola Superior de Guerra (ESG), a military think-tank founded in 1949 with the help of French and U.S. advisers, General Golbery do Couto e Silva began developing ideas that stressed both the possibility of "indirect attack" from the Soviet Union and the dangers of subversion and/or revolution. Under current conditions, he wrote, the concept of war must be expanded to include

> the entire territorial space of the belligerent states, thus involving the whole economic, political, cultural, and military capacity of the nation in the enormity of the struggle. All activities are focused on one single aim: victory and only victory. No distinction is made between soldiers and civilians, men, women, and children; they face the same danger, and identical sacrifices are demanded of them. They must all abdicate the secular liberties, which had been won at such high costs, and place them in the hands of the state, the all-powerful lord of war. . . . Above all total war has eliminated the time scale, incorporating in itself the time of prewar and postwar, which are in fact now only extensions of one sole and continuing state of war.

The world now faced a situation of "permanent war." As a result, "there is no longer a distinction between where peace ends and war begins."

In this setting, enemies of the Brazilian state would rely primarily upon "internal subversion"—particularly "revolutionary warfare," which Golbery defined as "a conflict, normally internal, that is stimulated and aided materially or psychologically from outside the nation, generally inspired by an ideology. It attempts to gain state power by progressive control of the nation." Revolutionary warfare did not necessarily entail the use of armed force. It was essentially a struggle over hearts and minds, a clash of psychological weapons: "A principal characteristic of Communist revolutionary war," Golbery said, "is the involvement of the population of the target country in a gradual, slow action—both progressive and continuous—which aims at the conquering of minds. It encompasses all aspects, from the exploitation of existing discontent and protest—with the incitement of the population against the constituted authorities—up to the actual organization of dominated and controlled zones or territories." Tactics of this sort would be especially effective in the developing world, "in countries of weak national power." In the face of such challenges, national security required internal security.

To this general argument, Golbery added innovative features. One focused on geopolitics. Latin America was essential to the West, and Brazil was the most important country in Latin America. This led Golbery to advocate tough bargaining with Washington: "when we see that the United States negotiates, using the weight of dollars, immense amounts of aid in order to gain the support of undecided people or even frankly hostile nations of the Western European region, in the Middle East, or in Asia—it seems to us to be only just that we should learn to bargain at high prices and to use the fact that we, as a nation, hold the trump card." Carried to its logical conclusion, the doctrine furnished the basis for an independent Brazilian foreign policy. ("We may also invoke a 'manifest destiny' theory," he suggested on one occasion, "especially since it does not collide directly with that of our bigger and more powerful brother in the North.") Second,

Golbery stressed the significance of economics. Industrialization offered a key to sovereignty and independence, in his view, and economic development could promote the integration and protection of national territory. It was therefore vitally important to develop the country's vast uninhabited expanses, which he categorized as "paths of penetration," and it would be eventually desirable "to flood the Amazon region with civilization." In this conception the purpose of economic development was not so much to raise the standard of living for the populace as to secure national integrity.

Thus imbued by the Cold War, the Brazilian generals seized power in April 1964 with promises to "restore legality" and reinforce the "threatened democratic institutions"—and, above all, to "eliminate the danger of subversion and communism." A series of "institutional acts" then established a putative juridical basis for authoritarian rule. Institutional Act No. 1, right after the coup, centralized political authority, eliminated parliamentary immunity, and, in a revealing phrase, launched inquiries into individuals believed to have "engaged in acts of revolutionary war." Under General Humberto Castello Branco, the government promptly inaugurated "Operation Cleanup" (Operaçao Limpeza). Within a few months the regime arrested perhaps 50,000 persons. A professor of engineering was charged with "being really a Communist, subversive, and agitator, as is well known by public opinion." A public employee was condemned because "his father was always a militant of the Communist party and taught him this as a child." Gratified by such devout expressions of anticommunism, Washington would remain steadfastly loyal to its newfound allies in Brazil.

Nearly ten years later, in Chile, armed forces once again rose to strike down a communist threat. In a radio address on September 11, 1973 General Augusto Pinochet reassured listeners that "This is not a coup d'etat, but a military movement" aimed at "salvaging the country," while one of his coconspirators, General Bernardo Leigh, vowed to "struggle against Marxism and to extirpate it to the last consequences." An edict the following day proclaimed that anyone displaying a "belligerent attitude" would be "executed on the spot." Like the Brazilians, Chilean military officers were utterly convinced that they were engaged in a permanent war. As Pinochet declared in a press conference on September 21: "Marxist resistance is not finished. There are still extremists left. Chile continues in a state of internal war." Leftists in Chile were "masters of subterranean struggle," in Pinochet's words, and communism was "not just another party" but a "system that turned everything upside down, without leaving any belief or faith." Anticommunism thus became a tenet of religious faith. In 1974 the regime established the Dirección de Inteligencia Nacional (DINA) whose mission was nothing less than the "total extermination of Marxism." Years later, Pinochet would look back on the early months of his government with satisfaction: "If the extremists believed the moment of confrontation was coming, so did I. They wanted triumph to take total power; I wanted it to save Chile from Communism."

Argentina experienced this now-familiar pattern in 1976, when a military coup ousted the government of Isabel Martínez de Perón. Upon seizing power, the generals claimed to have brought back the country from the brink of "dissolution and anarchy" and, like their Brazilian and Chilean counterparts, vowed to combat "subversion." What Argentina required, in their view, was a fundamental reorganization of economic, social, and political life. Hence they christened their regime as the "Proceso de Reorganización Nacional," and they sanctified their fight against subversion as the "Dirty War."

Aside from counterterrorist operations against leftist guerrillas, principally the Ejército Revolucionario del Pueblo (ERP), the Argentine generals unleashed a relentless campaign of repression against unarmed civilians. As explained by Ramón Camps, chief of Buenos Aires police during the height of the Dirty War: "You always have a latent element which awaits an opportune moment to reappear. . . . This is the thesis of Vo Nguyen Giap and of Mao Tse Tung." Even before taking power, General Jorge Videla had coolly foreseen the use of terror: "As many people will die in Argentina as necessary to restore order." Hundreds and thousands of victims simply vanished, becoming known, in the ungrammatical lexicon of the era, as "the disappeared." A human rights commission was subsequently able to document more than 9,000 cases of disappearances during the period from 1976 through 1982, acknowledging that " the true figure is much higher." Some observers estimated that there were as many as 15,000 *desaparecidos* and an additional 5,000 people who were murdered but identified. The scope of this official terror was as frightening as its scale: many of the arrests, detentions, and disappearances appeared to be almost at random, with deliberate disregard for guilt or innocence. Anyone could be a target; there was no sure means for self-protection. The purpose was intimidation of the whole society.

Thus did the Argentines fashion their doctrine of national security. As summarized by Jacobo Timerman, a journalist who was imprisoned in 1977, the creed was both straightforward and bizarre: "World War III has begun; the enemy is left-wing terrorism; and Argentina was the initial battleground chosen by the enemy. . . . World War III is not a confrontation between democracies and communism, but between the entire world and left-wing terrorism." Bringing the domino theory to its apogee, Argentina occupied a vanguard position in a titanic struggle on behalf of Western civilization. A particularly sinister feature of the Argentine ideology was its virulent anti-Semitism. As reported by Timerman: "It was clear that they hated Karl Marx, Che Guevara, Sigmund Freud, Theodor Herzl. But it was hard to understand why they hated Zionism more than communism, and considered it a more significant enemy; and that they regarded Israel as a more dangerous foe than Russia. . . . Communism was more visible than Zionism, therefore easier to identify, and hence less dangerous, although both ideologies had as their ultimate intention the destruction of nationality." Anti-Semitism had a long and ugly history in

Argentine society, and the generals summoned this legacy of darkness to justify their murderous insistence on national purification.

Throughout Latin America, one long-term effect of the Cold War became readily apparent: the polarization and intensification of political conflict. Applied to the regional context, the East-West conflict provoked and energized both the left and the right. As a consequence of its internal logic, the Cold War tended to encourage extremist forces—at the expense of centrist reform. Over a period of forty years, the Cold War incessantly promoted the radicalization of Latin American politics: both the revolutionary excesses of Sendero Luminoso and the national-security fantasies of the South American military were consummate, and probably inevitable, expressions of this relentless dialectic. Despite its extrahemispheric origins, the Cold War penetrated deeply, and painfully, into the core of Latin American society.

Human Rights and the United States

Just as unavoidably, the reactionary zeal of right-wing forces led to disagreements with the United States over the question of human rights. Throughout the Cold War period, U.S. policy pursued two goals that were often in conflict with one another—anticommunism and democracy. It was not until the mid-1970s that human rights became a major political issue. One fundamental reason for this change, in the wake of Vietnam and Watergate, was activism in the U.S. Congress. A 1975 amendment attached to the International Development and Food Assistance Act, sponsored by Representative Thomas Harkin (D-Iowa), called for an immediate halt in economic aid to countries engaged in gross violation of rights; and in 1978, after years of wrangling, Congress finally agreed that "no security assistance may be provided to any country the government of which engages in a consistent pattern of gross violations of internationally recognized human rights."

A second factor was the presidential election of Jimmy Carter. In his inaugural address of January 1977, Carter declared that "our commitment to human rights must be absolute. . . . Because we are free, we can never be indifferent to the fate of freedom elsewhere." And in 1978, on the thirtieth anniversary of the Universal Declaration of Human Rights, Carter went on to pledge: "As long as I am President, the government of the United States will continue throughout the world to enhance human rights. No force on earth can separate us from that commitment. . . . Our human rights policy is not a decoration. It is not something we have adopted to polish up our image abroad, or to put a fresh coat of moral paint on the discredited policies of the past. . . . Human rights is the soul of our foreign policy." Throughout its term, the Carter administration expressed profound unhappiness over human-rights violations in Brazil, Guatemala, Chile, and Argentina—but remained conspicuously silent about abuses in other countries, such as Iran and the Philippines, which were deemed to be of great strategic value in the East-West conflict. Practically speaking, Carter's stance on human rights was a policy for Latin America, not the world as a whole.

Within this context a crisis arose in September 1976, when the explosion of a car bomb in Washington, D. C., killed Orlando Letelier, an exiled official from the Allende government, and his young American assistant, Ronni Moffitt. There was little doubt that the assassination was the work of the Pinochet regime. The murder drew swift condemnation from the United Nations and from U.S. senator Edward Kennedy; in the House, Harkin redoubled efforts to have aid cut off. Eventually Congress agreed to the ban and approved Harkin's legislation, aimed principally at Chile, prohibiting all nonhumanitarian aid to governments that were violating human rights. The Letelier bombing continued to poison bilateral relations in 1979, when the Chilean Supreme Court refused to extradite three DINA suspects in the murder and authorized their release. Carter's State Department accused Chile of condoning "international terrorism," the U.S. ambassador was twice recalled, private commercial credits were cut, and the navy withdrew from annual exercises with Chile.

Pinochet adopted a defiant stance. Pointing to the Chinese ambassador across the room, Pinochet declared to U.S. ambassador George Landau in June 1978: "Believe me, Chile can go to China. We are not married to the United States. I could even turn to the Soviet Union. They would help. They would do anything to hurt you." When Landau asked for clarification about the prospect of an alignment with the USSR, Pinochet shot back: "Absolutely! I would do it to protect my country. The Soviet Union would always intervene against American interests. It is unfortunate that you Americans always fail to understand this."

Despite its bluster, Pinochet's response underscored the strength of nationalist sentiment within the South American military establishments. Unlike the satraps of the Caribbean, leaders of these bureaucratic-authoritarian regimes held deep beliefs in the sanctity of state and nation. Challenged by the United States on human rights, they reacted with combinations of annoyance, disdain, bewilderment—but not submission. Here they were, in their own mind-sets, fighting a crusade for the sake of Western civilization and receiving only condemnation for their efforts. Ironically, international ostracism merely heightened their determination to persevere. Protests by human-rights advocates served to further the cause of left-wing subversion, in the generals' eyes, and the only appropriate response was to stand fast. If necessary, right-wing authoritarians would defy the United States in the name of decency, morality, and anticommunism.

Option 3: Seeking a Third Way

Beyond the strategies of alliance with either the Soviet Union or the United States, of either communism or capitalism, Latin America sought a third alternative: refuge from the Cold War. As illustrated by the fates of Cuba and the Southern Cone, alignment with either the East or the West involved substantial costs.[6] What many leaders were seeking was an independent course of action, one that would maximize the range of policy choice and guarantee national sovereignty. Ultimately, this quest would take two complementary forms: one focusing on economic development, the other on foreign policy. In both endeavors, Latin America relied heavily upon—and joined together with—the emergence of new nations in Africa, Asia, and the Middle East.

A New International Economic Order?

Decolonization after World War II led to the appearance of new nation-states during the 1950s and 1960s that steadily swelled the ranks of the Third World. With political independence achieved, they faced the challenge of devising new policies for economic development—an area where Latin America came to play a major role. In 1948 the United Nations established the Economic Commission for Latin America (ECLA, with the Spanish acronym CEPAL) with its seat at Santiago de Chile.[7] Under the leadership of Raúl Prébisch, a brilliant Argentine economist, CEPAL formulated a powerful and compelling interpretation of the world economy. In schematic form, the Prébisch thesis maintained that the international division of labor, under which developing countries exported raw material goods and imported manufactures from abroad, was working to the disadvantage of Latin America. According to *cepalista* analyses, terms of trade were constantly moving against the primary producing countries: the value of their exports was declining but the cost of their imports was climbing. While productivity advances in the industrialized "center" of the global economy led to wage and other factor price increases, disguised unemployment and other tendencies resulted in commodity price declines in the "periphery." Meanwhile the income elasticity of demand for raw material imports was relatively low at the center (largely because of Engel's law, holding that proportional expenditures on food are on the average a decreasing function of income) while in the periphery it remained high—especially in view of the high import content of new investments. As income rose in the center, therefore, the percentage expenditure on imports from the periphery declined; but as income rose in the periphery, the percentage of income going for imports from the center was likely to increase.

CEPAL proposed a twofold solution. One was industrialization. As Prébisch sustained in a memorable manifesto of 1949, industrialization is "being forced upon [new countries] by events. Two world wars and a great economic crisis between them have shown the Latin American countries their opportunities, clearly pointing the way to industrial activity." Purposeful state planning and the judicious application of import restrictions could lead to industrial development that would eliminate losses from declining terms of trade, stimulate employment, and enhance the economic sovereignty of developing nations. The other solution was regional integration. As Prébisch clearly observed, one fundamental limitation to industrial growth in Latin America was "the present division of markets, with its consequent inefficiency," an obstacle that could only "be overcome by the combined efforts" of countries in the region. Industrialization required large markets. This vision came to fruition in 1960, with the formation of the Latin American Free Trade Area (LAFTA/ALALC). About twenty years later it would be replaced by the Latin American Integration Association (ALADI), headquartered in Montevideo. Neither experiment met with much practical success, though they came to represent Latin America's persisting desire for regional unification. In a significant sense, they served as contemporary formulations of the Bolivarian dream.

While CEPAL's empirical studies focused only on Latin America, its analytical framework applied to the developing areas as a whole. With the encouragement of Latin American delegates, Third World countries in 1961 pushed a resolution through the UN General Assembly designating the 1960s as the "United Nations Development Decade," a decision that led to the first United Nations Conference on Trade and Development (UNCTAD I) in Geneva in 1964. As differences emerged between the perspectives of industrialized and developing nations, representatives of Third World countries issued a "Joint Declaration of the Seventy-Seven" which proclaimed their own "unity" as "the outstanding feature of this Conference. . . . The developing countries have a strong conviction that there is a vital need to maintain, and further strengthen, this unity in the years ahead. It is an indispensable instrument for securing the adoption of new attitudes and new approaches in the international economic field." Thus emerged the Group of 77, whose membership would eventually grow to well over 100, a loose organization of developing nations intent upon collective action in the pursuit of social justice and economic development. Operating mainly within the United Nations, the Group of 77 came to be known as a "trade union for the poor." In effect, it represented the economic voice of the Third World.

Fittingly enough, Prébisch became the first secretary general of UNCTAD, a post he held until 1969. All countries of Latin America were among the original signatories of the 1964 declaration of the Group of 77. And because of its institutional capability, rendered through ECLA, Latin America often played a leading role in setting agendas and shaping deliberations at UNCTAD meetings.

Economic tensions between North and South came to a head in the early 1970s. For the Third World, developmental efforts and conventional strategies had yielded disappointing results. The breakdown of the Bretton Woods accords in 1971 (when Nixon took the United States off the gold standard) cast doubt upon the viability of the prevailing system. The success of OPEC countries in quadrupling the price of their product during the "oil crisis" of 1973–74 suggested that it might be time for confrontation, not accommodation. Nations of the South thus reached something of a consensus: economic fairness could come only through a global redistribution of resources and wealth.

In this spirit, G-77 countries and their supporters called for a special meeting of the General Assembly, which adopted, in May 1974, the "Declaration and Programme of Action on the Establishment of a New International Economic Order." Achievement of NIEO instantly became a key objective for the Third World. NIEO embodied five central demands:

- Regarding international trade, it called for higher relative prices of raw material exports and for greater volumes of raw material and manufactured exports from the Third World.
- Regarding foreign investment, it appealed for greater access to international capital, for the removal of legal constraints on expropriation, and for assistance in vigilance over multinational corporations.
- It established a target of 0.7 percent of GNP for economic assistance from industrialized countries (and also called for lenient debt renegotiations).
- It stressed the need for scientific and technological institutions in the developing world and appealed for assistance in persuading multinational corporations to promote technology transfer.
- It called for a greater voice in the reform and management of the international monetary system and for increased "automaticity" in access to loans from the International Monetary Fund (IMF).

For G-77 members, the fundamental goal of NIEO was to accelerate the pace of their own development and to shift the pattern of income distribution away from the rich nations of the North and in favor of the impoverished South.

For a brief time NIEO became a rallying cry for the Third World as a whole. Mexican president Luis Echeverría Álvarez became an especially vocal advocate. As part of a generally *tercermundista* foreign policy, Echeverría championed the adoption of a "Charter of Economic Rights and Duties" by the UN General Assembly.[8] (It was rumored, in fact, that he aspired to become secretary general of the United Nations.) And after stepping down from office in 1976, he founded the Centro de Estudios del Tercer Mundo. Mexico also hosted a number of UNCTAD and G-77 meetings, including a North-South "summit" at the resort town of Cancún in late 1981.

Yet the South made little real progress in reaching its goals. A central reason for this failure was the heterogeneity of the G-77 itself. The sheer size of the group, with more than 100 members from diverse regions and cultures, made consensus difficult enough. There were structural cleavages as well. The OPEC successes of 1973–74 and 1979–81 could not be easily achieved for other commodities, and the resulting price hikes for petroleum imposed serious balance-of-payments difficulties on oil-importing members of the Third World. Moreover, so-called upper-tier countries of the G-77 were closely connected with the industrialized world. As political economist Roger Hansen observed in the late 1970s: "The more the economically advanced members of the South are able to achieve their developmental goals within the present global economic system, the less interest they will have in changing it in the ways desired by other G-77 members."[9] This was especially true for Latin America, whose situation and interests had very little in common with South Asia and sub-Saharan Africa. The final death knell of the NIEO would come with the debt crisis of the 1980s.

Nonalignment and Foreign Policy

A frequent objective for Latin America, and for other countries in the developing world, was to avoid diplomatic entanglement in the Cold War. Taking sides implied subordination to one of the rival superpowers. An independent foreign policy, a "third way" of sorts, could expand the range of practical options, maintain flexibility, and assert national sovereignty.

Such was the impetus behind the Non-Aligned Movement, a gathering of Asian and African leaders who held their first major meeting at Bandung in 1955. The conference issued a summons for (1) nonalignment with East or West, (2) the international self-assertion of former colonial countries, and (3) militant anticolonialism. Strongly influenced by Josip Broz Tito of Yugoslavia and Jawaharlal Nehru of India, a subsequent meeting at Belgrade in 1961 emphasized the need for Third World countries to take active steps to prevent war between the United States and the USSR. Denouncing the "two imperialisms" of both East and West, the delegates proclaimed:

> Any attempt at imposing upon peoples one social or political system or another by force and from outside is a direct threat to world peace. The participating countries consider that under such conditions the principles of peaceful co-existence are the only alternative to the "cold war" and to a possible general nuclear catastrophe. Therefore these principles—which include the right of peoples to self-determination, to independence and to the free determination of the forms and methods of economic, social and cultural development—must be the only basis of all international relations.

A 1964 meeting in Cairo brought the theme of anticolonialism to the forefront of the agenda, where it remained for the rest of the decade. Just as the Group of 77 expressed the economic voice of the developing world, the Non-Aligned Movement (NAM) came to represent its political voice.

Latin America's role in NAM expanded over time. The most active participant was Cuba, which sent an official delegation to the Yugoslav meeting in 1961. (Several Latin American leaders were approached about Belgrade but did not attend because of the invitation to Cuba, which they regarded as a member of the Soviet bloc; Bolivia, Brazil, and Ecuador sent observers.) Democratic governments in Chile and Argentina sent observers to the Cairo meeting in 1964 and became full members in the early

1970s, under Allende and Perón. Peru became an observer in 1970 and a full member in 1973, under the radical military regime of Juan Velasco Alvarado. After the Sandinista revolution, Nicaragua joined in 1979. Bolivia and Ecuador became full members as well, and Colombia gained admission in the early 1980s. Most of the new Caribbean Commonwealth Countries took out membership after achieving independence. Despite Echeverría's militantly *tercermundista* policies, Mexico never went beyond observer status. Nor did Brazil, which maintained a scrupulous desire to avoid entangling alignments—even in the name of nonalignment![10]

Charismatic and ebullient, eager to maintain close ties to both the Third World and the USSR, Fidel Castro became NAM president for a four-year term and hosted a historic summit meeting at Havana in 1979. Under pressure from Moscow, Castro used the occasion to challenge the long-standing thesis of "two imperialisms" by proposing that the Soviet Union should be declared a "natural ally" of the Non-Aligned Movement. Tito of Yugoslavia led the attack on this idea, which found little support from other delegates, and the plan was summarily dropped. After the conference Cuba's chairmanship suffered an additional blow, when a planning session in New York failed to produce any clear priorities or substantive statements in preparation for the upcoming session of the UN General Assembly. Cuba's hope for election to a temporary seat on the UN Security Council was also countered by Colombia, and a deadlock ensued until both countries stood down in favor of Mexico—which was not a NAM member. As Ronald Reagan intensified the Cold War in the early 1980s Castro was succeeded as NAM president by Indira Gandhi, prime minister of India.

Perhaps the NAM's most significant contribution to Latin America was its powerful support of the NIEO in the early 1970s. At its Algiers conference of 1973 the NAM turned from its traditionally political agenda toward economic matters, adopting an "Action Programme for Economic Cooperation" as a basis for South-South unity and calling for the establishment of "a new international economic order." Anticipating subsequent arguments about a potential "peace dividend," NAM vehemently condemned the East-West arms race and envisioned disarmament as a means to free up resources that could be reallocated for the sake of global development.

By the 1980s the Non-Aligned Movement had more than 100 members. As with the G-77, its membership size was a double-edged sword: it gave the NAM enormous potential clout in international arenas, especially in the UN General Assembly, but it also led to lowest-common-denominator policy positions. Indeed, its general principles had become high-minded but vague: peace and disarmament, independence and self-determination, economic equality, cultural equality, universalism, and multilateralism. On practical policy issues, the NAM could not act as a unified bloc.

In the meantime several countries in Latin America took deliberate steps to pursue independent foreign policies on their own. Brazil sought to intensify relations with Japan and Western Europe in the 1970s, successfully resisting U.S. pressure to overturn a nuclear agreement with West Germany. Its reliance on imported petroleum prompted new diplomatic initiatives in the Middle East and Africa. Partly in response to declining military assistance from the United States, Brazil developed a formidable defense industry—and became one of the world's leading exporters of arms. And in frustration over the Carter administration's condemnation of human-rights abuses, the military rulers refused to join the U.S.-sponsored boycott of the 1980 Moscow Olympic Games in protest against the Soviet invasion of Afghanistan.

Mexico played for high stakes as well. In his continuing effort to establish solidarity with Arab and other Third World countries, Luis Echeverría instructed his representatives in 1975 to support a UN resolution—against Washington's vigorous opposition—denouncing Zionism as a form of racism. The U.S. reaction was swift. Jewish leaders and pro-Israeli groups began a campaign against tourism in Mexico. Bookings were canceled, vacations were changed, and Mexico had over 100,000 fewer visitors in 1976 than in 1975. Echeverría's diplomatic gesture cost his country millions of dollars in foreign exchange. Beginning in 1976 Mexico abstained or voted No on similar anti-Zionist resolutions in UN bodies. Economic pressure took its toll.

In general, Echeverría tempered his activism with a strong dose of caution. He aligned Mexico with leftist and progressive forces—in Chile, Spain, Cuba. Together with Carlos Andrés Pérez of Venezuela, he took the lead in forming the Sistema Económico Latinoamericano (SELA)—including Cuba but not the United States—which became a forum for regional consultation within UNCTAD. These matters were significant but to some extent symbolic. On most issues of major importance, Echeverría refrained from challenging Washington. After the 1973–74 oil crisis Echeverría did not, for example, seek full membership for Mexico in OPEC.

It was Echeverría's successor, José López Portillo, who nettled Washington by purporting to play an active role in Central America—the putative "backyard" of the United States. Openly supporting the Sandinista revolutionaries, López Portillo in May 1979 withdrew diplomatic recognition from the Somoza regime. In 1980 Mexico and Venezuela began shipping petroleum on preferential terms to Nicaragua as well as to other nations of the isthmus. In August 1981 Mexico joined together with France, an extrahemispheric power, to call for recognition of the Salvadoran FMLN as a "legitimate political force." And in February 1982 López Portillo unilaterally issued a plan to unravel "three knots that tie up the search for peace" in Central America—the internal conflict in El Salvador, distrust between the United States and Nicaragua, and hostility between the United States and Cuba. His proposal envisioned a negotiated settlement in El Salvador, a nonaggression treaty between the United

States and Nicaragua, and intensified dialogue between Havana and Washington. For all these purposes Mexico offered "to serve as a bridge," as foreign minister Jorge Castañeda explained, "as a communicator, between its friends and neighbors." Intent on imposing military solutions on Central America, the Reagan administration dismissed the Mexican initiative with annoyance and contempt.

From Contadora to Esquipulas

After taking office in December 1982 Mexican president Miguel de la Madrid embarked upon a path of multilateral negotiation. In early 1983 Mexico joined with Colombia, Panama, and Venezuela—the so-called Contadora Group, named for the island where they first met—to begin exploring possibilities for regional mediation of the Central American conflict. Through collective action and joint diplomacy, the Contadora countries strove to fashion a peaceful settlement that would acknowledge the legitimate interests of contending parties. Backing from a four-country *grupo de apoyo* (a "support group" composed of Argentina, Brazil, Uruguay, and Peru) gave additional impetus to the Contadora movement and reflected a new form of political *concertación* among Latin American nations.

The Reagan administration silently resisted these efforts. After the formation of the Contadora group, Washington launched its own Forum for Peace and Democracy under the auspices of Honduras and Costa Rica; the effort failed for lack of regional support. Washington then turned to the OAS, only to discover that the organization strongly supported the Contadora initiative. In the spring of 1983 Reagan appointed as special envoy for Central America former senator Richard Stone, a conservative Florida Democrat who had been previously registered as a lobbyist for the right-wing government of Guatemala. Later in the year the Reagan administration sought to resuscitate CONDECA, a discredited military alliance for Central American nations, in hopes of consolidating forces of the anticommunist right. Also in 1983 President Reagan appointed the National Bipartisan Commission on Central America, the blue-ribbon panel chaired by former secretary of state Henry A. Kissinger. In January 1984 its much-publicized report endorsed much of Reagan's policy toward the region and dismissed the Contadora effort with a single page of condescending adjectives, asserting that "the United States cannot use the Contadora process as a substitute for its own policies." In other words, Washington would pay no heed.

The Contadora countries nonetheless persisted. In September 1983 the group released a "Document of Objectives"—a list of twenty-one principles that were accepted by all five nations of Central America. A year later, in September 1984, the group presented its "Contadora Act for Peace and Cooperation in Central America," a broad proposal with three key provisions:

- All participating countries would hold free and fair elections, taking steps "to assure the equal participation of all political parties."
- Participating countries would suspend "all acquisition of military equipment," refrain from authorizing any new foreign military bases or schools, eliminate existing foreign military bases or schools within a half year, and establish schedules for the orderly withdrawal of foreign military advisers.
- Participating countries would desist from giving aid of any sort to irregular forces or armed bands "whose aim is the overthrow or destabilization of other governments."

In practical terms, the Contadora treaty meant that Nicaragua would have to repatriate Cuban and other military advisers and allow on-site inspection of its military facilities; Honduras would have to terminate U.S. military maneuvers and encampments; El Salvador would have to remove its U.S. military "trainers." In other words, all extraregional powers— Cuba, the Soviet Union, the United States—would have to withdraw from the isthmus. Under the aegis of the Contadora group, Central America would settle conflicts by itself.

Prospects for the treaty seemed excellent at first. On September 3 Guatemala announced its readiness to sign; Costa Rica concurred on September 14; El Salvador followed suit on September 19; and Honduras expressed a generally positive view pending "final adjustments." Two days later Nicaragua stunned the diplomatic world by endorsing the accord "in its totality, immediately and without modifications," on the sole condition that the United States would have to sign the supplementary protocol (whereby a number of nations, including Cuba and the USSR, would consent to abide by the terms of the treaty). The United Nations, the OAS, and the European Community all expressed their strong support.

Taken aback by this development, Washington set out to scuttle the plan. On October 10 Secretary of State Shultz made a sudden visit to Panama, El Salvador, and Mexico. By this time a U.S. client state, Honduras was persuaded to harden its insistence on adjustments, and pressure was applied to Costa Rica as well. On October 30 a confidential NSC memorandum exuded smug satisfaction: "We have effectively blocked Contadora group efforts to impose the second draft of the Revised Contadora Act." For public consumption, the Reagan administration contended that its objections to the treaty focused on the question of verifiability. The problem, claimed Shultz, was the inadequacy of safeguards to ensure compliance by participants; and the Sandinistas, being Soviet-inspired, would no doubt attempt to cheat. In contrast, most independent analysts thought the true reasons for Washington's intransigence were political: the Contadora accord entailed acceptance of the Sandinista regime and it implied a curtailment of U.S. hegemony throughout the region. (Moreover, the provision for Cuban and Soviet signatures on the supplementary protocols appeared to admit the importance of their roles.)

On points of this nature the Reagan White House was not prepared to surrender.

As the Contadora effort stalled, the U.S. government stepped up its activities. Military aid to El Salvador climbed from $33.5 million in 1983 to $176.8 million in 1984. Officer training picked up at the School of the Americas in Panama and at U.S. bases in Honduras. United States operatives planned the mining of Nicaragua's harbors, distributed manuals on the art of guerrilla warfare, and redoubled assistance to the neo-Somocista "freedom fighters." As the Sandinista-Contra war deepened, Nicaraguan refugees and Contra elements ensconced themselves in Costa Rica, another nation put at risk by the Cold War in Central America.

Oscar Arias Sánchez, elected to the presidency in 1986, chose to confront these problems directly. With skillful diplomacy and dogged determination, he persuaded chief executives from Central America to continue negotiations among themselves. The result of this process was the so-called Esquipulas accords, named after the town where the first meeting took place, that called on war-torn nations of the region to (1) initiate a cease-fire, (2) engage in dialogue with opposition movements, (3) prevent the use of their territory for aggression against other states, and (4) cease and prohibit aid to irregular forces or insurrectionary movements—these last two provisions aimed directly at Nicaragua and the United States. The August 1987 agreement also called for free elections and democratization of all nations in the region. It was an ambitious plan, one that incorporated key provisions from the Contadora documents, but it had the additional merit of representing a Central American solution to Central American problems. In fact it helped bring a measure of peace to the region, and it earned for Arias a Nobel Prize.

Legacies of War

The Cold War took a heavy toll on Latin America. It placed the region in the center of a worldwide East-West conflict. It subjected the hemisphere to U.S.–Soviet tension, sometimes real (as in the Cuban missile crisis of October 1962) but more often exaggerated or imaginary (as in Central America throughout the 1980s). It made the region susceptible to heavy-handed vigilance, covert action, and military intervention by the United States. Perhaps even more important, the Cold War deepened political schisms within countries of Latin America and promoted a spiraling process of polarization.

Chief beneficiaries of the Cold War, at least in the short run, were the forces of the political right. From the Caribbean to the Southern Cone, from Guatemala to Brazil, authoritarian governments were able to claim political legitimacy on the ground of anticommunism. With the brief and partial exception of the Carter administration, in the late 1970s, they were able to garner the support of the United States. Devoutly intolerant of political freedom and staunchly resistant to social change, reactionary rulers conducted ruthless campaigns to purge their nations of allegedly subversive, sinister, unpatriotic elements. One result, in some countries, was to deprive entire generations of imaginative, creative, progressive political leadership. Another was to set back the cause of economic development and social justice by incalculable margins.

The socialist alternative had costs and risks as well. Odds were, from the beginning, that revolutionary efforts would end in tragic failure. Only two out of nearly thirty guerrilla movements actually seized power; almost all the others were crushed by military force. And even those that triumphed, in Cuba and Nicaragua, soon encountered implacable hostility from the United States. Their only plausible option was to seek aid and support from the Soviet Union, but this only made them dependent on the USSR and drew them ever more deeply into the Cold War itself. Once the East-West conflict came to an end, they would be left on their own, orphans of a war that no longer existed.

At the outset the third way, the quest for economic and political independence, appeared to offer the fewest advantages. It meant forgoing all the benefits that would result from firm allegiance in one of the two camps, and it entailed the considerable risk of antagonizing both the superpowers, especially the United States (as happened to Arbenz in Guatemala, Bosch in the Dominican Republic, Allende in Chile, and others as well). Association with the Third World offered negligible economic compensation and, outside of such forums as the UN General Assembly, scant political power. But in the long run, the search for an independent stance proved to be the most productive course. It maintained the political integrity of Latin American nations, especially those under civilian and/or democratic governments, it enabled experimentation with a variety of economic policies, and, most important, it avoided the costs of wholehearted alignment with one or the other of the superpowers. Insistence on national sovereignty and Third World solidarity turned out to be more than demagogic appeal. It expanded, preserved, and maximized political room for maneuver.

III

AGE OF UNCERTAINTY

So, in sum, what do we see? . . . We see five great economic super powers: the United States, Western Europe, the Soviet Union, Mainland China, and, of course, Japan. . . . All nations are important . . . but these are the five that will determine the economic future and, because economic power will be the key to other kinds of power, the future of the world in other ways in the last third of this century.

Richard M. Nixon (1971)

9

Hegemony by Default

Out of these troubled times . . . a new world order can emerge: a new era—freer from the threat of terror, stronger in the pursuit of justice, and more secure in the quest for peace. An era in which the nations of the world, East and West, North and South, can live in harmony.
George Bush (1991)

In the post–Cold War era, no one knows what foreign policy ought to be.
Leslie Gelb (1994)

Sweeping transformations in the international order during the late 1980s ushered in an era of optimism, hope—and uncertainty. The crumbling of the Berlin Wall, the reunification of Germany, the liberation of East Europe, the consolidation of superpower détente, and the eventual implosion of the Soviet Union brought a sudden end to Cold War hostilities. This development had far-reaching implications not only for Europe but also for other parts of the world and, more generally, for the international system as a whole. Yet the *shape* and *content* of these ramifications remained far from clear. What kind of international order would emerge in the 1990s and beyond? How might this affect Latin America and its relationship with the United States? What forces and factors might affect the content of U.S. policy toward Latin America?

Ending the Cold War

The 1980s and 1990s altered the international arena in at least three fundamental ways. First was the emergence of multipolarity. As a result of long-term processes, the bipolar dominance of the United States and the Soviet

Union entered a phase of eclipse. The consolidation of the European Community, later European Union—including a suddenly reunified Germany—came to constitute a major power center. And the rise of Japan, with its burgeoning capital surplus, witnessed the accumulation of formidable economic might. The world of the 1990s clearly exhibited a multipolar distribution of power, not merely a bipolar one, with a qualitative shift in the bases of power as well. Military prowess was no longer the preeminent source of international standing; increasingly, economic and technological capacity were becoming key instruments of power.

Second was the process of "democratization," the transition of political regimes from authoritarianism toward pluralism. This tendency was perhaps most dramatic in East Europe—especially in the former East Germany, Poland, Hungary, and Czechoslovakia. It likewise appeared in Latin America—notably in Argentina, Chile, and Brazil—and, less visibly, in some parts of Asia—the Philippines, South Korea, to some extent even Taiwan. While self-congratulatory publicists often interpreted this tendency as a decisive triumph for the ideals of American democracy, there was good reason for caution. Many of these "democratic" governments showed lingering signs of authoritarian practices. They were also fragile and tentative experiments, by no means immune to reversal. And they resulted not so much from U.S. leadership as from complex combinations of internal and international factors. Only in Eastern Europe was there a relatively clear connection between the behavior of the superpowers, especially Mikhail Gorbachev's reforms in the Soviet Union, and the emergence of democratic polities. And even there, as shown by Rumania, Bulgaria, and Albania, the extent of democratization was incomplete.

Third was the decline of the Cold War itself, the conclusion of relentless and decades-long hostility between the Soviet Union and the United States. But this was not merely a big-power rivalry. As pointed out in chapter 5, it also involved:

- Intense ideological competition—between capitalism and communism, liberalism and populism, markets and states, doctrines of Adam Smith and Karl Marx.
- A division of the world into two broad, opposing camps—West vs. East, free world vs. peoples' republics.
- The occasional outbreaks of armed conflicts but within restricted limits and in permissible places—always on the periphery of the world arena, never at the center of the superpower rivalry.

The central reason for this containment and curtailment of armed hostility was, of course, the fact that the United States and the USSR possessed mutually deterrent nuclear arsenals. Any direct contest between them risked the possibility of nuclear exchange, something neither side could afford, and this led to a counterintuitive result: the principal contenders could never engage in open conflict. Notwithstanding its excesses and ambiguities, the Cold War established a fairly clear (if unstated) set of rules of the game for international discourse and interaction. Paradoxically enough, it also managed to maintain global security.

Pundits and politicians in the United States hastened to interpret the end of the Cold War (plus the spread of democracy) as a final victory of capitalism over communism. Francis Fukuyama gave highbrow formulation to this impulse in his celebrated 1989 essay "The End of History," which claimed that the world was bearing witness "not to an 'end of ideology' or a convergence between capitalism and socialism, but to an unabashed victory of economic and political liberalism." Communism was as dead as fascism; authoritarian doctrines were relics of the past. The implication, therefore, was that the world had reached "the end point of mankind's ideological evolution and the universalization of Western liberal democracy as the final form of human government." As a process of ideological and intellectual struggle, history had arrived at a terminal point.[1] While Fukuyama did *not* mean to imply that all forms of conflict and change would disappear, as some of his critics misclaimed, he underestimated the power of ideas and identities most likely to shape the newly emergent world: ethnicity, religion, and nationalism.

The demise of the Cold War did not result from spiritual uplift or from charitable sentiments or from the innate superiority of West over East. It resulted from hard-headed calculations on the part of national leaders. As historian Thomas Paterson has argued, "The Cold War waned because the contest had undermined the power of its two major protagonists." As the United States and the USSR confronted mounting challenges, "they gradually moved toward a cautious cooperation whose urgent goals were nothing less than the restoration of their economic well-being and the preservation of their diminishing global positions." From the perspective of the superpowers, the ending of the Cold War was simply a matter of enlightened self-interest. "The Soviet Union fell much harder than the United States," Paterson has noted, "but the implications of decline became unmistakable for both: The Cold War they made in the 1940s had to be unmade if the two nations were to remain prominent international superintendants."[2]

The principal burden was economic. Both the United States and the Soviet Union spent enormous (and increasing) sums of money to wage their Cold War, and neither side could keep it up. Washington paid out $12.4 billion for the Marshall Plan, $69.5 billion for the Korean War, $22.3 billion for the Alliance for Progress, and $172.2 billion for the Vietnam War. From 1946 through 1987 the United States dispensed more than $382 billion in economic and military foreign aid (about one-tenth of this amount, $38.4 billion, went to Latin America). Military expenditures were staggering: by the mid-1980s the annual defense budget was more than $300 billion—which meant that the Pentagon was spending an average of $28 million per hour, twenty-four hours a day, seven days a week. By 1986 the national debt climbed to more than $2.1 trillion, with 19 percent of the federal budget devoted exclusively to interest payments, and by 1990 the debt reached $3.2 trillion.

The USSR also allocated massive resources toward military preparedness and foreign ventures. Subsidies to Cuba rose from less than $400 million per year in the 1960s and 1970s to nearly $5 billion per year in the 1980s, by which time assistance to East Europe was running around $17 billion per year. During 1980 alone, according to one calculation, the total cost to the Soviet Union for maintaining its system of client-states was around $38 billion. This inflicted an enormous drain on an already-weakening Soviet economy. Concurrently, the rate of economic growth plunged from an average of 5.9 percent in the 1950s to 4.9 percent in 1969–73 to 2.6 percent in 1973–80 to merely 1.9 percent in 1981–85. Like the United States, the Soviet Union simply could not afford to sustain the Cold War.

What happened in East Europe did not occur in Asia. China and North Korea remained resolute communist states. Russia maintained its military presence in the region and the United States continued to deploy massive contingents and firepower. Instability, tension, and hostility prevailed along the Asia/Pacific front. Although it had historic consequences for the world as a whole, the fall of communism was an essentially European affair.

Rearrangements of Power: The Global Arena

The transition from a bipolar system to a multipolar structure was a gradual but inexorable process. At the end of World War II the United States was utterly dominant: it produced more than half the world's manufacturing, it produced more than one-third the world's total of all goods and services, and it held almost two-thirds the world's total of gold reserves. "Economically," as historian Paul Kennedy has written, "the world was its oyster."[3] This preeminence was not so much a sign of American superiority or know-how, however, as a result of wartime destruction suffered by other powers. It could not last forever.

The Soviet Union meanwhile confronted a crucial challenge in the reconstruction and reinvigoration of its economy, which had endured massive material and human losses during the war. In 1950 the Soviet gross domestic product (GDP) was barely one-third that of the United States; its per capita income was just over one-fourth the U.S. level. Nonetheless the USSR, and its powerful Red Army, remained a military giant. By 1949 the Soviet Union developed an atomic bomb, thus disrupting the U.S. monopoly. In 1950 the United States spent about $14.5 billion on defense, with a military force of 1.4 million; the USSR spent about $15.5 billion with a force of 4.3 million. Bipolarity prevailed.

The objective foundation of this two-power hegemony began to fade as other countries recovered from the economic devastation of World War

II. The relative supremacy of the United States underwent steady slippage from the 1950s through the 1990s (Table A6). Allied nations in Europe made swift strides during the 1950s and 1960s, thanks in part to U.S. assistance under the Marshall Plan, and consolidated their position through the formation and expansion of the European Economic Community. Stimulated first by the Korean War and guided afterward by firm government policy, Japan entered the ranks of advanced industrial nations during the 1960s and 1970s. And the People's Republic of China, prostrate in 1950 after years of Japanese occupation and decades of civil war, adopted a series of economic reforms in the late 1970s that transformed the country into a swiftly emerging world-class economic power.

United States economic hegemony lasted for about a quarter century. America's share of manufacturing declined from about one-half the world total in the late 1940s to less than one-third by the early 1980s—and was still falling. The U.S. share of gross world product dropped from 25.9 percent in 1960 to 21.5 percent in 1980. The U.S. share of world gold reserves (outside the communist bloc) fell from 68 percent in 1950 to 27 percent in 1973. Finally, the U.S. share of world trade slipped from 18.4 percent in 1950 to 13.4 percent in 1977. This erosion of economic preponderance represented a significant decline in relative resources and, by implication, a concomitant reduction in political power.

One source of mounting competition came from the European Community, whose combined GDP of 1990 was just about equivalent to that of the United States. Another came from Japan and, more broadly, the Pacific Rim. As of 1960 the combined gross domestic product of Asian-Pacific countries (excluding the United States) was merely 7.8 percent of world GDP; by 1982 it had more than doubled, to 16.4 percent, and by 1990 it had risen to 23.0 percent. Mimicking Henry Luce's ebullient 1941 comment about the coming "American century," many observers anticipated that the world was on the verge of a "Pacific century."

In addition, the United States and Soviet Union faced political challenges within their own camps. Against U.S. objections, Great Britain established diplomatic relations with the People's Republic of China in 1954 and took unilateral military action during the Suez crisis of 1956. Under Charles de Gaulle, France asserted its independence in the 1960s by developing its own nuclear capacity, withdrawing militarily from NATO, and requiring the removal of all alliance bases from French territory. And after Willy Brandt became chancellor in 1969, West Germany defied the Nixon administration by pursuing a policy of *Ostpolitik* which resulted in the Soviet-German nonaggression treaty of 1970.

The USSR encountered resistance from its client states as well. Marshall Tito of Yugoslavia faced down Joseph Stalin in the late 1940s and launched an independent foreign policy. Courageous citizens in 1956 mounted uprisings against communist rule in Poland and Hungary, where Stalin responded with a show of force. A profound political, diplomatic, and ideological split emerged in the late 1950s between the People's Republic of China and the USSR. Under Alexander Dubçek, Czechoslovakia attempted to chart its own path toward political and social reform during the "Prague spring" of 1968; once again the USSR responded with tanks and armed troops. Nationalism nonetheless persisted. During the late 1980s the tiny Baltic states—Estonia, Latvia, and Lithuania, long considered "captive" by the West—resisted Mikhail Gorbachev's blandishments and proclaimed national independence. Gorbachev fell from office in 1991 and his arch-rival, Boris Yeltsin, rose to power as a champion of Russian nationalism and political reform. Russia became a sovereign republic and, in short order, other members of the former USSR soon followed suit: Armenia, Azerbaijan, Georgia, Belarus, Kazakhstan, Kyrgyztan, Moldova, Tajikistan, Turkmenistan, Ukraine, Uzbekistan. What Ronald Reagan had once decried as an "evil empire" no longer existed. In its place were numerous countries struggling with massive challenges—economic revitalization, political order, control and dismantling of massive military machines.

The dispersion of global power from the 1950s through the 1980s received further impetus from the emergence of the Third World, which brought a host of new players into the international game. From 1943 through 1989, as erstwhile European empires succumbed to processes of "decolonization," no fewer than ninety-six countries acquired independence and entered the world community of nations. And while the Third World became a principal battleground for the Cold War, members of the Non-Aligned Movement made deliberate efforts to resist big-power domination. By sheer force of numbers, Third World countries exerted considerable influence and independence in global forums. In the General Assembly of the United Nations, for instance, Third World delegates voted along with the United States about 70 percent of the time during the 1950s; by the 1970s this coincidence rate had fallen to 30 percent, and by the 1980s it was only 20 percent.

The cumulative effect of these tendencies was to transform the shape and structure of the international system. In a sense the postwar recovery of European powers, especially in West Europe, tended to restore the historical and structural balance of power that existed in the 1920s and 1930s; cast in this light, U.S. supremacy was destined to be a temporary phenomenon. The appearance of the Third World, on the other hand, was an entirely new type of development, diffusing power and adding unprecedented complexity to world politics. In combination, these trends pointed toward one unmistakable economic and political outcome: the decline of U.S. hegemony on a world scale. With the conclusion of the Cold War, the political implications of these changes would at last become apparent.

At the same time the United States managed to consolidate, perhaps even to increase, its military preeminence. In this respect the implosion of the Soviet Union meant that the United States would have no serious military rival anywhere in the world: it could enjoy a "unipolar moment" of unchallenged superiority, as shown by its devastating performance during Operation Desert Storm against Iraq's Saddam Hussein in 1991. Temporarily, at least, there was sharp discontinuity between the global distribution of economic power, which had become emphatically multipolar, and the distribution of military power, which had become emphatically unipolar.

Yet this military picture had its complications. First was uncertainty about the control of nuclear weapons. During the Cold War only two command posts—one in the United States, the other in the Soviet Union—were positioned to launch a nuclear exchange. This power condominium was, naturally, the objective basis for their intermittent policies of rapprochement. Fragmentation of the USSR meant that its former dependencies, most conspicuously Ukraine, would acquire command and control of these weapons systems: the result was, in effect, a major increase in proliferation. The ending of the East-West contest moreover meant that allies and client states, no longer beholden to the major powers, could pursue nuclear strategies of their own. There thus emerged a growing number of "weapons states"—Iraq and North Korea among them—that threatened drastic alteration of the military calculus.

Adding to this irony, U.S. military preponderance had unusually limited political utility in the post–Cold War landscape. Challenges and conflicts of the 1990s did not lend themselves to military solutions. The Gulf War of 1991 was a glaring exception; the protracted, contradictory, and painful struggles of Somalia and Bosnia seemed more likely to represent the norm. Despite its position as the world's preeminent military power, in other words, the United States could not apply this strength to many situations. Military prowess was becoming a hollow shell.

The United States and Latin America: Hegemony Regained?

One of the most common assertions about inter-American relations, virtually a consensus among experts, is that the United States was losing regional hegemony throughout the Cold War period. "By 1980," one authority has written, "the United States exerted less dominance in the Western Hemisphere than at any time since World War II." The U.S. share of Latin America's exports was in steady decline, from 45 percent in 1958 to 34 percent in the late 1970s; the U.S. share of direct foreign investment was in decline, from over 50 percent in Brazil in 1965 to just 30 percent in 1979; the U.S. share of weapons sales to Latin America was also in decline. In 1979 Washington was unable to convince Latin America to support its proposal for an OAS mission in Nicaragua; in 1980 it was unable to persuade fifteen Latin American countries to join a boycott of the Moscow Olympics (in protest over the Soviet invasion of Afghanistan); in 1982 it was unable to prevent the Falklands/Malvinas war between Argentina and Britain. By the mid-1980s the verdict appeared to be clear: "The decline of

U.S. preponderance in the Western Hemisphere has been pervasive and fundamental."[4]

An important corollary of this thesis maintained that U.S. interventions in the hemisphere during the Cold War represented a *weakening* of American hegemony, rather than its consummate expression. Political scientist Abraham Lowenthal has contended that U.S. efforts to overthrow Allende in Chile were "anachronistic," since "U.S. preponderance in the Americas was already substantially diminished."[5] Similarly, historian Thomas Paterson has asserted that U.S. interventions in the 1970s and 1980s "attested not to U.S. strength but to the loosening of its imperial net."[6] If hegemony was operating smoothly, there would never have been any leftist challenge in the first place; there would never have arisen any *reason* for the United States to intervene. By this same standard, the survival of the Castro regime in Cuba represented a conspicuous sign of Washington's inability to exert its political will.

This notion of declining hegemony rests on dubious assumptions. One entails a working definition of "hegemony" which claims, in effect, near-total control over political events within the hemisphere. Another presumes that Latin American resistance to Washington was greater in the 1980s than in the 1950s, although the evidence is far from clear: the reluctance of Latin American nations to send troops to Korea, the anti-Nixon riot, and the triumph of the Cuban Revolution took place under Truman and Eisenhower.

In retrospect, the historical record reveals three basic points: first, the United States exercised a strong and continuous degree of hegemony over the Western Hemisphere from the 1950s to the 1990s; second, within this overall pattern, U.S. hegemony suffered a slight decline from the 1960s to the 1980s; and third, still within this pattern, U.S. hegemony climbed to an all-time high between the mid-1980s and the mid-1990s. Since World War II, in other words, the general trend has *always* been for the United States to exert a great degree of influence over Latin American countries, but the level of this influence revealed some oscillation (up, down, up) from the mid-1950s to the present time.

Data on gross domestic product (GDP) and population size for key Latin American countries, for the region as a whole, and for the United States support this interpretation (Table A7). The differences in demographic trajectories are startling: the populations of all Latin America and the United States were nearly the same size in 1950, just over 150 million, but by 1990 the population of Latin America was almost 75 percent larger, 436 million compared with 250 million. Yet the economic productivity of the United States has consistently overwhelmed Latin America's regional output: U.S. GDP was more than seven times as large as the Latin American GDP in 1950, seven times as large in 1970, and still over five times as large by 1990. In 1950 the GDP of the United States was thirty times that of Argentina, thirty-three times that of Brazil, thirty-seven times that of Mexico; by 1990 the GDP of the United States was fifty-eight times that of

Argentina, thirteen times that of Brazil, twenty-three times that of Mexico. Within the global arena, the United States lost a good deal of ground in relation to other major powers between 1950 and 1990; within the Western Hemisphere, by contrast, the United States managed to retain its position of preponderance.[7]

A similar picture emerges from data on trade (Table A8). The statistics yield several insights. One, perhaps most significant, is the fact that the United States was by this time the largest single trading partner for every country of the region. Second is the presence of the European Community, especially for countries of southern South America (Argentina, Brazil, and Chile), whose trade with the EC as a collective entity was greater than with the United States. Third is the virtual disappearance of the Soviet Union, which by 1990 captured only a minuscule portion of trade with Latin America: having been Argentina's largest customer in the 1980s due to its purchase of wheat, the Soviet Union (and former Soviet Union) faded out of view. Finally, the data reflect the commercial rise of Japan, which would by the early 1990s become the largest single customer for Chile, though it was elsewhere eclipsed by the United States. Investments revealed a similar story: during 1990–92 the United States poured about $22 billion into Latin America, nearly twice the combined amount from Europe and Japan. The United States thus asserted and affirmed its hemispheric position of economic supremacy; and while Europe and Japan continued and in some areas intensified economic relations with Latin America, they did not begin to pose a political challenge to Washington's preeminence in the Americas.[8]

United States predominance resulted in large part from a systematic retreat by extrahemispheric rivals. It is in precisely this respect that the United States came to reassert "hegemony by default." This occurred not so much because the end of the Cold War provoked the United States to do anything particularly bold, innovative, or effective; it happened, instead, because outside powers withdrew from the Americas and directed their attention elsewhere. The European Community focused on the rehabilitation and reincorporation of East Europe; the Soviet Union withdrew and then collapsed, leaving Russia to cope with enormous domestic challenges; Japan, ever mindful of its relationship with the United States (and beset by its own economic problems), proved reluctant to accelerate involvement in the hemisphere; and China, despite its headlong rush toward economic growth, was not yet in any position to pursue an aggressive strategy toward Latin America. There were no strong competitors for the United States. As a result, U.S. supremacy in the Americas was uncontested and complete.

Political Implications

This reassertion of U.S. hegemony would have far-reaching consequences. Conspicuous among them was dissipation in the appeal of Marxist, Leninist, and socialist ideology throughout Latin America. Long championed by the left as an antidote to U.S. imperialism and a recipe for social justice, Marxist doctrine came to be identified with the demise of the Soviet Union—and with the plight of both Cuba and Nicaragua. It was in Latin America, perhaps more than any other region of the world, where Fukuyama's portrayal of the "end of history" seemed most accurate (or least inaccurate): even as a utopian dream, the appeal of communism seemed to diminish.

Equally important was the collapse of its antithesis. Exploited by right-wing forces as justification for oppression, as shown in chapter 8, anticommunism no longer had any logical place within the political arena. This meant that political forces in Latin America—of both left and right— would eventually have to confront one another directly, without rhetorical recourse to Manichean global struggles; that reactionary groups would no longer be able to enlist support from Washington in common cause against the specter of communism; and, as a result, that there would be less distortion, polarization, and escalation of local conflict as a result of meddling by external powers.

Ultimately, the end of the Cold War signified that the United States would no longer have an archenemy within the hemisphere. To be sure, Washington policymakers and media pundits had for decades drastically exaggerated the extent of Soviet influence within the Americas. But even on these terms, the Soviet/Russian global reach underwent severe contraction. In 1991 Mikhail Gorbachev announced the end of an era by announcing the withdrawal of Soviet troops from Cuba; in June 1993 the famed and controversial Soviet combat brigade departed the island (leaving only 500–1,000 soldiers behind to protect an intelligence gathering facility).

The demise of the Cold War conveyed ambiguous implications about prospects for U.S. intervention in Latin America. Some observers argued that the new circumstance would lead to increased interference by the United States in Latin America, to more intermeddling rather than less. According to this view, it was precisely the logic of the Cold War—and the possibility of Soviet retaliation, at some distant point on the globe if not within the Americas—that acted as a deterrent to U.S. action throughout the hemisphere. Without any risk of Soviet (or other) response in the post–Cold War era, the United States would be able to do whatever it pleased throughout Latin America. Others maintained that the unmaking of the Cold War would reduce the likelihood of U.S. intervention: according to former NSC official Robert Pastor, for example, "The fear of Soviet involvement was probably the single most important *cause* of U.S. interventionism during the Cold War. . . . The Soviet Union was not a deterrent in the Western Hemisphere; its presence was a motive for intervention."[9] Of course this begs the question of whether the "fear of Soviet involvement" was justified. In virtually every case of U.S. intervention, with the partial exception of the Cuban missile crisis of October 1962, Washington greatly exaggerated the nature and extent of Soviet threat.

On balance, both arguments appeared to make sense. The retreat of the Soviet Union reduced the *incentives* for the United States to meddle in Latin American affairs; but it also lowered the anticipated *costs* of intervention. The balance of these calculations would most likely determine the actual course of action. In any event, the anticommunist crusade could no longer provide justification for U.S. interference. Washington would require new rationalizations for the imposition of its will on Latin America.

Rediscovering Latin America?

Evaporation of the presumed Soviet and/or communist threat raised fundamental questions about the nature and persistence of U.S. interests in Latin America. What importance would Latin America have for the United States in the wake of the Cold War? What incentives might establish guidelines for U.S. policy toward the region?

Economic Interests

As chapter 10 shows, a central axis of inter-American relations would come to deal with economic issues. These matters would acquire paramount importance for nations of Latin America. Measured in a global context, however, these issues were of only modest significance to the United States. As a share of total U.S. trade, for instance, U.S. commerce with Latin America declined from 28–35 percent in 1950 to 12–14 percent in the mid-1970s, hovering thereafter around this low level. By the early 1990s approximately half of U.S. trade with Latin America was with Mexico alone, which consolidated its position as the United States' third largest commercial partner—after Canada and Japan (Table A9).[10] Outside of Mexico, trade with Latin America was not very important to the United States, and it was much less important than it had been in the 1950s.

From the 1980s into the 1990s Latin America supplied approximately one-quarter of the petroleum imported by the United States. Oil continued to be of considerable economic, strategic, and geopolitical value to the United States—and to its major allies in Japan and Western Europe, which were almost wholly dependent on imported oil. As illustrated by the Gulf War in 1991, a central goal of U.S. foreign policy was maintaining sources of supply. Secure and steady access to Latin American petroleum could provide insurance against political instability in the Middle East, and it constituted a significant national interest for the United States. Yet most U.S. imports of Latin American oil, over 95 percent in 1992, came from Mexico and Venezuela. Concerns over petroleum might affect Washington's treatment of these two countries, but not so much of the region as a whole.

As with trade, patterns of investment also reflected a decline in relative importance for Latin America. In 1950 Latin America accounted for well over one-third of U.S. direct investment abroad; by 1970 Latin America received less than half that relative share, 16 percent, and by 1990 the figure had slipped to less than 10 percent (Figure 4). Western Europe, Canada, and "other" regions, especially Asia and the Pacific Rim, were all hosting substantially more U.S. investment than Latin America. To be

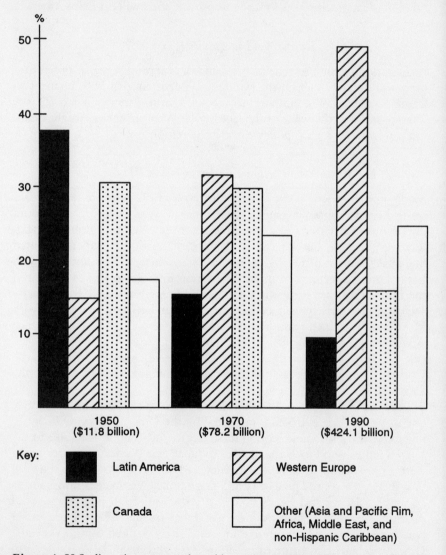

Figure 4. U.S. direct investment abroad by region, 1950–1990. [*Sources:* Data in U.S. Department of Commerce, *Historical Statistics of the United States, Colonial Times to 1970*, Part 2 (Washington, D.C.: U.S. Government Printing Office, 1975), series U 41–46, p. 870; and U.S. Department of Commerce, *Statistical Abstract of the United States, 1993* (Washington, D.C. Government Printing Office, 1993), p. 801.]

sure, the absolute value of U.S. investments in the region represented a substantial sum; adding investments in the English-speaking Caribbean (especially Bermuda), the figure rises from $41.8 billion to $71.6 billion. Within the global scheme, however, Latin America was of less significance to the United States than other world regions, and of much less significance than in the early postwar period.

This overall decline in Latin America's economic importance augmented its disparity with the United States. Trends in trade and investment meant that in comparison with previous periods the United States would have *less* at stake in its dealings with Latin America—at a time when Latin America would have *more* at stake in the United States. This growing asymmetry gave Washington great potential leverage over countries of the region.

Social Dimensions

In contrast to economics, Latin America was gaining relative importance to the United States in social and cultural realms. The most conspicuous manifestation of this trend was growth in the Latin-origin population within the United States. During the nineteenth century, the United States acquired Latino citizens as a result of territorial expansion and military conquest. During the twentieth century the Latino population swelled largely as a consequence of natural growth and especially of migration, the voluntary movement of labor across "invisible bridges" created through investments, trade, and political domination. Particularly striking was the close connection between U.S. overseas activity and consequent migratory flows. As sociologist Alejandro Portes has noted, countries that have supplied the major Spanish-origin groups in the United States

> were, each in its own time, targets of [an] expansionist pattern of U.S. intervention. . . . In a sense, the sending populations were Americanized before their members actually became immigrants to the United States. . . . The rise of Spanish working-class communities in the Southwest and Northeast may thus be seen as a dialectical consequence of past expansion of the United States into its immediate periphery. . . . Contemporary migration patterns tend to reflect precisely the character of past hegemonic actions by regional and global powers.[11]

Migrants thus came largely from Mexico, Puerto Rico, Cuba—and, in Asia, from the Philippines and Vietnam. The Mexican American writer Luis Valdés put it most succinctly: "We did not, in fact, come to the United States at all. The United States came to us."

By 1990 the "Hispanic" population in the United States amounted to 22.3 million, according to official census statistics, about 9 percent of the national total.[12] This represented an increase of 53 percent over the 1980 count of 14.6 million, making the Hispanic population one of the fastest-growing segments in U.S. society. About 60 percent were of Mexican origin, 12 percent of Puerto Rican origin, just under 5 percent of Cuban origin. In geographical terms the Hispanic population was highly concentrated, with nearly three-quarters living in only four states: California, Texas, New York, and Florida. In those areas, especially, the existence of sizable Hispanic communities led to multicultural social forms, to the enrichment of popular culture, to ethnic accommodation and tension—and, especially in California, to backlash from middle-class Anglos.

Hispanic influence reached from music to films and to sports, including the national pastime. By the end of the 1980s nearly 500 major league baseball players had come from Latin America—initially from Cuba, which accounted for 26 percent of the total, and then from Puerto Rico (25 percent), the Dominican Republic (23 percent), Venezuela, Mexico, Panama, Nicaragua, Colombia, and Honduras.[13] The Latin-born roster included such outstanding Hall of Famers as Roberto Clemente (Puerto Rico), Luis Aparicio (Venezuela), Juan Marichal (the Dominican Republic), and Rod Carew (Panama Canal Zone). Other prominent stars included José Canseco (born in Cuba), Andrés Galárraga (Venezuela), Fernando Valenzuela (Mexico), and George Bell, Tony Fernández, and Pedro Guerrero (all from the Dominican Republic). As with migration, Latin America's penchant for baseball reflected a clear-cut historic trend: it flourished in sites of U.S. investment and/or military occupation.

Hispanic influence extended to politics as well. This was largely a reflection of demographic trends, as Hispanics formed significant voting blocs in major states of the union. (They were not, however, unified: Mexican Americans tended to vote Democratic, Cuban Americans tended to vote Republican, Puerto Ricans tended not to vote.) In recognition of this reality President Clinton named two Latinos to cabinet positions. Even more significant, in the long run, was the growing influence of Hispanic groups over elements of foreign policy. Resident Cubans and Cuban Americans in Florida formed effective and visible lobbying groups that exerted major impact over U.S. policy toward Cuba; less obviously, but perhaps inexorably, Mexican Americans were acquiring influence on U.S. policy toward Mexico. The growth of the Hispanic community was not only transforming American popular culture. It was also shaping U.S. foreign policy.

U.S. Public Opinion

Equally important were the perceptions of mainstream American society. In the post–Cold War environment, the attitudes of U.S. citizens toward Latin America displayed three predominant features: ignorance, disdain, and indifference. Lack of knowledge about the region stemmed from underlying causes that ranged from shallow treatment in grade-school texts to erratic inclusion in college-level curricula to superficial coverage on television nightly news. For many if not most Americans, accurate information about Latin America was not readily available.

To aggravate this problem, popular media indulged in antiquated stereotypes. Such Hollywood films as *Butch Cassidy and the Sundance Kid* (1969) depicted Latins as inept and ridiculous, unable to cope with the derring-do of the characters played by Robert Redford and Paul Newman. Woody Allen's *Bananas* (1971) presented political dictatorship and instability as a form of comic opera. *Bring Me the Head of Alfredo Garcia* (1974) revived the image of Latin Americans as violent and bloodthirsty greasers. *Clear and Present Danger* (1994), from the novel by Tom Clancy, stressed the greed and ruthlessness of Colombian drug lords. There were exceptions to this general rule: as books and also as films, *The House of the Spirits* by Chilean Isabel Allende and *Like Water for Chocolate* by Mexican Laura Esquivel offered subtle and compelling views of Latin American life through the lens of "magical realism." But for the most part, stereotypes continued to prevail.

Together with a reassessment of world conditions, such images helped form U.S. public opinion toward countries of the region. A national poll in late 1994 showed that 65 percent of average American citizens—and 98 percent of the country's leaders—supported the idea that the United States should have an active role in global affairs. Within this framework, however, respondents took an ambivalent view of Latin America. About 76 percent of the general public agreed that Mexico represented a "vital interest" for the United States, but only 35 percent attributed similar importance to Brazil (Table A10). And while national leaders consistently accorded high significance to Mexico throughout all such surveys, they did not do so for Brazil: by 1994 only 49 percent of the leadership sample thought Brazil was an area of vital U.S. interest, compared with 73 percent in 1978 and 80 percent in 1982. Because of geographical proximity and socioeconomic interdependence, Mexico was something of a special case; as fears of international communism diminished, however, the rest of Latin America did not seem to matter very much. Public opinion appeared to reaffirm a historic dichotomy in U.S. perceptions of Latin America, expressing intense concern about nearby countries (especially Mexico) and lack of interest in South America.

In summary, according to a report on a 1990 survey, "The public accords relatively low priority to Latin America . . . in general, there is little desire to commit substantial U.S. resources, economic or otherwise, to the Latin American region." By 1990, only 2 percent of respondents expressed genuine concern for problems of Latin America, down from 10 percent in 1986. By 1994, preoccupation with material self-interest appeared to overwhelm altruism and idealism. For citizens in general, the leading purpose of U.S. foreign policy was held to be the deterrence of drug trafficking, cited by 85 percent as a "very important" policy goal; controlling and reducing illegal immigration was viewed as very important by 72 percent of the public; the promotion of democracy, by contrast, was seen as very important by merely 25 percent of the public (and just 21 percent of the leaders!). As described in chapter 11, drugs and migration would attract considerable (often wrathful) attention from U.S. citizens and policymakers alike. These issues also engendered negative feelings toward the region as a whole.

Power and Policy in the Age of Uncertainty

By the mid-1990s it was far from clear whether the post–Cold War world would manage to achieve a workable code for international behavior. The situation was confusing. As political scientist Joseph A. Nye, Jr., wrote in 1992, "No single hierarchy describes adequately a world politics with multiple structures. The distribution of power in world politics has become like a layer cake. The top military layer is largely unipolar, for there is no other military power comparable to the United States. The economic middle layer is tripolar and has been for two decades. The bottom layer of transnational interdependence shows a diffusion of power."[14] This configuration was unlikely to lead to world stability—not through a balance of power, mutual deterrence, or hegemonic imposition. The most likely outcome for the future, according to analyst Stephen Krasner, was "not a new order, but more of the older old order; that is, the pattern of international relations that existed before the Cold War."[15]

Uncertainty prevailed. One of the defining features of the international arena, as of the mid-1990s, was the absence of any firm or widely understood set of rules of the game. On this informal level, and especially in comparison with prior periods, the post–Cold War world was a relatively "lawless" arena. In their own way, both the Imperial Era and the Cold War established clear codes for conduct; the Age of Uncertainty could not. This circumstance both discouraged and justified quests for international cooperation.

A second feature of this panorama was the increasing importance of nongovernmental actors and forces—multinational business firms, international traders, migrant workers, private organizations, and other participants in what Nye referred to as the network of "transnational interdependence." Technological innovation, demographic expansion, spreading communications, atmospheric pollution, and other nonpolitical factors were coming to have more impact on the daily lives of citizens than the foreign policy of governments. The power of the economic market, in particular, was challenging (or, better said, disregarding) the power of the state. While the nation-state remained preeminent as a unit of organization, it no longer exercised a near-monopoly over international transactions.

Third, the post–Cold War arena was providing witness to the role and importance of international "regimes" in the conventional sense—as a set of "implicit or explicit principles, norms, rules and decision-making procedures around which actors' expectations converge in a given area of international relations." In a sense the development of regimes reflected long-term trends: an increasing reliance upon institutionalization (as in

NATO and the European Union), an increasing reluctance for great powers to use force against one another, and an increasing willingness, especially in Europe, to sacrifice or at least "pool" national sovereignty for the sake of supranational organization. As of the mid-1990s these regimes were more effective in the economic arena than in dealing with political questions. In the Americas, they would become especially relevant to the conduct of international trade, but not in other issue-areas.

A fourth characteristic was the persistence and growth of illicit transnational activities. Arms trafficking, drug smuggling, and clandestine migration took place in explicit violation of sovereign state policies and/or multilateral regimes. Much of this activity, especially unauthorized migration, resulted from individual decisions and behavior. Criminal organizations and terrorist groups flourished as well, not only in less developed areas, including Latin America, but especially in the ex-communist world. Gangster operations represented a formidable obstacle to the construction of a new international order and, especially, to effective governance by nation-states.

In the context of these global realities, inter-American relations revealed three defining features. First was an emerging emphasis on socioeconomic issues rather than political conflicts. At least in public, leaders throughout the hemisphere expressed virtually unanimous support for democracy at home and U.S. leadership abroad. Ideology was no longer a matter of contention. As explained in chapters to follow, U.S.–Latin American relations would focus not on grandiose matters of state but on "low politics"—such uninspiring issues as economic development, environmental protection, international migration, and drug trafficking.

Second, the end of the Cold War and the consequent complexity of the world arena had crucial ramifications for the formulation of U.S. policy toward Latin America. Without any clear sense of mission or purpose, without guiding principles or practical doctrines, foreign policy became closely linked to domestic polities. This became especially apparent for Latin America precisely because it was seen as a region of ambiguous importance rather than the location of soaring state interests. And in contrast to the late nineteenth and early twentieth centuries, when the business community played a key part in Washington's outlook toward Latin America, the making of foreign policy at the end of the twentieth century responded more and more to the demands of social groups and electoral blocs and interest associations—including Cuban Americans, African Americans, and Mexican Americans.

Third, realities within the Western Hemisphere would display a simple and pervasive fact: renewed hegemony of the United States. Without any threat from extrahemispheric powers, and without any likelihood of collective challenge from Latin America itself, the United States was free to impose its will throughout the Americas. More than any time in the past, Washington could now live up to Richard Olney's oft-quoted remark of 1895: the United States could rule the continent "by fiat."

The question was how the United States would exercise its power. Three possibilities loomed large. One was that Washington would effectively abandon the region, since it no longer played a major role in geopolitical strategy, consigning Latin America to a marginal position in the global arena. A second was that, in the absence of the Cold War, Washington would discover new reasons to care about Latin America—such as migration and trade—and that this evolving agenda would reveal an underlying coincidence of interests between North and South America. This would lead to increasing engagement by the United States and to increasing cooperation between Washington and governments throughout the region. A third possibility was that the United States would identify pressing national interests within the hemisphere and pursue them in unilateral fashion. And in a sense, attention to the hemisphere would comprise a reaction to developments in other parts of the globe. As historian Thomas Paterson has observed:

> Overall, because the three worlds have fragmented, because there no one hegemon rules, because world disorder looms large, Americans nervous about the stormy post–Cold War era are likely to seek to batten down their traditional sphere of influence in Latin America.

"The U.S. quest for hegemony has been constant in the twentieth century," Paterson adds; "what has changed is the rationale. With or without a Cold War, the United States will likely continue its unilateral, interventionist role in Latin America."[16] Only time would tell.

10

The New Economic Agenda

Love and free trade.
    Economist's slogan (1992)

*Freedom of trade is fair only if it is subject to the demands of social
justice.*
    Pope Paul VI (1967)

By the early 1990s a spirit of optimism suffused Washington and many
capitals of Latin America. As economic matters moved to the forefront of
the inter-American agenda, officials came to agree that the Cold War had
distorted U.S.–Latin American relations by introducing an ideological
factor that was extraneous, artificial, and deleterious. In the newly emerging world, they also concurred, the economic interests of the United States
and Latin America converged with one another. Steadfast pursuit of economic interests would therefore lead to a happy and harmonious relationship. It was economics, rather than politics, that defined true and legitimate national interests. And with the United States and Latin America
both intent on economic gain, the prospects for hemispheric collaboration
were better than ever before.

Three factors determined the basic framework for inter-American economic relations in the 1990s. One, as described in chapter 9, was the
reshaping of the international arena with the rise to power of Europe and
Japan. Second was the legacy of Latin America's debt crisis of the 1980s.
Third was a worldwide concern to reconcile processes of economic development with the need for environmental protection.

The Debt Crisis

What came to be known as "the debt crisis" had its origins in the 1970s.
Seeking to increase their profits and exert their political power, members of

235

the Organization of Petroleum Exporting Countries (OPEC) reduced production and shipments in 1973–74 and again in 1979–81. The result on
both occasions was a shortage of petroleum throughout the West, long
waiting lines at gasoline stations in Europe and the United States, a sharp
increase in prices—and windfall profits for oil-producing countries. Unable to absorb all these funds, OPEC governments deposited massive
amounts of dollars into U.S. and European banks. Obliged to pay interest
on these deposits, the banks then had to lend these sums out to borrowers
who would pay higher rates of interest.

The moneylenders turned to Latin America. Since advanced industrial
countries were facing recession, the most logical targets for lending were
relatively unsophisticated borrowers in the developing world who were
willing to accept higher rates of interest than their industrial country counterparts. This meant especially the so-called upper tier of Third World
countries—Argentina, Brazil, Venezuela, and Mexico. Bankers were quite
comfortable in dealing with public agencies and state enterprises, in the
belief that repayment would be guaranteed by governments; countries may
not be able to pay, according to a well-known dictum, but neither they nor
their debts disappear. Meanwhile borrowers were encouraged by modest
interest rates (at some points in the mid-1970s real interest rates, as measured by the difference between nominal rates and worldwide inflation,
were actually negative). Under these circumstances, Latin America's total
foreign debt swelled from around $30 billion in 1970 to more than $240
billion in 1980.

The general assumption, shared by lenders and borrowers alike, was
that the world economy would continue on a path of moderate growth
with low real interest rates. This prediction turned out to be wrong. Economic growth in industrialized countries declined from 4.9 percent in the
1960s to 3.4 percent in the 1970s; expansion in world trade dropped from
9 percent in the 1960s to just 4 percent in the 1970s. In the early 1980s the
U.S. economy fell into a serious recession. Stagnation in the industrialized
world reduced imports of raw materials from the developing world, while
structural transformation—especially the decline of smokestack industries
and growth in the service sector—further weakened demand for traditional
goods. For Latin American countries, these trends led to a substantial
decline in exports and export earnings—which were required in order to
service their loans.

As global inflation was accelerating, U.S. Federal Reserve chairman
Paul Volcker responded with a "tight money" policy entailing a substantial
increase in interest rates. This had serious impacts on Latin America. Most
of the region's loans were contracted at variable interest rates, periodically
adjusted in accordance with the movement of some widely accepted international yardstick. For example, operative interest rates might be established as the London Inter-Bank Offered Rate (LIBOR) plus an additional
margin of 0.5 percent to 2.0 percent (depending on the creditworthiness
of the borrower). As a result of fluctuations in the international market,

actual average interest rates paid by Latin American lenders climbed from 10 percent in 1978 to 15 percent in 1980 and 18 percent in 1981. Costs of debt service therefore rose dramatically. According to one calculation, the accumulation of extra debt due to increases in interest rates (above 10 percent) during the five-year period 1978–82 came to $40 billion–$50 billion!

In the meantime, the value as well as the volume of traditional Latin American exports—from coffee to nonferrous metals to petroleum—was sharply plummeting. A steady strengthening of the U.S. dollar intensified the trend. By the mid-1980s international commodity prices reached their lowest point in real terms since World War II; as a result, Latin American nations were earning less hard currency from exports. As the cost of debt service was rising, in other words, Latin America's capacity to pay was declining. In 1984 debt service amounted to 46 percent of the region's total earnings from exports.

Oscillations in the price of petroleum were particularly volatile. Largely as a consequence of OPEC-induced shocks, the average price climbed from $10 per barrel in the early 1970s to more than $40 per barrel in 1981. This stimulated a new wave of borrowing. Oil importers, like Brazil, borrowed money in order to purchase petroleum and continue their drive toward industrialization; exporters, like Mexico and Venezuela, borrowed money with anticipated income as collateral. Then the bottom dropped out of the market, as prices for oil plunged to less than $20 per barrel (a level where they stayed until the early 1990s). As a result of price fluctuations, both importers and exporters piled up substantial debts; and for different reasons, both would find it difficult to pay.

By the early 1980s both lenders and borrowers were overextended. Indebted countries were caught in a vicious squeeze between declining export prices and rising interest rates, so they began to borrow more and more money just to keep up with payments on debt service. Loans piled upon loans: between 1975 and 1985 Latin America's external debt spiraled from $99 billion to $384 billion (Table A11). "You borrowed money like a bunch of drunken sailors," one prominent banker is reported to have said during a subsequent session with Latin America's finance managers. "Yes," came the tart reply, "but we had a drunken bartender."

The Mexican Crisis

On Thursday, August 12, 1982 Mexican finance minister Jesús Silva Herzog placed telephone calls to Paul Volcker of the U.S. Federal Reserve, U.S. treasury secretary Donald Regan, and IMF director Jacques de Larosière. His urgent message: Mexico could no longer meet its obligations on debt. That night Silva Herzog hurried to Washington for pressing consultations. By Sunday the negotiators could announce agreement on two points: a moratorium on the amortization of Mexico's debt to commercial banks, and an international package of emergency loans. The most important point was implicit: interest payments would continue as scheduled.

Central to the ensuing negotiations was the creation of a mechanism for communication between Mexico and its creditor banks—between 800 and 1,000 institutions in all. Discussions eventually led to the formation of a centralized advisory committee dominated by large-scale "money center" banks, and placed under the chairmanship of William Rhodes of Citicorp. Nominally charged with providing advice to the Mexican government, the committee actually served to coordinate the negotiating stance of the banks. In effect, the bankers succeeded in forming a cartel.

Complications ensued on September 1, when President José López Portillo abruptly announced the nationalization of Mexico's banks. His goal was to halt capital flight by financial speculators—"vultures" (*buitres*), as he angrily proclaimed—which led him to impose mandatory exchange controls as well. While business communities in Mexico and the United States greeted the news with an admixture of hostility and disbelief, most international bankers maintained discreet silence: many of Mexico's creditors were not at all displeased that the debts of the Mexican banks, which had made doubtful loans to businesses in trouble, were now in the hands of the Mexican state.

Negotiations soon resumed, based on the premise that Mexico's predicament represented a "liquidity crisis" (a cash squeeze) rather than a "solvency crisis" (a basic inability to pay). The first step was to strengthen Mexico's foreign exchange reserves in order to enable continued payments on interest. This was accomplished through an advance payment by the United States of $1 billion on purchases for its strategic oil reserve; a $1 billion credit guarantee for the acquisition of agricultural commodities from the United States; and a loan of $1.85 billion from various sources, principally the U.S. Federal Reserve.

The second step was to provide long-term financing, and here the International Monetary Fund stepped in to play a crucial role. The IMF agreed to provide Mexico with an authorization of $3.96 billion in exchange for a stringent stabilization program to combat inflation, then running around 100 percent per year. And in November, de Larosière used this agreement as a means of forcing Mexico's creditors to provide a total of $5 billion in new funds. Come up with the money, he threatened them at a meeting in Toronto, or the IMF will withdraw its authorization—thus endangering all their currently outstanding loans. Within a month the banks complied. The IMF thus initiated a cycle of involuntary or "nonmarket" lending by creditor banks.

The third step was renegotiation of terms and timing of debt repayments. Discussions eventually led to a rescheduling of the $19.5 billion in public debt due before the end of 1984 and agreements on a staggered grace period for repayments on other principal. Mexico and its creditors could heave a collective sigh of relief. Seized with self-congratulation, participants in these deliberations regarded their handling of the Mexican crisis as a major success.

In Search of Solutions

As other countries in Latin America announced their inability to meet debt obligations, the international community sought to find a workable response. During the first stage of the decade-long crisis, from 1982 to 1985, bankers and debtors attempted to "muddle through" what they saw as problems of "liquidity." The reaction nonetheless formed a clear pattern, with the International Monetary Fund performing a key role as catalyst and monitor. Once a country proclaimed inability to pay, the IMF would negotiate an austerity package. IMF authorities were especially eager to attack both inflation and public-sector deficits (even though interest payments alone accounted for 15 to 20 percent of public outlays, equivalent to 4 to 5 percent of GNP). Approval of an IMF package would then persuade otherwise reluctant creditor banks to provide fresh loans, which enabled debtor countries to keep up their payments.

The IMF and the banking community dealt with each country on a case-by-case basis. Each of the major debtors—Mexico, Brazil, Venezuela, and Argentina—had somewhat different schedules and problems. As a result creditors could negotiate with individual governments rather than with a coalition. The bankers could also reduce the incentive for collective action by offering slightly better terms in each successive round of negotiation. Through such means the international community was able to prevent the formation of a debtors' cartel.

These tactics assured successful rescue of the banks. Negotiators proudly proclaimed that their purpose was to avoid financial panic, which could have harmful consequences for the entire international community, but in practice the pursuit of this goal entailed protection of private banks, some of which were seriously overexposed. A central premise of all negotiations was the continuation of interest payments. And as a result, the banks managed to survive: as international economist Pedro-Pablo Kuczynski has observed, no major bank failed during the 1980s because of its Latin American loans.[1]

A second stage in response to the crisis began in 1985. At a major meeting in Seoul, then-U.S. treasury secretary James A. Baker III stressed the importance of economic growth for indebted countries—acknowledging in effect that countries faced crises of solvency, not just liquidity. Recognizing the dearth of commercial lending, Baker called for an injection of $20 billion in developing countries that were willing to undertake market reforms. For this task he assigned a major role to the World Bank, which had construed its concern with long-term development as a reason for staying on the sidelines of the debt crisis. The Baker Plan led to scant practical results, mainly because the $20 billion proved to be unavailable, but it marked an important shift in the definition and conceptualization of the debt crisis.

It fell to Baker's successor, Nicholas F. Brady, to carry on the process. Announced in March 1989, the Brady Plan proposed a broad portfolio of debt reduction and restructuring alternatives and offered U.S. government support to countries undertaking market-based economic policies. The Brady Plan had two distinct features: one was its flexibility and open-endedness, expressed in its expansive menu of policy options, which created greater willingness among borrowers and lenders than under the Baker Plan; another was its explicit recognition that debt reduction would have to be an integral element in any lasting resolution of the debt crisis. Long anathema to the banks and to the Reagan administration, debt relief was thus legitimized on the basis that it could provide efficiency gains for both the debtors and the banks.

By February 1990 the Brady Plan resulted in the restructuring of nearly $50 billion of Mexican debt. Creditor banks were able to choose from three options: first, they could swap current bank loans at face value for new bonds paying the relatively modest rate of 6.25 percent interest ("par bonds"); second, they could swap old loans for new bonds at a respectable rate of interest (LIBOR + $^{13}/_{16}$ percent) but at a 35 percent discount on face value ("discount bonds"); third, they could exchange old debt for new debt at face value by agreeing to provide new loans (up to 25 percent of their total exposure). With thirty-year zero-coupon bonds, the U.S. government agreed to guarantee payment on all these new bonds. (Creditors were also entitled to recapture Mexican profits on oil sales over $14 per barrel after July 1996.) Most banks chose the debt reduction options. As a result, the face value of Mexico's external commercial debt declined by $5.5 billion.

Negotiations under the Brady Plan also led to agreements with Costa Rica, Venezuela, Uruguay, Argentina—and, in mid-1992, Brazil. With the exception of Costa Rica and Mexico, however, implementation of the plan did not bring much significant debt reduction. One result was paradoxical: partial reduction and successful restructuring of the *commercial* debt tended to increase the face value of *total* debt, including official debt, since these measures strengthened the value of outstanding debt shares in financial markets. To be sure, the burdens of debt service became less onerous in time, but more as a result of economic growth and export expansion by countries of Latin America (plus declining worldwide intrest rates) than negotiated debt reduction.

Social Implications

For Latin America the 1980s came to be known as the "lost decade." Economic and social progress was negligible at best, negative at worst. Renegotiations and restructurings led to reliance upon continuous lending (and borrowing), which forced the region's external debt up from $242 billion in 1980 to $431 billion by 1990. Meeting their contractual obligations, Latin American countries transferred a net amount of more than $200 billion to advanced industrial countries. They slashed imports—from $98 billion in 1981 to $59 billion in 1984—and doled out one-third to one-half their export earnings in the form of interest payments.

Economic growth for Latin America came to a virtual halt. Growth rates of gross domestic product (GDP) per capita for the region were actually negative for 1981, 1982, 1983, 1988, and 1989; for 1983 alone the figure was −5.0 percent (Table A12). For the decade as a whole per capita output declined by 8.3 percent, and for individual countries the performance was much worse: −23.5 percent for Argentina and −24.9 percent for Venezuela. (For entirely different reasons, mostly associated with the Contra war, Nicaragua suffered a staggering decline of −33.1 percent.) Unemployment swelled and wages plummeted. For Mexico, whose conduct set a model of good behavior for other debtor countries, real wages declined by nearly 50 percent during the course of the decade.

By 1989 nearly a third of the region's population lived in poverty, according to a World Bank study, up from 27 percent a decade earlier. This increase was especially apparent in the cities, where the proportion of poor climbed from 16.8 percent of the urban population in 1980 to 23.0 percent in 1989. Misery persisted in the countryside, where the poverty rate went from 45.1 percent of the rural population to 52.5 percent. And over the course of the decade, the bottom 20 percent saw their share of the region's income drop to just 4 percent of the total. Using slightly different statistical criteria, analysts at the UN's Economic Commission for Latin America and the Caribbean (ECLAC/CEPAL) reached an essentially identical conclusion, finding that the relative proportion of Latin American families living in poverty swelled from 35 percent in 1980 to 39 percent in 1990; in absolute terms, this meant that the number of impoverished individuals increased by 45 million–50 million. No matter what the measurement, the social reality was clear: for peasants, workers, and downwardly mobile segments of the middle class, the debt crisis had a devastating impact.

The Washington Consensus

Eventually, the international financial community arrived at the conclusion that Latin America required fundamental economic reform. A principal source of the region's difficulty was held to be structural distortions resulting from the strategy of "import-substitution industrialization" (ISI) through which Latin American countries sought to manufacture goods once imported from abroad. To a considerable extent, ISI grew out of *cepalista* studies in the 1950s showing that secular terms of trade were running against commodity producers: the real price of raw materials was declining while the cost of manufactures was increasing. Domestic industrialization under state protection offered a practical and logical response to these conditions. Through the 1970s ISI produced high rates of growth, and observers referred glowingly to economic "miracles" in such countries as Mexico and Brazil.

During the 1980s, however, officials and analysts began to attribute numerous deficiencies to ISI—as a result of its emphasis upon the state, its reliance upon domestic markets, and its protection of the private sector. Of course the debt crisis itself was largely due to factors outside of (and outside the control of) Latin America. Notwithstanding this self-evident truth, economists and policymakers in major international institutions—from the U.S. Treasury to the World Bank and the International Monetary Fund—issued a clarion call for economic restructuring in Latin America.

What came to be known as the "Washington consensus" entailed three sets of prescriptions.[2] First, it called for reduction and revision in the economic role of the state. Latin American governments should exercise fiscal discipline (as commonly preached, but rarely practiced, by Washington itself), and they should concentrate their resources not on social subsidies but on health, education, and infrastructural investment. They should also deregulate their national economies, letting market forces operate without political or bureaucratic constraints.

Second, the Washington consensus advocated support for the private sector. Latin American governments should sell off state-owned enterprises, which could reduce public deficits through proceeds from the sales and through the elimination of wasteful subsidies. The governments should also remove restrictions on foreign capital. Behind the consensus was a doctrinaire belief that private management, driven by profit motivation and market competition, was inherently more efficient than public administration.

Third, Latin American governments should drastically revise policies on trade. They should look outward, not inward, for markets. The reduction of tariffs and other barriers to imports would improve access to intermediate inputs, which was necessary for the ability to export finished products at competitive prices. Excessive protection of domestic industry created costly distortions that penalized exports, punished domestic consumers, and encouraged inefficiencies. (It was assumed that Latin America's recovery required the expansion of nontraditional exports, especially manufactured goods, rather than traditional commodities and raw materials.) In this regard, trade policy and the encouragement of private enterprise went hand-in-hand: both would stimulate competition, efficiency, and active participation in the international economy.

In sum, the Washington consensus advocated the adoption of free-market capitalism by Latin America. Yet this neoliberal vision contained at least one major paradox. A centerpiece of the entire program was reducing the role of the state; but at the same time, implementation of these policies could be accomplished only by a powerful state. Economic reform was bound to encounter resistance from entrenched groups—sheltered entrepreneurs, unionized workers, public-sector employees. Imposition of broad, equitable, and effective tax codes, another of the Washington proposals, would generate opposition from almost everyone. It would take a strong and autonomous state to overcome such pressures. Proponents of the consensus often sought to resolve this paradox by advocating small but efficient government, "lean and mean," but this formulation did not clearly address fundamental questions about the *role* and the *extent* of state participation in economic affairs.

To an extent, Washington's orthodox wisdom represented an extension and formalization of the recipes for economic readjustment foisted on Latin America by the International Monetary Fund and by bankers' advisory committees during the course of the 1980s. Faced with little choice, Latin American governments accepted many of these policy recommendations. Privatization became especially fashionable. By the end of 1990 more than $15 billion of foreign debt had been retired through debt/equity conversions in privatizations of state-owned companies in Argentina, Brazil, and Mexico. And during 1991 around $10 billion of foreign investment flowed into the region, an increase of more than 20 percent in existing foreign investment stock. The business of Latin America, it seemed, was coming to be business.

The Mantra of Free Trade

A movement in favor of "free trade" simultaneously swept through the Americas. In the mid-1980s Argentina and Brazil initiated negotiations for what would ultimately become a four-country partnership including Uruguay and Paraguay. In 1990 the United States and Canada accepted Mexico's proposal to begin discussions for the creation of a North American free trade area; within two years negotiators reached agreement on a formal treaty. Also in 1990 then-U.S. president George Bush proposed the development of a free trade zone embracing the entire Western Hemisphere. Seeking to overcome the painful crisis of the 1980s, leaders throughout Latin America came to regard "free trade" as a central part of any long-term solution to the continent's economic woes.

This movement immersed the Western Hemisphere in processes of "regional economic integration," which entailed the removal of state-imposed barriers to the mutual exchange of goods, services, capital, or persons. According to standard usage, the removal of barriers to the exchange of goods alone would be sufficient to create a "free trade area" (FTA). That plus the erection of common external tariffs would constitute a "customs union." Establishment of a "common market" would require the removal of barriers to the free flow of all factors of production, especially services and capital. As chapter 11 explains, the mutual exchange of persons—that is, the free flow of labor—would constitute one of the most contentious issues in contemporary processes of integration.

North American Free Trade

The most ambitious and far-reaching instance of regional integration concerned the North American Free Trade Agreement (NAFTA). Unveiled in August 1992, the pact was signed that October by leaders of the three countries in San Antonio, Texas, in the midst of the U.S. presidential campaign. After ratification by legislatures of the three governments, it took effect in January 1994. Building on a bilateral free trade accord between Canada and the United States (approved in 1988, initiated January 1989), NAFTA created one of the two largest trading blocs in the world—with a population of 370 million and combined economic production of approximately $6 trillion as of 1992, North America could be a worthy rival to the European Union.[3]

NAFTA promoted a free flow of goods between member countries by eliminating duties, tariffs, and trade barriers over a period of fifteen years. Sixty-five percent of U.S. goods gained duty-free status immediately or within five years; half of U.S. farm goods exported to Mexico immediately became duty-free. There were special exceptions for certain "highly sensitive" products in agriculture, typically one of the sectors most resistant to economic integration; phase-outs on tariffs for corn and dry beans in Mexico and orange juice and sugar in the United States would extend to the year 2009. Tariffs on all automobiles within North America would be phased out over ten years, but rules of origin stipulated that local content would have to be at least 62.5 percent for vehicles to qualify. Not surprisingly, spokespersons for Asian governments regarded this clause as highly "protectionist," a thinly disguised effort to exclude Japanese industries and products from the North American market.

NAFTA opened Mexico to U.S. investments in various ways. Under the treaty U.S. banks and securities firms could establish branch offices in Mexico, and U.S. citizens could invest in Mexico's banking and insurance industries. While Mexico continued to prohibit foreign ownership of oil fields, in accordance with its constitution, U.S. firms became eligible to compete for contracts with Petróleos Mexicanos (PEMEX) and to operate, in general, under the same provisions as Mexican companies.

One item was most conspicuous by its absence: beyond a narrowly written provision for movement of corporate executives and selected professionals, the treaty made no reference at all to large-scale migration of labor. The continuing flow of "undocumented workers" from Mexico into the United States—where they were customarily classified as "illegal aliens," in a suggestive turn of phrase—remained a major source of conflict and contention in the bilateral relationship. Apparently sensing that there was no ground for reasonable compromise, NAFTA negotiators decided to avoid the question altogether. But as the next chapter shows, avoidance did not make the issue disappear.

One of the most revealing features of NAFTA was its provision for governance and, especially, the resolution of disputes. NAFTA established a Trade Commission, with ministers or cabinet-level officials, to meet at least once a year, and assigned day-to-day oversight of operations to a trilateral secretariat. In case of disagreement (for example, over the degree of local content in an automobile), the complaining country could request "consultations" with the allegedly offending country. (The third party may or may not choose to join the deliberations.) If these consultations failed to resolve the matter within thirty to forty-five days, any one of the countries could convene a meeting of the Trade Commission (with all three countries present). If the commission was unable to find a solution to the problem, it turned the matter over to a panel of experts—which, after careful study, would propose recommendations for settling the dispute. Upon receiving the panel's report, the contending countries were then supposed to come to an agreement. And if *that* could not be done, the complaining country could impose unilateral trade sanctions against the defending country until the issue was somehow resolved.

NAFTA precipitated strenuous debate within the United States (and to a somewhat lesser extent in Canada, where organized labor and small business were feeling ill effects from the U.S.–Canadian agreement). In the heat of the 1992 presidential campaign, Democratic candidate Bill Clinton pledged to support NAFTA on condition that there be effective safeguards for environmental protection and worker rights; by September 1993 the governments reached "supplemental" or side agreements on labor and environment. As the U.S. Congress prepared to vote on ratification, NAFTA moved to the center of the political stage. Texas billionaire (and erstwhile presidential hopeful) Ross Perot led the charge against the treaty, claiming that NAFTA would entice business to seek low-wage Mexican labor and thus lose jobs for millions of American workers. Proponents insisted that NAFTA would stimulate U.S. exports, achieve economies of scale, and enhance U.S. competitiveness. Disregarding vociferous opposition from unionized labor, a historic bastion of support for Democrats, Clinton lobbied tirelessly on behalf of the treaty. And after Perot stumbled badly during a memorable television debate with Vice President Al Gore, the House of Representatives finally approved the NAFTA accord by the surprisingly lopsided margin of 234–200; the Senate followed with a vote of 61–38.

In final form, the NAFTA accord had three outstanding characteristics. One was its implicit commitment to regional economic integration. Despite its title, NAFTA was not primarily concerned with "free trade." By 1990 tariff and even nontariff barriers to U.S.–Mexican commerce were already low. NAFTA was primarily concerned with investment. By obtaining preferential access to U.S. markets and a formal "seal of approval" through NAFTA, Mexico was hoping to attract sizable flows of direct foreign investment—from Japan and Europe as well as from the United States. By obtaining untrammeled access to low-wage (but highly skilled) Mexican labor, the United States was hoping to create an export platform for manufactured goods to improve its competitive position in the global economy. It was for these reasons that the NAFTA treaty contained extensive chapters about investment, competition, telecommunications, and financial services. Commerce was only one part of the picture. Implicitly, NAFTA envisioned a substantially more profound form of integration than its label acknowledged.

Second, NAFTA was essentially an intergovernmental accord. Unlike the European Community (later European Union), which created an elaborate structure for governance with genuine supranational authority,

NAFTA relied on negotiations and presumed consensus between national governments. As revealed in the provisions for dispute resolution, NAFTA did not entail any "pooling" or "sharing" or "delegation" of political sovereignty along European lines. The result was inconsistency, some thought, between the relatively "deep" level of economic integration envisioned by NAFTA and its distinctly "shallow" level of political integration. Ultimately, it appeared that this disjuncture was likely either to paralyze processes of economic integration and/or exert enormous pressure for supranational authority—which could itself become an instrument for the assertion of U.S. hegemony. One way or another, it seemed likely that NAFTA would have to confront its own internal contradictions.

Third, NAFTA possessed an underlying political rationale. In this respect it shared a trait that was characteristic of all enduring integration schemes. From the time of its foundation in the late 1950s, for instance, the European Union had two major political goals: placing constraints on Germany, in order to preserve postwar stability, and strengthening West Europe against the Soviet bloc, in order to contain communism. As a recent study has concluded, "Regional integration builds upon political foundations. Integration is not merely an economic enterprise. It is also a political compact. . . . Integration requires a clear and recognized convergence of political interests for all participant states. This does not mean that political interests must be identical. It means that they must be compatible and clearly understood."[4]

Political Dimensions of NAFTA

For both the United States and Mexico, political concerns were driving the NAFTA agenda. This was less true for Canada, which had just reached its own bilateral free trade agreement with the United States, and was unhappy to learn in mid-1990 about ongoing discussions between Mexico City and Washington. Although reluctant to encourage this initiative, Ottawa eventually decided to join the NAFTA negotiations for defensive reasons: to prevent Mexico and the United States from devising a bilateral accord of their own that would damage Canadian interests. Economically, Canada appeared to have little to gain (and something to lose) from the inclusion of Mexico in an expanded North American market; politically, Ottawa could hope to trim its losses only by taking part in the process.

The United States, for its part, had four basic political goals. One was the preservation of stability on its southern border. This had been the cornerstone of U.S. policy toward Mexico ever since the revolution of 1910. The idea was that NAFTA would stimulate economic growth in Mexico, easing social pressure and sustaining the regime. Notwithstanding public rhetoric, it was not Washington's primary intent to promote democratic change; it was to uphold political peace.

Second, the United States sought to assure itself of increasing access to petroleum from Mexico, one of the five leading sources of U.S. imports.

(Mexican shipments in the late 1980s and early 1990s were roughly half as large as those from the topmost source, Saudi Arabia.) Petroleum continued to have major geostrategic significance, as the Persian Gulf War eloquently testified, and secure and steady access to sources within the hemisphere could counterbalance the potential costs of political turbulence elsewhere in the world. During the NAFTA negotiations Washington strenuously attempted to obtain rights for U.S. firms to engage in excavation. Mexico firmly resisted this demand, on the ground that it would contravene the constitution of 1917, but opened other opportunities for U.S. participation in the petrochemical sector.

Third, NAFTA provided the United States with an important bargaining chip in its trade negotiations with Europe, Japan, and the General Agreement on Tariffs and Trade. In confronting a potential "fortress Europe" or a resistant Japan, in other words, Washington could threaten to form an exclusive economic bloc in North America—or perhaps the Western Hemisphere as a whole—and pursue highly protectionist policies. Ironically, the international community eventually interpreted the ratification of NAFTA as a vote in favor of free trade, rather than protectionism, a development that helped restore U.S. leadership in the world arena.

And fourth, the United States wanted to consolidate diplomatic support from Mexico on foreign policy in general. As demonstrated by disagreements over Central America during the 1980s, foreign policy had long been a source of bilateral tension. And with NAFTA in place, Mexico became unlikely to express serious disagreement with the United States on major issues of international diplomacy. None other than the U.S. ambassador to Mexico, John D. Negroponte, said as much in a controversial (originally confidential) memorandum to Washington in April 1991. "Mexico is in the process of changing the substance and image of its foreign policy," he wrote to Bernard Aronson, the assistant secretary for inter-American affairs: "It has switched from an ideological, nationalistic and protectionist approach to a pragmatic, outreaching and competitive view of world affairs. . . . The proposal for an FTA is in a way the capstone of these new policy approaches. *From a foreign policy perspective, an FTA would institutionalize acceptance of a North American orientation to Mexico's foreign relations*" (emphasis added). That Negroponte made this statement does not necessarily mean that it is correct. But it does, at the least, convey a sense of expectations within the U.S. government.

On the other side, Mexico was seeking, first and foremost, preservation of its social peace. The hope was that NAFTA would attract investment, stimulate employment, and provide meaningful opportunity for the one million persons entering the job market every year. This would alleviate poverty, reduce social tension, and perpetuate the country's political regime. In this sense the goal of the PRI was thoroughly compatible with Washington's desire to prolong stability in Mexico.

Second, NAFTA offered President Carlos Salinas de Gortari an opportunity to institutionalize and perpetuate his economic reforms. Under his leadership Mexico had taken aggressive steps in accordance with (if not in response to) the Washington consensus—liberalizing trade, privatizing the parastatal sector, encouraging foreign investment, redefining the role of the state. Such policies were threatening to long-established interests in Mexico and caused a good deal of resentment. In order to preserve his innovations, Salinas wanted to insulate them from the historic vagaries of presidential succession, which permitted each new chief executive to reverse or ignore predecessor policies. Under NAFTA, however, the Salinista program of "structural readjustment" now became part of an international treaty—one that was subscribed to by the world's only remaining superpower. These circumstances would sharply narrow the plausible range of choice for opponents of this model and for Salinas' successors. With NAFTA, the Salinista reforms were cast in bronze.

Third, Mexico was seeking international benediction for its not-quite-democratic political regime. Such acceptance was especially important because, in comparison with Argentina, Chile, Brazil, and other countries undergoing processes of "democratization," Mexico no longer looked like a paragon of political civility. Prospects for democratization in Mexico became a matter of prominent debate.[5] Skeptics insisted that NAFTA would strengthen and consolidate Mexico's authoritarian system. Advocates maintained that NAFTA would promote democracy by unleashing social forces that would ultimately lay the foundation for democratic development in Mexico. According to this logic, the Mexican political regime deserved approbation not because of its authoritarian present but because of its democratic future. Mexico was seeking legitimation through anticipation.

Finally, Mexico believed that NAFTA would provide the country with diplomatic leverage vis-à-vis the rest of Latin America and, by extension, the Third World as a whole. Association with Canada and the United States would link Mexico with advanced industrial democracies and leaders of the "first world." Consequently Mexico could serve as a "bridge" between the developing world and the developed world, as a representative and interlocutor for aspiring peoples of the South. The negotiation of NAFTA prompted some analysts to charge that Mexico was turning its back on Latin America and the Third World. The assumption in Mexico City, however, was that NAFTA would in the long run strengthen Mexico's diplomatic and political prestige.

All these calculations were suddenly upset. On January 1, 1994—the day that NAFTA went into effect—a guerrilla movement in the poverty-stricken state of Chiapas rose up to denounce the free trade accord, the Salinista economic model, and the undemocratic character of the political regime. With colorful and able leadership, the Zapatista National Liberation Army (EZLN) captured national and international attention during the course of highly publicized negotiations with governmental authorities. On March 17 an assassin's bullet struck down Luis Donaldo Colosio, Salinas' handpicked successor and the presidential candidate of the PRI.

Salinas hastily chose another candidate, the forty-two-year-old Ernesto Zedillo Ponce de León, who scurried to develop a credible campaign for the upcoming August election. And on September 28 another shooting took the life of José Francisco Ruiz Massieu, the number-two leader of the PRI and one of Zedillo's most trusted political allies.

These shocking developments inflicted a devastating blow to Mexico's international image. Mexico could no longer be seen as an up-and-coming country on the brink of joining the first world; it looked, instead, like a Third World society threatening to come apart at the seams. Had these events occurred before the U.S. Congress voted on NAFTA, most analysts agreed, the pact would have faced certain rejection.

Under these new and tragic circumstances, NAFTA confronted a highly uncertain future. Some reassurance came from the August 1994 presidential elections, by all accounts the cleanest in Mexican history, in which Zedillo triumphed with 48.8 percent of the vote (compared with 26.0 percent for the rightist PAN and only 16.6 percent for the populist PRD).[6] Zedillo's capacity to govern still remained open to doubt: within a month of taking office he would be severely tested by a renewal of tensions in Chiapas, a collapse of confidence among investors, and a precipitous decline in the dollar value of the peso. Despite the popular mandate for continuity, Mexico seemed to be in the midst of major change.

From NAFTA to WHFTA?

Also unclear were the prospects for creation of a free trade zone embracing all of the Americas. Almost from the beginning, NAFTA was envisioned not only as a three-way partnership but also as the stepping-stone toward a hemispheric accord (soon nicknamed WHFTA, for Western Hemisphere Free Trade Area). As George Bush proclaimed when launching the Enterprise for the Americas Initiative in June 1990, the ultimate goal was to be a free trade zone "stretching from the port of Anchorage to the Tierra del Fuego." Bush and later Bill Clinton announced that the process of expansion would commence with Chile. And in December 1993 Vice President Gore pronounced his vision of "a Western Hemisphere Community of Democracies" that would consolidate political and economic harmony throughout the region, with NAFTA as "a starting point." Eager to gain access to this privileged circle, Latin American leaders came to regard eventual accession to NAFTA as a key part of their development strategy. Expectations were soon running high.

The question was whether they might be fulfilled. The United States had substantial interests in the region, in both investment and trade, and many analysts were predicting that the Latin American market had potential for high rates of expansion. Latin America, for its part, wanted a WHFTA as a quid pro quo for major transformations in development strategies. In keeping with the Washington consensus, countries of the region were lowering barriers to trade, privatizing state-owned companies, promoting foreign investment, and reshaping the role of the state. It was not clear whether governments were undertaking these changes on the basis of unilateral and voluntary decisions or in response to pressure from the international community; in either case, they had reason to want something in return. A WHFTA would enable them to achieve some degree of commercial reciprocity on the part of the United States, thus assuring access to the North American market. More important, accession to WHFTA would provide new members with an internationally recognized seal of approval as suitable sites for foreign investment.

Creation of a WHFTA could occur in various ways. One possibility would be for countries of the Americas to enter NAFTA directly through accession: if NAFTA eventually were to include all countries of the hemisphere, it would automatically become a WHFTA. A second means would be for the United States (or Mexico) to form a series of "hub-and-spoke" arrangements with Latin American countries which could ultimately lead to integration of the region by "filling in the rims." A third possibility would be for Latin American countries to accelerate their own processes of subregional integration (MERCOSUR, the Andean Pact, etc.) so these groupings could then negotiate free-trade agreements with NAFTA. There was more than one route to a WHFTA.

Yet formation of WHFTA faced formidable obstacles, both economic and political. The commercial rationale was much less compelling than in the case of NAFTA. As shown in chapter 9, trade relations between the United States and Latin America *outside of Mexico* were declining in importance to the United States over time. Moreover, a WHFTA could result in substantial trade diversion, especially for countries of South America (most notably Brazil).

Institutional and political impediments seemed even more compelling than economic factors. In final form, NAFTA did not establish criteria for admission. In a deliberately uninformative accession clause, the treaty simply held that new countries may join NAFTA "subject to such terms and conditions as may be agreed" by the member countries, and "following approval in accordance with the applicable approval procedures in each country." This vague language meant that member countries retained the right to establish arbitrary or impossible accession criteria if they so chose—and that it would take considerable time to develop any criteria at all. One especially difficult question was whether admission would be restricted to "democratic" states, in which case there would have to be serious and significant provisions for oversight. This was of course greatly complicated by the fact that a founding member of NAFTA was Mexico, which had one of the most durable nondemocratic regimes in the Americas; democracy as a criterion for accession to NAFTA by other countries would thus appear to set a double standard.

Any expansion of NAFTA would have to be in the interests of all the member states, of course, as well as in the interests of the applicants. In this respect the interests of NAFTA partners appeared to be ambiguous.

Canada had resisted negotiations with Mexico in the first place, and was unlikely to welcome the accession of still more Latin American countries. The United States might regard expansion of NAFTA as a means of consolidating economic and political influence—and of gaining access to new markets—but would have to balance these advantages against potentially negative impacts on relations with Europe and Japan. Mexico presumably wanted to be the only NAFTA-approved site in Latin America for foreign investment, and would therefore oppose new accessions (admission of new members from the region would also dilute Mexico's political status as a unique interlocutor between Latin America and the United States). Decisions on accession would have to be unanimous, at any rate, which meant that each of the three member countries was in possession of a veto. And it seemed most doubtful that, in the wake of the Chiapas uprising and the Colosio/Ruiz Massieu assassinations, either Washington or Ottawa would be eager to expand the risks associated with new membership.

Finally, and perhaps most fundamentally, WHFTA lacked clear political motivation. As explained, NAFTA had the makings of a credible political bargain; WHFTA did not. Geopolitical motivation could come about in response to major events, realignments, or developments in the international arena, but it was not apparent by the mid-1990s. This weakness constituted a major obstacle. Without strong political motivation, there could be no lasting integration.

Environmental Protection

The free trade movement in the Americas coincided with the emergence of a global movement on behalf of the environment. Ecological disasters such as the meltdown of nuclear reactors at Ukraine's Chernobyl, in April 1986, and the *Exxon Valdez* oil spill in Alaska's Prince William Sound, in March 1989, captured worldwide headlines and provoked expressions of popular outrage. From Europe to the United States to Latin America, there emerged citizens' public interest groups with the avowed intent of bringing a halt to environmental degradation. The international community took up the cause, and by the early 1990s a broad array of institutions claimed a role in "correcting" environmental abuses throughout the Third World.

Hemispheric Challenges

Rising awareness about the environment led to the inescapable conclusion that, especially during the twentieth century, economic development wrought havoc with the planet Earth. One of the most startling realizations concerned depletion of the ozone layer. Damage came from the release of gases reacting aggressively to destroy ozone molecules that accumulate in the stratosphere and establish a protective shield that absorbs a large part of the sun's ultraviolet rays. By the early 1990s scientists could

confirm a 50 percent erosion of the ozone layer over the Antarctic, a hole
that covered about 10 percent of the Southern Hemisphere. The resulting
penetration of ultraviolet rays would increase the frequency of skin cancer
and cataracts, inflict harm on algae and microscopic marine animals that
make up basic food for the fish population, and have negative effects on
land plants, including major crops. The source of this problem was the
industrialized world, which produced 95 percent of the gases—known as
chlorofluorocarbons (CFCs) and halons—responsible for the destruction
of ozone molecules. (CFCs were used as aerosol propellants, refrigerants,
and solvents, and in the manufacture of plastic foams; halons for fire
extinguishers.) Prosperous countries were also the largest users of CFCs:
with only 5 percent of the world's population the United States alone
accounted for 29 percent of consumption.

Of more immediate relevance to the inter-American agenda was the
threat of "global warming," which occurs as the earth's atmosphere traps
more and more gases—mainly carbon dioxide from fossil fuels (coal and
oil) but also natural gas, nitrous oxide, and the ubiquitous CFCs. Creating
a "greenhouse effect," the resultant canopy of gas causes the atmosphere to
reflect heat back to the earth's surface rather than allowing it to escape.
Experts predicted that gas accumulations could, in consequence, produce
an increase in the global mean temperature of three to eight degrees Fahr-
enheit during the twenty-first century, a fundamental climate change
which could (by melting glaciers) raise sea levels by as much as two feet.
This would lead to coastal flooding, which, in turn, would cause enormous
damage to the United States and other countries; it could totally engulf
some small low-lying island states, causing them literally to disappear from
the map; and it would provoke massive human displacement and suffering
in such nations as Bangladesh, India, China, Indonesia, and Egypt.

One significant source of global warming was deforestation, which
contributed approximately 14 percent of the overall effect. On average, 17
million hectares of tropical forests (an area equivalent to Virginia plus
West Virginia) disappeared every year between 1981 and 1990. Deforestation resulted from transient cultivation by subsistence farmers and use of
wood for fuel and, more importantly, from the inroads of commercial
logging, cattle ranching, road construction, and permanent agriculture and
colonization schemes. Clearing was done mainly by burning, rather than
cutting, which poured millions of tons of carbon dioxide into the world's
atmosphere. Despoliation of forests was especially flagrant in Latin
America, which accounted for 40 percent of net carbon emissions from this
process.

Deforestation had a devastating impact on biodiversity. Forests covered only one-sixteenth of the earth's surface but held 50 to 90 percent of
the world's plant and animal species, which may range from 5 million to
100 million. Largely as a result of deforestation, 100 species were becoming extinct every single day of the year. This destroyed genetic material
essential for industrial, agricultural, and especially pharmaceutical pro-

cesses and goods. Concern focused in large part on Latin America because five of the world's "ecologically mega-diverse" countries were located in the region: Brazil, Colombia, Mexico, Peru, and Ecuador.

Deforestation in Brazil became an international cause célèbre. Of special concern was the Amazon River Basin, host to the world's largest tropical rain forest. To promote economic development (and to alleviate poverty) the Brazilian government encouraged migration to the region by constructing a TransAmazon highway and by offering tax relief, production subsidies, and titles to free or inexpensive land. Between 1975 and 1987 over 3 million hectares of tropical forest, roughly equivalent in size to the state of Maine, went up in flames. At this rate, according to one forecast, about 15 percent of the world's plant species would be forever lost by the end of the century. Moreover, surveys revealed that over half the cleared land was used for raising beef cattle on large-scale farms, not for small-scale agriculture. Invasion of the Amazon also led to the forcible displacement of indigenous peoples, which prompted denunciations of human-rights violations, and resulted in the highly publicized assassination in 1988 of Chico Mendes, who had championed the rights of local rubber tappers against the demands of speculators and ranchers. For a whole host of reasons, environmentalists and activists heaped near-universal scorn on Brazil's mismanagement of its precious natural resource.

Some arguments about the Amazon employed bodily metaphors. One maintained that it served as the world's "lungs," generating a significant share of the global supply of oxygen; Brazilians insisted that there was no factual basis for this claim, however, since the forest consumed practically all the oxygen it produced. A second contention held that the Amazon functioned as a kind of global "kidney," inhaling impurities from the atmosphere and recycling them back into nature; deforestation thus reduced the earth's capacity to absorb pollution. Implicitly, both analogies suggested that the Amazon was of legitimate concern to the world as a whole; appealing to national sovereignty, Brazilians claimed that it belonged to them.

Environmental degradation affected Latin America in numerous ways. Carbon dioxide emissions from automobiles, industrial waste, acid rain, and lack of sanitation and social services posed palpable threats to public health throughout the region, especially in such major metropolises as Mexico City, São Paulo, and Santiago de Chile. In rural areas overexploitation of land was leading to rapid desertification through erosion of soil and loss of fertility. By the 1990s approximately 70 percent of the productive arid lands of South America and Mexico had suffered desertification. Agricultural production relied upon excessive use of fertilizer and pesticides derived from fossil fuels, which were often harmful to human health as well as to the soil. About 75 percent of the pesticides used in Central America were either prohibited or restricted in the United States.

In summary, the Western Hemisphere faced four broad types of environmental challenge by the early 1990s. One consisted of problems affecting the entire world, such as depletion of the ozone layer, caused almost entirely by the industrialized countries. The second consisted of worldwide problems, such as global warming, caused partly by Latin America but more so by the United States. The third consisted of bilateral problems, such as cross-border pollution, caused mainly by Latin America (though often as a result of joint undertakings with the United States). The fourth consisted of continental problems, such as air pollution, caused largely by economic activity and public policy within Latin America itself.

The United States became concerned about environmental devastation in Latin America during the 1980s for a simple reason: because environmental abuse in Latin America could cause harm to the United States. Depletion of the ozone layer, global warming from the greenhouse effect, and the loss of biodiversity threatened the United States as much as other countries. Moreover, the proximity of Latin America to the United States meant that there could be spillover effects, especially across the U.S.–Mexican border. While a good deal of international discourse spoke loftily about common purpose and global community, one underlying fact was apparent: the United States perceived a matter of national interest.

North-South Tensions and the Rio Summit

Environmental issues provoked substantial controversy and, particularly, differences in outlook between the industrialized countries of the North and the developing countries of the South. The lack of scientific consensus on a number of key questions, such as the likely rate of global warming or the precise role of CFCs, only added to the intensity of these debates. Disagreements centered around three sets of closely related concerns: definition of the global agenda, the assignment of responsibility, and the prescription of remedies.

Each side wanted to place its own concerns at the top of the international agenda and to blame the other for its contribution to environmental deterioration. The North was eager to talk about species extinction and climate change, especially ozone thinning and global warming. The North thus tended to focus on such issues as the destruction of the Amazon rain forest and also stressed imminent dangers from the potential role of the South in *future* patterns of degradation, as from industrial expansion in China, India, or Brazil. The North was particularly inclined to call for population control—meaning, of course, population control in the Third World. Projections showed that the world's population, around 5.5 billion in 1990, was likely to reach 8.5 billion by 2025 and 10 billion by 2050. In quasi-Malthusian fashion, analysts warned that this kind of demographic explosion would place impossible demands on the earth's supply of natural resources. Particularly disturbing, in their view, was the fact that so much of this growth would take place in less developed countries of the world. On occasion these alarms took on a racist tinge.

The South strove to discuss water pollution, air pollution, and the degradation of agricultural lands. Threats to the planet came not from the

South's population but from excessive consumption by the industrial countries. With only 26 percent of the world's population, spokesmen for the South observed, developed countries consumed 80 percent of the world's commercial energy, 79 percent of its steel, 86 percent of other metals, and 85 percent of its paper. The United States alone emitted more than one-fifth of the world's carbon dioxide in 1989, and advanced industrial countries together produced nearly one-half the total. By contrast Latin America, despite its abuse of tropical forests and its fondness for automobiles, contributed only 13 to 14 percent of total carbon dioxide emissions. By every conceivable measure, the North had done much more to cause problems of ozone depletion and global warming than had the South.

The basic problem for the Third World was not its people, spokesmen insisted, but its poverty. "For the majority of the world population," declared a Brazilian official in the early 1970s, "the betterment of conditions is much more a question of mitigating poverty, counting on more food, better clothing, housing, medical assistance, and employment, than seeing atmospheric pollution reduced." It was callous and misleading to compare "luxury emissions" in the North with "survival emissions" from the South. Snorted a representative from India: "The wealthy worry about car fumes; we worry about starvation."

Many Latin Americans identified the debt crisis of the 1980s as a critical reason for environmental abuse. Insistence on debt service and the consequent transfer of more than $200 billion to international creditors placed excruciating demands on the region's economies. In response Latin American countries desperately sought to increase exports, and this resulted in overexploitation of resources. According to this argument, debt alleviation was essential for dealing with environmental problems.

Seeking to reconcile views of North and South, the UN's World Commission on Environment and Development in 1987 articulated the notion of what it called "sustainable development," defined as economic development that "meets the needs of the present without compromising the ability of future generations to meet their own needs."[7] It should be possible, in other words, to reconcile economic development with environmental responsibility. In practice, however, the principle of "sustainable development" was subject to a vast array of definitions.[8]

Not surprisingly, the differing viewpoints of North and South led to different prescriptions for remedies—and different financial obligations. Often condescendingly, the North opined that countries of the developing world could fund their own efforts at environmental protection by reallocating resources—by reducing military expenditures, by privatizing public enterprises, by rooting out corruption, by revising economic priorities in line with the Washington consensus, and by "improved governance in general." The South responded by charging that a long history of heedless development and predatory resource exploitation on the part of the North meant that "the industrialized countries have incurred an ecological debt with the world." It was not for poor nations to bear the costs of correcting problems they did not create. That was up to the North. After all, polluters ought to pay.

In view of these disagreements, many observers anticipated that the June 1992 UN Conference on Environment and Development in Rio de Janeiro would deteriorate into a bitter clash of North and South. Indeed, this "Earth Summit" proved to be the largest international conference ever held—with more than 100 heads of state or government in attendance, 8,000 delegates, 9,000 members of the press, and 3,000 accredited representatives of nongovernmental organizations (NGOs). The conference approved several charters, including some nonbinding statements of principle, but its central task was the adoption of Agenda 21, a comprehensive action plan to guide the policies of governments for the remainder of this century and the next. With 40 chapters covering 115 program areas in more than 400 pages of text, Agenda 21 spanned a broad range of environment and development issues—from atmosphere, soil, forests, and oceans to population, consumption, toxic and solid fuel disposal, technology transfer, and financing. Its purpose was to forge a partnership between developed and developing countries in search of "sustainable development." Its central premise was that alleviation of poverty in poor countries *and* changes in consumption patterns in rich countries would be required in order to achieve this goal.

Agenda 21 ran into difficulty, however, partly because all decisions required complete consensus (among the 178 countries in attendance). In one area after another, small coalitions vetoed or diluted key provisions. Saudi Arabia, Kuwait, Iran, and other members of OPEC watered down references to energy taxes and renewable energy sources. The Holy See, Argentina, Ireland, and Colombia eliminated the population chapter's references to family planning and contraceptives. But the anticipated North-South standoff failed to materialize. While the Group of 77 (G-77) (now 129 countries) continued to represent the Third World, it accepted many moderate positions. Latin American countries on the whole exercised a mellowing influence within the G-77, and Brazil acted as a skillful and gracious host. One factor behind the relatively cooperative stand of the South may have been the collapse of the Soviet-led bloc, whose erstwhile members were now competing with Third World countries for international assistance in order to clean up their own environmental problems.

It was the Biodiversity Convention resulting from the Rio summit that exposed the Bush administration's half-hearted commitment to environmental cooperation. As drafted, the convention had two basic weaknesses: it failed to provide adequate protection for intellectual property rights, and it gave an unacceptable degree of financial control to developing countries (with decisions to be made on the basis of one-nation one-vote, regardless of the magnitude of financial contributions). As head of the U.S. delegation, Environmental Protection Agency director William Reilly cabled Washington in an effort to find a way to approve the accord, but his memorandum was leaked to the press and his position undermined. "For me personally," Reilly later recalled, "it was like a bungee jump. You dive into space secured by a line on your leg and trust it pulls you up before you smash into the ground. It doesn't typically occur to you that someone might cut your line." Adding to Reilly's dismay, the Bush administration refused to accept a binding commitment, embraced by Europe and Japan, to reduce carbon dioxide emissions by the year 2000 to their 1990 levels.

The financing of Agenda 21 presented yet another challenge. Its average annual costs were projected to be $600 billion; $475 billion would come from developing countries but the remaining $125 billion, or 20 percent, would have to be from the developed world. With the current volume of worldwide development assistance around $55 billion, this meant that Agenda 21 required an increase of $70 billion. When the United States refused to make any commitments on aid, G-77 countries pointed out that the additional increment represented a proportional increase in foreign aid from 0.35 percent of GNP to 0.70 percent (precisely the level once envisioned by NIEO and subsequently endorsed by the UN General Assembly; the United States had not only opposed this resolution but proceeded to reduce its foreign aid to only 0.15 percent of GNP). A major confrontation was avoided through intercession by the World Bank, which volunteered to support developing countries in carrying out the UNCED agenda through an annual "earth increment" of about $18 billion to $22 billion for 1993–95. Despite the fragility of its support and its financing, many experts concluded that Agenda 21 represented a workable framework for international collaboration on environmental matters.

NAFTA *and the Environment*

Mounting concern over the compatibility of economic development and environmental protection drew public attention to the relationship between environment and trade. Many analysts maintained that an emphasis on export-oriented development, as promoted by the Washington consensus, would accentuate abuse of natural resources in Latin America. They further insisted that economic liberalization, including privatization and foreign investment, would promote the formation of "pollution havens" (analogous to "tax havens") in countries of the region. In contrast, trade advocates argued that economic opening and international competition would lead to widespread adoption of "clean" technologies and improved production techniques. They also charged that excessive concern for the environment could furnish a transparent disguise for economic protectionism on behalf of selfish interest groups.

The debate intensified in 1991, when the General Agreement on Tariffs and Trade ruled against a U.S. ban on the importation of tuna from Mexico and several other countries whose fishermen used nets that were dangerous for dolphins. Washington pointed out that its action was consistent with its Marine Mammal Protection Act; drawing a distinction between the environmental suitability of a "process" versus that of a "product," however, GATT maintained that the prohibition violated rules of commerce and insisted on its repeal. The ruling heightened anti-GATT sentiment within the environmental community and convinced many observers that trade and environment were essentially incompatible.

This question came to a head during NAFTA negotiations in the early 1990s. As originally drafted, NAFTA made only passing reference to environmental concerns, as in the provision that its member countries "recognize that it is inappropriate to encourage investment by relaxing domestic health, safety or environmental measures." Like GATT, NAFTA was not intended to be an ecological charter, but environmental groups protested that the so-called green language in NAFTA was vague and inadequate. In response, the three NAFTA countries announced in September 1992 the creation of a trilateral commission on environment to assist in implementation of the trade agreement, known as the North American Commission on the Environment (NACE). This body was charged with issuing an annual report and making recommendations on environmental matters, including the sensitive issue of pollution havens. The establishment of NACE proved instrumental in winning support for NAFTA from the National Wildlife Federation, which, with 5.3 million members, was the largest conservation organization in the United States. Even so, the prospects for congressional ratification of NAFTA remained far from clear.

In keeping with his campaign pledge, President Clinton oversaw the initiation of negotiations on a supplementary NAFTA accord on environmental protection in March 1993. In May the U.S. team presented its full offer, which envisioned, first, establishment of a ministerial council and creation of a relatively independent commission with important fact-finding capacities; given the importance of their role, commission members should have diplomatic privileges and immunities to ensure "the independent exercise of their functions." Second, Washington insisted on empowerment for private groups to file submissions and complaints. Third, the Clinton proposal sought to define a NAFTA violation as "a persistent and unjustifiable pattern of non-enforcement" of domestic environmental legislation. Fourth, and perhaps most important, the United States called for the potential use of trade sanctions; if a dispute were not resolved, according to the U.S. formula, "a complaining party may suspend an appropriate level of benefits under NAFTA." Mexico and Canada called for a weaker commission and a less independent secretariat, with no provision for diplomatic immunities or for private petitions; neither wanted trade sanctions.

The key issue centered on sanctions. The Canadian team proposed the levying of fines against offending governments rather than trade sanctions—which, by definition, appeared to violate the very spirit of a "free trade" agreement. And for the enforcement of payment, Canada suggested the use of domestic courts; Mexico staunchly opposed this procedure as an infringement on national sovereignty. Eventually the United

States prevailed upon its partners to agree to the idea of trade sanctions, although Canada managed to retain its form of court-mandated fines (or "assessments") rather than sanctions themselves.

The final accord was, in the words of one observer, "significantly narrower" than the original U.S. position.[9] The environmental secretariat became subordinate to the ministerial council, rather than a truly independent entity, without the power to initiate dispute settlement and sanction procedures; it could still establish a factual record, however, which could become the basis for a complaint by a two-thirds vote of the ministerial council. (Officials of the secretariat were granted diplomatic privileges and immunities, but these seemed less important in view of its less intrusive role.) Private groups were authorized to make submissions, within carefully specified limits, but they could not initiate legal action on their own; they could also press their views before a Commission on Environmental Cooperation (the successor to NACE), an officially recognized forum for lobbying. A violation of standards was ultimately defined as a "persistent pattern of failure . . . to effectively enforce" domestic environmental law. (Even so, the accord explicitly acknowledged the need for "reasonable" discretion in the application of laws, and the starting point for tracing violations would be January 1, 1994, which meant that it would take substantial time to accumulate a record of "persistent" transgression.) Penalties could be imposed on an offending party only by an arbitration panel established by a ministerial decision of two countries out of three, and only after a lengthy and cumbersome quasi-legal process.

It was far from evident what such sanctions would mean. One curious feature was that, if applied, commercial sanctions would actually penalize private producers (and consumers), rather than the governments that had failed to enforce their own laws. Nor were the punishments very strict: the accord established a maximum of $20 million (the first year) or .007 percent of trade (in subsequent years)—with proceeds earmarked for the benefit of the transgressor, since they were to be used "to improve or enhance the environment or environmental law enforcement in the Party complained against, consistent with its law." Only in cases of noncompliance could a country suspend NAFTA benefits to an offending country—by returning to pre-NAFTA or most-favored-nation tariff levels, whichever was the lesser, for a sufficient time to generate the amount of the fine. To paraphrase Bill Clinton, these sanctions did not seem to have a lot of teeth.

The U.S.–Mexican border received special attention as a consequence of NAFTA. The frontier had for decades posed serious environmental hazards, including problems of renegade sewage (mainly from Tijuana toward San Diego), industrial pollution (especially in the "gray triangle" of southern Arizona-northern Sonora), air contamination (as in the twin cities of El Paso and Ciudad Juárez), and water pollution (in rivers and underwater aquifers). To confront these harsh realities the United States and Mexico developed an Integrated Environmental Plan for the U.S.–

Mexico Border Areas, a multiyear program of intensified cooperation under the direction of a Border Environmental Cooperation Commission
(BECC) composed of twenty-four members representing various districts
of the border region. To assist these efforts Mexico committed $460 mil-
lion for border cleanup during 1993–95 and the United States pledged
$379 million. One key question was whether this program would work.
Another concerned hope for potential creation of a precedent: as one U.S.
government memorandum speculated in early 1994, "With its concepts of
private sector involvement, public input and bottom-up project development, should the BECC be a model for application elsewhere in the
Americas?"

Whatever its practical outcome, negotiation of the NAFTA side agreement made one point clear: by the 1990s, trade and environment were
inextricably intertwined. As one analyst has written, these developments
forcefully demonstrated

> that the environment has become a staple of trade politics in the 1990s, for it
> was politically impossible to contemplate the completion of the NAFTA trade
> accord without a complementary agreement on the environment. Thus, trade
> liberalization became dependent on parallel efforts to protect the environ-
> ment. However, it could also be argued that environmental progress became
> dependent on trade liberalization, in that NAFTA focused attention on prob-
> lems such as pollution along the U.S.–Mexico border—problems that would
> have been less visible without a trade agreement.[10]

The terms of debate had thus shifted. Instead of focusing on the potentially
deleterious effects of untrammeled commerce and export promotion, attention now fastened on the potentially constructive consequences of the
government-to-government *negotiation* of free trade agreements.

Whatever else it spawned, the free trade movement had one clear
political consequence: it provided the United States with a new kind of
opportunity to impose its will upon Latin America. As nations of the
region aspired to "free trade" agreements with the United States, or to
membership in NAFTA, Washington could establish suitable environmental policy as a price of admission. And since environmental concerns were
subject to ample definition, leverage on this range of issues could become
intrusive and extensive. In exchange for access to the U.S. market, in other
words, Latin America would have to accede to U.S. demands on the
environmentally related matters that could reach far into realms of domestic public policy.

The Miami Summit

Seeking to capitalize upon the apparent spirit of inter-American harmony
surrounding the new economic agenda, the Clinton adminstration promoted and hosted a grandiose "Summit of the Americas" in the Latinized
city of Miami in December 1994. Attended by thirty-four heads of state,

with the conspicous exception of Cuba's Fidel Castro, this was the first such gathering since 1967, when the United States and Latin America concurred on a stillborn plan for economic integration. The ostensible goal of the Miami summit was to develop a blueprint for hemispheric collaboration into the twenty-first century. An implicit purpose, from Washington's perspective, was to provide assurances that the United States would neither neglect nor abandon Latin American countries outside of Mexico.

As the date of the meeting approached, the U.S. government proposed a complex fourteen-point agenda. Under the Clintonesque rubric of "reinventing government," one set of recommendations called for attacks on corruption and drug trafficking. A second series focused on the strengthening of financial linkages and the promotion of free trade, to be based upon the principles of "open regionalism." And a third category, under the always-elastic label of "sustainable development," envisioned commitments in the areas of public health, education, resource management, and environmental protection—to "reduce environmental problems and negative impacts, promote a level playing field for industries operating in the hemisphere, increase demand for environmental technologies and services, and offer opportunities for public participation in the environmental policy-making." Moreover, the "upward" harmonization of environmental standards in the Americas "would strengthen legal frameworks, enhance environmental compliance and enforcement capacity, and build institutions through technical cooperation, training, and education."

Latin American leaders regarded the Clinton agenda as unfocused, intrusive, and irrelevant. Fearful of possible exclusion from the anticipated benefits of free trade with Canada and the United States, countries other than Mexico were overwhelmingly concerned with questions and anxieties about the terms, timing, and conditions for accession to NAFTA or to some form of WHFTA. They were particularly insistent that the Miami gathering should establish a specific timetable for hemispheric integration. As pressure mounted, the Miami agenda eventually came to focus on a centerpiece: the extension of free trade.

As arranged just prior to the conclave, heads of state accordingly agreed to the formation of FTAA, a Free Trade Area of the Americas (rather than the less mellifluous WHFTA).[11] As a sign of good faith, NAFTA members also invited Chile to commence negotiations on accession. Confidently predicting that FTAA "will stretch from Alaska to Argentina," Clinton boasted that the accord marked "a watershed in the history of the hemisphere." With a combination of amnesia and hyperbole, the American president went on to proclaim "The so-called lost decade of Latin America is a fading memory." With the exception of Cuba, he exulted, the region had "freed itself from dictatorship and debt, and embraced democracy and development."

What happened in fact was that signatories in Miami designated the year 2005 as a deadline for the conclusion of *negotiations* for a free trade area—with implementation to follow in subsequent years. This was an ambiguous result. Advocates hailed the agreement for its high-minded principles and ambitious goals. Skeptics lamented its vagueness and its drawn-out timetable, which meant that official talks could drag on for a decade or more. Complained Gonzalo Sánchez de Losada, the president of Bolivia: "It would be a tragic mistake to engage in a prolonged process where struggling nations with fragile democracies must wait 10, 15, maybe 20 years in an economic purgatory. The cost could be nothing less than the democratic foundations of our countries."

Ironically enough, the principal resistance to the practical realization of an FTAA was likely to come not from Latin America but from the United States. "The fact of the matter," admitted one Clinton aide in Miami, "is that three-quarters of the countries here would join NAFTA tomorrow morning if they could. But we do not think they are ready." And as political scientist Mark B. Rosenberg remarked, "The real pitfalls are the U.S. Congress and the U.S. public. . . . The public is not ready for a free-trade agreement with Latin America. In the post–Cold War environment, they don't understand what the dominant values are. The pace of change is so rapid, and Americans are very insecure." Despite Miami's lofty rhetoric, the road to hemispheric integration was bound to be uneven, difficult, and slow.

11

Illicit Flows and Military Force

The only law the narco-terrorists do not break is the law of supply and demand.

Virgilio Barco (1990)

International migration is ultimately driven by economic realities. Whether "pushed" by untenable conditions in Mexico or "pulled" by opportunities in the United States, workers face an essentially economic decision.

Bilateral Commission on the Future of United States–Mexican Relations (1988)

The risk remains that the United States may intervene anywhere in the world, especially Latin America.

La República, Lima, Peru (1994)

Increasing interdependence between the United States and Latin America greatly broadened the inter-American agenda during the 1980s and 1990s. Human interaction on a routine, day-to-day basis penetrated deeply into both societies. These connections resulted not from governmental initiatives or diplomatic negotiations but from decisions and actions on the part of private citizens. Such linkages arose apart from the state and, in some cases, in spite of the state. In the post–Cold War environment, the resolute persistence of these ties betrayed the continuing inability of governments to exert control over social dimensions of the inter-American relationship.

Outstanding among these issues were drug trafficking and undocumented migration. Both resulted from the interplay of economic forces: drug trafficking responded to consumer demand for hallucinogenic substances; migration reflected the search by labor for employment. Both had visible impacts on the social order in Latin America and the United States. Both were unwelcome to the U.S. government, which declared them to be illegal. In vain, too, Washington sought to establish international regulations in an effort to halt both types of interaction. As frustration mounted, drugs and migration led to calls for military action; eventually, public concern over these issues established rationales for a U.S. invasion of Panama and an armed occupation of Haiti.

Drugs and Drug Trafficking

Commerce in illicit drugs long resisted governmental efforts at control. Despite the public declaration of a "war on drugs," annual sales in the United States in the early 1990s hovered around $50 billion per year. The economic toll from drug abuse and drug-related accidents was approaching $60 billion per year. About 200,000 children were born to drug-dependent mothers every year; nearly half these infants were "crack babies." Meantime the costs of law enforcement were steadily rising, while violence was surging in major cities of America—in Miami, New York, Chicago, Los Angeles, and Washington, D. C.

Dimensions of Demand

The fundamental source of the drug problem, of *narcotráfico* in the Americas, was the presence and power of consumer demand. Demand for drugs was most conspicuous in advanced industrial countries, in Europe and—especially important for Latin America—in the United States. The legal status of specific drugs derived from social convention, not scientific deduction. While the sale and use of tobacco and alcohol were permitted under U.S. law, prohibition was placed on other substances: marijuana, cocaine, heroin, and so-called designer drugs such as phencyclidine (PCP), lysergic acid diethylamide (LSD or "acid"), or methaqualone (Quaalude). As a consequence, the U.S. legal structure declared that two of the world's most harmful and widely used drugs were acceptable while other drugs of varying potency and danger were impermissible.

There was considerable uncertainty about the level and location of consumer demand for illicit drugs in the United States. Government reports estimated the number of users through a periodic survey conducted by the National Institute on Drug Abuse (NIDA), an official agency whose representatives administered a questionnaire to willing respondents about drug use by household members. Resulting data showed a substantial decline in the number of current users (defined as those who had taken drugs within the past thirty days) from over 24 million in 1979 to 12.9 million in 1990 and 11.4 million in 1992. This implied a drop of more than 50 percent in overall drug usage. Current users of marijuana, by far the most popular of the illicit drugs, declined from over 18 million in 1985 to just 9 million in 1992. Past-month users of cocaine followed a similar trend, dropping from 5.8 million in 1985 to 1.3 million in 1992 (Table A13). Casual drug usage was apparently declining within the American middle class, especially the white suburban middle class. Judged by these standards, the "war on drugs" would appear to have been a success.

At the same time, levels of hard-core addiction were holding fast. While past-month users of cocaine dropped off sharply from the mid-1980s to the early 1990s, according to the NIDA surveys, the estimated number of weekly users held steady at 600,000 or so. Other studies estimated the number of heavy users of cocaine around 2 million, with a slight rise from 1990 to 1991, while the number of emergency-room visits for cocaine-related problems climbed to record heights in 1992.[1] In the meantime heroin was regaining popularity as a drug of choice. The NIDA results estimated the population ever to have used heroin around 2 million; more refined studies calculated the number of casual users of heroin around 380,000 in 1991 and the number of heavy users around 590,000, up from 515,000 just the previous year. And among the teenage population, the overall number of drug users declined from 4.1 million in 1979, at which time nearly 40 percent of graduating seniors acknowledged current use of illicit substances, to just 1.3 million in 1992. By 1994, however, drug use among high-school seniors was reported to be on the rise, with LSD and cocaine regaining popularity.

Drug traffic was also reaching markets in other parts of the world. A U.S. government report painted a somber picture in early 1994: "Multiton shipments of cocaine, which once flowed mainly to the United States and Canada, now reach every corner of the globe. All major European capitals report a growing influx of the drug, with Russian authorities seizing over a metric ton of Colombian cocaine in St. Petersburg alone. No place seems exempt. The heroin situation is no more reassuring. The drug which cocaine displaced in the 1980s is making a comeback everywhere." Despite government efforts and publicity campaigns, the worldwide market was thriving.

Sources of Supply

Over the years, especially during the 1970s and 1980s, the United States consistently promoted attempts to suppress the production of illicit drugs throughout the hemisphere. In pursuit of this goal the U.S. government advocated two approaches: first, elimination of the sources of supply, by destroying crops and laboratory facilities; second, interdiction of shipments bound for the U.S. market, by conducting surveillance at the border and on the high seas. The idea was to reduce the flow of illicit drugs into the United States, drive prices upward, harass the traffickers, discourage consumption, and push the users out of the market.

During the 1980s public concern over drug abuse and drug-related violence mounted steadily until, characteristically enough, the Reagan/

Bush administrations chose to declare a "war" on drugs. At stake was not only the health of U.S. citizens. According to William J. Bennett, head of the Office of National Drug Control Policy, it was a matter of national sovereignty:

> The source of the most dangerous drugs threatening our nation is principally international. Few foreign threats are more costly to the U.S. economy. None does more damage to our national values and institutions and destroys more American lives. While most international threats are potential, the damage and violence caused by the drug trade are actual and pervasive. Drugs are a major threat to our national security.

Thus draped in the banner of "national security," U.S. international policy on drugs justified its long-standing emphasis on supply control.

Almost by definition, this strategy focused mainly on Latin America. Countries of the region produced or transshipped over 80 percent of the cocaine and 90 percent of the marijuana that entered the United States. (It is to be observed that the United States produced at least one-third of the marijuana consumed in the United States by the early 1990s, and became one of the world's leading producers of methamphetamines and designer drugs.) In particular, the concern with cocaine prompted U.S. authorities to devote special attention toward coca leaf production in nations of the Andes—Bolivia, Peru, Colombia, and Ecuador to a lesser extent—and toward the processing and trafficking "cartels" residing in Colombia.

By official U.S. estimates, coca leaf production nonetheless continued to increase (Table A14). Output grew from 291,100 metric tons in 1987 to more than 305,000 metric tons in 1990 and over 333,000 in 1992; a subsequent drop in 1993 occurred largely because of a natural fungus in Peru, not as a result of policy, and there was every reason to believe that production would soon recuperate. Partly because of expanding output within the United States, marijuana cultivation in Latin America underwent a cyclical pattern, rising from 1987 to 1990 and then falling back by 1993 to just under 15,000 metric tons. Meantime the production of heroin was picking up throughout the region. While the world's largest source of opium remained the "Golden Triangle" (Thailand, Laos, and Myanmar), Latin American entrepreneurs moved quickly into the burgeoning U.S. market. Producing high-quality heroin at relatively low prices, the Colombian cartels suddenly began to offer stiff competition to their Asian counterparts.

Eradication campaigns had substantial effect on marijuana but almost no consequential impact on cocaine. During 1992 an estimated 217,808 hectares of land were devoted to coca leaf production; only 6,108 hectares—less than 3 percent of the total—were actually eradicated. In 1993 less than 2 percent of coca leaf crops were eradicated. Nor did seizures make much difference in availability. In 1991, for instance, Latin American authorities seized a record-setting level of nearly 200 metric tons of potential cocaine products, but the total available for export was still over 700 metric tons, just about the same as in previous years. Of this amount perhaps 400 to 500 metric tons were shipped to the United States, where federal officials confiscated more than 100 additional metric tons, leaving the total available for consumption between 274 metric tons and 442 metric tons—much the same quantity as in prior years, and at much the same retail prices. In anticipation of eradication and interdiction campaigns, producers simply stepped up their output.

The allocation of profits varied according to distribution channels for each product. Earnings from cocaine and heroin tended to be concentrated in the hands of the cartels; profits from marijuana and designer drugs were more dispersed. Such patterns underscored key features of the trafficking phenomenon. First, economic values of drug shipments correlated with perceived levels of risk, which in turn responded to the likelihood of law enforcement. Second, most of the profits stayed in the hands of distributors, of middlemen, rather than the producers. Third, the largest share of profits accrued not in Latin America but at the retail end of the market, suggesting that a great deal of drug money stayed in the United States. For this reason money laundering became a central issue, especially in the United States.

Finally, trafficking and distribution routes became extremely flexible. In response to new obstacles or opportunities, traffickers switched routes from one country to another, or from one form of transportation to another. Increased risk of apprehension in the Caribbean led the Colombian cartels to move transit routes from Florida to Mexico. During much of the 1980s substantial shipments entered the United States on low-flying aircraft using clandestine landing strips. Distributors were making frequent use of elaborate hiding devices (such as hollowed-out lumber), of cargo containers, and, in many cases, of individual "swallowers" traveling on international airlines with stashes inside their body, often in condoms filled with cocaine or heroin. In this form there appeared, early in the 1990s, a "Nigerian connection" for heroin traffic, while newly independent Russia became a rising entrepôt for the distribution of heroin from the Golden Crescent (Afghanistan, Iran, Pakistan) through Eurasia to western Europe and beyond. Transit routes and new cartels could thus emerge almost overnight.

Policies and Wars

The United States devoted massive resources to its war on drugs. In the international arena, U.S. policy stressed the control of supply, especially through (1) suppression of production, including crop eradication, (2) interdiction of shipments, especially at the U.S. border, and (3) encouragement for other nations to join in these efforts, usually through bilateral arrangements but also through multilateral treaties. On the domestic front U.S. efforts emphasized law enforcement, including the incarceration of illicit drug users. (Partly as a result, the United States came to have the highest rate of incarceration in the world; by 1992 nearly 60 percent of federal prisoners were drug offenders.)[2] Demand reduction—through education and treatment—received much less attention than application of the law. As political pressure continued to mount, so did federal expenditures—the annual drug control budget climbed from $4.7 billion in 1988 to nearly $12 billion in 1992. Together, the Reagan and Bush administrations spent nearly $65 billion in support of these strategies.

More than a year after taking office, the Clinton administration announced its general antidrug policy in early 1994. The plan called for a record-high budget of $13.2 billion in fiscal year 1995. Drug policy director Lee Brown proposed a slight revision in spending priorities, targeting just 59 percent for supply control and 41 percent for demand reduction— the first time that demand control activities received 40 percent or more of the budget. Domestically, Brown expressed special concern for hard-core users in the inner cities and pledged to provide more education and treatment. Internationally, the Clinton program placed less emphasis on interdiction of drugs, except along the U.S.–Mexican border, and instead planned to move directly against the cartels (without indicating how this would be done). One of the most significant changes came at the rhetorical level: instead of depicting drug abuse as the result of moral failure, Brown and his associates interpreted inner-city drug addiction as a response to poverty and hopelessness.

Despite this shift in emphasis, the Clinton policy provoked persistent tension with Latin American governments. Washington expressed continual frustration with the government of Alberto Fujimori in Peru, which refused to conduct eradication campaigns against peasant growers in the Andes, and occasional frustration with the government of César Gaviria in Colombia, which negotiated terms of amnesty with leading drug entrepreneurs. Yet the Clinton planners clearly recognized the existence of a dilemma: "how to encourage the political leadership in economically troubled countries to give up the vast revenue from a lucrative but illegal industry in exchange for limited foreign assistance, international recognition that it has made the right choice, and the promise of future benefits for a drug-free society." Quite simply, Latin American leaders had little to gain—and a great deal to lose—from acceptance of the U.S. line on drugs.

In actual practice, antidrug policies produced complex and contradictory results. In the United States, repeated public declaration of a "war" on drugs led to demands for "total victory" (whatever that might be), it encouraged calls for enlistment of the military, and it often led to ostracism of those who disagreed with governmental policy—as though their patriotism and/or sanity were in question. In Latin America, campaigns of repression erupted in organized violence between armed groups, including the military and the police. To provide a sense of this complexity, Table 2 outlines seven simultaneous kinds of drug wars waged throughout the region in the 1980s and 1990s.[3] In the first, the United States took on drug suppliers in one way or another, most conspicuously through agents

Table 2. Drug Wars in Latin America

Conflict	Combatants
War No. 1	United States versus suppliers
War No. 2	Latin American governments versus narcoterrorists
War No. 3	Latin American governments versus guerrillas
War No. 4	Latin American governments versus narcotraffickers
War No. 5	Narcotraffickers versus narcotraffickers
War No. 6	Narcotraffickers versus guerrillas
War No. 7	Narcotraffickers versus political left

Source: Reprinted from *Drug Policy in the Americas,* Peter H. Smith (ed.), 1992, by permission of Westview Press, Boulder, Colorado.

of the Drug Enforcement Administration. In the second, Latin American governments responded to challenges by "narcoterrorists," agents of drug cartels who used terror, violence, and intimidation to assert raw political power. (This was most apparent in Colombia, where the government achieved a major political victory by killing Medellín kingpin Pablo Escobar in December 1993.) In the third drug war, Latin American governments engaged in struggles with armed guerrilla movements that formed unholy alliances with traffickers. In the fourth, Latin American governments waged armed campaigns against narcotraffickers—those who produced and exported illicit drugs but did not engage in systematic political terrorism. In the fifth war, drug cartels fought among themselves, usually over market share. This explained much of the violence in Colombia, where Escobar's former associates played a major role in exposing him to government authorities, and also in the cities of America, where rival distributors waged campaigns of attrition against one another. In the sixth confrontation, drug traffickers engaged in conflict with their sometime allies, armed guerrilla groups; this often occurred once the *traficantes* began to use their profits to purchase land and join the socioeconomic establishment—against which the guerrillas had taken arms in the first place. In the seventh and last kind of war, unique to Colombia in the 1980s, *narcotraficantes* declared war against political opponents, in this case left-wing parties. For the most part, however, drug operations obeyed no single ideology.

The diversity in drug wars underlined the range and variability of interests involved in public policy. The "drug problem" in Colombia was markedly different from the "drug problem" in Peru, Bolivia, or Mexico (not to mention the United States). Also striking was the ubiquity of unintended consequences. Colombia's crackdown on the Medellín cartel produced a temporary decline in the price of coca leaf in Peru and Bolivia; instead of enticing coca producers to turn to cultivation of licit crops, however, it encouraged them to process their products (thus increasing value-added) and to export coca base instead of coca leaves. In this fashion, a "success" in the Colombian drug war could exacerbate the problem in Bolivia—or in other neighboring countries. Indeed, it appears that the

Colombian crackdown accelerated the dispersion of drug-trafficking activities throughout the continent, from Chile and Argentina to Costa Rica
and Belize, especially as transit routes and as sites for money laundering.
"Latin America as a whole is sliding into the drug war," said one well-
informed observer in the early 1990s. "Argentina and Brazil can see their
future in Bolivia. Bolivia sees its own [future] in Peru, Peru in Colombia,
and Colombia in Lebanon. It's an endless cycle."

Although the U.S.-sponsored drug wars failed to achieve the goals of
reducing supply and raising prices for illicit drugs in the American market,
they had serious effects on Latin American society and politics. First, they
subjected the countries and peoples of the region to staggering levels of
violence and intimidation—not only in Colombia, but also in Peru and
Mexico, where antidrug campaigns produced large-scale violations of human rights. Second, the drug wars exposed national institutions to corruption. One of the lessons of antidrug campaigns, around the world, was that
law-enforcement agencies risked corruption by drug traffickers and lords;
increased contact with *traficantes,* even in an adversarial manner, increased
the possibility of compromise and subversion. Third, prosecution of the
drug wars placed increasing autonomy and authority in the hands of the
Latin American armed forces. Drug wars encouraged militarization. This
could pose a substantial threat to still-fragile democracies throughout the
region.

Finally, the drug wars created major complications for U.S.–Latin
American relations. For reasons of its own, the United States strongly
encouraged Latin American governments to enlist in the antidrug wars.
And Latin American leaders responded, but for differing reasons. Sometimes, as in the case of Bolivia, they were reluctant to precipitate what they
regarded as all-out wars against the peasantry. Sometimes, as in the case of
Colombia, they reacted to challenges from drug cartels with considerable
force—but even then, *they were not waging the same war that the United
States was advocating.* The U.S. government was asking Latin American
governments to join ranks in a war against the narcotraffickers, and thus to
forge an alliance with the United States. (In terms of Table 2, this would
mean a combination of War No. 1, waged by the United States, with War
No. 4, to be waged by Latin America.) But as successive Colombian
presidents have shown, the concern in Colombia was not so much with
narcotraffic as with narcoterror (War No. 2 in Table 2). This challenge
entailed different purposes, strategies, and policies. Such incongruity in
antidrug campaigns not only led to confusion. It also led to missed opportunities and, in one conspicuous instance, it helped provoke armed conflict
between governments.

Panama: Operation Just Cause

Panama seemed an improbable place for a U.S. invasion. The country
owed its very existence to pressure from the United States, which in 1903

openly promoted a secessionist rebellion against the government of Colombia in order to acquire a site for construction of a transisthmian waterway. Universally hailed as an engineering miracle, the Panama Canal immediately became a major economic and political asset for the United States. The original treaty established U.S. control of the canal and its associated Zone "in perpetuity"; under President Jimmy Carter, negotiations led to an agreement for a gradual transfer of the canal to Panama by the end of the year 1999. To uphold its position, to protect the canal, and to project U.S. power throughout the surrounding region, the Pentagon located the headquarters for its Southern Command within the Zone. United States influence permeated virtually every layer of Panamanian society and politics. With a population in the late 1980s of 2.4 million and a military force of 14,000, Panama seemed unlikely to pose a legitimate threat to U.S. interests.

Moreover the country's political strongman, Manuel Antonio Noriega, had close links with the United States. A protegé of Omar Torrijos, the swaggering soldier-populist who seized power in 1968, Noriega became the National Guard's chief of intelligence in 1970. After Torrijos died in a helicopter crash in 1981, Noriega patiently maneuvered to gain command of the guard by 1983. Around this time he began cooperation with the Reagan administration, allowing the United States to use Panama as a staging area for its military operations in Nicaragua and El Salvador and assisting the CIA in its efforts to strengthen Contra resistance to the Sandinista regime. (In this role Noriega would eventually have meetings with Oliver North, William Casey, and other top U.S. officials; ever the double agent, he had good connections with Fidel Castro as well.) Noriega also opened Panama to money laundering for drug profits, protected by the nation's strict secrecy laws for banks, and established a working relationship with the Medellín cartel, which used the country as a transit route for occasional shipments, as a temporary site of operations, and as a sanctuary to escape pressure from Colombian authorities. Mercurial and cunning, Noriega reached a tacit understanding with the U.S. government: in a display of *realpolitik* and/or hypocrisy, Washington would ignore his drug business as long as he supported U.S. anticommunist policies in Central America. To avoid suspicion Noriega cooperated from time to time with the antinarcotics efforts of the U.S. Drug Enforcement Administration, earning the "highest commendation" for Panama from Attorney General Edwin Meese III in 1987.

As commander of the National Guard, renamed the Panamanian Defense Forces, Noriega wielded supreme political power. His situation began to unravel in June 1987, when Colonel Roberto Díaz Herrera, retiring second-in-command of the PDF, denounced Noriega for participation in electoral fraud, personal corruption, and the assassination of opponents. Then a bombshell fell in February 1988, when federal prosecutors in Miami secured a twelve-count indictment against Noriega under the conspiracy statute known as RICO (Racketeer Influenced and Corrupt Organizations Act). If convicted on all charges, Noriega could receive up to 145 years in jail and $1,145,000 in fines. The charges claimed that Noriega had taken part in shipping drugs and laundering money, but the heart of the case rested on the accusation that he had accepted a $4 million payoff to shelter and protect the Medellín cartel. With the exception of one drugs-for-arms deal in March 1986, all these transactions had taken place between October 1982 and June 1984.

The indictments sent shock waves through Washington as well as Panama City. Noriega was by far the most powerful foreign official ever to have been indicted by the United States. His collaborators in the U.S. government—including the CIA, the NSC, the Pentagon, and many in the DEA—were stunned by these developments. The State Department proposed asking the Department of Justice to drop the charges if Noriega would go into exile, but the general rejected the offer.

In late February 1988 President Eric Arturo Delvalle, in an uncustomary act of bravado, relieved the general of his duties as PDF commander. Within eight hours a pro-Noriega National Assembly abruptly dismissed Delvalle and installed the pliant Manuel Solís Palma. Despite Delvalle's dubious political credentials—becoming vice president as a result of fraud in 1984 and president as a result of Noriega's interference in 1986—the U.S. government announced its "unqualified support for civilian constitutional rule in Panama" and continued to recognize Delvalle as the legitimate president. Thus emboldened, Delvalle issued a proclamation through the U.S. embassy in Panama City ordering that all money payable to Panama should be placed in escrow and that his government would not recognize any payments made to the Noriega-controlled regime. With the aid of high-priced lawyers and well-placed friends in Washington, the Delvalle team took control of $35 million–$40 million in four New York banks, and a cooperative U.S. government announced that all Canal Commission payments, about $7 million per month, would go into Delvalle's escrow accounts. The effect of these measures and subsequent sanctions was impressive: the Panamanian gross domestic product contracted by a staggering 15.8 percent in 1988 alone, and the total loss in its governmental revenue mounted to $450 million.

Washington stepped up its rhetoric as well. In May 1988 President Reagan declared that the U.S. goal in Panama "must be the removal of Noriega from power." Vice President Bush, running hard for the presidency, maintained that the United States should be prepared to do "whatever is necessary, including military force," to protect "sacred" U.S. interests in Panama. The CIA took active part in covert-action plots—perhaps as many as five separate plots—to get rid of Noriega.

Elections in Panama were scheduled for May 1989. Noriega considered a run for the presidency but eventually handed his party's nomination to one of his long-time associates, Carlos Duque. The opposition supported a coalition headed by Guillermo Endara and supported by Ricardo Arias Calderón and Guillermo "Billy" Ford as vice presidential candidates.

As Panamanian citizens turned out to vote in large numbers, the Catholic Church organized a "quick count" showing that Duque was losing by a 3:1 margin. When the electoral council began replacing actual results with counterfeits, an observation team under former president Jimmy Carter denounced the fraud and returned to Washington. Tension mounted in Panama City, and during one pro-opposition demonstration Noriega's "Dignity Battalions" inflicted a bloody beating on Billy Ford and roughed up other participants in the rally.

In mid-May the Organization of American States formally condemned "the grave events and the abuses by General Manuel Antonio Noriega in the crisis and the electoral process in Panama," and dispatched a mission to negotiate a peaceful transfer of power. Denouncing U.S. interference in Panamanian politics, Noriega refused to cooperate with the OAS delegation. Latin American governments were nonetheless reluctant to impose sanctions against Panama, although the Inter-American Commission on Human Rights issued a report in November 1989 calling Noriega's regime "devoid of constitutional legitimacy." The United States increased troop levels in the canal area, but Noriega refused to buckle under the pressure.

Offended by Noriega's insolence, President George Bush discovered a strong political motive for action on Panama: the antidrug campaign. In September 1989 he delivered a major speech in which he called drugs the country's "gravest domestic threat." Polls reported that 64 percent of the American people identified drugs as the nation's number-one problem. Having renewed the war against drugs, Bush needed some sort of victory. By November an exasperated Bush was determined to invade: as one official on the scene recalled, it was "a decision in search of an excuse."

A pretext soon arrived. On December 15 the Noriega-controlled National Assembly proclaimed that a "state of war" existed with the United States and named Noriega for the first time as chief of government. With tensions high, members of the PDF the next day opened fire on a car carrying four U.S. military officers when it refused to stop at a roadblock. One officer was killed, a second was injured, and a third who witnessed the event was arrested and beaten. That same day an American Navy lieutenant was detained and beaten, while his wife was subjected to sexual harassment. Bush professed "enormous outrage" and soon gave his approval to invasion plans.

Attack!

At 1:00 A.M. on Friday, December 20 the United States struck Panama with overwhelming force. Backed by helicopter gunships and sophisticated aircraft, 13,000 troops flew into Panama to join the 13,000 comrades already at U.S. bases in the canal area. Parachute drops and amphibious assaults allowed the Americans to gain quick advantage over the PDF, while the air force—including two F-117A Stealth fighter-bombers carrying laser-guided 2,000-pound bombs—rained 422 bombs on Panama within a span of thirteen hours. Flames engulfed the slum neighborhoods of Chorrillo and San Miguelito, both bastions of pro-Noriega sentiment. The PDF put up little resistance, and U.S. forces secured control of the country within five days. Neighborhood sweeps by American troops rounded up nearly 5,000 prisoners, more than the entire number of combat troops within the PDF. The Pentagon decided to call the action "Operation Just Cause."

Its proclaimed objectives were to capture Noriega, to install the government of Guillermo Endara that had been elected in May, and to protect American citizens. Noriega at first managed to elude the U.S. dragnet, however, and Bush put a $1 million bounty on the general's head. On Christmas Day an exhausted Noriega sought asylum in the Papal Nunciature, and the Vatican refused to turn him over to the "occupying army." American forces then laid siege to the Nunciature, playing rock music at a deafening volume. Inside, Archbishop José Sebastián Laboa adopted the role of confessor-counselor with Noriega. Finally, on January 4 Noriega donned a clean uniform, strode through the embassy's gates, and offered his formal surrender to General Maxwell Thurman. The next day Noriega was arraigned in Miami on multiple counts of drug trafficking and conspiracy, the charges listed in the indictment handed down in February 1988.

From Chile to Mexico, reaction to the invasion was swift and negative. Bush had not bothered to consult any Latin leaders beforehand. On December 22 the OAS passed a resolution that "deeply regrets the military intervention in Panama" and urged the withdrawal of American troops. Twenty nations voted for the resolution, seven abstained, and the United States was alone in opposing it. The UN General Assembly passed a stronger resolution, condemning the intervention with a vote of 70–20–40. Essentially, however, these were rhetorical gestures. The U.S. intervention was a fait accompli, and no one was about to take action against it; in the post–Cold War world, the United States could wield its power in the hemisphere with relative impunity.

The Panama operation gained widespread support from the American people, as confirmed by public opinion polls, though the death toll became an object of bitter dispute. Critics expressed dismay over the extent of devastation, all for the alleged purpose of capturing one man. Former U.S. attorney general Ramsay Clark, among others, charged that thousands of innocent civilians had been killed. The Pentagon released official figures of 23 American soldiers dead and over 100 wounded; 314 Panamanian military killed and 125 wounded; and 202 Panamanian civilians killed. In time, however, independent human rights groups were able to demonstrate that the U.S. government figures greatly overestimated the number of Panamanian military killed—which was more like 50, rather than 300-plus, indicating that the level of resistance was much less than originally reported. Similarly, Americas Watch put the number of civilians killed at 300, with as many as 3,000 wounded, and rendered a harsh critique of U.S.

violation of the "ever-present duty to minimize harm to the civilian population."

Nonetheless, the ultimate rationale was that Just Cause represented a successful operation in the war on drugs. Exulted Representative Ike Skelton (D-Missouri): "The international snake Noriega has finally been put in his cage." Intoned Republican Senate leader Bob Dole of Kansas: "Noriega's bad news is good news for our war on drugs. It proves America won't cave in to anyone, no matter how powerful or corrupt." Added Senator Carl Levin (D-Michigan): "All Americans rejoice that the United States armed forces have brought this indicted drug-running thug to justice." Concurred Representative Morris K. Udall (D-Arizona): "Until the U.S. action taken today, an entire country had been held hostage by a drug dealer." Chimed Representative Jim Kolbe (R-Arizona): "Noriega has removed himself from the civilized world. One hopes this puts a good scare into some of the drug warlords. Noriega was a drug warlord. He just happened to run a country."

Aftermath

Operation Just Cause had virtually no impact on drug trafficking. Noriega had been a minor player in the narcotics business, and even according to the Miami indictment he had retired from active participation in March 1986. In this sense his removal was totally insignificant. Nor did the arrest of Noriega, the presence of U.S. troops, or the installation of the Endara administration have any observable effect on Panama's role as a site for drug transit and money laundering. According to congressional testimony in March 1990 by State Department official Michael Kozak, who had played a key role in Panamanian events, "Our law enforcement people would say that it has picked back up to the level where it existed before Just Cause."

The trial of Manuel Noriega had more enduring significance. His lawyers immediately launched a broad challenge to the U.S. case, asserting that his arrest was illegal, that his status as chief of state made him immune to prosecution, that he was a political prisoner captured in an invasion that violated international law. At issue was the fundamental question of whether U.S. agents could seize suspected drug traffickers in foreign countries and forcibly bring them to the United States for trial. (Much the same question arose in the case of Humberto Álvarez Machaín, a Mexican doctor accused of participating in the 1985 murder of DEA agent Enrique Camarena; the case was eventually dismissed on grounds of flimsy evidence, not on the principle of illegal seizure.) Noriega's legal team also sought the release of classified documents about the general's longstanding relationship with the CIA, a subject of great potential embarrassment to former agency director George Bush. The presiding judge ultimately refused to allow Noriega to demonstrate the strength of his past ties to the CIA, on the ground that it had no bearing on the charges in question, but the issue persisted: if a person committed legal transgressions in the course of cooperating with one agency of the U.S. government, was it appropriate for a different government agency to bring that individual to a criminal trial? In mid-1992 a jury finally convicted Noriega on eight charges of drug trafficking and racketeering, and he received a sentence of forty years in prison without parole. A relieved and self-righteous George Bush declared that this was "fitting punishment for drug crimes that have harmed all America. It demonstrates that international drug felons are not above the law, no matter how great their wealth, their status or their armed might."

Notwithstanding the imprisonment of Noriega, the benefits from Just Cause did not extend to much of Panama. Overweight and uninspiring, President Endara was unable to provide firm leadership. Only one year after taking office he had to call on U.S. troops to help put down a military uprising on behalf of the popular Colonel Eduardo Herrera, who had been dismissed and then imprisoned by the government. As the Panamanian economy took longer than expected to recover, unemployment and poverty remained at staggering levels. Endara's approval rating plunged from 73 percent in mid-1989 (just after the contested elections) to 17 percent in March 1991, and it continued to slide after that. According to a popular refrain, "General Noriega has been replaced by General Discontent."

Presidential elections in May 1994 added yet another twist. Victory went to Ernesto Pérez Balladares, a former Noriega crony who earned 33.3 percent of the votes by appealing to widespread frustration. "There is runaway unemployment and runaway corruption here," as a resident of San Miguelito explained, "and Toro [Pérez Balladares] is the only one who can stop that." During the campaign Pérez Balladares distanced both himself and his party from Noriega, invoking instead the legacy of Omar Torrijos, but the basic fact remained: Noriega loyalists were back in power. Second in the balloting was Mireya Moscoso, the widow of three-time president Arnulfo Arias, with 29.1 percent; third was salsa star Rubén Blades, with 17.1 percent, followed by Rubén Darío Carlés, with 16.1 percent. Had Moscoso and Carlés joined forces, a progovernment candidate might have won; this failure simply emphasized the persistence of narrow-minded bickering within and between the traditional parties. Years after the U.S. invasion, politics in Panama was much the same.

The Process of Migration

Like drug traffic and consumption, international migration occurred throughout history in nearly all parts of the world. During the nineteenth century vast waves of people left Europe in search of a better life in the Americas, settling in the United States and, in the Southern Hemisphere, in Argentina and Brazil. Migration continued into the twentieth century and spread to all corners of the globe: Turkish workers moved to Germany, Algerians to France, Commonwealth citizens to England, Salvadorans to

Honduras, Colombians to Venezuela. Out of a world population of nearly 5.5 billion, there were by the mid-1990s between 80 million and 100 million immigrants, refugees, and legal and documented workers living outside their country of citizenship.

The United States developed as a nation on the basis of migration. Between 1900 and 1910 the United States accepted 8.8 million additional immigrants, mostly from Europe, and over the following two decades the country granted legal access to nearly 10 million more new arrivals. This influx came to a near-halt in the 1930s, under pressure from the Great Depression, and resumed after the close of World War II.

Figure 5 displays trends in the magnitude and composition of legal immigration from the 1950s through the 1980s, a period through which the United States attempted to set strict limits on migratory flows. Several patterns stand out. One is a steady increase in the volume of legal migration, from 2.5 million in the 1950s to 6.0 million in the 1980s—the highest figure in the world, it might be said, but well below the levels of the early 1900s. Another is the precipitous decline in the proportion of immigrants from Europe and Canada (mostly Europe), from 66 percent in the 1950s to 14 percent in the 1980s, and the concomitant rise in Asian immigration from 6 percent to 44 percent. Legal immigration from Mexico held steady, 12 to 14 percent of the total, while flows from elsewhere in Latin America increased sharply during the 1960s and subsequently hovered around 26 to 27 percent of the total.

These trends underline important points. First, there was—and continues to be—a significant volume of legal migration from Mexico and Latin America to the United States. Indeed, the inflow of Mexicans in the 1920s was just about as large as during the 1960s, and legal admissions increased markedly in the 1970s and 1980s. Even in the absence of illegal immigration, these flows would have a considerable impact on American society.

Second, alterations in the composition of the immigrant stream— especially the relative decline of the component from Europe—prompted xenophobic, nativistic reactions among the U.S. public. Often this response took overtly racist form. As conservative presidential candidate Patrick J. Buchanan opined in 1992, "I think God made all people good, but if we had to take a million immigrants in, say Zulus, next year, or Englishmen, and put them in Virginia, what group would be easier to assimilate and would cause less problems for the people of Virginia?" In some parts of the country, particularly California, racist feelings erupted in virulent denunciation of Mexicans, condemned as "illegal aliens" in a land that once was theirs.

Third, the establishment of numerical quotas proved to be an illusory exercise. Even the increase in legal entries—which nearly doubled between the 1960s and the 1980s—could not accommodate growing pressures for migration to the United States. As a result many people chose to enter the United States without official authorization, in violation of the law. It is by

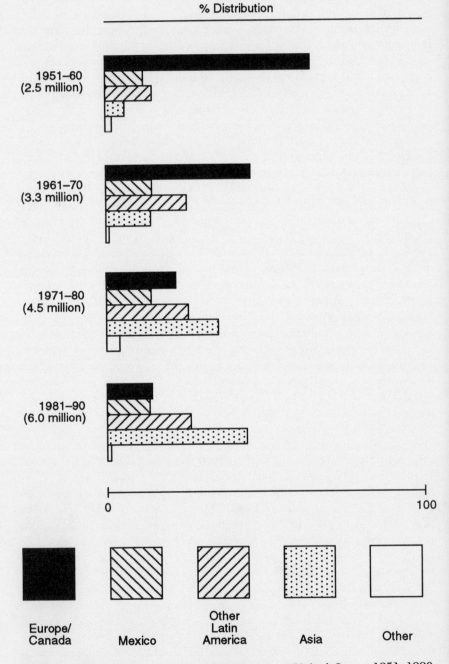

% Distribution

1951–60
(2.5 million)

1961–70
(3.3 million)

1971–80
(4.5 million)

1981–90
(6.0 million)

0   100

Europe/
Canada   Mexico

Other
Latin
America   Asia   Other

Figure 5. Regional origins of legal immigrants to United States, 1951–1990. [*Source:* Data published by U.S. Immigration and Naturalization Service.]

definition impossible to gauge the magnitude of this population with much precision, but responsible demographers have settled on a rough estimate of 2.5 million to 4.0 million "illegal aliens" from all parts of the world in early 1992. (This was lower than the estimated range of 3.0 million to 5.0 million for 1986, but higher than the figure of 1.8 million to 3.0 million for 1989.) Particularly conspicuous was illegal migration from Mexico, estimated to account for 55 to 60 percent of unauthorized residents in the United States by the early 1990s. Others came from all points of the globe, from Haiti to Ireland to China, frequently entering the country legally and then overstaying their visas.

Trends in U.S. Policy

Within the Americas, U.S. policy on migration devoted special attention to Mexico. From the turn of the century until the 1930s, an informal "open border" policy toward Mexico provided U.S. employers with an immense pool of unskilled workers to accommodate seasonal and cyclical variations in labor demand, primarily in agriculture, mining, and construction. Mexican workers met special needs for temporary labor during World War I and, more generally, played a valuable role in the development of the American Southwest. Restrictions during the 1930s came as a direct consequence of the Great Depression. Not only did Mexican migration come to a screeching halt; amidst anti-Mexican sentiment, the forcible deportation of a half million Mexicans led to a reversal of the flow. Despite its unseemly conclusion, this first migration cycle convinced U.S. employers of the economic advantages that derived from access to an unregulated, flexible, and inexpensive supply of labor.

World War II began a second cycle of Mexican immigration. In response to labor shortages in agriculture, the U.S. government in 1942 proposed a formal agreement to utilize Mexican workers. Formally legislated as U.S. Public Law 45, but more popularly known as the *bracero* program, this temporary-worker agreement between Mexico and the United States began as an emergency measure to replenish labor lost to military service. The accord continued without significant interruption until 1964, when Washington allowed the agreement to lapse.

The Walter-McCarran Immigration Act of 1952 continued and tightened the quota system first established in the 1920s. By establishing a preference system which gave priority to prospective immigrants with special skills in short supply in the United States, Walter-McCarran explicitly acknowledged the principle that immigration should be coordinated with labor demand in the United States. But the statute also revealed internal contradictions. Most glaring was the "Texas Proviso," which enabled growers in that state to hire undocumented field hands from Mexico; as a result, Walter-McCarran made it illegal to *be* an undocumented alien but not to *hire* one. In actual practice, Mexicans were largely exempted from these regulations.

Next came the immigration reforms of 1965. Passed in the midst of the Civil Rights movement, this legislation set the stage for dramatic changes in the size and composition of migrant streams. To abolish the discriminatory quota system, the 1965 amendments nearly doubled the worldwide number of annual U.S. visas, from 158,000 to 290,000; established a more equitable distribution of visas by region, allotting 170,000 to the Eastern Hemisphere and 120,000 to the Western Hemisphere; and reordered priorities for visa preference categories, giving relatively greater emphasis to family reunification over labor market considerations. The original legislation set a maximum of 20,000 visas per nation from the Eastern Hemisphere but placed no ceiling on individual countries in the Western Hemisphere, a provision which allowed Mexico to acquire a disproportionate share. In 1976, however, supplementary legislation applied the 20,000 limit to nations of the Western Hemisphere—to the direct detriment of Mexico.

Impacts of IRCA

Against this backdrop, the Immigration Reform and Control Act of 1986 culminated a succession of attempts to curtail undocumented immigration. Passage came amidst a national clamor to "take control of our borders," in President Reagan's telling phrase, and as persistent unemployment fueled public resentment against workers from Mexico and other countries. Attorney General Edwin Meese III also proclaimed, in the face of both logic and fact, that restrictions on illegal immigration would reduce the flow of illicit drugs to the United States. Sponsored by Senator Alan Simpson (R-Wyoming) and Representative Peter Rodino (D-New Jersey), the bill contained three principal provisions:

- Economic sanctions against U.S. employers who "knowingly employ, recruit, or refer for a fee" undocumented workers.
- Permanent amnesty for undocumented workers who could prove continuous residence in the United States since any time prior to January 1, 1982.
- Partial amnesty for undocumented workers in the agricultural sector who had worked for at least ninety consecutive days in the three consecutive years 1984, 1985, and 1986 (SAW I) or during the year between May 1985 and May 1986 (SAW II); and a provision for the readmission of "replenishment agricultural workers" (RAWs) in 1990–92.

Ultimately, IRCA represented a compromise between those political forces opposing unauthorized migration (from organized labor to racist reactionaries), those who benefited from its existence (mostly employers), and Hispanic leaders expressing concern about the potential aggravation of ethnic prejudice.

IRCA achieved mixed results. The employer-sanctions portion of the law proved to be toothless. It remained possible for employers to comply with the law—and still hire undocumented workers. For instance, Simpson-Rodino obliged employers to request official papers from job applicants, but did not require them to verify the authenticity of the documents: merely by inspecting any one of twenty-plus possible documents, widely available in counterfeit form, employers could technically satisfy their legal requirements. As a consequence, employer sanctions had only marginal impact on illegal migration.

Support for this point comes from data on annual apprehensions of illegal aliens from the mid-1970s through the early 1990s (most apprehensions took place along or near the U.S.–Mexican border, so 90 percent or more of the detainees were Mexican). The figures suggest that IRCA posed a temporary deterrent to illegal migration, as the total number of apprehensions declined from 1.76 million in 1986 to 1.2 million in 1987 and less than 1 million by 1989, a drop of 45 percent; but then the figures began to inch up, climbing to 1.2 million in 1991 and 1.3 million by 1993—which was just around the pre-IRCA level of 1985 (Figure 6). (The 1993 figure for apprehensions of Mexicans was almost exactly the same as in 1985.) In other words, IRCA appeared to have a dual impact on illegal migration: first, it led to an increase of unauthorized flows in 1985 and especially 1986, as anxious migrants sought to gain access prior to

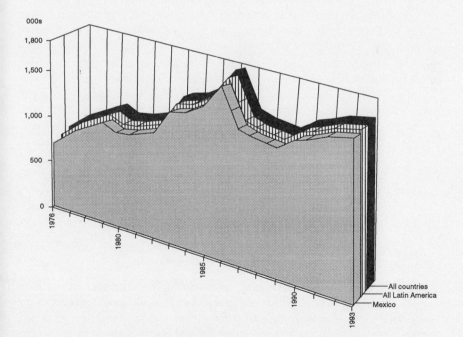

Figure 6. Apprehensions of illegal aliens in the United States, 1976–1993. [*Source:* Data supplied by U.S. Immigration and Naturalization Service.]

implementation of the much-discussed law; and second, it led to a temporary reduction in illicit crossings in 1987–89, but this almost certainly resulted more from the extension of amnesty to formerly illegal migrants than from the effect of employer sanctions.

It must be said, if only in passing, that the number of arrests in Figure 6 provides a less-than-perfect guide to the number of illegal entries. Conventional wisdom holds that there are two (or three or four) entries for each arrest; multiplied by one of these ratios, data on arrests yield semiofficial estimates on unauthorized flows. But apprehension statistics refer to *events*—that is, to the number of arrests—rather than to *people*. They make no allowance for multiple arrests (anecdotal evidence indicates that individuals can be arrested more than once in the same day). They make no adjustment for voluntary returns to Mexico or other homelands (while survey data indicate that the majority of migrants come only for temporary periods). And they are bound to respond to the varying intensity and magnitude of enforcement efforts by the U.S. Border Patrol.

In contrast to employer sanctions, the amnesty portion of IRCA turned out to be highly successful. Partly seeking to improve its public image, the Immigration and Naturalization Service (INS) gave high priority to the program, opening 109 new offices to handle an eventual volume of 3.9 million inquiries. Approximately 1.7 million applications were submitted under the "pre-1982" program and 1.3 million under the SAW program, for a total of 3 million. More than 90 percent of the pre-1982 applicants had their status adjusted from temporary to permanent resident. All SAWs approved for temporary residence automatically received permanent resident status. In other words, nearly 3 million people acquired legal status in the United States as a result of Simpson-Rodino.

In the meantime there continued a historic shift in the nature and composition of *indocumentados* from Mexico, away from the temporary or seasonal migration of single working-age males toward the longer-term settlement of families, women, and children. But as one expert has concluded, "There is no evidence that IRCA has reduced the total pool of Mexican migrants employed or seeking work in U.S. labor markets."[4] While sharpening the distinction between migrant workers with and without legal status, in fact, IRCA might even have served to increase the size of the overall pool, and in so doing, it may have exacerbated social and political tensions within American society over unauthorized immigration.

The Refugee Question

Yet another stream of foreigners came to the United States not as economic migrants but as political refugees, people seeking to escape persecution and repression in their native lands. As a matter of U.S. law, individuals were entitled to asylum in the United States if they could demonstrate a "well-founded fear of persecution on account of race, religion, nationality, membership in a particular social group or political opinion." And as a matter of U.S. tradition, acceptance of refugees reinforced the nation's self-image as a bastion of political freedom. Unlike economic migrants, refugees were coming to this country not merely for wages or employment; like America's forefathers, they were seeking the full expression of their fundamental human rights.

By its nature, the granting of asylum was an explicitly political decision—and it was inevitable, perhaps, that it would be used (and abused) for political purposes. Since there was no scientific means for discerning whether someone had a "well-founded fear of persecution," judgments tended to be arbitrary. In general, the U.S. government was quick to grant asylum to people fleeing from hostile regimes and loath to give asylum to people fleeing from its allies. During the Cold War, this meant that Washington was happy to embrace refugees from the Soviet Union, the People's Republic of China, or Fidelista Cuba and Sandinista Nicaragua, but it was notoriously inhospitable to applicants from Guatemala, El Salvador, or Chile under Pinochet. The actual hazard to human rights had little or no bearing on such cases. What mattered was Washington's desire to embarrass its enemies, support its friends, and reap propaganda value on behalf of the "free world."

Termination of the Cold War threw the refugee question into total disarray, leaving the United States without any guidepost for its hemispheric asylum policy. By the early 1990s only Castro's Cuba remained an enemy of the United States. And while other nations in Latin America were undergoing processes of "democratization" (for which Washington often took credit), human-rights abuses continued to occur. In fact some of the most egregious violations, as in Colombia and Mexico, resulted from governmental cooperation in the U.S.-sponsored "war on drugs." In this topsy-turvy world, policy decisions on human rights and refugees were likely to become more arbitrary than ever.

Equally disturbing, from Washington's standpoint, was the prospect of massive waves of refugees from nearby countries of the region. At the outset, policymakers had imagined that actual numbers of refugees would be modest enough to avoid entanglement in questions about assimilation into U.S. society. Indeed, the preference was for high-profile individuals whose defection from enemy states would endorse the superiority of Western capitalism and the wisdom of U.S. policy. In 1980 the Mariel boatlift challenged that happy assumption by suddenly unloading 128,000 Cubans in the United States, creating numerous episodes of social turbulence and turmoil. Refugees en masse posed questions not only about respect for human rights in foreign countries but also about U.S. attitudes toward foreigners. Arriving in large scale, political refugees from Latin America encountered the same kind of rancor, resistance, and reaction as did economic migrants. With xenophobia on the rise, the refugee issue became a migration issue as well.

Haiti: Operation Uphold Democracy

One of the most cynical acts of the Cold War was a 1981 compact between the Reagan administration and the right-wing regime of Jean-Claude ("Baby Doc") Duvalier, an agreement under which the U.S. Coast Guard would repatriate Haitian citizens after perfunctory on-board hearings. Over the next ten years the United States picked up 22,716 Haitians on the high seas, most attempting to flee their country in small boats or makeshift rafts—and admitted only 28 (0.12 percent!) for political asylum. The purpose of this accord, in the name of anticommunism, was to spare embarrassment for the murderous Duvalier regime, to intimidate its political opponents, and to minimize the number of unwanted arrivals on Florida shores.

In the eyes of American society, Haitians were especially undesirable. They were poor. They were black. And they were identified as carriers of AIDS, a stigmatization that intensified anti-Haitian sentiment during the course of the 1980s. By the early 1990s it was estimated that as much as 9 percent of the Haitian population might be HIV-positive, a proportion that was bound to be much higher among the young adult males most likely to take to the seas. Victims of manifold prejudice, Haitians found themselves unwelcome in the United States.

After Duvalier's fall in 1986, Haiti finally held a free and fair election in December 1990. The undisputed winner, with two-thirds of the vote, was Jean-Bertrand Aristide, a thirty-seven-year-old Catholic priest who curried support from the popular masses. A devotee of liberation theology, a Christian doctrine espousing drastic social change, Aristide expressed profound resentment of the mulatto elite, the armed forces, and the historic role of the United States. "I cannot forgive what your country has done to Haiti," he said to a group of distinguished Americans shortly after his election. Inaugurated in February 1991, Aristide proceeded to antagonize opponents without consolidating power. In September 1991, less than nine months into his term, he was forced into exile by a military coup. Haiti once again fell under the heel of the armed forces, led by General Raoul Cédras.

The overthrow drew sharp condemnation from the Organization of American States, which called for Aristide's prompt reinstatement and imposed a trade embargo in November 1991. United States Secretary of State James A. Baker III proclaimed that Haiti's illegal regime had "no future." The OAS began a ceaseless round of negotiations with Aristide, Cédras, and other political forces in Haiti. The Inter-American Commission on Human Rights dispatched a team to the country, issued statements, and denounced violations of human rights. An already-poor populace suffered from the embargo while illicit commerce flourished. Nurturing anti-Aristide sentiment, Cédras managed to consolidate support within the business elite. Discussions continued but there was no movement.

As repression mounted, Haitians set out for the United States. By January 1992 the U.S. Coast Guard had taken at least 12,600 Haitians into custody at sea, providing "safe haven" for thousands at Camp Guantánamo (in Cuba). By May 1992 U.S. authorities had processed 34,000 requests for asylum, granting about one-third, while Guantánamo was bursting at the seams. Citing a "dangerous and unmanageable situation," President George Bush that same month ordered the Coast Guard to pick up all Haitians on the seas and return them to their homeland without any screening at all. Democratic presidential candidate Bill Clinton denounced the Bush policy as immoral, "a callous response to a terrible human tragedy." In one of his more memorable malapropisms, Bush defended his stance by explaining: "We're not trying to starve the people of Haiti and we're not trying to freeze them or cook them or do anything of that nature." The Coast Guard held the line.

The refugee problem confronted U.S. authorities with a serious dilemma. In order to justify forcible repatriation, they would have to deny political asylum on the ground that Haitians were taking to the seas for economic reasons; that is, they would have to maintain that applicants had no "well-grounded fear of persecution" from the Cédras regime. In making this case, however, they would implicitly have to concede that there was no systematic denial of human rights in Haiti. Washington was unable to have it both ways: there was a stark choice between rejecting the migrants or denouncing the regime. Bureaucrats and politicians attempted to obscure the issue, contradicting themselves from time to time, but the dilemma persisted nonetheless.

Emboldened by Clinton's campaign rhetoric, Haitians began taking to the sea after his election in November 1992. Judging from the number of boats and rafts under construction, Coast Guard analysts estimated that as many as 200,000 Haitians were preparing to set sail for the United States. Notified by Bush of this development even before his own inauguration, Clinton ruefully announced that the Bush policy of forced repatriation would stay in place. An aide to Aristide denounced the "floating Berlin Wall," especially in light of a U.S. policy granting automatic asylum to refugees from Cuba, and Aristide himself expressed impatience at inaction by the OAS: "History will never forgive thirty-four countries if they continue to just talk instead of doing what they have to do."

The initiative then moved from the OAS to the United Nations, which appointed Argentina's former foreign minister Dante Caputo as chief negotiator and intermediary. In June 1993 the UN Security Council imposed a worldwide embargo on shipments of petroleum to Haiti. Within a month Caputo persuaded both Aristide and Cédras to accept a compromise: Aristide would regain the presidency by October 30, Cédras would step down as army chieftain, Aristide would appoint a prime minister (with the approval of the Haitian parliament), and there would be a general amnesty for involvement in the September 1991 coup. Signed in July 1993, the so-called Governors Island accords appeared to offer a workable solution. But as the time approached for Aristide's return, Cédras realized that the Clinton White House was in no position to enforce the UN plan. On October 3 eighteen American soldiers had been killed during a peace-keeping mission in Somalia, an event that led to instantaneous demands for the recall of U.S. troops from foreign lands. In the meantime, the United States prepared to meet its obligations under the Governors Island accords by providing military advisers to help professionalize the Haitian armed forces and police. With about 200 lightly armed troops aboard, the USS *Harlan County* steamed into Port-au-Prince on October 11—only to find that its berth was blocked by small boats and a menacing crowd of heavily armed civilians threatened violence. Unwilling to risk confrontation, Washington ordered the *Harlan County* to withdraw from the harbor. Cédras and his paramilitary attachés had faced down the United States and the United Nations. As an American official would later reflect, "When we caved, we pulled the plug on Governors Island."

With the collapse of UN mediation, the Clinton administration turned toward bilateral negotiations under veteran diplomat Lawrence Pezzullo. The U.S. goal was to find a centrist solution that would resolve the crisis without restoring Aristide to power. Around this time Aristide was falling into disfavor in Washington. In October 1993 word leaked out about a CIA report depicting Aristide as politically vengeful and mentally unstable. And as part of its search for a centrist solution, Washington began to equivocate on the assessment of human rights in Haiti. An official at the U.S. embassy in Port-au-Prince scornfully denounced independent human-rights reporting as "all bullshit." "If any of it were true, I'd be tripping over bodies on my way to work every morning." The reevaluation reached its pinnacle in April 1994, in the unlikely form of a diplomatic cable dismissing concerns over human rights as political exaggeration: "The Haitian Left, including President Aristide and his supporters in Washington and here, consistently manipulate or even fabricate human rights abuses as a propaganda tool." Composed by Ellen Cosgrove, the U.S. embassy's human rights officer, the cable cast doubt on widespread reports of political rape: "For a range of cultural reasons (not pleasant to contemplate) rape has never been considered or reported as a serious crime here. . . . We are frankly suspicious of the sudden high number of re-ported rapes, particularly in this culture, occurring at the same time that Aristide activists seek to draw a comparison between Haiti and Bosnia." While acknowledging the presence of abuse, Cosgrove emphasized the theme of manipulation: "President Aristide and his lobbying apparatus in Washington have increasing substantiation for charges that the human rights situation here is getting worse—and what they cannot substantiate they will fabricate." In this malign endeavor, she added, "they are wittingly or unwittingly assisted by Human Rights and by [the UN and OAS]." Signed and sent by Ambassador William L. Swing, the cable not only expressed profound antipathy toward Aristide but also yielded an unmis-takable conclusion: Haitians seeking political asylum were economic migrants posing as victims of persecution. After news reports about the missive produced a public furor, the State Department disavowed its implications and Swing, without explanation, simply retracted the document. Key U.S. officials nonetheless defended its interpretation. As Pezzullo maintained, "Certainly there has been a great deal of hype put into the human-rights situation . . . the situation isn't a pretty one, but it's being overplayed by people on the left in Haiti and by human-rights groups."

The U.S. search for a centrist solution came to naught, however, and the Clinton administration then returned to a hard line against the regime. Domestic politics became the driving force behind U.S. policy, especially as black American leaders stepped to the fore. In April 1994 Randall Robinson, the head of an activist organization known as TransAfrica, began a hunger strike in protest against the policy on refugees, declaring that Clinton "has set up a dragnet around Haiti to catch Haitians and return them to the killing fields." As Robinson's condition weakened, Clinton revised the policy by announcing that U.S. authorities would now process rafters at sea, offering asylum to victims of political repression. Clinton also replaced Pezzullo as special envoy with William Gray, a former member of the Black Congressional Caucus, which had long been demanding strong action on Haiti. To tighten the screws on Haiti, Washington then pressed for a resolution by the UN Security Council imposing new economic sanctions and condemning "any attempt illegally to remove legal authority" from Aristide and declaring "that it would consider illegitimate any proposed government resulting from such an attempt."

News of this policy shift led to yet another wave of rafters in search of asylum. The U.S. Coast Guard was suddenly picking up 2,000 Haitians per day. Hundreds drowned. Guantánamo was reopened, and the administration began looking for other countries to provide "safe haven" until Aristide could be restored.

Clinton was running out of options. The only choice was to remove Cédras and reinstate Aristide, and to use force if necessary. On July 31, after Haiti expelled a UN team of human rights monitors, the Security Council approved a new resolution authorizing the United States "to use all necessary means to facilitate the departure from Haiti of the military leadership." United States ambassador Madeleine Albright summarized its message to the junta: "You can depart voluntarily and soon, or you can depart involuntarily and soon." Disturbances at the refugee camp in Guantánamo added to the growing pressure. In late August Cédras refused to accept another UN mediation effort, and paramilitary gunmen shot down yet another prominent ally of Aristide. After a short visit to the Caribbean Community, a few of whose leaders volunteered token participation in a multinational force, a top Pentagon official proclaimed: "The multinational force is going to Haiti. The [only] issue is the circumstance under which that force enters Haiti."

By this time the White House was actively planning for an invasion, and the United States began stepping up its military pressure. In early

September 1994 naval ships and other forces were readied to move closer to Haiti. United States warplanes increased window-rattling flights over the island. On September 11 Warren Christopher said once again: "Time is running out." Having issued so many public warnings, the United States would now have to take military action. "We've tried everything else," one U.S. official said glumly. "This is the only option we have left."

As the countdown continued, U.S. politicians began to express reservations. Republicans called for a congressional vote on any possible invasion. Senator Bob Dole put it bluntly: "Is there any real national interest in Haiti?" An ABC News poll showed that 73 percent of Americans opposed the idea of an invasion of Haiti. Even Senator Claiborne Pell (D-Rhode Island), chairman of the Senate Foreign Relations Committee and a staunch Clinton supporter, pronounced misgivings: "I find it hard to identify a palpable U.S. interest in expending blood and treasure in restoring democracy in Haiti when we have not done that elsewhere in Latin America over the past 40 years or so," he said in a letter to Clinton. "I keep asking myself why it is so important to restore democracy in Haiti when we took no such steps in countries such as Chile, Argentina, El Salvador and Bolivia, to cite just a few examples of countries that have experienced anti-democracy coups over the years."

On Thursday, September 15 Clinton attempted to explain his position in a nationally televised speech. Denouncing the Cédras government as "the most violent regime in our hemisphere," the president cited several reasons for concern over Haiti: "to stop the brutal atrocities that threaten tens of thousands of Haitians, to secure our borders, and to preserve stability and promote democracy in our hemisphere, and to uphold the reliability of the commitments we make and the commitments others make to us." The moment of decision had arrived: "The message of the United States to the Haitian dictators is clear: Your time is up. Leave now, or we will force you from power."

Beneath the presidential rhetoric, it was the refugee issue that defined the fundamental interest of the United States. "I know that the United States cannot, indeed we should not, be the world's policeman," Clinton conceded, "and I know that this is a time, with the Cold War over, that so many Americans are reluctant to commit military resources and our personnel beyond our borders. But when brutality occurs close to our shores it affects our national interest and we have a responsibility to act." He went on to explain the logic behind this deduction:

> Thousands of Haitians have already fled toward the United States, risking their lives to escape the reign of terror. As long as Cédras rules, Haitians will continue to seek sanctuary in our nation. This year, in less than two months, more than 21,000 Haitians were rescued at sea by our Coast Guard and Navy. Today, more than 14,000 refugees are living at our naval base in Guantánamo. The American people have already expended almost $200 million to support them, to maintain the economic embargo, and the prospect of millions and millions being spent every month for an indefinite period of time looms ahead

unless we act. Three hundred thousand more Haitians, 5 percent of their entire population, are in hiding in their own country. If we don't act, they could be the next wave of refugees at our door. We will continue to face the threat of a mass exodus of refugees and its constant threat to stability in our region and control of our borders.

No American should be surprised that the recent tide of migrants seeking refuge on our shores comes from Haiti and from Cuba. After all, they are the only nations left in the Western Hemisphere where democratic government is denied, the only countries where dictators have managed to hold back the waves of democracy and progress that have swept over our entire region.

Ultimately, it was the prospect of 300,000 refugees that determined U.S. policy. As Doyle McManus of the *Los Angeles Times* would remark, "Never before has the United States gone to war to stop refugees from coming to our shores." Haitian journalist Anne-christine d'Adesky concurred with this judgment, arguing that Clinton's stance reflected "less his concern about human rights or democracy, than his belated assessment that the only way to keep refugees away from Miami is to stop the murders in Haiti."

Cédras countered Clinton's warning with expressions of defiance, and an invasion seemed imminent. Clinton agonized: "I know it is unpopular. I know the timing is unpopular. I know the whole thing is unpopular. But I believe it is the right thing." Then he dispatched a high-level delegation, led by former president Jimmy Carter, for a last-ditch effort at negotiation. At first the talks went poorly. At 1:00 P.M. on Sunday, September 18 Clinton gave orders for an invasion to commence at one minute past midnight. Carter continued his negotiations and presented the Haitians with a draft agreement that called for Aristide's return to power by October 15 and amnesty for the military rulers. At 5:30 P.M. one of the Haitian leaders burst into the room with news of mobilization of U.S. para-troopers at Fort Bragg, North Carolina, and denounced the Carter mission as a deceptive trap. At 6:45 P.M. U.S. commanders launched sixty-one planes toward Haiti with troops aboard. As talks were about to break up, negotiators paid a final call on President Émile Jonaissant. "We'll have peace, not war," the octogenarian executive said. Though Cédras and his chief of staff refused to sign the document, the deal was nonetheless done. A relieved Clinton recalled the planes and canceled the invasion.

The next day U.S. troops would occupy the country without any organized resistance. In less than a week there were more than 15,000 American troops on the ground. The nature of this operation, called by some an "intervasion," was elusive and expanding. It began as a limited military occupation with the name of Uphold Democracy, but, even after Aristide took office on schedule in mid-October, it developed into an extensive takeover of the governmental apparatus. Most volatile was Haitian-on-Haitian violence, as pro- and anti-Aristide forces engaged in bitter recriminations, and most distressing was the ubiquity of crushing poverty. By the end of March 1995 President Clinton celebrated the replacement of U.S. troops by a UN peacekeeping force—a contingent including 2,400 American soldiers, however, with a U.S. commander in charge. It remained unclear whether, how, or when the United States would eventually manage to extricate itself from this desperate and beautiful land.

Reflections: On Power and Hegemony

As the first U.S. military actions in Latin America of the post–Cold War era, the American operations in Panama and Haiti cast much light on the dynamics of the contemporary age. First, Just Cause and Uphold Democracy demonstrated the absence of international rules of the game and, in particular, of concerns for national sovereignty. From the 1890s through the 1920s, the United States launched repeated interventions in order to protect business and commercial interests. The calculation was economic and the rationale focused on democracy and international law. During the Cold War, the United States launched systematic interventions against governments perceived to be leftist, socialist, procommunist, or communist. The calculation was geopolitical and the rationale was ideological. In a way the Panama and Haiti operations bore considerable resemblance to those interventions of the bygone Imperial Era, but in another sense they represented applications of raw power, unconstrained by international protocol and undisguised by diplomatic niceties. In both instances the United States arrogated for itself the right, if not the duty, of overthrowing governments in the Americas.

Second, Just Cause and Uphold Democracy were both undertaken in the name of democratic restoration, which imbued them with an aura of Wilsonian high-mindedness. Yet the restitution of democracy itself was insufficient cause for military action; were that the case, American troops would have been scattered all over the globe. In each of these two cases, there were pressing political considerations as well: the need for visible progress in the drug wars and the clamor for stoppage of illegal immigration. It was the power of these social issues within the United States, filtered through the lens of domestic politics, that provided the ultimate motivation for operations in Panama and Haiti. Democracy alone was not enough; democracy plus a domestic political problem could provide a recipe for intervention.

Third, in the absence of grand politics, these actions revealed a heightened emphasis on personality. In many ways the Panama invasion resulted from a clash of individual wills, with the diminutive Noriega upholding his macho credentials and the worrisome Bush struggling to shed his persisting image as a "wimp."[5] Indeed, official portrayals and media depictions of Noriega in the United States presented him as the embodiment of malice—"a man so black of heart," as journalist John Dinges has written, "so evil of soul, that any means necessary, even invasion, was justified to consummate his exorcism."[6] And in Haiti, similarly, the cool defiance of General Cédras

challenged the authority of a stumbling Bill Clinton, who repeatedly denounced the "thugs" and "dictators" in power (although, to the great
consternation of the White House, Carter would praise Cédras as a patriot). In the absence of a contest over ideology, without any conceivable
communist threat, the U.S. government needed to vilify its opponents to
justify its chosen course. Satanization of rivals appeared to become a fixture
of the post–Cold War period.

Fourth, these two operations underlined the extent and character of
U.S. hegemony within the Western Hemisphere. Despite murmurings and
resolutions in august international bodies, from the OAS to the United
Nations, there was never any prospect of meaningful retaliation against the
American actions. In practical terms, the international community tacitly
accepted the U.S. claim to uncontested dominance in the Americas. And
for these very reasons, these two operations appeared to settle any questions about U.S. interventionism in the post–Cold War period. Regardless
of how small the stakes, the United States would clearly intervene throughout the region.

At the same time, Just Cause and Uphold Democracy revealed the
limitations of U.S. power. These applications of military force did not, and
could not, bring a halt to the illicit flows they were intended to deter. Long
after the invasion of Panama, drug trafficking continued without abate-
ment; and while military occupation brought a virtual (but incomplete)
end to the tide of rafters from Haiti, it hardly offered a plausible recipe for
stanching undocumented migration from all of Latin America. What these
episodes showed, in other words, was that Washington wielded great
hegemony over *governments* throughout the hemisphere, but that the
United States could neither control nor deter undesirable *social forces*
within the region. To this extent post–Cold War hegemony displayed a
hollow quality.

12

Latin America: In Quest of Alternatives

Latin America's community is the Third World.
Colombian foreign minister (1974)

We want Mexico to be part of the first world, not the third.
Carlos Salinas de Gortari (1990)

We want to be part of the first world, the only possible world. . . . I don't want to belong to the Third World. Argentina has to be in the First World, which is the only world that should exist.
Carlos Saúl Menem (1990)

Termination of the Cold War brought mixed blessings to Latin America. The end of East-West conflict meant that the region would no longer serve as a battleground for superpower rivalry. Within Latin America, passage of the Cold War relaxed the terms of ideological contention, weakening forces of left and right and reducing levels of polarization in domestic politics. By strengthening centrist elements, it reinforced processes of liberalization under way throughout the 1980s and enhanced the prospects for democratic consolidation.[1] The end of the Cold War prompted the hope, as well, that Washington could come to evaluate and appreciate Latin America on its own terms, respecting regional aspirations and supporting indigenous efforts for social and political development.

While many observers initially imagined that conclusion of the Cold War would expand the range and quality of plausible policy options for Latin America, this optimistic assumption soon came into question. Leaders in the region faced two pressing imperatives. One was to identify and occupy a viable position in the newly emerging global economy, to locate a niche that could provide a foundation for long-term development and growth. A second challenge was to confront changing patterns in the distribution of international power and, in particular, the intensification of U.S. hegemony within the Western Hemisphere. Within these contexts, the quest for policy alternatives was greatly complicated by uncertainty and drift throughout the world arena and by the absence of rules of the game. How could (or should) Latin America respond to these realities?

Global Maneuvering

As in other historical periods, the dynamics of inter-American relations would reflect conditions and events around the world at large. As the international community searched for order in the post–Cold War environment, there emerged several possible modes of interaction and alignment. In theory, at least, one such form was virtual anarchy, a rivalry of all against all, but in practice it seemed likely that international relations would eventually coalesce according to a discernible pattern.[2] Consolidation of one or more of these structures would fix the parameters for U.S.–Latin American relations and determine the range of viable policy options available to Latin America. Stated in schematic fashion, they took the form of three distinct scenarios.

Scenario 1: Global Development

The most optimistic view, widely held in the late 1980s and early 1990s, predicted that the end of the Cold War would augur an era of peace, prosperity, and harmony. The great powers, including the United States, would devote fewer resources to the arms race and more to the cause of economic development. There would be a productive (and efficient) reinvestment of the "peace dividend" into social equity and human welfare. Swords would be beaten into ploughshares, spears into pruning hooks. By creating a positive-sum game, the promotion of economic development would in turn reduce the likelihood of international conflict; the curtailment of military spending would diminish the need for armed defense. No longer burdened by East-West hostility, the world would become a gentler, kinder, more livable place. As George Bush proclaimed after victory in the Persian Gulf, there would emerge a "new world order."

At least two underlying forces would help bring about this outcome. One was the fact of global economic interdependence: autarky was not a viable option, and all nations needed each other. This condition would encourage cooperation and peaceful negotiation. Second was the omnipresence of mass communications, which could help nurture and perpetuate a cosmopolitan popular culture. By the early 1990s this effect was becoming apparent among the young—who tended everywhere to wear the same clothes, listen to the same music, cultivate the same lifestyles. Mass communications could also acquaint people with international trends and, more specifically, with the promise and possibility of life without dictatorship, thus enhancing the strength and universality of democratic values.

The pursuit of global development would bring fundamental changes in the tone and content of U.S.–Latin American relations. The United States would become more open, accepting, and tolerant of political diversity. It could disband the rigid anticommunism that guided U.S. policy from the 1940s through the 1980s. Without the Red menace, real or imagined, the United States would no longer oppose reformist or even revolutionary movements and would be able to achieve a new understanding of political trends in the Third World and in Latin America. No longer afflicted by ideological blinders, the United States would accept increasing pluralism in the world arena.

The global-development forecast rested on two essential premises: first, that international competition would become economic, rather than military or political; second, that economic conditions would oblige the United States to concede major roles to Japan and Europe within the Americas. As a result, Latin American countries would have opportunities to establish closer economic ties with powers outside the Western Hemisphere, thus reducing historic tensions in the bilateral U.S.–Latin American relationship. On occasion, Japan and Europe could even agree to disagree with the United States on issues relating to Latin America. An increased presence of friendly external powers in the Western Hemisphere would not be regarded as an intrusion into a traditional U.S. domain but as a constructive contribution to the common tasks of worldwide development.

Under this scenario, the U.S.–Latin American relationship would be based on voluntary collaboration. Cooperation would revolve around perceptions of convergent interests, rather than coercion by the United States or enlistment in an ideological crusade. And for these same reasons, collaboration would be *selective* in nature. Some Latin American countries might concur with the United States on some issues, other countries might concur on a different set of issues. No nation in the region would be obliged to accept the kind of all-or-nothing ultimatum presented to Cuba and Nicaragua during the Cold War era.

Scenario 2: Spheres of Influence

Hopes for the achievement of global development were fading by the early 1990s. A second possible outcome, far less optimistic than the first, would entail a reestablishment of traditional spheres of influence. As explained in chapter 1, the classic arrangement of spheres had two defining elements: first, the exertion of informal hegemony by a major power within a demarcated geopolitical region, and second, the acceptance of that hegemony by other major powers (which had other spheres of their own). It was the reciprocal acceptance of hegemonic claims that made the system viable; otherwise, disagreement over imperial boundaries could lead to serious conflict among the major powers.

This system offered several attractions in the new international environment. One related to security. Without the bipolar dominance and firm alliances characteristic of the Cold War, there was an increasing likelihood of ethnic struggle and regional warfare. The Iraqi-Kuwaiti conflict of the early 1990s was only the most conspicuous example. Other dangerous rivalries included Algeria-Egypt, India-Pakistan, Syria-Israel, North Korea-South Korea, and, as epitomized by the tragic devastation of Yugoslavia, myriad ethnic tensions within East Europe that had long been suppressed by the Cold War itself. To confront such challenges, leading powers might revert to a division of the world into spheres of influence—with each responsible for keeping the peace within its given sphere, and for coordinating its actions with other regional sentries.

The second underlying factor was economic, and grew out of contemporary movements toward commercial regionalization. While this trend took many forms, the most widely predicted development would lead to the formation of three massive and separate trading blocs:

- A European bloc, eventually including East Europe and possibly part of the ex-Soviet Union.
- A North American bloc, including Canada and Mexico as well as the United States, or possibly a hemispheric bloc embracing all of the Americas.
- A Pacific/Asia bloc, including Japan and its rapidly growing neighbors and eventually China.

The creation of trading blocs could provide both an objective basis and a political justification for reasserting spheres of influence. The global order would take shape as a consequence of regional initiatives.

This would not be an easy arrangement to manage. Alarmists predicted that "the twenty-first century will be a century of economic warfare," while the respected economist C. Fred Bergsten made a similar point with more caution: "The end of the Cold War could sharply heighten the prospect of trade war." Without the common cause of anticommunism, leading powers would be tempted to seek economic advantage from one another. Moreover, three-player games tend to be notoriously unstable, since everyone fears that the other two will line up against it on a permanent basis: "Given the inevitable self-perception of vulnerability on the part of each of the three parties, two will tend to ally against the third under conditions of rough tripolar equality—perhaps in an effort to create their own so-called 'bipolar' dominance." This would strengthen the hand of parochial forces—protectionists in America, traditionalists in Japan, regionalists in Europe—and precipitate a self-destructive cycle. "The target would probably seek to form (or expand) its bloc of nearby supporters, and the other areas would respond in kind. All economies would suffer, and risks of trade warfare would become real."[3]

Fulfillment of this scenario would have negative consequences for U.S.–Latin American relations—which would revolve around U.S. efforts to assert (or reassert) its sphere of influence throughout the Americas. Without the Cold War, however, this policy would no longer have its ideological justification in resistance to communism. It would stand revealed for what it would be: an exercise of raw power, an effort by the strong to dominate the weak and to exclude rival powers from the region. For all practical intents and purposes, it would be tantamount to restoration of the Monroe Doctrine.

Scenario 3: North-South Separation

A third scenario would extend the termination of the Cold War to its logical conclusion. In this perspective there could develop a "North-North" axis of economic and political cooperation that would encircle the upper half of the globe—from the United States to the European Community through East (or Central) Europe to Russia and Japan. Capital and commerce would flow relatively freely around this circuit and result in accelerated rates of growth for all concerned.

The South would be left out. Except for raw materials, countries of the South would have little to offer the hyper-developing nations of the North. To be sure, some members of the South would have special tickets of admission to the North-North economy. Oil-producing countries, especially cooperative ones, would have access to the northern circle. So would postapartheid South Africa, partly because of raw materials and partly for political and cultural reasons. With their cheap labor, abundant savings, and high technology, the Asian "gang of four" (Hong Kong, Singapore, South Korea, and Taiwan, also known as the "four little tigers") would be assured their own admission. But less developed countries, from India to Africa to South America, would face virtual exclusion from the privileged axis. As a result, the benefits of economic growth would be increasingly concentrated in the North; East-West conflict would give way to a North-South division of the world. As Charles William Maynes observed in 1990: "The key division in world politics is likely to become the North-South divide. The reasons are the relationship between poverty and people and the clash between economics and demographics."[4]

Realization of this scenario would depend upon two hard-nosed premises. First was the economic logic of an open market. Capital flows in the direction of opportunity—toward consumer markets, skilled labor forces, and entrepreneurial capacity. These advantages tended to be concentrated in the North, whereas the South offered uncertainty and risk. Second was the political logic of capitalist society. Power tends to follow and accommodate financial and commercial flows; indeed, some say, the supreme task of government in a liberal society is to protect capital, not to guide or control it. The more widespread the global tendency to privatize industry and reduce the economic role of the state, the more likely the trend toward subordination of governmental interests to market forces—and the ratification of the North-North axis by its member states.

Consolidation of a North-North axis could provoke serious problems. An abandoned South would be liable to become ever more dispirited, desperate, and reckless. Moderate leaders would lose credibility. Radicals of one stripe or another—nationalists, populists, *ayatollahs* (if not leftists)—would come into power. With little to lose, they would be tempted to pursue high-risk strategies of confrontation. The world would become increasingly dangerous, especially if nuclear weapons were to proliferate, and temptations for military action would escalate. Clearly, it would not be in the long-term interests of the North to have an angered and impoverished South on the other side of the equator.

The formation of a North-North axis would pose cruel choices for Latin America. For it was conceivable that, without the East-West conflict and/or the Soviet threat, the United States would lose interest in Latin America. As Jorge Castañeda once noted, this possibility created a serious dilemma for the region:

> Paradoxically, after so many years of worrying about excessive U.S. involvement, Latin America may soon suffer from U.S. indifference, compounded by the rest of the world's traditional, relative lack of interest. As the geopolitical motivation for U.S. policy toward Latin America fades, its economic component could also shrink. The hemisphere could well face the prospect of "Africanization"—condemnation to the margins of world financial and trade flows but also, inevitably, to neglect and irrelevance. It may well find itself caught in the bind of a perverse, contradictory tension: between new forms of U.S. intervention in domestic Latin American policies and new expressions of U.S. and world indifference to its needs.[5]

Without the Cold War, Latin America was confronting the possibility of marginalization.

These three scenarios outlined broad hypothetical trends. They were not mutually exclusive. They could emerge in complex combination or in chronological succession. Scenario 2 (Spheres) could lead to realization of Scenario 1 (Development) if advanced industrial nations exerted leadership in such a way as to accelerate growth among the less-developed countries within their areas of regional responsibility. Scenario 3 (Separation) could give way to Scenario 2 (Spheres) if rivalry and discord were to appear within the North-North axis and losing parties resorted to the formation of regional blocs. Alternatively, Scenario 2 (Spheres) could give way to Scenario 3 (Separation) if the costs of regional hegemony were to become unacceptable to major powers—especially, in comparison to the relative temptations of a North-North axis. Combinations could also occur. To meet the security challenge, major powers might impose Scenario 2 (Spheres), appointing and supporting regional sentries at key points on the globe; and to meet the development challenge, these same powers might resort to Scenario 3 (Separation). In other words, maintenance and protection of a North-North economic axis might require the capability to impose peace on abandoned areas of the South through the use of military force.

Narrowing Options

As major powers wrestled with reconfiguration of the world community and struggled to devise new rules of the game, Latin America found itself at a distinct disadvantage. The continent was not a major power center. It would have only a modest role in determining which general scenario would give shape to the post–Cold War world. *Ceteris paribus,* the most favorable outcome for Latin America would be Scenario 1 (Development); the least favorable was Scenario 3 (Separation); an intermediate possibility was Scenario 2 (Spheres). Amid uncertain prospects, the principal challenge for Latin America was to approximate the benefits that might have been available under Scenario 1, were this vision feasible, and to avoid the costs of abandonment and marginalization under Scenario 3. It was by no means self-evident how to accomplish these goals. Notwithstanding an initial burst of continental optimism in the late 1980s, it soon became apparent that the post–Cold War environment provided Latin America with a distressingly slim range of practical options.

It was no longer possible, as Bolívar fervently hoped, to seek protection from an extrahemispheric power. In full enjoyment of its "unipolar moment," the United States held uncontested military supremacy throughout the world. And despite the redistribution of global economic power, all major powers were elsewhere predisposed: the Soviet Union had collapsed, West Europe was promoting the rehabilitation and incorporation of East Europe, Japan was focusing attention on its Asian neighbors and especially on its bilateral relationship with the United States. There was nowhere for Latin America to turn.

Nor could Third World solidarity provide a plausible substitute. Indeed, the "developing world" was becoming increasingly fragmented into differing strata—between the conventional Third World and what came to be known as the "Fourth World," including countries such as Ethiopia, Burkina Faso, and Bangladesh, an area of bone-crushing poverty and structural underdevelopment. Within Latin America, the World Bank classified only Haiti (with a GNP/per capita of $360 in 1989) as a "low-income" country; most countries of the region stood above the international median; Venezuela and Brazil both qualified as "upper-middle-income" (with GNP/per capita of greater than $2,400), in fact, with Mexico and Argentina close behind.[6] And as foreshadowed by struggles over the "new international economic order" in the 1970s, Latin America's strategic and economic interests would not always converge with those of Asia, the Middle East, and Africa. In the wake of the debt crisis of the 1980s the region's economic destiny was, for better or worse, inextricably tied to the North.

South-South cooperation offered gratifying opportunities for rhetorical expressions of political solidarity; perhaps in search of leverage, too, Argentina, Brazil, Mexico, and Peru joined with other prominent Third World countries to form a so-called G-15 in 1989. In practical terms, however, the South could not provide a durable solution.

Nor was there a clear-cut formula for attracting attention and support from the United States. During the Cold War, political rulers of all stripes, from centrist reformers to rightist dictators, could invoke the threat of communism in order to obtain moral and material assistance from Washington. This was no longer possible. Leaders of Latin America would have to find some other means of engaging attention from Washington. It was not obvious what this could be.

Farewell to Revolution

Moreover, the end of the Cold War brought an end to revolutionary ferment in Latin America. As detailed in chapter 8, the intrinsic appeals of Marxist ideology plus long-standing resistance to the United States helped foment guerrilla uprisings and socialist movements from the 1950s through the 1980s. With the collapse of communism, however, Marxism-Leninism lost legitimacy as both a diagnosis of social ills and (especially) as a prescription for their remedy. Without the Soviet Union, there was no external patron for revolutionary movements. And without any fear of retaliation, either in Latin America or (more likely) in some other part of the world, the United States was free to wage unremitting war against revolutionary groups and socialist states.

Guerrilla movements throughout the hemisphere quickly lost force. As a rule, only those movements with continuing sources of income—usually obtained through collaboration with *narcotraficantes,* particularly in Peru and Colombia—could keep up operations. And even then they were able to interpret the handwriting on the wall. In Colombia, the 19th of April Movement (M-19) turned in its arms in order to join the electoral arena; its leader, Antonio Navarro Wolf, ran a respectable campaign in the presidential race of 1994. In Peru, Sendero Luminoso lost momentum and popular support after the capture in 1992 of its enigmatic leader, Abimael Guzmán. The only new guerrilla movement of the 1990s appeared in Mexico, in the southernmost state of Chiapas, but with an essentially reformist agenda. Armed revolution no longer offered a path to redemption.

Socialist states faced difficulties too. In Nicaragua, the Sandinista government fell victim to final vestiges of the Cold War itself. Unceasing campaigns against the U.S.-supported Contras obliged the government to spend nearly half its budget on defense and to alienate its citizens with the imposition of a military draft and other wartime measures. As a result of such factors plus the U.S. embargo, the Nicaraguan economy went into a serious tailspin. In February 1990 presidential elections pitted Daniel Ortega, the Sandinista leader, against Violeta Barrios de Chamorro, widow of Pedro Joaquín Chamorro and representative of a fragmented opposition coalition (UNO from its Spanish initials). Most pollsters announced that Ortega's lead was widening as the election approached. Then came the stunning results: UNO captured 54.7 percent of the vote, against 40.8 percent for the Sandinistas. At the urging of Jimmy Carter, in attendance as an international observer, Ortega made a gracious concession speech. Buffeted by the U.S.-imposed economic embargo and harassed by the U.S.-sponsored Contras, the Sandinista revolution came to an end with a whimper.

It was in Cuba, perhaps, that the end of the Cold War had its most decisive effect. East-West détente and collapse of the Soviet Union led to the abrupt disappearance of commercial ties and economic subsidies for Cuba. During the Cold War the USSR had consistently overpaid Cuba for sugar, while Cuba underpaid the Soviets for petroleum: the result was an annual subsidy estimated between $3.5 and $4.5 billion per year. Termination of this arrangement led to economic devastation. Critical industrial, raw material, and food imports from Russia plummeted by over 70 percent between 1989 and 1992, and continued declining in 1993. Petroleum imports from Russia dropped by more than half—from 13.3 million metric tons in 1989 to 5.7 million metric tons in 1993—leading Cuba to import bicycles from the People's Republic of China. Largely due to inclement weather, sugar production fell from 8.4 million metric tons in 1990 to merely 4.3 million in 1993. Together with the long-standing U.S. boycott, the implosion of communism imposed the equivalent of a "double embargo" on the beleaguered island. As a result, the estimated gross domestic product dropped by 45 percent between 1989 and 1993—and, according to responsible projections, continued its downward slide in 1994. This meant penury for millions of Cuban citizens: in 1992, according to one official source, 65 percent of Cuban families had monthly incomes equivalent to less than two dollars (U.S.) per capita at prevailing black-market rates of exchange.

Fidel responded to this adversity with an ambiguous stance, alternating between liberalization and crackdown. Seeking to find a new niche in the global economy, the government began attempting to attract foreign capital, technology, and tourism and to promote rapid growth among nontraditional exports. In 1993 the regime granted permission for Cubans to possess hard currency, allowed self-employment in trades and crafts, and created relatively autonomous cooperatives for sugar and agricultural production. To ease the pains of economic hardship, Castro also declared the initiation of a "special period in a time of peace."

But there were limits to these innovations. Having promulgated the slogan of *Socialismo o Muerte* in 1989, Fidel and his advisers concluded that Mikhail Gorbachev's eventual undoing resulted from excessive reformist zeal. Anxious to avoid this fate, Fidel took an uncompromising stance at the December 1993 meeting of the National Assembly of People's Power, contemptuously dismissing "the idea that capitalism can solve some of our problems" as "a crazy and absurd dream." *El Líder* continued:

> I believe in socialism and despise capitalism. What I feel is repugnance toward capitalists. . . . The better I know capitalism, the more I love socialism. I have such a concept of the garbage, unfairness, baseness, alienation, and immorality that capitalism is in all its forms, including its politicians.

To emphasize the point, a new constitution in late 1992 affirmed that the Cuban economy would rest on the "socialist ownership of the means of production." In general, it appeared that Cuba was moving toward hybrid market-Leninism along the lines of post-Mao China.

Political conformity accompanied these economic measures. After the Fourth Party Congress (October 1991), dissident poet María Elena Cruz-Varela was assaulted and then imprisoned. Numerous critics and human rights activists came under attack in 1992 and afterward. Within the leadership there existed an uneasy truce between three groups—reformists, centrists, and hard-line Fidelistas—with Castro retaining the decisive hand, occasionally dismissing independent-minded colleagues for reasons of personal caprice. In the February 1993 elections for the People's Assembly, 88.4 percent of voters throughout Cuba cast ballots for the entire list of official candidates.

It seemed, to many, that Castro was in an untenable situation. As early as 1991 one knowledgeable observer confidently proclaimed: "It is only a matter of time before Cuban communism collapses. While the date of its demise is obviously unknown in advance, it can be expected sooner rather than later." But Fidel displayed remarkable resilience, especially in the face of scattered opposition, and he was able to capitalize upon widespread resistance (within Cuba and around the world) to the perpetuation and intensification of the U.S. commercial embargo.[7] As policy analyst Jorge Domínguez shrewdly observed, "Washington's rigid opposition continued to allow Castro to rally citizens to defend what many Cubans are able to recognize as the regime's legitimate successes. The United States has been a staunch enemy of Castro, but with an enemy like this one, he may not need friends."[8]

Cuban citizens faced three alternatives: they could endure the hardships stoically; they could erupt in protest, as in April 1994; or they could escape to the United States. First hundreds, then thousands, attempted to traverse the Florida Straits in homemade rafts. The number of *balseros* climbed from just under 500 in 1990 to approximately 2,500 in 1991 to nearly 3,500 in 1993—then escalated sharply in mid-1994. During August 1994 the U.S. Coast Guard rescued more than 3,500 Cubans from the dangerous waters of the straits. Governor Lawton Chiles of Florida declared a statewide emergency and appealed to President Clinton for help.

In late August 1994 the Clinton administration responded by announcing the end of a thirty-year policy giving preferential treatment to refugees from Cuba, ordering instead their detention in Guantánamo and in Florida. Recalling the so-called Mariel exodus of 1980, when 128,000 people left Cuba for the United States, Clinton denounced the wave of *balseros* as "a cold-blooded attempt to maintain the Castro grip on Cuba and to divert attention from his failed communist policies. . . . Let me be clear: The Cuban government will not succeed in any attempt to dictate American immigration policy." Within days Clinton also announced a ban on dollar remittances to Cuba, often sent home to family members by Cubans in the United States, and a plan to increase and amplify anti-Castro broadcasts by Radio Martí. To justify these steps, Clinton offered his interpretation of reasons behind the *balsero* exodus: "The real problem is the stubborn refusal of the Castro regime to have an open democracy and an open economy, and I think the policies we are following will hasten the day when that occurs." Another top official made no secret of Washington's ultimate purpose:

> The goal is to try to encourage a peaceful evolution to a democracy with free markets. We think it [Cuba] is a failed regime which is continuing political and economic repression, and which does not have the support of the Cuban people. . . . In general, we want to try to find ways to support independent groups in Cuba in any way that is lawful and peaceful, and we will continue to do so.

As on so many prior occasions, the U.S. intent was Castro's overthrow. But as pointed out in chapter 11, such open disregard for the political sovereignty of a Latin American nation was uniquely characteristic of the post–Cold War period.

In September 1994 the United States and Cuba reached an interim accord. Negotiated by midlevel officials, the agreement specified that the United States would accept a minimum of 20,000 Cubans per year on a regular basis and for one year all eligible Cubans then on the waiting list at the American diplomatic mission in Havana (4,000 to 6,000). In exchange, Cuba agreed to "take effective measures in every way it possibly can to prevent unsafe departures using mainly persuasive methods."[9] The accord offered no immediate solace to the 25,000 Cubans being held at Guantánamo and made no reference to the ban on dollar remittances or to the thirty-two-year old embargo. Such items could be taken up only after Cuba began taking steps toward democracy and open markets, crowed Undersecretary of State Peter Tarnoff: "If it is seriously interested in reform, the government of Cuba must agree to be in touch with its own people."[10]

Under pressures of this kind, the revolutionary option tended to evaporate. Disenchanted by politics in general, Latin Americans gravitated toward social movements instead of partisan campaigns. Having endured human-rights abuses by authoritarian regimes and economic deprivation during the years of debt crisis, citizens became increasingly skeptical about the uses of the state. No longer inclined to seek utopian solutions, they came to rely on local grass-roots movements for the sake of pragmatic, practical change. Paradoxically, the gradual emergence of civil society in Latin America thus coincided with a downsizing of political ambitions, a focus on self-help, and an acceptance of incremental change.

For national leaders in Latin America, however, the question still remained: how to attract attention and support from the United States? Interpreting the inter-American agenda of the post–Cold War era, they fastened on economic relations. There was almost no other choice: unlike the communist threat, migration and drugs furnished weak bargaining chips; and as Panama and Haiti served to demonstrate, tension along these lines could lead to U.S. military intervention. The emphasis then turned to economics and instruments for commercial cooperation. Free trade became the watchword of the day.

In the absence of a worldwide commitment to global development, it thus became apparent by the mid-1990s that nations of Latin America were left with three alternatives: first, they could undertake unilateral attempts to cultivate ties with Europe and Japan as well as with the United States; second, they could construct regional or subregional communities through economic integration; or third, they could align themselves with the United States. Aptly reflecting contemporary idioms, all these strategies emphasized economics over politics, opportunity over principle, pragmatism over ideology. They also concealed a fundamental danger, represented by the possibility of North-South separation: that some countries (and many people) might face isolation and abandonment.

Option 1: Unilateral Liberalization

One potential strategy for nations of Latin America was to undertake unilateral programs of economic liberalization, more or less according to the Washington consensus, and to strengthen commercial and financial ties with major power centers. A "plurilateral" approach toward economic intercourse seemed to comply with multipolar realities of the new global economy, especially the rise of Europe and Japan. Systematic reduction of commercial barriers promised to achieve the anticipated benefits of free trade. Moreover, unilateral action had the advantage of maintaining flexibility. Within a general strategy of export-led development, the corresponding policy prescriptions were relatively straightforward: diversify products and partners, seek foreign investment from multiple sources, avoid restrictive entanglements; in other words, embark on a unilateral project in the name of free trade.

Among all countries of Latin America, Chile was in the best position to pursue this option. Like other nations, Chile had adopted an increasingly protectionist trade policy from the 1930s to the early 1970s—by 1973 the modal tariff was 90 percent, with a maximum of 750 percent, accompanied by an extensive network of nontariff barriers (NTBs) as well. From 1974 onward the Pinochet regime imposed a radical change in policy. Most nontariff barriers were eliminated at the outset, and tariffs were steadily lowered to a flat rate of 10 percent for nearly all items by 1979. In reaction to the debt crisis the government temporarily hiked tariffs back up to 35 percent in 1984, while avoiding NTBs, and subsequent steps brought tariffs back down to 11 percent by the early 1990s.

The democratic governments of Patricio Aylwin and Eduardo Frei (Jr.) continued the Pinochet emphasis on commercial liberalization. "Free trade has been widely accepted as an integral part of Chile's development model," according to one well-informed analysis, "and there is consensus that a return to protectionism is not a reasonable option." In demonstration of this point, there was no meaningful opposition to reduction of the tariff rate from 15 percent to 11 percent in mid-1991.

Results of this outward-looking strategy were dramatic. Exports as a share of Chile's GDP grew from 31 percent in 1974 to 71 percent in 1990. After sharp contractions in the early 1980s, the economy achieved strong and steady rates of economic growth—reaching a maximum of 10 percent in 1989, and far out-performing the region as a whole from 1986 through 1992. The dependence on raw materials was still fairly high, however, and value added to natural resources continued to be low. During the 1960s mining accounted for 85.6 percent of exports, for instance, and in the late 1980s this sector still accounted for 53.1 percent. In the meantime, the share of industrial products in exports grew from 10.5 percent to 32.8 percent—not as strong a performance as might have been hoped but nonetheless a positive trend.

Chile furthermore achieved unusual success in the diversification of its commercial partnerships. By 1991 Japan replaced the United States as Chile's largest customer (as shown in Table A8, Japan was closing in on the United States by 1990). Chile also had extensive trade connections with the European Community, especially with Germany, and imported about as many goods from the EC as a whole as from the United States. By the early 1990s Chile had thus managed to forge exceptional balance in the structure of its international trade.

At the same time Chile developed a selective network of bilateral free trade agreements (FTAs) with countries of Latin America. In 1991 the Aylwin administration reached an agreement with Mexico, for the purpose of establishing an FTA by January 1996. In 1993 the government forged compacts with Colombia, for an operational FTA by 1994, and with Venezuela, for the realization of free trade by 1999. Chile also concluded a less ambitious agreement with Argentina and initiated additional consultations with Bolivia, Costa Rica, Ecuador, and Uruguay. The goals of these bilateral negotiations were manifold: to open new markets, to assure supplies of critical products (such as petroleum), and to establish Chile's position as a continental leader. As free trade became the clarion call of the 1990s, Chile assumed a position of preeminence.

A central issue, for Chile, was its relationship with the United States. Finance minister Alejandro Foxley reacted enthusiastically to Bush's announcement of the Enterprise for the Americas Initiative (EAI) in mid-1990, and Chile was the first country in Latin America to benefit— with a $150 million sectoral loan from the Inter-American Development Bank, a debt-reduction plan of $16 million, and the signing of a bilateral "framework agreement" for trade negotiations in September 1990. In June 1991, on the first anniversary of the EAI pronouncement, the two governments established a bilateral working group to clear the way for an eventual FTA. During President Aylwin's official visit to Washington in May 1992, it was further announced that Chile would be first in line for an FTA with the United States after completion of the NAFTA negotiations with Mexico.

What Chile wanted from an FTA with the United States was not so much trade as investment. Indeed, there was concern in Santiago about the potential for trade diversion, since the elimination of tariffs on U.S. goods would amount to an 11 percent margin of favoritism vis-à-vis other sources. The result of this preference could be systematic bias against Japan, the European Community, and other trade partners, with a consequent distortion in commercial flows. But the benefit would come in the form of an international "seal of approval," a certification that Chile offered the world a safe and sound site for direct foreign investment. In the words of one analysis, an FTA with the United States "would show that democracy is good for business because it offers continuity and stability and legitimizes market liberalization policies."

By the mid-1990s there were two major questions confronting Chilean policy. One was whether to pursue a bilateral FTA with the United States alone or to join the North American Free Trade Agreement, as proposed at the Miami summit of December 1994. According to most observers, Chile would have preferred a bilateral agreement with the United States, which could expand Chile's room for maneuver regarding MERCOSUR and which would also avoid the complexity and density of the NAFTA accord (which, it will be remembered, offered no clear guidelines for accession). For reasons of its own, Mexico might want to oppose or postpone any expansion of NAFTA, although Chile may have been a special case—it would not provide Mexico with serious economic competition, it would offer association with a highly touted democracy, and it would strengthen Mexico's diplomatic hand in South America. As of mid-1995 Chile appeared to be heading for eventual membership in NAFTA, but the timing and form of its accession were far from self-evident.

The second question, not unrelated to the first, was whether an FTA would contain environmental stipulations. On this there was uneasiness. According to one analysis:

People, both in and out of government, view this constraint with mixed feelings. Some Chilean environmental groups argue that the overall environmental impact of the FTA is dubious because the benefit from debt-for-nature swaps, the environment tool of the EAI, is likely to be small compared to the environmental damage of the FTA caused by increased trade and investment. Some industries are reluctant to accept U.S. environmental standards that might compromise their operations. On the other hand, others argue that U.S. pressure and, eventually, support might help clean up the environment and improve Chilean standards in the future.

In effect, the incorporation of environmental guidelines within NAFTA provided resolution on this point. Either to join NAFTA or to reach an FTA with the United States, Chile would have to accept negotiation on environmental standards.

Despite these uncertainties, Chile managed to forge a workable and productive policy response to circumstances of the 1990s. By developing commercial ties with Europe and Japan as well as the United States, Chile was not beholden to any single trade partner. By negotiating selective bilateral agreements, Chile maintained flexibility in its international policy. And by publicly advocating the virtues of free trade, Chile claimed a leadership role throughout the region. Having restored its traditions of democracy, Chile became a political model as well. The international community looked upon Chile with benign approval, just as neighboring countries may have felt a bit of envy: in meeting after meeting, Chile came to be viewed as the *vedette* of Latin America.

Other nations of the region would probably have liked to pursue the Chilean path. There is substantial, though anecdotal, evidence that Carlos Salinas de Gortari wanted to adopt a similar policy after taking office in 1988. Unlike Chile, however, the Mexican economy was heavily dependent upon the United States. Such realities imposed constraints and narrowed policy options.[11] As things turned out, only Chile was in a position to adopt the Chilean model.

Option 2: Subregional Integration

A second strategic alternative was the promotion of regional (or subregional) economic integration. Latin America had a long history of efforts in this area, of course, dating back to the formation of LAFTA in 1960. Subregional projects also abounded, from the Central American Common Market (successful in the 1960s) to the Andean Pact (1969) to the Caribbean Common Market (1972). Most of these schemes sought to promote industrial development by expanding markets and erecting protectionist barriers against outside competition. Partly because the economies of member countries tended to be more competitive than complementary, however, regional markets never became especially important: intraregional market shares peaked at 26 percent for the Central American Common Market, 14 percent within LAFTA/ALADI, and merely 4.8 percent for the Andean Group.

In the aftermath of debt crisis and Cold War, Latin American leaders sought to promote new forms of regional integration. Their idea was not to foster growth through market protection, however, but integration with the global economy. As economist Sylvia Saborio described the integrationist revival of the early 1990s:

> As part of the broader agenda of economic reforms, it is outward-oriented rather than inward-looking. It seeks rather than shuns foreign investment as a source of capital, technology, and distribution outlets. It relies primarily on market signals and competitive forces rather than on policy interventions to allocate resources. And, last but not least, it favors across-the-board, automatic measures over selective, piecemeal approaches to minimize backsliding and special interest pressure.

Regional integration thus received a new impetus, based not on the expansion of internal markets but on competitive connections with the world economy.

Construed as a program for all of Latin America, regional integration harkened back to Simón Bolívar's vision of unification: as a Central American diplomat once said, "This would give us an opportunity to achieve the Bolivarian dream of continental unity." It would also constitute a plausible defensive measure against the potential formation of a North-North axis. Integration of Latin America would strengthen the regional hand in dealing with the North, especially with the United States, and thus minimize the prospects of isolation and abandonment.

Yet continental unification seemed a long way off. Not every nation sought immediate participation: it was to Chile's advantage to pursue its unilateral options, just as it would be Mexico's choice (for different reasons) to enter into NAFTA. And not every country was prepared to follow a regional strategy: around 1990, for instance, Peru was widely regarded as an economic basket case. As Bolívar had himself discovered, regional collaboration was more easily imagined than achieved.

Under these circumstances the most reasonable strategy called for subregional integration—projects for economic cooperation among groups of Latin American countries, rather than for the continent as a whole. The Central American Common Market was resuscitated, CARICOM was reinvigorated, and the Andean Pact was reshaped and revitalized. Surprisingly, perhaps, the most ambitious and influential of these subregional schemes emerged in South America's Southern Cone.

MERCOSUR

The movement for creation of the Common Market of the South, known from its Spanish acronym as MERCOSUR, drew on integration efforts dating from the 1960s. Specific steps began with the bilateral Programa de Integración y Cooperación Argentino-Brasileño (PICAB) in 1985. Formalized in 1988 through a treaty that was ratified in 1989, this Argentine-Brazilian accord initially set a ten-year timetable for creation of a binational common market. In November 1990 Presidents Carlos Saúl Menem and

Fernando Collor de Melo decided to accelerate the schedule, cutting back the phase-in period by four years and introducing automatic tariff reductions (thus imposing a kind of "tariff shock"). They also agreed to undertake negotiations with Uruguay and Paraguay.

Under the Treaty of Asunción, reached in March 1991, the four member countries—Argentina, Brazil, Paraguay, and Uruguay—committed themselves to construct by December 1994 a customs union, with a common external tariff, and to move onward to a full-fledged common market in subsequent years. Especially in view of long-standing rivalries among its constituent members, MERCOSUR was a truly remarkable development. Its partner countries comprised nearly one-half of Latin America's gross domestic product, more than 40 percent of its total population, and about one-third its foreign trade. More important than its size, however, was its strategic orientation. According to Argentine analyst Félix Peña, one of the project's original architects, the principal innovation of MERCOSUR stemmed from its commitment to "outward-oriented integration"—that is, from its determination to make member states more competitive in the international arena rather than to rely on closed markets via import-substitution industrialization. Moreover, wrote Peña, "The MERCOSUR is not merely an instrument to facilitate trade expansion. On the contrary, it is oriented towards cooperation on investment and job creation. In essence, it is a tool for technological modernization and industrial restructuring." In other words, it extends and promotes simultaneous and compatible strategies for liberalization: "The basic assumption underlying the MERCOSUR is that the four countries have chosen a path from which there is no turning back."

In addition, MERCOSUR had clear political goals: the consolidation of democracy and the maintenance of peace throughout the Southern Cone. At the same time that MERCOSUR was taking shape, agreements were reached in the nuclear field between Argentina and Brazil, countries that shared significant nuclear capacity as well as historic rivalry. To quote Peña once again: MERCOSUR was "not simply an economic project. . . . although its principal measures related to trade, production, and investment, it transcends economics and penetrates the broadest of political issues." In a sense, MERCOSUR would provide civilian democrats throughout the subregion with a regular opportunity for consultation and mutual support, thus offsetting the long-established conclaves for representatives of the armed forces.

Unlike the North American Free Trade Agreement, MERCOSUR established a complex structure of decision-making institutions. A Common Market Group, coordinated by the foreign ministries, constituted the executive organ. General policy was set by a Council of the Common Market, under the foreign and economy ministers, with biannual meetings attended by the four presidents. There was also a Joint Parliamentary Commission drawn from members of the respective national parliaments. From the start, MERCOSUR's designers saw it as a dynamic institution, one that would evolve rapidly over time and also crystallize relations with economies of the North. Once President Bush announced the Enterprise for the Americas Initiative, MERCOSUR became a potential instrument for collective bargaining: as a Brazilian observer recalled, "There was the perception that it would be interesting to concentrate efforts to negotiate *en bloc.*" Contradictory tendencies also emerged: having undergone a harsh program of structural adjustment, Argentina expressed eagerness to negotiate its own FTA with the United States (and/or seek membership within NAFTA), an act that would logically lead to the dismantlement of MERCOSUR. Within all such subregional groupings, the tradeoffs between unilateral initiative and multilateral solidarity presented individual countries with agonizing policy dilemmas.

Open Regionalism

A persisting rationale for the contemporary integrationist movement in Latin America espoused the notion of "open regionalism"—patterns of regional integration that would be outward-oriented, not inward-looking, designed to achieve integration with the world economy rather than protection from it. Throughout the Western Hemisphere, as in the Pacific Basin, insistence on open regionalism became something of a mantra. As construed in Latin America, open regionalism implied at least two policy orientations:

- External tariffs (and NTBs) must not be raised for any member country.
- Opportunities for accession by nonmembers should be clearly available.

In both these senses, the integration schemes must be "open" to participation by nonmembers. The purpose must be to increase the volume of trade, not merely to divert it, and participation in the benefits should be available to nonmembers.

These simple principles were more easily invoked than respected, however. By the mid-1990s it was possible to imagine rollbacks in trade liberalization, especially in view of the short-term hardships imposed by readjustment programs. And even then the negotiation of common external tariffs could lead to raises in rates for individual member countries (probably smaller ones) within an overall reduction for the group as a whole.

Similarly, openness to new members posed practical problems as well. None of the existing subregional agreements had transparent accession clauses, and some—such as the Central American Common Market and CARICOM—were meant to have identifiable geographical limits. There were also structural disincentives for taking on new members. First, the countries most apt to seek admission were likely to be the least desirable: all groupings would probably welcome Chile, which had no reason to join, but they would not want to accept basket cases, which would have the most reason to join. Second, there would be scant motivation to share existing benefits with nonmember countries if the integration scheme were working well. Despite the rhetoric of openness, membership in a collective arrangement implied access to benefits that nonmembers would not have; otherwise there would be no purpose to the organization in the first place. Admission of new members necessarily meant sharing these benefits with someone else. Of course the situation might be different if the integration scheme were not working well, in which case new members might give it new life, but under those circumstances there would be no reason for any outside country to apply for admission. Either way, the achievement of genuinely "open" regionalism proved to be a daunting task.

Even so, the insistence on open regionalism served a crucial political purpose: maintaining access to linkages with major economic powers, especially the United States. As President Bush indicated in his proclamation of the Enterprise for the Americas Initiative, there would be encouragement for groups of countries to apply for membership in a free trade zone stretching "from Anchorage to the Tierra del Fuego." Subregional groupings in Latin America all wanted to pursue this possibility. Moreover, there was considerable concern about the fate of the Uruguay Round of GATT negotiations, successfully concluded in late 1993, and the possible formation of rivalrous blocs in the world economy, still an open question as of 1995. As a matter of self-protection, subregional groups in Latin America wanted to keep their options open.

Option 3: Joining with the North

A third strategy for Latin America was to find a way to join with the North, or more specifically, with the United States. In the early 1990s Washington encouraged this prospect, first by engaging in free trade discussions with Mexico and then by launching the Enterprise for the Americas Initiative. Indeed, one of the most notable features of new integrationist movements was the proactive stance by the United States, which was now seeking "to steer them, support them, and eventually join them." It seemed apparent that the United States was adopting this course more as a means of confronting economic rivals elsewhere in the world, especially Europe and Japan, rather than of proclaiming fundamental solidarity with neighbors in the hemisphere, but the resulting opportunity was nonetheless apparent. It was now possible, under these new conditions, for countries of Latin America to align themselves with the United States on economic grounds.

This alternative seemed attractive because it would assure some form of integration in the world economy, thus preventing exclusion from a potential North-North axis. Affiliation with the North would naturally entail costs. Admission to this club would carry a substantial price, probably consisting of multiple elements:

- Acceptance, at least in broad outline, of the economic tenets of the "Washington consensus."
- Liberal opportunities for foreign investment to operate within the local market.
- Advantageous concessions for foreign access to raw materials.
- Low-cost labor for foreign investment.
- In the political realm, loyal cooperation on foreign-policy issues.

Bidding could lead to competition and differences among the countries of Latin America rather than to solidarity. As a Central American legislator ruefully predicted: "We will each vie to become the fifth little tiger."

Among all nations of the region, Mexico was in by far the best position to pursue this option. It had a number of built-in advantages—geographical proximity to the United States, petroleum deposits, a relatively skilled work force, and a large and growing market. The complexity of the bilateral agenda, ranging from drugs to migration to foreign-policy questions, added further incentives for Washington.

The negotiation of NAFTA, described in chapter 10, made it possible for Mexico to jump upon the economic bandwagon of North-North development, but as a conspicuously junior partner. (It goes without saying that this was not the same thing as "joining the first world.") In exchange, Mexico would have to abdicate many of its pretensions to independent political leadership in Latin America or the Third World. And within the bilateral arena, in instances of conflict arising from economic integration, Mexico would face an even greater asymmetry in power resources than in the past. This was perhaps a bitter trade-off, but it was the essence of the bargain.

Precisely for these reasons NAFTA was not, in fact, Mexico's first choice. Early in his term Carlos Salinas de Gortari attempted to pursue the kind of "plurilateral" strategy pioneered by Chile, reaching out through commerce and investment to multiple centers of world economic power (and, at the same time, carefully tailoring economic relations with the United States through a series of limited sectoral agreements). But this option proved not to be viable. Financiers in Europe were directing their resources toward the rehabilitation and reincorporation of Eastern Europe, as Salinas learned to his dismay at a memorable meeting in Davos, Switzerland, in February 1990, and Japanese investors were proving reluctant to meddle in what they saw as a U.S. sphere of interest. Anxious to attract investment capital, Salinas then turned toward the United States. NAFTA would insure future access to the U.S. market, ensure the continuation of his economic policies, and, most important, send a crucial signal to the business community. In one analyst's summation, an FTA with the United States would provide "an excellent chance to advertise to the world the business opportunities available in Mexico."

At issue, in the mid-1990s, was whether this kind of institutionalized alignment with the United States offered an appropriate alternative for

other nations of the hemisphere. This was the central idea behind the
Enterprise for the Americas Initiative. Several countries—Chile, Argentina, Costa Rica among them—expressed immediate interest in the possibility of free trade arrangements with the United States. These overtures
raised three practical questions: the assessment of likely costs and benefits;
the utility of NAFTA versus a separate bilateral compact; and the likelihood of ratification by the United States.

The principal concern about costs and benefits focused on potential
trade diversion. This risk was substantial for countries with major commercial partners outside the hemisphere. Chile thus insisted that any FTA
involving the United States should represent a form of "open" regionalism: its goal was to attract foreign investment, to secure access to the U.S.
market, and to maintain its commercial ties with Europe and Japan. The
lower the unilateral barriers to imports, of course, the more plausible this
approach; and the greater the prior concentration of trade with the United
States, as in the case of Costa Rica, the less the room for trade diversion.
For a country like Brazil, however, with extensive European connections
and substantial import barriers, the prospects of trade diversion were genuinely worrisome. For this reason policymakers in Brasília displayed considerable reticence toward the idea of special trade agreements with the
United States.

A second concern focused on NAFTA itself. This was a highly spe-
cialized treaty, adorned with special provisions and festooned with supplementary agreements on environmental and labor issues. While it met the
particular concerns of its three members, it seemed to offer an exceptionally cumbersome instrument for accession by other countries. What
Chile and Costa Rica and Argentina really wanted were bilateral FTAs
with the United States, straightforward and simple accords that would
certify the signatories as appropriate and desirable sites for foreign investment. NAFTA, with complex provisions ranging from rules of origin to
environmental protection, was both more and less than what they wanted.
As explained in chapter 10, the expansion of NAFTA into a hemispheric
WHFTA would be a complicated process.

Third was uncertainty about attitudes in the United States. Despite all
the compelling reasons in favor of a free trade agreement with Mexico, the
U.S. Congress ratified NAFTA with a substantial degree of reluctance, and
only under intense political pressure from the White House. (Clinton won
approval for NAFTA in the House of Representatives from 75 percent of
Republicans, but only 40 percent of Democrats.) Subsequent crises
throughout 1994—the January uprising in Chiapas, the March assassination of presidential candidate Luis Donaldo Colosio, the September slay-
ing of PRI leader José Francisco Ruiz Massieu—led many lawmakers to
revise their views of Mexico. The peso's sudden plunge in December only
added to this disenchantment: as Mexican historian Lorenzo Meyer would
later remark, "The First World paradise promised by Carlos Salinas was
transformed in a moment into one more chapter of our Third World hell."

Concurrent events in other countries, including the late-summer crisis in Haiti, reinforced popular American stereotypes about violence and instability throughout the region. It was not at all clear, in other words, that accession to NAFTA or bilateral government-to-government accords would receive final approval from the U.S. Congress. In addition to other caveats, this uncertainty posed strong disincentives for Latin America. For any national leader, the political costs of rejection by the U.S. legislature were bound to be enormous: better to avoid the possibility than to have tried and lost.

Even without such dire prospects, the stance of the U.S. government was critical. As economist Nora Lustig wrote in early 1994:

> The future of regional integration crucially depends on the position of the United States. Is the U.S. going to follow suit with its earlier promises and promote a free trade area in the hemisphere? Is it going to do it by extending NAFTA or through bilateral agreements? Is NAFTA an open bloc? The answer is not clear. . . . Until the U.S. government defines its position and strategy, the process of hemispheric integration will continue to be haphazard and the prospects of lowering trade barriers *between* the regional integration arrangements will be small.[12]

As in other historic eras, the range of options available to Latin America was contingent on the performance of the United States.

Hubs and Spokes

The plethora of integrationist agreements emerging in the 1990s raised the possibility of so-called hub-and-spoke formations. Under this system a central country, or "hub," would enjoy special preference in the market of each "spoke" country under a series of separate bilateral agreements. The spokes, however, would not have preferential access to each other's markets; even worse, they would have to compete among themselves for preferences within the hub market. What was good for the hub, in other words, was not so good for the spokes.

There were initial fears that the United States was intent upon the formation of a hub-and-spoke system in the Americas with itself at the center. It was this concern, in fact, that prompted a reluctant Canadian government to join the U.S.–Mexican negotiations over what would eventually become NAFTA. Rather than become one of two competitive spokes in a North American market, it was preferable for Ottawa to take full part in the creation of a trilateral arrangement.

Efforts to avoid a U.S.-centric system did not, however, prevent Latin American countries from attempting to create their own hub-and-spoke arrangements. There were economic and, especially, political advantages in the hub position. By virtue of size and strategic location, only two nations had realistic opportunities to pursue this strategy: Mexico and Brazil.[13]

The Mexican idea was to establish itself as the central interlocutor between the United States and Latin America. This position could be welcome to Washington, given its long and troubled history of relations with Latin America, and it could provide considerable leverage for Mexico as well. In a political sense, this role could compensate for Mexico's loss of independence in other areas of foreign policy. As a founding member of NAFTA, Mexico could exercise a veto over applications for accession to the North American area. This veto alone represented a substantial source of hemispheric influence. In addition, Mexico began pursuing a series of subregional agreements: a bilateral pact with Chile (1991), a bilateral pact with Costa Rica (1991), a regional pact with Central America (1992), and a trilateral arrangement with Venezuela and Colombia (1993) to form the Grupo de los Tres. The resulting pattern created a good deal of confusion, since the compatibility of all these schemes was not self-evident, but their political meaning was clear: any road to the U.S. market would have to go through Mexico.

Brazil took a somewhat different tack, attempting to affirm its position as a subregional hegemon rather than as an interlocutor with the United States. Already the dominant country within MERCOSUR, Brazil officially launched in April 1994 its proposal for a South American Free Trade Area, or SAFTA (Área de Libre Comercio Sudamericana, ALCSA). President Itamar Franco first outlined the idea in September 1993, and government representatives took informal soundings throughout the region. SAFTA instantly became a major topic of discussion within MERCOSUR, and with authorization from its partners Brazil pursued the project with energy and animation.

The goal of SAFTA was to create a free trade zone for "substantially all trade" within the continent (in GATTspeak)—that is, on all products except those touching on "sensitive" national interests. This meant about 80 percent of intraregional trade. SAFTA would accomplish this target largely through a linear, automatic, and progressive schedule of liberalization over the ten-year period from 1995 to 2005. It would remove non-tariff as well as tariff barriers, though it would deal only with goods and not with labor or services. The principal forum for negotiations would be the Asociación Latinoamericana de Integración, headquartered in Uruguay.

Public intentions behind SAFTA were manifold: to capitalize on the experience of MERCOSUR, which had led to growth of intraregional trade; to avoid the "isolation" of MERCOSUR, especially from Chile and the Andean Group; and to accumulate negotiating power for dealing with the possibility of broader integration schemes in the Americas.[14] Continental membership in SAFTA, it was argued, would "strengthen capacity . . . to face the prospect of integration on a hemispheric scale, through NAFTA, revealing not only the desire but the capability among South American countries to overcome obstacles and to develop in partnership."

There was a political motivation as well. SAFTA would confirm Brazil's historic claim to be a continental hegemon, its long-standing sense of manifest destiny. By itself, without any formal link to North America or the United States, SAFTA would reflect and ratify regional domination by Brazil. Alternatively, during the course of any ensuing negotiations with the North, Brazil would become the principal intermediary between the continent and the United States. Either way, SAFTA would lead to the strengthening of Brazil's international position. In a political sense, Brazil would thus become the hub of South America.

Outlooks for the Americas

As a result of all these trends and developments, it was possible by the mid-1990s to imagine three general outlines for the future structure of the Western Hemisphere. While based on economic factors, especially ongoing processes of regional integration, the scenarios had profound political, social, and diplomatic implications.

One would envision prolongation of the status quo, with a three-member NAFTA as the only formal trade accord linking Latin America to the United States. This result could come about for a variety of reasons, as explained in chapter 10, including resistance on the part of the U.S. Congress. In this eventuality other countries of Latin America would be free to pursue alternative strategies, such as "plurilateral" opening to extra-hemispheric trading partners or the promotion of subregional integration schemes. South-South cooperation of the 1970s vintage was not, however, a serious option. And with Mexico ensconced in North America, the Bolivarian dream of unification was a logical impossibility. The most ambitious conceivable model for regional integration without the United States appeared to be SAFTA, the Brazilian project for a South American Free Trade Area.

A second general scenario envisioned the achievement of WHFTA, despite all obstacles and problems. In this case all countries of the hemisphere would join together in a free trade area that would accelerate the flow of goods and services, promote development, and, it would be hoped, contribute to the consolidation of democracy. Via links with the United States, all countries of Latin America would have access to capital and markets of the advanced industrial North. This could come about either through successive accessions to NAFTA, in which case the resultant extent of hemispheric integration would be relatively deep, or possibly through the promulgation of a new hemispheric organization, in which case the degree of integration would be relatively shallow. To be viable, however, any meaningful form of WHFTA would have to include and accommodate Brazil. Whether Washington, Brasília, and other capitals of Latin America could all come to terms on such an initiative was a highly uncertain prospect as of 1995.

A third possibility might be called "NAFTA-plus"—that is, a scenario under which NAFTA would undergo limited expansion to include three or

four other countries of Latin America. The process might begin with
Chile, as many observers predicted, then move on to Costa Rica, everyone's favorite small country. But the list of viable candidates grew short
after that. The admission of Argentina would lead to the automatic destruction of MERCOSUR. Venezuela, despite its oil, was showing signs
of political instability. Colombia, despite its macroeconomic moderation,
remained the headquarters for traffic in cocaine. In other words, it was not
hard to see how the expansion of NAFTA might start, but it was hard to
see where it might end—or how it might come to embrace all countries of
the hemisphere.

On balance, the NAFTA-plus scenario seemed perhaps the most
realistic—and in some respects the most pessimistic. NAFTA-plus could
eventually lead to fragmentation, stratification, and division of the hemisphere by constructing a two-tiered system of "ins" vs. "outs." This system
could lead to social resentment in excluded countries and to expressions of
political anger, what one analyst has called "movements of rage." In the
long run this animosity would have serious economic and political consequences for the future of all countries in the hemisphere.

The possibilities of NAFTA-plus had serious implications for Latin
America. Neither Argentina nor Venezuela nor Colombia could count on
prompt accession to NAFTA (or creation of WHFTA). Such countries
would have to define and pursue alternative strategies for themselves.
Waiting on line for NAFTA did not constitute a policy.

There were equally important implications for the United States.
NAFTA may have constituted a coherent policy toward Mexico, but it did
not provide a meaningful policy with regard to other countries of the
region. For the short to medium term, Washington would have to develop
new and feasible policies for dealing with Latin American countries that
did not belong to either NAFTA or a fledgling WHFTA. A potential
outline for such a policy emerged from the Miami summit of December
1994, with its proclamation of a Free Trade Area of the Americas, but this
commitment was exceedingly vague—and its implementation was bound
to face numerous obstacles and hazards. Notwithstanding official optimism, prospects for a hemispheric "community of democracies" seemed
tenuous indeed.

Cultures of Accommodation

Partly because of its uncertainty, the post–Cold War environment stimulated intellectual and attitudinal ferment throughout Latin America. This
was a time for rethinking orthodox wisdom, reassessing long-held assumptions, discarding outmoded shibboleths. As leaders and citizens searched
for new ideas and solutions, the very meanings of standard political
categories—left, right, center—were coming into question. Rearrangements of power in the global and hemispheric arena not only altered the
terms of diplomatic and commercial intercourse; they revised perceptions

and outlooks as well, altering "cognitive maps" that Latin Americans had constructed about their world, their continent, and themselves. Amid swirling intellectual currents, one classic theme persisted: the preservation of cultural identity.

At the most practical level, analysts sought to articulate a strategy of economic development that would build upon, but move beyond, the policy prescriptions of the Washington consensus. One of the most disagreeable, and potentially simplistic, notions within this conventional wisdom was that Latin America could find the keys to development merely by "opening" its economies—by enabling external forces to reshape and reinvigorate factors of production through trade and investment. Latin America's principal task, according to this prescription, was to become a passive recipient of these benevolent influences. There was little room for positive initiative on the part of continental governments. Latin states should merely get out of the way and, in the most literal sense, adopt a laissez-faire stance.

Gradually, economists and social scientists throughout the region developed a deliberate and thoughtful response to this challenge. Under the influence of the late Fernando Fajnzylber and his colleagues at the UN's Economic Commission for Latin America and the Caribbean (ECLAC), policymakers fashioned a series of ideas that stressed the centrality of national development policies. As explained by sympathetic observers:

> The new paradigm is as different from the stylised version of import substitution industrialisation identified with Latin America since the 1950s as it is from the stylised version of export-oriented growth identified with East Asia more recently. National competitiveness is conceived of as a project that originates internally as a means of mobilising the society towards economic transformation and dynamism which would result in international competitiveness rather than the other way round. It is built on the idea that no market, sector or industry is insulated from the world and that relative efficiency is relevant to all economic actors. The idea is to combine internal and external elements in highly productive, synergistic modes so as to achieve the maximum stimulus to output growth. Whereas the orthodox view advocates export-led growth through uniform trade liberalisation, the new paradigm articulates a path of growth-led exports through nationally differentiated strategies for achieving competitiveness. Whereas market forces *are* the centrepiece of the orthodox view, they are but one of several crucial means of achieving national competitiveness.

ECLAC analysts expressed profound concerns with questions of social equity, not just economic growth. Analyzing the much-heralded models of East Asia, especially the "four tigers" (Hong Kong, Taiwan, Singapore, and South Korea), Fajnzylber and his associates argued that Latin America suffered from the relative lack of investment in technology, especially in its exploitation of natural resources. They also perceived that strategies for economic development contained political implications, and that the region faced a dual challenge: the need to reinforce nascent democratic structures in Latin America and the need to provide effective support for opening national economies within the global system. These imperatives called for substantial investment in human resources, particularly education, which ECLAC regarded as a critical priority.[15]

Economic stimulus could not come merely from outside. On the contrary, according to this view, "Growth is from inside outward and is supply-driven." The key issues confronting Latin America were matters of national policy—not so much commercial arrangements as internal development strategies, with trade constituting a derivative rather than a determining issue. Free trade alone was not the answer: the challenge was to define Latin America's optimal position in the world economy and to implement policies accordingly. Even in the global economy of the 1990s, with all its uncertainties and ambiguities, Latin America could and should take charge of its future.

Outside this policy realm, there were broader intellectual changes as well. Conspicuous among them was a relaxation of the concept of nationalism. Throughout Latin America, ruling elites were busily engaged in the redefinition (or dismissal) of the traditional nationalism that sought to uphold historic principles of sovereignty and self-determination. In pragmatic and flexible fashion, they were tending to define national interests in terms of economic opportunity, not political principle, and they seemed fully prepared to surrender portions of sovereignty in the interests of regional integration. This transformation may have been more thorough among ruling elites than among the citizenry as a whole, but it was nonetheless a remarkable change.

A parallel shift took place in views of the United States. In the wake of the Cold War, peoples of Latin America tended to adopt increasingly favorable opinions about their northern neighbor. The implosion of the Soviet Union and the collapse of socialist ideology appeared, for many, to confirm the legitimacy (or at least the inevitability) of U.S. leadership throughout the hemisphere. In this new context, the United States was not so much a resented Colossus of the North; it was a triumphant major power. Intimacy with U.S. presidents, rather than anti-imperialist rhetoric, suddenly became a positive commodity in Latin American politics.

This revision was somewhat puzzling. It reflected, in part, increasing degrees of societal interdependence—from trade and migration to popular film, music, and sports. It reflected a pragmatic recognition of global realities. And it may have represented, at least for some, the only available alternative. One means of accommodating the reassertion of U.S. hegemony was to relabel it, to give it a new name and diminish its threatening quality. The power of the United States thus came to represent not a source of danger, as it had for so long, but a source of hope and opportunity. In theory, there was no other way for Latin Americans to make sense of the post–Cold War world.

In practice, however, such cultural concessions were not likely to achieve hemispheric harmony. While Latin America was becoming *less* nationalistic in the 1990s, the United States was becoming *more* nationalistic. Within the United States, the end of the Cold War and victory in the Gulf War set off demonstrations of patriotic triumphalism, just as economic rivalry with Japan prompted expressions of defensive nativism. Indeed, many observers in the United States were interpreting the movement toward orthodox liberalism and free trade within the hemisphere—from NAFTA to the EAI—as yet another confirmation of the wisdom and superiority of U. S.–style capitalism. While Latin Americans were seeking a new partnership with the United States, in other words, the United States was anticipating unilateral dominion throughout the Western Hemisphere. This disjuncture could lead to serious frictions.

As they scanned the international arena, commentators from Latin America came to reassess the content of regional as well as national identity. Increasingly, according to some analysts, countries of Latin America were following divergent paths: Brazil was reaching into South America, Chile was moving toward the Pacific Rim, and Mexico was entering North America. The range of policy options and the diversity of national interests were pulling countries of the region apart rather than together. This was the time, some said, to reevaluate the concept of "Latin America" and its practical significance. Perhaps it was an outmoded construct, a conceptual notion whose relevance was in the past. More forcefully than ever before, the underlying assumption of the Bolivarian dream was coming under challenge: continental unification may have been a chimera.

Underneath these responses to changing realities, there was resistance and ambiguity as well. Even as their options narrowed, Latin American governments refused to comply with Washington's directives on some key policy questions. In 1992 and again in 1993 and 1994 they voted unanimously for a resolution in the UN General Assembly condemning the U.S. embargo of Cuba. In mid-1994 fourteen presidents of Latin American governments—members of the so-called Rio Group—called for suspension of the U.S. embargo in exchange for "a peaceful transition toward a democratic and pluralist system in Cuba." And while Washington was able to cobble together international support for its September 1994 occupation of Haiti, as described in chapter 11, the United States drew no substantive backing from any major countries of the hemisphere. Beneath the protestations of harmony, lingering tensions prevailed.

The ultimate challenge, in the viewpoint of many, was to preserve and sustain the autonomy of Latin American culture. In the eloquent words delivered in mid-1993 by Fernando Solana, Mexico's former secretary of foreign relations:

> Above all, we seek the defense of our sovereignty. We are aware of the globalism that characterizes telecommunications, information, and business. At the same time, we do not want to see any dilution of our nationality [*nuestra mexicanidad*], of our distinct and special culture, of our capacity to take decisions and to shape the destiny of our resources and our territory.
>
> We firmly believe that cultural and philosophical diversity enriches the

world. It is the alternative, the idea of a homogeneous world with uniform customs and means of confronting challenges, that would mean the true end of History.

Here was a quest without end. Come what may, citizens and leaders of Latin America would continue their struggles for identity, empowerment, and dignity.

Conclusion: Structure and Change in U.S.–Latin American Relations

The evolution of U.S.–Latin American relations reveals patterns of continuity, consistency, and change from the 1790s to the 1990s. Long-term historical trends also provide a basis for looking ahead to the future. The purpose of this chapter is not to prescribe policy nostrums, however, but to reexamine fundamental questions: What have been the driving forces behind U.S. policy toward Latin America? What have been the key determinants of Latin America's response? What has been the nature of this interaction? And, by extension, what are likely to be major factors in shaping U.S.–Latin American relations in years to come?

Looking Back: Summation

As postulated at the outset, the dynamics of U.S.–Latin American relations complied closely with what I have interpreted as prevailing rules of conduct in the global arena. Transformation in these rules reflected changing global realities and gave sharp definition to three distinct chronological periods: the Imperial Era, stretching from the 1790s through the 1930s; the Cold War, lasting from the late 1940s through the late 1980s; and the current era, what I have called the Age of Uncertainty, starting in the 1990s. Each of these epochs contained its own rules of the game—codes that informed not only U.S. behavior toward Latin America but also the Latin American response. This conceptual framework shapes and supports the fundamental contentions of this book: that U.S.–Latin American interactions revealed structural regularities, that these regularities followed principles of logic, and that these regularities changed over time in under-standable ways. United States–Latin American relations have responded not to cultural whimsy or psychological caprice but to objective realities and governing norms in the international scene.

During the Imperial Era major powers promulgated an operative code of conduct that sought to maintain a balance of power among themselves and to preserve their sovereignty. Each of these powers acquired colonial possessions that ultimately figured in the calculus of power, and each therefore controlled a clearly defined and widely recognized sphere of influence. The United States entered this contest in the early 1800s as an aspiring challenger and soon began to advance its claims by acquiring territory mostly from Spain (Florida) or from ex-Spanish colonies (Mexico). United States politicians, publicists, and theologians justified this expansionist policy on the grounds of "manifest destiny," with its presumptive mission to extend the reach of political democracy throughout the hemisphere. The Monroe Doctrine and its subsequent corollaries established rationales for restricting Europe's presence in the New World and securing the U.S. sphere of influence. Since curtailment of European power in the Caribbean area was of paramount importance, the island of Cuba became an object of special imperial desire. At the end of the nineteenth century Washington shifted its overall strategy from territorial expansion toward the promotion of economic and commercial interests, adjusting its political tactics toward the installation of protectorates and the periodic use of military intervention. In contrast to most European powers, the United States rarely created formal colonies, with the conspicuous exceptions of Puerto Rico and the Philippines, while continuing to proclaim its dedication to democratic principle. FDR's Good Neighbor policy represented a culmination of U.S. imperial strategy, not a departure from it, as Washington managed to consolidate its sphere of influence through commercial exchange, hemispheric diplomacy, inculcations of Pan-American solidarity, and the cultivation of goodwill.

Confronted by this steady rise of U.S. power, Latin America had several plausible responses at its disposal. One enshrined the Bolivarian dream of continental unification, a theme that would appear and reappear in varying guise over time; another sought extrahemispheric protection; still others included aspirations for subregional hegemony, entertained mainly by Argentina and Brazil, and reliance on legalistic codes of international behavior. Expressions of cultures of resistance, with special emphases on national self-determination and the rejection of American society and values, were not quixotic manifestations of collective envy; they offered meaningful counterinterpretations to North American claims of manifest destiny, exposing ideological tensions that would persist in decades to come. As cultivated by the weak against the strong, doctrines of resistance constituted a substantial power resource for Latin America and its leadership.

Beginning in the late 1940s, the Cold War led to major rearrangements of the global arena. The United States and the Soviet Union emerged from the ashes of victory in World War II to dominate a bipolar world. Locked in a nuclear standoff, the United States and the USSR would engage in a geopolitical and ideological rivalry that interpreted the Third World as a global battleground. Reflecting the intensity of this struggle, the rules of this international game acquired remarkable transparency and clarity. Within Latin America, by now established as a U.S. sphere of influence, Washington pursued relentless but coherent policies— banishing or outlawing what it regarded as suspect forces, supporting friendly governments, and overthrowing allegedly dangerous regimes. The anticommunist crusade pervaded virtually every facet of U.S. policy toward the region, from the cultivation of moderate labor movements in the 1960s to the promotion of counterrevolutionary guerrilla movements in the 1980s. For Washington, the Cold War was an obsession.

These circumstances left Latin America with a limited range of strategic alternatives. The most daring and dangerous was the quest for socialist revolution, an effort that could succeed only with the protection of an extrahemispheric superpower—meaning, in practice, the Soviet Union. The fate of revolution thus became hostage to big-power politics. A second alternative, pursued with energy and verve by an unseemly assortment of dictators, was to join the anticommunist crusade. This tactic offered the great advantage of defining one's rivals as enemies of capitalism, democracy, and therefore the United States, whose power could then be brought into play. A third kind of option was to seek an independent path, a "third way," often through political affiliation with the Non-Aligned Movement or economic membership in the G-77. While this alternative made some significant strides, as in the Contadora Group's efforts to mediate the Central American conflict of the 1980s, it usually drew expressions of wrath or disdain from the United States. In a bipolar world, there was not much room for maneuver.

In the late 1980s the end of the Cold War brought another transformation to the international arena. The distribution of global power became multilayered and complex—unipolar in the military sense, where the United States remained supreme, and multipolar in the economic sense, where Europe and Japan (and other burgeoning regions) vied for global preeminence. In this Age of Uncertainty, there existed no coherent or recognized rules of the game. Around the world, patterns of conflict and major-power behavior became disturbingly unpredictable. Within the Western Hemisphere, by contrast, U.S. hegemony was uncontested and complete: there were no significant extrahemispheric rivals, and the power differential between the United States and Latin America reached unprecedented heights. As U.S. interests shifted from military security toward economic and social concerns, domestic constituencies came to have conspicuous impacts on U.S. foreign policy: the business community promoted free trade, environmentalists pushed for biological diversity, a disparate coalition supported a sometimes hysterical crusade against illicit drugs, nativists joined an equally hysterical crusade against undocumented immigration. Largely in response to such domestic political pressures, but always in the name of democracy, the United States took military action against Panama in 1989 and Haiti in 1994.

In this post–Cold War context, Latin America had even fewer options than before. There was no way to avoid or evade the fact of U.S. power. There were no extrahemispheric patrons available. Revolution was out of the question. In a world without established codes, international law and multilateral organization would have little serious impact. Essentially, the alternative for countries of Latin America was economic—to adopt the growing emphasis on liberalization and "free trade." They could seek to implement this strategy in one (or more) of several ways: by expanding commercial ties with Europe and Japan as well as the United States, as Chile did; by seeking an institutionalized relationship with the United States, as Mexico did; or by resuscitating dreams of subregional unification, as Brazil attempted to do through MERCOSUR and SAFTA. There still lingered traces of cultural resistance to U.S. power, as shown by the Chiapas uprising in January 1994, but these were relatively few and far between. The Age of Uncertainty was perhaps not the end of history, as some analysts surmised, but it may have signaled the triumph of neoliberal ideology.

Looking Back: Analysis

The central thesis of this book is that the dynamics of U.S.–Latin American relations reflected prevailing rules of the international game within each historical period, and that these dynamics underwent change in accordance with alterations in the rules of the game. Transformations in these operative rules, or codes, came about in response to change in three factors: the number of major powers, the nature of power resources, and the goals of international policy (Table 3). The number of powers determined whether global contests would be multipolar, as in the Imperial Era; bipolar, as in the Cold War; or multilayered, a combination of unipolar and multipolar, as in the Age of Uncertainty. The nature of power resources varied in complex ways: military capacity ranged from conventional forces to thermonuclear capability to a combination of the two, though military prowess lost much of its practical utility after the end of the Cold War; economic capacity ranged from commercial penetration to direct investment to financial linkages, all employed in varying degrees over the time spans in question. The principal goals of international rivalry evolved from the acquisition of territory (either as colonies or possessions) to the cultivation of political affinity (especially during the Cold War) to the development of economic cooperation and alignment (in the post–Cold War era).

Throughout these transformations the invocation of ideology played an important but essentially subordinate role in these contests. The United States proclaimed its "manifest destiny" as the diffusion of democratic

Table 3.   Global Contexts for U. S.–Latin American Relations

Factor	Imperial Era 1790s–1930s	Cold War 1940s–1980s	Age of Uncertainty 1990s–
Distribution of power	Multipolar	Bipolar	Unipolar/multipolar
Policy goals	Territorial, commercial	Geopolitical, ideological	Economic, social
Rules of the game	Balance of power	Global containment	Undetermined

politics, European powers embarked on civilizing missions, the Soviet Union insisted that its goal was the socialist liberation of downtrodden peoples. During the early twentieth century, too, racist doctrine helped to rationalize the U.S. tendency to impose protectorates (or military governments) on countries in Central America and the Caribbean. Ideological claims provided essential and significant justifications for big-power actions, though they rarely determined the course of such policies.

In its broad international contexts, the conduct of U.S.–Latin American relations was essentially derivative. Notwithstanding the Monroe Doctrine, the Western Hemisphere was not an isolated arena; on the contrary, the doctrine itself can best be understood as a challenge to European powers. The United States sought to impose a sphere of influence in the Americas not so much for its own sake but as a power resource for dealing with extrahemispheric rivals. The evolving drama of inter-American relations played out on a broad international stage.

Explaining U.S. Policies

Within these global schemes, there were significant sources of variation in U.S. conduct toward Latin America. Four factors, or variables, helped determine patterns and changes in U.S. behavior over time: (1) the relative importance of Latin America vis-à-vis other world regions, (2) perceptions of extrahemispheric rivalry, (3) definitions of U.S. national interest, and (4) the relationship between state actors and social groups in policy formation. These factors were closely interrelated.

The historical record demonstrates that Latin America commanded considerable attention from the United States throughout the nineteenth and twentieth centuries, but that there was significant variation in the relative degree of importance ascribed to the region. During the Imperial Era, Latin America was a central policy concern for Washington: it was the region where the United States expressed its own imperial ambitions and sought to eradicate all vestiges of European power. By the late 1920s and throughout the 1930s, when the United States appeared isolationist in respect to Europe and the rest of the world, Latin America came to occupy "first place" in the nation's diplomacy. During the Cold War, the dynamics of East-West competition transformed Latin America into an arena for struggle, a prize in the superpower contest, a status it shared with the

Third World as a whole: Latin America commanded special attention from Washington because of geographical propinquity and alleged "security" interests, but it was less unique or privileged in this sense than at previous times. Once the Cold War ended, Latin America occupied an ambiguous position in the eyes of Washington. In ways that were reminiscent of the imperial contest, the region came to constitute a sphere of U.S. influence, uncontested at last, a place where the United States could exercise its hemispheric hegemony for the purpose of confronting a complex and multipolar world; but attention to Latin America became selective as well, more focused on Mexico and the Caribbean than on South America, more attuned to social and economic interactions than to broad geopolitical concerns. In summary, Latin America was always important to the United States, but its relative degree of importance varied across these three historical periods—roughly speaking, from very high to high to rather mixed.

Washington's view of Latin America depended upon its rivalry with extrahemispheric powers. The basic rule was straightforward: the greater the perception of extrahemispheric threat, the greater the attention to Latin America. During the Imperial Era, the United States was explicitly and consciously engaged in an effort to banish European influence from the Western Hemisphere: in a multipolar world, Britain and Germany were the most powerful rivals, though other Continental powers—Italy, Holland, France—also played meaningful roles. During the Cold War, the United States steadfastly pursued its policy of "containment," seeking to prevent the Soviet Union—and/or its allies or puppets—from gaining influence in the Americas. The perception of danger was greatly exaggerated, as a result of anticommunist hysteria, but it had profound political meaning: Washington saw itself as the leader of a worldwide crusade, and it formed policies in accordance with this sense of purpose. With the end of the Cold War, extrahemispheric influence in the Americas virtually vanished. For the first time in history Washington had no rivals (real or imagined) in the hemisphere, though it confronted a multipolar challenge on the global scene. By the 1990s the United States had finally realized its ambition of the 1790s: to create a zone of uncontested influence within the Western Hemisphere.

A third key factor behind U.S. policy concerned prevalent definitions of national interests. At the most general level, these interests were constant: the accumulation and expression of international power. Yet the content of U.S. national interests varied over time. During the Imperial Era, the United States pursued two goals: territorial expansion and commercial influence. The overall purpose was to achieve rank as a major power. During the Cold War, as one of two rival superpowers, the United States sought geopolitical and ideological advantage in a worldwide struggle. And in the contemporary period, the United States has been attempting to consolidate economic hegemony in the Americas, partly as a tool for bargaining with other powers in a multipolar world. In light of increasing interdependence, Washington has also been attempting to protect the

United States from unwelcome social influences, such as illicit drugs and undocumented migration. In long-term perspective, the primary impetus behind U.S. policy thus shifted from territorial and commercial motivations from the 1800s to the 1930s, to ideological and geopolitical purposes from the 1940s through the 1980s, to economic and social concerns from the 1990s onward.

Throughout this sweep of history the United States steadfastly professed its intention of fostering democracy throughout the Americas, often invoking notions of hemispheric solidarity and the existence of a "Western Hemisphere idea." The promotion of democracy supplied a useful, sometimes crucial, rationalization for the application of American power. In this particular respect, the post–Cold War era came to bear an exceedingly strong resemblance to the pre–Cold War period. No longer able to appeal to anticommunism for ideological orientation, Washington now proclaimed the extension of democracy as its guidepost in foreign affairs. Bill Clinton's earnest pronouncements about democracy had more in common with the lofty declarations of Woodrow Wilson than with the Machiavellian calculations of Cold Warriors. United States efforts to promote democracy had been conspicuously unsuccessful in the Imperial Era, however, and there was little sign that Washington had learned any lessons from this history by the 1990s.

A fourth factor shaping U.S. policy concerned the relative roles of state elites and social actors. During the early nineteenth century, when the United States embarked on territorial expansion, the governmental apparatus defined and implemented American foreign policy. It was statesmen of the time—Jefferson, Adams, Polk, and others—who steadfastly pursued the acquisition of land; and while they enjoyed considerable popular support in this enterprise, they did so largely on their own initiative. Later in this era, from the 1890s through the 1930s, state elites operated in close collaboration with the business community, especially banking interests. Intent upon the extension and consolidation of economic influence, rather than the expansion of physical boundaries, governmental elites and financial representatives developed joint strategies that ranged from diplomatic pressure to military intervention. This partnership was especially evident in Central America and the Caribbean, where private bankers assumed control of outstanding national debts, thus eliminating the primary motivation for European powers to meddle in the hemisphere, while the U.S. government backed up the bankers with American military force. Though its goals may seem nefarious in retrospect, this was a smooth and effective public-private alliance.

The Cold War brought governmental elites to a supreme and unchallenged position in policy-making. In light of the bipolar U.S.–Soviet rivalry, international strategy derived from a geopolitical and ideological calculus stressing the containment and curtailment of communist influence. Application of this doctrine was the preserve par excellence of professional bureaucrats, career diplomats, and seasoned politicians. Business interests (and organized labor) occasionally played a strong supporting role: United Fruit promoted U.S. intervention in Guatemala, ITT clamored for action in Chile, the AFL-CIO trained and supported anticommunist labor leaders. Yet investors and financiers tended to have subordinate parts in policy formation during this period: U.S. interventions in Cuba, the Dominican Republic, and Grenada came about as a result of ideological and geopolitical considerations, not for economic reasons. State elites dominated the policy arena throughout the East-West conflict. For better or worse, one consequence of this monopoly was a clear, even rigid, consistency in U.S. policy.

Termination of the Cold War brought a sudden end to this bureaucratic stranglehold. No longer governed by a geopolitical calculus, no longer guided by a coherent doctrine, foreign policy became vulnerable to the interplay of domestic interests. Ethnic groups with growing importance in the electoral arena—Cuban Americans, Mexican Americans, African Americans—came to have a crucial impact on America's policies toward Castro's Cuba, the NAFTA agreement with Mexico, and the Cédras regime in Haiti. Popular condemnation of drug trafficking and undocumented migration helped stiffen governmental resolve to halt these flows, while business interests avidly supported promotion of the Washington consensus on free trade and on economic policy. Such influence was not so much a deliberate and voluntary partnership, as in the 1910s and 1920s, as a result of grass-roots mobilization and electoral blackmail. By the 1990s pressure groups were able to penetrate (if not to capture) specific issue-areas in foreign policy. Washington fell into a decidedly reactive mode, responding not only to the outbreak of international crises but also to the clamor of domestic interests. As a result, and in sharp contrast to the Cold War, U.S. policy acquired a decidedly ad hoc, makeshift quality.

Table 4 summarizes the determinants of U.S. policy toward Latin America for each time period and demonstrates that a combination of

Table 4. Principal Determinants of U.S. Policy

Determinant	Imperial Era 1790s–1930s	Cold War 1940s–1980s	Age of Uncertainty 1990s–
Importance of Latin America	Growing to very high	High	Ambiguous
Extrahemispheric rivals	European powers	Soviet Union	—
Primary goals	Spheres of influence	Anticommunism	Economic gain, social exclusion
Policy actors	Government + business	Government alone	Government + interest groups
General strategy	Territorial, commercial incorporation	Political penetration	Economic integration

factors—the relative importance of Latin America, the presence (or perception) of extrahemispheric rivals, the definition of national interests, and the composition of policy actors—had a determining influence upon the resultant set of strategies and policies. Even in schematic form, Table 4 serves to emphasize two central points: first, that there was an underlying logic behind the construction of U.S. policy *within* each historical period, and second, that there was an underlying logic to the transformation of U.S. policies *between* these periods as well.

Understanding Latin American Responses

As U.S. strategies underwent long-term change over time, so did Latin America's capacity to respond. There were continuities as well. A central premise of this analysis has stressed the presence and significance of power inequalities. From the mid-nineteenth century onward the United States was stronger than all countries of Latin America—economically, militarily, and politically—and by the early twentieth century the United States became more powerful than the region as a whole. The conduct of inter-American relations reflected and reasserted this fundamental asymmetry in myriad ways. Interaction took place not between equal partners but between the strong and the relatively weak. Individually and collectively, Latin American countries were constantly confronting a more powerful and better endowed adversary, a sometime ally engaged in a quest for constant advantage, a hemispheric neighbor smitten by global ambitions, an expansive power proclaiming the virtues of democracy: the Colossus of the North.

To counter the United States, and to pursue its own destiny, Latin America over time developed a cumulative total of six distinct strategic alternatives. One was the Bolivarian notion of collective unification. Though it never took full institutional form, the idea persisted over time and could claim some notable success—in the insistence on principles of self-determination and nonintervention from the 1890s to the 1930s, in the formulation of economic doctrines in the 1940s and 1950s, and in the settlement of Central American conflicts in the 1980s. A second broad strategy consisted of a search for support, protection, and patronage from extrahemispheric powers—especially the United Kingdom in the nineteenth century and the Soviet Union during the Cold War. A third strategy entailed a quest for subregional hegemony, visions entertained by Argentina and Brazil in the nineteenth century and by Brazil in the contemporary era. A fourth stressed the uses of international law and/or international organization, the principles of which could protect weaker countries from predatory or arbitrary actions by the strong; relatively successful during the Imperial Era, these efforts foundered during the Cold War and show little prospect for realization during the contemporary age.[1] A fifth strategic alternative, especially plausible during the Cold War, sought South-South solidarity with other nations of the so-called Third World. Sixth was the quest for social revolution, especially socialist revolution, that also reached its peak during the period of East-West confrontation.

Beyond these assertions of defiance and autonomy there remained, of course, another kind of option—alignment with the United States, either in deference to Washington's power or in pursuit of tactical advantage. During the Imperial Era Brazil sought an alliance with the United States as a matter of grand geopolitical strategy, while client rulers in Central America and the Caribbean accepted Washington's tutelage as a matter of political survival (and personal profit). The Cold War offered association with the United States as a strategic opportunity for the authoritarian right, which, with notable success, invoked the cause of anticommunism to justify its claims on power. And now, during the Age of Uncertainty, Mexico has most categorically thrown itself into the arms of the United States; other countries of the region, from Costa Rica to Argentina, seem prepared to follow this same course. It should be noted, however, that leaders and peoples of Latin America have not chosen affiliation with the United States out of admiration, loyalty, or affection—but because it has appeared to suit their purposes. This implies a portent for the future: if reliance on the United States does not produce the anticipated results for Latin America, or if other plausible options emerge, the public display of inter-American harmony that characterized the early 1990s may not endure forever.

Strategic alternatives became available in differing degrees and combinations at different periods of time (Table 5). During the Imperial Era, leaders of Latin America could entertain a fairly broad array of choices, achieving a substantial measure of success in the area of international law (partly as a result of diplomatic unity). The Cold War narrowed the range of maneuver, pressuring Latin American countries into alignments with either the United States or the USSR, though courageous and enterprising leaders pursued an independent path, often in collaboration with other Third World countries, and were able to help mediate conflicts in Central America and elsewhere. During the present era, ironically, the inventory of options appears to be even more restricted: whether they want to or not, Latin American leaders have little choice other than to implement policy prescriptions of the Washington consensus and to seek economic accommodation with the United States and the advanced industrial nations of the North.

In summary, the display in Table 5 demonstrates yet another basic thesis of this book: Latin America's reactions to the United States reflected just as much logic and regularity as did U.S. policies. Both the United States and Latin America were forging reasonable responses to their prevailing environments. The dynamics of their interaction, as well as of their policy initiatives, revealed regularity and structure.

Yet another essential component of Latin America's response to the United States took the form not of practical policy measures but of cultural interpretations of reality. Latin American politicians, pundits, and intellec-

Table 5.   Strategic Options for Latin America

Strategy	Imperial Era 1790s–1930s	Cold War 1940s–1980s	Age of Uncertainty 1990s–
Collective unity	Attempted (political integration)	Attempted (economic integration)	Unlikely
Extrahemispheric protection	Attempted (Europe)	Attempted (USSR)	—
Subregional hegemony	Attempted (Brazil, Argentina)	—	Possible (Brazil)
International law/ organization	Successful	Attempted	—
Social revolution:			
Nonsocialist	Mexico	Bolivia[a]	—
Socialist	—	Cuba, Nicaragua	—
Third World solidarity	—	Attempted (NAM, G-77)	—
Alignment with United States	Attempted (Brazil + client rulers)	Successful (authoritarian right)	Attempted (Mexico + others?)

— : not available or not feasible.

[a] The Bolivian Revolution of 1952 had socialist tendencies, among others, but soon gave way to close cooperation with the United States.

tuals developed a series of ideological and attitudinal outlooks. During the Imperial Era, leaders and representatives of Latin America forged cultures of "resistance." During the Cold War, many expressed resentment of the United States by subscribing to Marxist beliefs. And in the post–Cold War period, an era most notable for its absence of ideological contentiousness, many Latin Americans have been forging cultures of "accommodation" that recognize realities of U.S. power but also sustain the value and integrity of Latin America's social identity.

Differentiating Latin America

Some countries of Latin America, in some situations, were better prepared than others to confront the United States. Variations in capability reflected the impact of four related factors: (1) size and strength, (2) geographical proximity, (3) links to extrahemispheric powers, and (4) intellectual and cultural resources.

In terms of population size, economic output, and military capability, some nations of Latin America were stronger than others. Argentina and Brazil possessed resources that Honduras, Haiti, and Cuba did not. Such capacities enabled these countries not only to avert outright U.S. interventionism but also, at times, to entertain visions of continental grandeur and subregional hegemony. In the nineteenth century Argentina and Brazil each nurtured notions of challenging, or at least offsetting, the rise of U.S. power, and in the twentieth century Brazil has continued to see itself as the natural leader of South America. The resulting proposition borders on the circular: differential levels of power meant differential capacity to resist pressures from the United States. Size and power also exercised a deterrent effect: while the United States displayed recurring willingness to launch military invasions of small countries, Washington never considered sending troops into Brazil.

Geography supplied a second key determinant. Countries surrounding the Caribbean Rim—Mexico, Central America, the islands of the Caribbean—were much more likely to feel the weight of U.S. power than were South American nations. From the 1790s onward, and especially from the 1890s through the 1990s, policymakers in Washington ascribed particular importance to the greater Caribbean Basin—because of maritime routes, commercial ties, financial investments, natural resources, geographical propinquity, and (for all these reasons) national security. From the start, Washington was more predisposed to project its power in this area than in South America. Exceptions to this rule occurred mainly during the Cold War, when all countries of Latin America became squares on a global checkerboard; hence U.S. support for the Brazilian coup of 1964 and, even more conspicuously, for the Allende overthrow of 1973. With the ending of the anticommunist crusade, the United States reduced its interest in South America and refocused its attention on the Caribbean Basin. Geographical location did much to shape the tenor and tone of bilateral and continental relations: the closer to the United States, the greater the degree of attention from Washington—and the greater the consequent level of conflict.

A third factor concerned linkages with extrahemispheric powers. For historic and economic reasons some countries, such as the ABC nations of South America, enjoyed close and significant ties to Europe, especially in the late nineteenth and early twentieth centuries. As Simón Bolívar anticipated in the 1820s, these connections furnished a significant amount of diplomatic and political leverage in dealing with the United States. During the Cold War, Cuba and (to a lesser degree) Nicaragua turned toward the Soviet Union in search of protection. This was a high-risk strategy, however, since it ran directly counter to anticommunist ideology and to Washington's persisting quest for undisputed hegemony within the hemisphere. (Latin American nations did not have the luxury enjoyed by other Third World countries, such as Egypt, that were able to play the superpowers off against each other: located within the putative "backyard" of the United States, Latin American countries would generally have to follow Washington's lead—or move into the rival camp.) And with the end of the Cold War and the virtual withdrawal of extrahemispheric powers, this alternative collapsed. By the 1990s Latin America had no choice but to confront the United States.

Yet another differentiating factor among Latin American countries was cultural tradition. This was an amorphous concept, to be sure, one that embraced intellectual resources, educational institutions, and historical legacies. Yet in actual practice it was a factor that provided some countries, such as Mexico and Cuba and Nicaragua, with the capacity to construct powerful cultures of resistance that ultimately laid the ideological foundations for social revolution. In different form, it was a factor that shaped the cosmopolitan and European outlook of such distinguished jurists as Chile's Andrés Bello and Argentina's Carlos Calvo, who devised legal doctrines of national sovereignty and nonintervention. And it was a factor that, still more recently, permitted the rise of subtle and complex cultures of accommodation in the wake of the Cold War.

In this respect there was a countervailing factor at work. Because of traditions of continental solidarity, dating back to Bolivarian dreams of unification, intellectual and cultural achievements in any one part of Latin America quickly became assets for the region as a whole. Jose Martí spoke not only for Cuba but for what he called *"nuestra América";* Víctor Raúl Haya de la Torre sought reform not only in Peru but across the entire continent; César Augusto Sandino became a martyr not only for Nicaragua but for all revolutionary activists; Fidel Castro and Salvador Allende fired political imagination not only in their own countries but throughout the region; in different ways, Raúl Prébisch and Carlos Salinas de Gortari charted paths of economic development for all of Latin America; and writers of the left and right, from Gabriel García Márquez and Carlos Fuentes to Jorge Luis Borges, gained renown as interpreters and representatives for Latin America as a whole. Each national struggle had regional dimensions, each voice became the clamor of a continent at large. A defining paradox of Latin American nationalism was its ability to transcend national borders, especially insofar as it focused on the paramount challenge of common concern: the overweening power of the United States.

In retrospect, the determinants of U.S. policies and of Latin America's options combined to establish the dynamic structure of *interactions* between the United States and Latin America. During the Imperial Era, the United States was attempting to *incorporate* all or parts of Latin America into its own sphere of interest, through either conquest or commerce, while Latin American leaders engaged in various forms of resistance. During the Cold War the United States attempted to *penetrate* into Latin American societies and governments, to purge them of undesirable political and ideological elements and thus rid the hemisphere of putative threats to national security; right-wing Latin Americans responded by exploiting the resultant opportunities, leftists reacted with calls for revolution, reformists attempted to identify intermediate paths. And in the 1990s the United States has sought to *integrate* Latin America into its economic community, and at the same time to repel unwanted social interactions. Confronted by this ambivalent message, Latin American leaders have responded by seeking selective cooperation with the United States— choosing to cooperate on economic matters, in other words, but to retain freedom of action in other areas. In so many ways, the Age of Uncertainty was proving to be the most complex of all eras.

Looking Ahead: What Now?

The principal outlook for the future of U.S.–Latin American relations flows directly from this book's central argument: it will be conditioned by the nature, form, and implicit rules of global politics. As the post–Cold War world continues its search for a "new international order," if one is ever to appear, it is the worldwide pattern and conduct of international relations that will determine the shape and substance of inter-American relations. As in previous eras, hemispheric affairs beyond the year 2000 are likely to be cast within a global framework. As from the beginning to the present, U.S.–Latin American relations will be intimately linked to trends and developments in the global arena. More to the point, the underlying codes for hemispheric interaction will be essentially derivative from the international rules of the game.

In many senses the Age of Uncertainty bears more resemblance to the Imperial Era than to the Cold War. Like the late nineteenth century, the end of the twentieth century displays a complex and multipolar distribution of power, at least in the economic arena. In the absence of established rules of the game, the current environment places fewer constraints on big-power action than did the Cold War. And the countries of the South, or Third World, have little power and few strategic options. Their major concern at present is not so much that they will be colonized, however, as the fear that they will be neglected and abandoned. During the Cold War, especially in Asia and Africa, developing countries at least could entertain hopes of taking advantage of the superpower rivalry, of playing off the United States and the Soviet Union against one another. Such leverage no longer exists.

A principal difference between the Imperial Age and the present is the fact of uncontested U.S. hegemony within the hemisphere. During the earlier period, as shown in Part I, the presence of European nations established a multipolar distribution of power within the Americas. It was a complex contest, a long-term struggle in which the United States sought consistently to banish or reduce European influence in order to construct its own sphere of influence. That struggle no longer prevails. With the implosion of the Soviet Union, the withdrawal of extrahemispheric powers, and the triumph of neoliberal ideology, the United States now stands supreme within the hemisphere. As a result, there are few constraints on Washington. In the post–Cold War world, the United States can intervene at will. It has done so in Panama and Haiti; it will probably do so again.

It is pointless to hazard specific prognostications about the future of U.S.–Latin American relations. In a global environment without established rules of the game, almost anything could happen. To anticipate possible trends in the twenty-first century, however, it should be useful to identify key factors at both the global and hemispheric levels that seem most likely to affect the shape of future developments.

The most critical variable in the worldwide arena concerns the formation (or not) of regional blocs. As sketched out in chapter 11, there are several alternative scenarios at work. One envisions a broad, open, liberalized economic and political arrangement in quest of "global development." A second anticipates the formation of three rivalrous blocs—in Europe, the Americas, and the Asia/Pacific Rim—arrayed in an economic competition that would lead to political conflict as well. A third view contemplates the possible formation of a North-North axis that would, with various exceptions, exclude the countries of the South. The resolution of these possibilities will come not so much from the Western Hemisphere, or from Latin America, as from interactions and arrangements among the major global economic powers (although, to be sure, the formation of a free-trade zone in the Americas could provoke either retaliation or accommodation from Europe and Japan). Settlement of this issue will have a critical effect on the conduct and tone of inter-American relations over the next half century at least.

A subsidiary question concerns the extent to which economic blocs, if they appear, will be open or closed. Closed blocs would limit countries of Latin America to dealing with the United States; at least in principle, open blocs could permit them to cultivate economic and political relations with other major powers of the world. Similarly, the creation of loose and informal blocs might leave latitude and flexibility for countries of Latin America; rigid, highly institutionalized blocs would be more likely to curtail their freedom of action. Once again, however, decisions on these matters are not likely to originate from Latin America; they will emerge from tacit understandings among the major world powers.

Within the Western Hemisphere there is every reason to anticipate the perpetuation, and perhaps the accentuation, of U.S. hegemony. In this event, a key determinant of U.S. policy toward Latin America will be the relative importance of the region within the overall global arena. This value will depend largely on U.S. relationships with major extrahemispheric powers and its own position in the world system. The more important Latin America is for purposes of U.S. policy, the more attention the area will receive; the less important the region, the less the attention. Here again, Latin America must contemplate a bitter irony: having long endured excessive attention and meddling by the United States, in the post–Cold War environment it faces the unsettling prospect of neglect.

Whatever the ultimate shape of the international system, the character of U.S.–Latin American diplomacy will depend largely upon the U.S. management of social issues. For the foreseeable future, inter-American economic relations will probably generate positive feelings in the United States, since Latin America will be depicted and seen as an asset for America's recovery and growth; moreover, the negotiation of arcane treaties on trade and investment usually stays within bureaucratic circles and does not become fodder for public political battles (though this was not true for NAFTA, and it may not pertain to the future). Social and cultural relations are another matter. Continuation of illegal flows of unwelcome products and people—that is, of drugs and migrants and refugees—is likely to generate disagreement and tension. The spread of Latin American culture, from language to music and everyday fashion, may also produce a nativist backlash. And it is in these areas, more than others, that the popular voices of American citizens tend to be loudest. The more responsive U.S. foreign policy becomes to domestic clienteles, the more likely the emergence of serious agitation over sociocultural issues—and the greater the likelihood of conflict with Latin America.

To some degree this outcome seems inevitable. Largely to improve its position vis-à-vis other major powers, the United States appears intent on intensifying, consolidating, and deepening economic contact with countries of Latin America. This process will necessarily have important social consequences. Accelerations in the exchange of goods, capital, and services stimulate flows of labor and other items, including unauthorized migrants, refugees, drugs, and expressions of popular culture. In other words, increasing economic interdependence will lead to increasing sociocultural interdependence, which often provokes volatile political reactions. To exaggerate the point: as a result of increasing economic collaboration, the United States and Latin America may find themselves on a social and cultural collision course.

A central challenge for Latin America concerns collective solidarity. The more unified the countries of the region, the greater their overall bargaining power with the United States (and other world powers); the less the unification, the less the bargaining power. The principal difficulty, in the contemporary era, is that there are so many incentives in favor of pursuit of individual gain; this is especially apparent in the economic realm, where some nations are better positioned to form links with the United States and the North than others. The ultimate risk is that the pursuit of individual advantage will contribute to fragmentation of the hemisphere, to a two-tier system of ins vs. outs, haves vs. have-nots, that could eventually provoke serious and sustained conflict within the Western Hemisphere. Perhaps the most effective means to avoid this danger would come from the promotion of regional solidarity among nations of Latin America on their own, not under the tutelage of the United States. The eventual achievement of a hemispheric "community of democracies," as envisioned by Washington, may require revitalization of the Bolivarian dream of Latin American unity.

Appendix:
Statistical Tables

Table A1. Major Trading Partners for Latin America: Selected Countries, 1913

	Partner (% Share of Trade)				Total (Millions U.S. $)
	United Kingdom	Germany	France	United States	
Caribbean Basin					
Colombia					
Imports	20.3	14.1	15.6	26.8	27.6
Exports	13.6	7.2	2.1	44.3	33.2
Cuba					
Imports	12.3	6.9	5.2	53.7	140.1
Exports	11.2	2.8	1.0	79.7	164.6
Mexico					
Imports	11.8	13.0	8.6	53.9	90.7
Exports	13.5	3.4	2.8	75.2	148.0
Venezuela					
Imports	25.5	16.6	9.1	32.8	77.8
Exports	9.9	19.4	34.6	29.3	28.3
South America					
Argentina					
Imports	31.0	16.9	9.0	14.7	487.7
Exports	24.9	12.0	7.8	4.7	510.3
Brazil					
Imports	24.5	17.5	9.8	15.7	324.0
Exports	13.3	14.0	12.2	32.2	315.7
Chile					
Imports	29.9	24.6	5.5	16.7	120.3
Exports	38.9	21.6	6.2	21.3	142.8
Peru					
Imports	26.2	17.2	4.5	28.9	29.0
Exports	37.2	6.7	3.4	33.3	43.6

Source: Division of Economic Research, Pan American Union, *The Foreign Trade of Latin America since 1913* (Washington: Pan American Union, 1952), pp. 37–50.

Table A2. Major Trading Partners for Latin America: Selected Countries, 1938

	Partner (% Share of Trade)				Total (Millions U.S. $)
	United Kingdom	Germany	France	United States	
Caribbean Basin					
Colombia					
Imports	11.1	17.4	3.4	49.8	89.1
Exports	0.5	14.6	4.7	52.7	80.8
Cuba					
Imports	4.2	4.4	2.6	70.9	106.0
Exports	13.7	2.0	1.5	76.0	142.7
Mexico					
Imports	4.1	18.9	4.0	57.6	109.3
Exports	9.4	7.7	2.3	67.4	185.4
Venezuela					
Imports	7.1	12.0	3.0	56.3	97.5
Exports	3.2	3.2	1.3	13.2	280.4
South America					
Argentina					
Imports	20.1	10.3	4.7	17.4	428.2
Exports	32.8	11.7	5.4	8.5	409.2
Brazil					
Imports	10.4	25.0	3.2	24.2	295.4
Exports	8.8	19.0	6.4	34.3	295.6
Chile					
Imports	10.1	25.8	1.9	27.9	103.0
Exports	21.8	10.0	4.5	15.7	141.0
Peru					
Imports	10.0	20.2	2.7	34.3	58.3
Exports	20.0	10.6	6.4	26.9	76.7

Source: Division of Economic Research, Pan American Union, *The Foreign Trade of Latin America since 1913* (Washington: Pan American Union, 1952), pp. 37–50.

Table A3. Estimated Membership of Communist Parties in Latin America, 1947–1957

	1947	1952	1957
Argentina	30,000	30,000	90,000
Brazil	150,000	60,000	50,000
Chile	50,000	35,000	25,000
Cuba	50,000	25,000	12,000
Mexico	10,000	5,000	5,000
Peru	30,000	10,000	6,000
Venezuela	20,000	10,000	9,000
Latin America	375,500	197,500	214,000

Source: Data in Rollie Poppino, *International Communism in Latin America: A History of the Movement, 1917–1963* (Glencoe: The Free Press, 1964), Appendix II, p. 231.

Table A4. Trends in Latin America's Per Capita Gross Domestic Product: Selected Countries, 1961–1970

	Average Annual Growth Rate (%)	
	1961–65	1966–70
Argentina	2.1	2.1
Brazil	1.6	4.3
Chile	2.4	1.3
Colombia	1.3	2.3
Mexico	3.6	3.6
Peru	3.4	1.0
Venezuela	1.6	0.9
Central America		
Costa Rica	1.8	3.3
El Salvador	3.7	1.6
Guatemala	2.1	2.4
Honduras	1.9	1.5
Nicaragua	5.7	2.2

Source: L. Ronald Scheman, "The Alliance for Progress: Concept and Creativity," in Scheman (ed.), *The Alliance for Progress: A Retrospective* (New York: Praeger, 1988), p. 15.

Table A5. Infant Mortality Rates in Latin America: Selected Countries, 1960–1968

	Death Rate per 1,000 Births, Under One Year		
	Average 1960–62	Goal 1968[a]	Level 1968
Argentina	61.0	42.7	60.8
Chile	117.8	76.6	86.6
Colombia	92.8	65.0	78.3
Mexico	71.4	46.4	64.2
Peru	92.9	65.0	75.3
Venezuela	52.1	33.9	44.4
Central America			
Costa Rica	66.1	46.3	62.3
El Salvador	72.5	47.1	59.2
Guatemala	89.3	58.0	93.8
Honduras	43.4	33.9	35.5
Nicaragua	63.1	41.0	53.2

Source: Data in L. Ronald Scheman, "The Alliance for Progress: Concept and Creativity," in Scheman (ed.), *The Alliance for Progress: A Retrospective* (New York: Praeger, 1988), p. 28.
[a]"Goal 1968" refers to respective proportion of Alliance for Progress overall goal, which was to reduce by one-half the prevailing child mortality rate by 1968.

Table A6. Gross Domestic Product and Population Size: Major World Powers, 1950–1990

	1950[a]		1970		1990	
	GDP (Billions U.S. $)	Population (Millions)	GDP (Billions U.S. $)	Population (Millions)	GDP (Billions U.S. $)	Population (Millions)
United States	381	152.3	1,011.6	204.8	5,392.2	250.0
Soviet Union[b]	126	211.4	230.5	241.8	1,259.3	289.0
United Kingdom	71	50.0	106.5	55.7	975.2	57.4
Italy	29	45.7	107.5	53.7	1,090.8	57.7
France	50	41.5	142.9	50.8	1,190.8	56.4
Germany	48	67.0	184.5	61.6	1,574.3	79.5
European Community[c]			499.4	189.3	5,996.7	344.8
Japan	32	80.5	203.7	103.5	2,942.9	123.5
China	33	463.5	93.2	750.0	364.9	1,133.7

Sources: Paul Kennedy, *The Rise and Fall of World Powers*, p. 369; World Bank, *World Development Report 1992:Development and the Environment* (New York: Oxford University Press, 1992), Tables 1 and 3, pp. 218–219 and 222–223; World Bank, *World Development Report 1993: Investing in Health* (New York: Oxford University Press, 1993), Table, pp. 242–243; Economist Intelligence Unit, *USSR Country Report* 1991, 4; Satwar Lateef, *Economic Growth in China and India 1950–1980*, vol. 2 (London: Economist Intelligence Unit, 1976),4; *World Almanac and Book of Facts* 1950, 1970.

[a]Economic data for 1950 are expressed in dollars of 1964; some refer to GNP rather than GDP.

[b]The Soviet Union dissolved in 1991.

[c]Formed in 1957, the European Economic Community had six members as of 1970: Belgium, France, West Germany, Italy, Luxembourg, and the Netherlands; by 1990 the European Community had twelve members, following the accession of Denmark, Ireland, Greece, Spain, Portugal, and the United Kingdom (East Germany became part of Germany as a result of reunification in 1990); in 1993 the EC was renamed the European Union.

Table A7. Gross Domestic Product and Population Size: Latin America and the United States, 1950–1990

	1950		1970		1990	
	GDP (Billions U.S. $)	Population (Millions)	GDP (Billions U.S. $)	Population (Millions)	GDP (Billions U.S. $)	Population (Millions)
Argentina	9.5	17.1	20.5	23.8	93.3	32.3
Brazil	8.8	52.2	35.5	92.5	414.1	150.4
Chile	2.6	6.1	8.2	9.4	27.8	13.2
Colombia	2.0	11.3	7.2	20.5	41.1	33.0
Mexico	7.8	25.8	35.5	50.7	237.8	86.2
Peru	1.5	8.0	7.2	13.5	36.6	22.3
Venezuela	4.6	5.0	13.4	10.3	48.3	19.7
Latin America	40.9	155.1	143.9	269.0	1,015.2	435.7
United States	287.0	152.3	1,011.5	204.8	5,392.2	250.0

Sources: James W. Wilkie, Carlos Alberto Contreras, and Christof Anders Weber (eds.), *Statistical Abstract of Latin America* 30 (Los Angeles: UCLA Latin American Center, 1993), Part 1, Tables 601–623, pp. 106–117, and Part 2, Table 3423, pp. 1240–1241; World Bank, *World Development Report 1993: Investing in Health* (New York: Oxford University Press, 1993), Table 3, pp. 242–243; and the *Economic Report of the President*, various years.

Table A8. Major Trading Partners for Latin America: Selected Countries, 1990

		Partner (% Share of Trade)				
			Europe			
	United States	United Kingdom	Germany	European Community	Japan	USSR
Caribbean Basin						
Colombia						
Exports	45.8	1.9	9.8	26.2	3.9	1.3
Imports	37.7	2.6	7.4	20.2	9.3	0.2
Mexico						
Exports	73.1	0.8	1.5	10.2	5.4	0.2
Imports	70.8	1.2	4.5	12.6	5.1	0.03
Venezuela						
Exports	54.7	1.0	5.3	12.3	3.4	0.01
Imports	44.5	4.0	8.7	29.7	4.7	0.2
South America						
Argentina						
Exports	13.8	1.5	5.2	30.5	3.2	4.0
Imports	21.5	1.0	10.0	27.4	3.3	0.3
Brazil						
Exports	23.4	3.4	6.6	30.9	8.3	0.9
Imports	21.1	2.0	8.6	20.6	6.0	0.3
Chile						
Exports	16.9	4.6	10.9	34.7	14.6	0.2
Imports	19.2	2.9	6.9	19.8	7.0	0.6
Peru						
Exports	22.2	5.6	6.9	28.5	12.9	1.1
Imports	30.4	2.7	7.1	19.9	4.2	0.1

Source: James W. Wilkie, Carlos Alberto Contreras, and Christof Anders Weber (eds.), *Statistical Abstract of Latin America,* 30 (Los Angeles: UCLA Latin American Center, 1993), Part 2, Table 2602 and 2612–2633, pp. 850–852, 862–923.

Table A9. Trade with Latin America as Percentage of Total U.S. Trade, 1950–1991

	U. S. Exports to Latin America (as % of Total U.S. Exports)	U. S. Imports from Latin America (as % of Total U.S. Exports)
1950	28	35
1958–59	23	28
1963–65	16	21
1974–76	14	12
1979–81	17	14
1984–86	14	13
1989–91	14	13

Source: Joseph Grunwald, "The Rocky Road toward Hemispheric Economic Integration: A Regional Backgrounder with Attention to the Future," in Roy E. Green (ed.), *The Enterprise for the Americas Initiative* (Westport: Praeger, 1993), ch. 8, Table 8.1. Reproduced by permission of the author and of Greenwood Publishing Group, Inc., Westport, CT.

Table A10. Perceptions of U.S. Vital Interests, 1978–1994

	1978		1982		1986		1990		1994	
	Public	Leaders	Public	Leaders	Public	Leaders	Public	Leaders	Public	Leaders
USSR/Russia	74	95	—	—	—	—	83	93	79	98
Japan	78	99	82	97	78	98	79	95	85	96
Canada	69	95	82	95	78	96	77	90	71	93
Egypt	75	91	66	90	61	—	53	76	45	78
China (PRC)	70	93	64	87	61	89	47	73	68	95
Mexico	60	90	74	98	74	96	63	94	76	98
Brazil	38	73	45	80	45	63	39	51	35	49

% Perceiving Vital Interests[a]

Source: Based on data in John E. Rielly (ed.), *American Public Opinion and U.S. Foreign Policy 1979, 1983, 1987, 1991, 1995* (Chicago: Chicago Council on Foreign Relations, 1979, 1983, 1987, 1991, 1995).

[a]In response to the following question: "Many people believe that the United States has a vital interest in certain areas of the world and not in others. That is, certain countries of the world are important to the U.S. for political, economic or security reasons. I am going to read a list of countries. For each, tell me whether you feel the U.S. does or does not have a vital interest in that country."

Table A11. Latin America's External Debt, 1970–1985

	Billions of U.S. Dollars		
	1975	1980	1985
Argentina	6.0	27.3	48.4
Brazil	25.0	70.0	106.7
Mexico	16.9	57.1	97.4
Venezuela	17.2	29.6	32.1
Latin America	98.9	241.5	383.9

Source: Data in Pedro-Pablo Kuczynski, *Latin American Debt* (Baltimore: Johns Hopkins University Press/Twentieth Century Fund, 1988), p. 217.

Table A12. Trends in Latin America's Per Capita Gross Domestic Product: Selected Countries, 1981–1989

	Annual % Change									Total 1981–1989
	1981	1982	1983	1984	1985	1986	1987	1988	1989	
Argentina	−8.4	−7.2	1.1	0.9	−5.9	4.4	0.5	−4.4	−6.7	−23.5
Brazil	−6.5	−1.6	−5.6	2.8	6.1	5.2	1.5	−2.4	0.9	−0.4
Mexico	6.1	−3.0	−6.5	1.2	0.2	−6.0	−0.8	−1.1	0.8	−9.2
Venezuela	−4.0	−4.0	−8.1	−4.2	−1.0	3.1	−0.5	2.1	−10.8	−24.9
Latin America[a]	−1.9	−3.5	−5.0	1.2	1.3	1.4	0.7	−1.5	−1.0	−8.3

Source: United Nations, Economic Commission for Latin American and the Caribbean, *Changing Production Patterns with Social Equity* (Santiago de Chile: ECLAC, 1990), p. 20.

[a] Excluding Cuba.

Table A13. Drug Use in the United States, 1979–1992

	Estimated Millions of Users						
	1979	1982	1985	1988	1990	1991	1992
Any illicit drug use (past month)	24.3	22.4	23.0	14.5	12.9	12.8	11.4
Past month marijuana	22.5	20.0	18.2	11.6	10.2	9.7	9.0
Past month cocaine	4.3	4.2	5.8	2.9	1.6	1.9	1.3
Weekly cocaine	na	na	0.6	0.9	0.7	0.6	0.6
Lifetime heroin	2.4	1.9	1.9	1.9	1.7	2.7	1.8
Adolescent past month	4.1	2.8	3.3	1.9	1.6	1.4	1.3

Source: Data in Office of National Drug Control Strategy, *National Drug Control Strategy: Reclaiming Our Communities from Drugs and Violence* (Washington: The White House, February 1994), p. 100.

Table A14. Latin American Production of Illicit Drugs, 1987–1993

	Metric Tons		
Country	1987	1990	1993
	Coca Leaf		
Bolivia	79,200	76,800	84,400
Colombia	20,500	32,100	31,700
Peru	191,000	196,900	155,500
Ecuador	400	170	100
Totals	291,100	305,170	271,700
	Marijuana		
Mexico	5,933	9,715	6,280
Colombia	5,600	1,500	4,125
Jamaica	460	825	502
Belize	200	60	0
Others	1,500	3,500	3,500
Totals	13,693	25,600	14,407
	Opium		
Mexico	50	62	49
Guatemala	3	13	4
Colombia	0	0	20
Totals	53	75	73

Sources: U.S. Department of State, Bureau of International Narcotics Matters, *International Narcotics Control Strategy Report, March 1991* (Washington: U.S. Government Printing Office, 1991), 22; and *International Narcotics Control Strategy Report, April 1994* (1994), 20.

Notes

Introduction

1. Stephen Krasner, "Structural Causes and Regime Consequences: Regimes as Intervening Variables," in Krasner (ed.), *International Regimes* (Ithaca: Cornell University Press, 1983), p. 2. As Stephan Haggard and Beth A. Simmons have observed, Krasner's emphasis on norms takes an intermediate stance between two other notions of regime—one that interprets a regime as any form of regular and patterned behavior, another that insists on the existence of explicit multilateral agreements; see Haggard and Simmons, "Theories of International Regimes," *International Organization* 41, no. 3 (Summer 1987): 491–517.

2. Also in contrast to Krasner, I do not regard the acceptance of recognized "decision-making procedures" as essential to the existence of a regime—unless competition and conflict, even military conflict, could be considered as a decision-making procedures.

3. Robert Gilpin, *War and Change in World Politics* (Cambridge: Cambridge University Press, 1981); and Richard Rosecrance, *Action and Reaction in World Politics—International Systems in Perspective* (Boston: Little, Brown, 1963).

4. In *Action and Reaction*, for example, Richard Rosecrance finds nine different systems in operation from the eighteenth century to the mid-twentieth century; for his assessment of the post–Cold War period see Richard Rosecrance, "A New Concert of Powers," *Foreign Affairs* 71, no. 2 (Spring 1992): 64–82.

5. I employ the concept of "system" in a general way, to refer to a specific and regular pattern of interaction among diverse units according to some principle or method of coherence or control; it is closely related to the idea of "structure." For sophisticated discussion of these issues see Kenneth Waltz, *Theory of International Politics* (Reading: Addison-Wesley, 1979) and Robert O. Keohane (ed.), *Neorealism and Its Critics* (New York: Columbia University Press, 1986).

6. I employ the term *hegemony* in its broadest sense, as the capacity of an actor (or nation) to impose its will over others without significant challenge.

7. For use of this metaphor see Robert A. Pastor, *Whirlpool: U.S. Foreign Policy toward Latin America and the Caribbean* (Princeton: Princeton University Press, 1992).

Chapter 1

1. William Appleman Williams, *The Tragedy of American Diplomacy*, 2nd ed. (New York: Franklin Watts, 1976), p. 21.

2. On this concept see John Gallagher and Ronald Robinson, "The Imperialism of Free Trade," *Economic History Review* 2nd series, 6, no. 1 (1953): 1–15.

3. Jefferson felt especially betrayed because he had favored France in foreign policy, strongly condemning a proindependence uprising against French rule in Haiti—partly because he thought it would set a nefarious example for American slaves.

4. Haiti acquired independence from France in 1804, after a black rebellion led by ex-slave Toussaint L'Ouverture, and took control of the Dominican Republic from 1822 to 1844; under Faustin Soulouque (1847–59), Haiti made two unsuccessful attempts to recapture Santo Domingo.

5. After the period of Haitian rule (1822–44), the Dominican Republic was briefly retaken by Spain from 1861 to 1865, when political revolts and yellow fever persuaded Isabella II to withdraw voluntarily. In 1868 Ulysses Grant proposed annexation of the Dominican Republic by the United States, but the U.S. Senate voted down the plan.

6. The precise terms of his boast remain a matter of scholarly controversy: see James F. Vivian, "The 'Taking' of the Panama Canal Zone: Myth and Reality," *Diplomatic History* 4, no. 1 (Winter 1980): 95–100.

Chapter 2

1. Paul W. Drake, "From Good Men to Good Neighbors: 1912–1932," in Abraham F. Lowenthal (ed.), *Exporting Democracy: The United States and Latin America* (Baltimore: Johns Hopkins University Press, 1991), pp. 3–40.

2. *Los Angeles Times,* September 18, 1994.

Chapter 3

1. Still the standard source is Bryce Wood, *The Making of the Good Neighbor Policy* (New York: Columbia University Press, 1961).

2. Franklin and Theodore Roosevelt were distant family cousins; Franklin's wife, Eleanor, was also Theodore's niece.

3. Arthur P. Whitaker, *The Western Hemisphere Idea: Its Rise and Decline* (Ithaca: Cornell University Press, 1954). This view drew considerable support during the 1930s from popularization of the historical thesis of Herbert Eugene Bolton, a prominent scholar who contended that the Americas had more in common with each other than with Europe. See Lewis Hanke (ed.), *Do the Americas*

Have a Common History? A Critique of the Bolton Theory (New York: Alfred A. Knopf, 1964).

4. See Gerald K. Haines, "Under the Eagle's Wing: The Franklin Roosevelt Administration Forges an American Hemisphere," *Diplomatic History* 1, no. 4 (Fall 1977):373–388.

5. Allen L. Woll, *The Latin Image in American Film* (Los Angeles: UCLA Latin American Center Publications, University of California, Los Angeles, 1977), p. 60.

6. "Chica Chica Boom Chic," by Mack Gordon and Harry Warren © 1941 Twentieth Century Music Corporation © Renewed 1969 and assigned to EMI Miller Catalog Inc. All rights reserved. Used by permission. Warner Bros. Publications USA Inc., Miami, Fl 33014.

7. Irwin F. Gellman, *Good Neighbor Diplomacy: United States Policies in Latin America, 1933–1945* (Baltimore: Johns Hopkins University Press, 1979), p. 38.

Chapter 4

1. Reflecting racial tenets of the time, Bolívar insisted that the United States and Haiti should be excluded from this union, as they would be "a foreign substance in our body." He was silent on the question of Brazil, at this time the seat of the Portuguese empire.

2. Throughout this book, the adjective *regional* embraces all of Latin America; *subregional* applies to portions of Latin America (such as Central America or South America); and the term *hemispheric* refers to all of Latin America plus North America (in principle, though not always in practice, including Canada as well as the United States).

3. The U.S. view of international law shifted according to convenience. Early in the nineteenth century American leaders dismissed European "black-letter" law as antiquated and irrelevant, as shown in chapter 2, because it conflicted with expansionist policy; by the end of the century, at least in this context, American spokesmen supported principles of international law that reflected national interests.

Chapter 5

1. Thomas G. Paterson, *On Every Front: The Making and Unmaking of the Cold War,* rev. ed. (New York: W. W. Norton, 1992), ch. 3, "Spheres: The Quest for Influence to 1947," pp. 41–69.

2. It is thus revealing that the "bureaucratic politics" interpretation of U.S. foreign policy-making arose during and in reference to the Cold War; see Graham T. Allison, *Essence of Decision: Explaining the Cuban Missile Crisis* (Boston: Little, Brown, 1971), and Abraham F. Lowenthal, "United States Policy toward Latin America: 'Liberal,' 'Radical,' and 'Bureaucratic' Perspectives," *Latin American Research Review* 8 (Fall 1973): 3–25.

3. Stephen G. Rabe, *Eisenhower and Latin America: The Foreign Policy of Anticommunism* (Chapel Hill: University of North Carolina Press, 1988), p. 13.

4. Leslie Bethell, "From the Second World War to the Cold War: 1944–1954," in Abraham F. Lowenthal (ed.), *Exporting Democracy: The United States and Latin America* (Baltimore: Johns Hopkins University Press, 1991), p. 48.

5. Rollie Poppino, *International Communism in Latin America: A History of the Movement, 1917–1963* (Glencoe: The Free Press, 1964), p. 36.

6. Poppino, *International Communism*, p. 195.

Chapter 6

1. Convinced of the existence of a worldwide communist conspiracy, Western analysts usually put the People's Republic of China in the "second" world; especially after their late-1950s split with the Soviet Union, Chinese leaders saw their country as part of the "third" world. An alternative classification stressed not political allegiance but economic development, categorizing countries on a continuum from "most" to "least" developed; in practice, the least developed countries tended to correspond to membership in the "third" world.

2. Stephen G. Rabe, *Eisenhower and Latin America: The Foreign Policy of Anticommunism* (Chapel Hill: University of North Carolina Press, 1988), p. 16–17.

3. Despite the president's evident goodwill, his omission of the pronoun *"el"* before the word *Progreso* was a poignant reminder of Washington's inattention to Latin America; somewhere in the White House, one might have thought, there must have been someone with a working knowledge of Spanish grammar.

4. Tony Smith, "The Alliance for Progress: The 1960s," in Abraham F. Lowenthal (ed.), *Exporting Democracy: The United States and Latin America* (Baltimore: Johns Hopkins University Press, 1991), p. 74.

5. William D. Rogers, *The Twilight Struggle: The Alliance for Progress and the Politics of Development in Latin America* (New York: Random House, 1967), p. 199.

6. Smith, "Alliance, " p. 72; and L. Ronald Scheman (ed.), *The Alliance for Progress: A Retrospective* (New York: Praeger, 1988), pp. 10–11.

7. Estimates for net resource flows range from roughly $4 billion to $10 billion.

8. L. Ronald Scheman, "The Alliance for Progress: Concept and Creativity," in Scheman (ed.), *Alliance for Progress,* p. 18.

9. According to Jerome Levinson and Juan de Onís, "There is no official transcript of the meeting, but Mann's remarks were reported by Tad Szulc in the *New York Times* of March 19, 1964. Mann was later to claim that the Szulc report was distorted, but other participants in the meeting (who ask that their names be withheld) have corroborated Szulc's report." *The Alliance That Lost Its Way: A Critical Report on the Alliance for Progress* (Chicago: Quadrangle Books, 1970), p. 88, note 7.

10. Jeane J. Kirkpatrick, *Dictatorship and Double Standards: Rationalism and Reason in Politics* (New York: Simon & Schuster, 1982), p. 26.

Chapter 7

1. Eisenhower, in fact, was prepared to uphold the Ydígoras Fuentes regime for this very reason. Hearing of a near-revolt in Guatemala in late 1960, he later recalled his determination "that if we received a request from Guatemala for assistance, we would move in without delay."

2. Hugh Thomas, *The Cuban Revolution* (New York: Harper & Row, 1977), p. 585.

3. U.S. Congress, Senate Select Committee to Study Governmental Operations with Respect to Intelligence Activities, *Alleged Assassination Plots Involving Foreign Leaders*, Senate Report No. 465, 94th Congress, 1st Session (Washington, D.C.: U.S. Government Printing Office, 1975), p. 71. Underworld figures were prepared to cooperate with plans to eliminate Castro because they had lost extensive gambling and prostitution operations in Havana as a result of the Cuban Revolution.

4. Ibid., pp. 191–215.

5. There was some discussion of a possible assassination of Allende, as reported by Seymour Hersh in *The Price of Power: Kissinger in the Nixon White House* (New York: Simon & Schuster, 1983), pp. 258–259, though this is largely discounted by Paul E. Sigmund in *The United States and Democracy in Chile* (Baltimore: Johns Hopkins University Press, 1993), p. 51. All we know from prior episodes is that an assassination plot was not outside the bounds of possibility.

6. See William LeoGrande, "Through the Looking Glass: The Kissinger Report on Central America," *World Policy Journal* (Winter 1984): 251–284.

7. To complete this picture, the United States also took covert action against the government of Cheddi Jagan in British Guiana in the early 1960s; see Robert A. Packenham, *Liberal America and the Third World: Political Development Ideas in Foreign Aid and Social Science* (Princeton: Princeton University Press, 1973), pp. 75–81.

Chapter 8

1. Jorge G. Castañeda, *Utopia Unarmed: The Latin American Left after the Cold War* (New York: Alfred A. Knopf, 1993), p. 38.

2. Timothy Wickham-Crowley, *Guerrilla Movements and Revolution in Latin America* (Princeton: Princeton University Press, 1992), esp. pp. 209–220.

3. On this see Wickham-Crowley, *Guerrilla Movements,* esp. ch. 12; and Margaret E. Crahan and Peter H. Smith, "The State of Revolution," in Alfred Stepan (ed.), *Americas: New Interpretive Essays* (New York: Oxford University Press, 1992), pp. 79–108.

4. Castañeda, *Utopia,* p. 111.

5. U.S. Congress, Senate Select Committee to Study Governmental Operations with Respect to Intelligence Activities, *Alleged Assassination Plots Involving Foreign Leaders*, Senate Report No. 465, 94th Congress, 1st Session (Washington, D.C.: U.S. Government Printing Office, 1975), pp. 191–215.

6. Strictly speaking, the "Southern Cone" of South America embraces Chile, Argentina, and Uruguay (which also fell under military rule during the 1970s); in colloquial usage, the term sometimes includes Paraguay and even Brazil.

7. As former European colonies in the Caribbean acquired independence, the organization changed its name to the Economic Commission for Latin America and the Caribbean (ECLAC).

8. The charter was opposed by only six industrialized countries—the United States, Great Britain, West Germany, Belgium, Denmark, and Luxembourg—on the ground that it would lead to more expropriation of foreign investment and to more Third World producer associations like OPEC.

9. Roger D. Hansen, *Beyond the North-South Stalemate* (New York: McGraw-Hill, 1979), p. 101.

10. By 1989 sixteen Latin American states were full members of the Non-Aligned Movement: Argentina, Belize, Bolivia, Chile, Colombia, Cuba, Ecuador, Grenada, Guyana, Jamaica, Nicaragua, Panama, Peru, St. Lucia, Suriname, Trinidad-Tobago. Eight were observers: Barbados, Brazil, Costa Rica, Dominica, El Salvador, Mexico, Uruguay, Venezuela, as were three regional organizations: ECLAC, SELA, and OLADE (the Latin American Energy Organization). Non-members included Antigua-Bermuda, Bahamas, Dominican Republic, Guatemala, Haiti, Honduras, Paraguay, St. Kitt-Nevis, St. Vincent.

Chapter 9

1. Francis Fukuyama, "The End of History?" *The National Interest* 16 (Summer 1989): 3–18.

2. Thomas G. Paterson, *On Every Front: The Making and Unmaking of the Cold War*, rev. ed. (New York: W. W. Norton, 1992), pp. 192–193.

3. Paul Kennedy, *The Rise and Fall of the Great Powers: Economic Change and Military Conflict from 1500 to 2000* (New York: Random House, 1987), p. 358.

4. Abraham F. Lowenthal, *Partners in Conflict: The United States and Latin America* (Baltimore: Johns Hopkins University Press, 1987), p. 33; also in the revised edition, *Partners in Conflict: The United States and Latin America in the 1990s* (Baltimore: John Hopkins University Press, 1990), p. 36.

5. Lowenthal, *Partners,* p. 32; and revised edition, p. 35.

6. Paterson, *On Every Front,* p. 213; also Paterson, "Why the Cold War Ended: The Latin American Dimension" (unpublished paper, 1993), p. 23.

7. In relation to population size, the spread in per capita output grew steadily: in 1950 per capita GDP in the United States was just over seven times as large as in Latin America, and by 1990 it was nearly ten times as large. By this standard, U.S. preponderance was *increasing* over time.

8. See Alberto Van Klaveren, "Europe and Latin America in the 1990s," and Barbara Stallings and Kotaro Horisaka, "Japan and Latin America: New Patterns in the 1990s," both in Abraham F. Lowenthal and Gregory Treverton (eds.), *Latin America in a New World* (Boulder: Westview Press, 1994), pp. 81–104 and 126–149; and Peter H. Smith, "Japan, Latin America, and the New International Order," Institute of Developing Economies, Visiting Research Scholar Series 179 (Tokyo: Institute of Developing Economies, 1990).

9. Robert A. Pastor, *Whirlpool: U.S. Foreign Policy toward Latin America and the Caribbean* (Princeton: Princeton University Press, 1992), p. 230.

10. In 1992 Mexican trade with the United States, in third place overall, amounted to $75.8 billion; Venezuela was in sixteenth place with $13.6 billion, Brazil in seventeenth place with $13.4 billion, Colombia in twenty-seventh place with $6.1 billion, and Argentina in forty-second place with $4.5 billion.

11. Quoted in Rubén G. Rumbaut, "The Americans: Latin American and Caribbean Peoples in the United States," in Alfred Stepan (ed.), *Americas: New Interpretive Essays* (New York: Oxford University Press, 1992), pp. 278–279.

12. This figure refers to U.S. citizens or to persons legally present in the United States; understandably, the practical definition of the "Hispanic" population is subject to uncertainty and debate.

13. Puerto Rico is not customarily regarded as a political or economic member of Latin America, but its inclusion seems appropriate in this social context.

14. Joseph S. Nye, Jr., "What New World Order?" *Foreign Affairs* 71, no. 2 (Spring 1991): 83–96, with quote on p. 88.

15. As quoted in Peter H. Smith and Peter Zung, "The Third World after the Cold War: A Conference Report," *CILAS Working Papers,* 1 (Center for Iberian and Latin American Studies, University of California, San Diego, 1992), p. 13.

16. Paterson, "Why the Cold War Ended," pp. 40–41.

Chapter 10

1. Pedro-Pablo Kuczynski, *Latin American Debt* (Baltimore: Johns Hopkins University Press/Twentieth Century Fund, 1988), p. 86.

2. The classic (and controversial) formulation of this consensus appears in John Williamson, "What Washington Means by Policy Reform," in Williamson (ed.), *Latin American Economic Adjustment: How Much Has Happened?* (Washington, D.C.: Institute for International Economics, 1990), pp. 7–20.

3. Comparison of the economic size of these two blocs was highly contingent on exchange rates for the U.S. dollar; according to some calculations (at some moments) NAFTA was larger than the European Union, according to others it was smaller.

4. Peter H. Smith, "Conclusion—The Politics of Integration: Guidelines for Policy," in Smith (ed.), *The Challenge of Integration: Europe and the Americas* (Miami: North–South Center, 1993), p. 393.

5. Peter H. Smith, "The Political Impact of Free Trade on Mexico," *Journal of Interamerican Studies and World Affairs* (July 1992): 1–24.

6. Discounting invalid (*nulos*) ballots, Zedillo received 50.2 percent of the vote—just enough to claim a majority.

7. World Commission on Environment and Development, *Our Common Future* (New York: Oxford University Press, 1987), p. 8.

8. David Goodman and Michael Redclift (eds.), *Environment and Development in Latin America* (New York: Manchester University Press, 1991), pp. 3–4.

9. Gilbert R. Winham, "Enforcement of Environmental Measures: Negotiating the NAFTA Environmental Side Agreement," *Journal of Environment and Development* 3, no. 1 (Winter 1994): 35.

10. Winham, "Enforcement," 30.

11. Organizers originally thought to entitle the initiative as the Americas Free Trade Area, but the acronym AFTA had been already usurped by the ASEAN Free Trade Area. Members of ASEAN, the Association of Southeast Asian Nations, are Brunei, Indonesia, Malaysia, the Philippines, Singapore, Thailand and, as of mid-1995, Vietnam.

Chapter 11

1. The NIDA surveys raise serious problems of measurement. Candor in response might well vary over time: the greater the level of social intolerance about drugs, the less likely it is that people will provide complete information. And NIDA

surveys deal only with households; by definition, they do not cover the homeless, the prison population, students in dormitories, and those downtrodden segments of society most likely to be engaged in "doing" drugs.

2. By 1993 Russia moved into first place, with the United States in second—with more than 60 percent of all federal inmates and more than 25 percent of state prisoners in jail for drug charges.

3. Note that Table 2 does *not* refer to educational or therapeutic campaigns, though politicians frequently described such activities as part of the antidrug "wars." It refers only to organized violence.

4. Wayne A. Cornelius, "From Sojourners to Settlers: The Changing Profile of Mexican Immigration to the United States," in Jorge A. Bustamante, Clark W. Reynolds, and Raúl A. Hinojosa Ojeda (eds.), *U.S.–Mexico Relations: Labor Market Interdependence* (Stanford: Stanford University Press, 1992), p. 184.

5. Also important, witnesses say, was Bush's quaint sense of chivalry. "If they kill an American Marine," he said at a news conference, "that's real bad. And if they threaten and brutalize the wife of an American citizen, sexually threatening the lieutenant's wife while kicking him in the groin over and over again—then . . . this president is going to do something about it."

6. John Dinges, *Our Man in Panama: The Shrewd Rise and Brutal Fall of Manuel Noriega* (New York: Random House, 1991), p. 319.

Chapter 12

1. The end of the Cold War was not responsible for Latin American democratization movements; as mentioned in chapter 9, the major transitions—in Argentina, Brazil, Chile, Uruguay—all took place prior to the communist collapse.

2. There are, of course, many different ways of construing the post–Cold War scene. For one especially influential (and controversial) interpretation see Samuel P. Huntington, "The Clash of Civilizations?" *Foreign Affairs* 72, no. 3 (Summer 1993): 22–49.

3. *Japan Times,* May 27, 1990.

4. Charles William Maynes, "America without the Cold War," *Foreign Policy* 78 (Spring 1990): 3–25, with quote on pp. 22–23.

5. Jorge Castañeda, "Latin America and the End of the Cold War," *World Policy Journal* 7, no. 3 (Summer 1990): 469–492, with quote on p. 477.

6. World Bank, *World Development Report 1991: The Challenge of Development* (New York: Oxford University Press, 1991), Table 1, pp. 204–205.

7. In October 1994 the UN General Assembly overwhelmingly disapproved of the American embargo by a vote of 101 to 2 with 48 abstentions, with only Israel supporting the United States; in 1992 the vote was 59 to 3 with 71 abstentions.

8. For differing interpretations see Susan Kaufman Purcell, "Collapsing Cuba," *Foreign Affairs* 71, no. 1 (1992): 130–145, and Jorge Domínguez, "Secrets of Castro's Staying Power," *Foreign Affairs* 72, no. 2 (Spring 1993): 97–107.

9. In fact, it was not clear precisely how the Cuban government could stem the tide of *balseros.* Apparently Castro first relaxed strictures against emigration because he was greatly (and understandably) annoyed by U.S. official welcomes to Cuban refugees who had hijacked ferry boats in Havana.

10. In May 1995 the Clinton administration announced that it would admit to the United States approximately 20,000 Cubans still held at Guantánamo, presumably in accordance with the September 1994 agreement, but that it would henceforth return to Cuba any new *balseros* picked up on the high seas—thus overturning the thirty-year policy of embracing Cuban emigrants as refugees. Although this decision drew harsh criticism from leaders of the Cuban American community, it was calculated to capitalize on anti-immigration sentiment throughout the state—especially in veiw of Florida's likely importance in the electoral campaign of 1996.

11. Like Chile, Mexico became a member of the forum for Asia-Pacific Economic Cooperation (APEC), but the Mexican economy remains closely tied to the United States.

12. Nora Lustig, "The Future of Trade Policy in Latin America," unpublished paper (Brookings Institution, March 1994), p. 17.

13. In principle Chile's negotiation of multiple FTAs throughout Latin America was consistent with a hub-and-spoke strategy, but the country was simply not big or strong enough to constitute a continental "hub."

14. Intraregional trade among MERCOSUR countries rose from less than $2 billion in 1985 to more than $7 billion in 1992, thus climbing from 5.7 percent of total exports in 1985 to 14.3 percent in 1992.

15. See Fernando Fajnzylber, *Unavoidable Industrial Restructuring in Latin America* (Durham: Duke University Press, 1990); Economic Commission for Latin America and the Caribbean, *Changing Production Patterns with Social Equity* (Santiago de Chile: ECLAC, 1990); ECLAC, *Social Equity and Changing Production Patterns: An Integrated Approach* (Santiago de Chile: ECLAC, 1992); and ECLAC, *Education and Knowledge: Basic Pillars of Changing Production Patterns with Social Equity* (Santiago de Chile: ECLAC, 1992).

Conclusion

1. Hopes lingered in some quarters for multilateral organization, especially the OAS, and to some extent NAFTA may have represented an attempt by Mexico to set rules and restrictions on the United States in areas of economic policy; by mid-1995, however, there was little indication that such strategies were likely to succeed.

Select Bibliography

This bibliography offers an introductory guide to further reading on U.S.–Latin American relations. Listings appear under four headings: International Relations: Concepts and Trends, The United States in the Global Arena, U.S. Policy toward Latin America, and Latin America: Politics, Strategies, and Policies. While these categories overlap to some extent, individual entries are listed only once.

International Relations: Concepts and Trends

Dougherty, James E., and Robert L. Pfaltzgraff, Jr. *Contending Theories of International Relations: A Comprehensive Survey,* 3rd ed. New York: Harper & Row, 1990.

Gilpin, Robert. *War and Change in World Politics.* Cambridge: Cambridge University Press, 1981.

———. *The Political Economy of International Relations.* Princeton: Princeton University Press, 1987.

Haggard, Stephan, and Robert R. Kaufman (eds.). *The Politics of Economic Adjustment.* Princeton: Princeton University Press, 1992.

Hansen, Roger D. *Beyond the North-South Stalemate.* New York: McGraw-Hill, 1979.

Holsti, Ole R. "Models of International Relations and Foreign Policy." *Diplomatic History* 13, no. 1 (Winter 1989): 15–43.

Kennedy, Paul. *Preparing for the Twenty-First Century.* New York: Random House, 1993.

———. *The Rise and Fall of the Great Powers: Economic Change and Military Conflict from 1500 to 2000.* New York: Random House, 1988.

Keohane, Robert O. *After Hegemony: Cooperation and Discord in the World Political Economy.* Princeton: Princeton University Press, 1984.

Keohane, Robert O. (ed.). *Neorealism and Its Critics.* New York: Columbia University Press, 1986.

Keohane, Robert O., and Joseph S. Nye. *Power and Interdependence,* 2nd ed. Glenview: Scott, Foresman, 1989.

Krasner, Stephen (ed.) *International Regimes.* Ithaca: Cornell University Press, 1983.

———. *Structural Conflict: The Third World Against Global Liberalism.* Berkeley and Los Angeles: University of California Press, 1985.

Nye, Joseph S., Jr. *Bound to Lead: The Changing Nature of American Power.* New York: Basic Books, 1990.

Oye, Kenneth A. (ed.). *Cooperation under Anarchy.* Princeton: Princeton University Press, 1986.

Rosecrance, Richard. *Action and Reaction in World Politics: International Systems in Perspective.* Boston: Little, Brown, 1963.

Rothstein, Robert L. *Global Bargaining: UNCTAD and the Quest for a New International Order.* Princeton: Princeton University Press, 1979.

Smith, Peter H. (ed.). *The Challenge of Integration: Europe and the Americas.* Miami: North-South Center/Transaction Publishers, 1993.

Smith, Tony. *America's Mission: The United States and the Worldwide Struggle for Democracy in the Twentieth Century.* Princeton: Princeton University Press, 1994.

———. *The Pattern of Imperialism: The United States, Great Britain, and the Late-Industrializing World since 1815.* Cambridge: Cambridge University Press, 1981.

The United States in the Global Arena

Ambrose, Stephen E. *Rise to Globalism: American Foreign Policy, 1938–1980,* 2nd rev. ed. New York: Penguin Books, 1980.

Desch, Michael C. *When the Third World Matters: Latin America and United States Grand Strategy.* Baltimore: Johns Hopkins University Press, 1993.

Gardner, Lloyd C. *Economic Aspects of New Deal Diplomacy.* Madison: University of Wisconsin Press, 1964.

Goldstein, Judith. *Ideas, Interests, and American Trade Policy.* Ithaca: Cornell University Press, 1993.

Haass, Richard N. *Intervention: The Use of American Military Force in the Post–Cold War World.* Washington, D.C.: Brookings Institution, 1995.

Hunt, Michael H. *Ideology and U.S. Foreign Policy.* New Haven: Yale University Press, 1987.

Lake, David A. *Power, Protection, and Free Trade: International Sources of U.S. Commercial Stategy, 1887–1939.* Ithaca: Cornell University Press, 1988.

McCormick, Thomas J. *America's Half Century: United States Foreign Policy in the Cold War.* Baltimore: Johns Hopkins University Press, 1989.

Merk, Frederick. *Manifest Destiny and Mission in American History: A Reinterpretation.* New York: Alfred A. Knopf, 1963.

Oye, Kenneth A., Robert J. Lieber, and Donald Rothchild (eds.). *Eagle Resurgent? The Reagan Era in American Foreign Policy.* Boston: Little, Brown, 1983.

————. *Eagle Defiant: United States Foreign Policy in the 1980s.* Boston: Little, Brown, 1983.

Packenham, Robert A. *Liberal America and the Third World: Political Development Ideas in Foreign Aid and Social Science.* Princeton: Princeton University Press, 1973.

Paterson, Thomas G. *On Every Front: The Making and Unmaking of the Cold War,* rev. ed. New York: W. W. Norton, 1992.

Tucker, Robert W., and David C. Hendrickson. *The Imperial Temptation: The New World Order and America's Purpose.* New York: Council on Foreign Relations, 1992.

U.S. Congress. Senate Select Committee to Study Governmental Operations with Respect to Intelligence Activities. *Alleged Assassination Plots Involving Foreign Leaders.* Senate Report No. 465. 94th Congress, 1st Session. Washington, D.C.: U.S. Government Printing Office, 1975.

Van Alstyne, R. W. *The Rising American Empire.* New York: Oxford University Press, 1960.

Weinberg, Albert K. *Manifest Destiny: A Study of Nationalist Expansionism in American History.* Baltimore: Johns Hopkins University Press, 1935.

Weston, Rubin Francis. *Racism in U.S. Imperialism.* Columbia: University of South Carolina Press, 1972.

Williams, William Appleman. *Empire as a Way of Life.* New York: Oxford University Press, 1980.

————. *The Tragedy of American Diplomacy,* 2nd ed. New York: Dell Publishing, 1972.

U.S. Policy Toward Latin America

Aguilar, Alonso. *Pan-Americanism from Monroe to the Present: A View from the Other Side.* New York: Monthly Review Press, 1968.

Baily, Samuel L. *The United States and the Development of South America, 1945–1975.* New York: Franklin Watts, 1976.

Bemis, Samuel Flagg. *The Latin American Policy of the United States: An Historical Interpretation.* New York: Harcourt, Brace and Company, 1943.

Benjamin, Jules R. *The United States and the Origins of the Cuban Revolution: An Empire of Liberty in an Age of National Liberation.* Princeton: Princeton University Press, 1990.

Bilateral Commission on the Future of United States–Mexican Relations. *The Challenge of Interdependence: Mexico and the United States.* Lanham, MD: University Press of America, 1989.

Blachman, Morris J., William M. LeoGrande, and Kenneth Sharpe (eds.). *Confronting Revolution: Security through Diplomacy in Central America.* New York: Pantheon, 1986.

Blasier, Cole. *The Hovering Giant: U.S. Responses to Revolutionary Change in Latin America.* Pittsburgh: University of Pittsburgh Press, 1976.

Bustamante, Jorge A., Clark W. Reynolds, and Raúl A. Hinojosa Ojeda (eds.). *U.S.–Mexico Relations: Labor Market Interdependence.* Stanford: Stanford University Press, 1992.

Carothers, Thomas. *In the Name of Democracy: U.S. Policy toward Latin America in the Reagan Years*. Berkeley and Los Angeles: University of California Press, 1991.

Coatsworth, John H. *Central America and the United States: The Clients and the Colossus*. New York: Twayne, 1994.

Connell-Smith, Gordon. *The United States and Latin America: An Historical Analysis of Inter-American Relations*. New York: Wiley, 1974.

Dinges, John. *Our Man in Panama: The Shrewd Rise and Brutal Fall of Manuel Noriega*. New York: Random House, 1991.

Foner, Philip S. *The Spanish-Cuban-American War and the Birth of American Imperialism, 1895–1902*, 2 vols. New York: Monthly Review Press, 1972.

Gellman, Irwin F. *Good Neighbor Diplomacy: United States Policies in Latin America, 1933–1945*. Baltimore: Johns Hopkins University Press, 1979.

Gilderhus, Mark T. *Pan American Visions: Woodrow Wilson in the Western Hemisphere, 1913–1921*. Tucson: University of Arizona Press, 1986.

Gleijeses, Piero. *Shattered Hope: The Guatemalan Revolution and the United States, 1944–1954*. Princeton: Princeton University Press, 1991.

Green, David. *The Containment of Latin America: A History of the Myths and Reality of the Good Neighbor Policy*. Chicago: Quadrangle Books, 1971.

Hartlyn, Jonathan, Lars Schoultz, and Augusto Varas (eds.). *The United States and Latin America in the 1990s: Beyond the Cold War*. Chapel Hill: University of North Carolina Press, 1992.

Healy, David. *U.S. Expansionism: The Imperialist Urge in the 1890s*. Madison: University of Wisconsin Press, 1970.

Johnson, John J. *A Hemisphere Apart: The Foundations of United States Policy toward Latin America*. Baltimore: Johns Hopkins University Press, 1990.

LaFeber, Walter. *Inevitable Revolutions: The United States in Central America*. New York: W. W. Norton, 1983; and 2nd ed., revised and expanded, 1993.

———. *The New Empire: An Interpretation of American Expansion, 1860–1898*. Ithaca: Cornell University Press, 1963.

Lake, Anthony. *Somoza Falling*. Boston: Houghton Mifflin, 1989.

Langley, Lester D. *Struggle for the American Mediterranean: United States–European Rivalry in the Gulf-Caribbean, 1776–1904*. Athens: University of Georgia Press, 1976.

———. *The United States and the Caribbean in the Twentieth Century*. Athens: University of Georgia Press, 1982.

Levinson, Jerome, and Juan de Onís. *The Alliance That Lost Its Way: A Critical Report on the Alliance for Progress*. Chicago: Quadrangle Books, 1970.

Lowenthal, Abraham F. *The Dominican Intervention*. Cambridge: Harvard University Press, 1972.

Lowenthal, Abraham F. (ed.). *Exporting Democracy: The United States and Latin America, Themes and Issues*. Baltimore: Johns Hopkins University Press, 1991.

———. *Partners in Conflict: The United States and Latin America*. Baltimore: Johns Hopkins University Press, 1987. Revised edition, *Partners in Conflict: The United States and Latin Amrica in the 1990s*. Baltimore: Johns Hopkins University Press, 1990.

Martz, John D. (ed.). *United States Policy in Latin America: A Quarter Century of Crisis and Challenge, 1961–1986*. Lincoln: University of Nebraska Press, 1988.

Molineu, Harold. *U.S. Policy toward Latin America: From Regionalism to Globalism*, 2nd ed. Boulder: Westview Press, 1990.

Munro, Dana G. *Intervention and Dollar Diplomacy in the Caribbean, 1900–1921*. Princeton: Princeton University Press, 1964.

———. *The United States and the Caribbean Republics, 1921–1933*. Princeton: Princeton University Press, 1974.

Pastor, Robert A. *Condemned to Repetition: The United States and Nicaragua*. Princeton: Princeton University Press, 1987.

———. *Whirlpool: U.S. Foreign Policy toward Latin America and the Caribbean*. Princeton: Princeton University Press, 1992.

Perkins, Dexter. *A History of the Monroe Doctrine,* rev. ed. Boston: Little, Brown, 1963.

Rabe, Stephen G. *Eisenhower and Latin America: The Foreign Policy of Anticommunism*. Chapel Hill: University of North Carolina Press, 1988.

Rogers, William D. *The Twilight Struggle: The Alliance for Progress and the Politics of Development in Latin America*. New York: Random House, 1967.

Romualdi, Serafino. *Presidents and Peons: Recollections of a Labor Ambassador in Latin America*. New York: Funk & Wagnalls, 1967.

Scheman, L. Ronald (ed.). *The Alliance for Progress: A Retrospective*. New York: Praeger, 1988.

Schoultz, Lars. *Human Rights and United States Policy toward Latin America*. Princeton: Princeton University Press, 1981.

———. *National Security and United States Policy toward Latin America*. Princeton: Princeton University Press, 1987.

Schoultz, Lars, William C. Smith, and Augusto Varas (eds.). *Security, Democracy, and Development in U.S.–Latin American Relations*. Miami: North-South Center/Transaction Publishers, 1994.

Sigmund, Paul E. *The United States and Democracy in Chile*. Baltimore: Johns Hopkins University Press, 1993.

Smith, Gaddis. *The Last Years of the Monroe Doctrine, 1945–1993*. New York: Hill and Wang, 1994.

Smith, Peter H. (ed.). *Drug Policy in the Americas*. Boulder: Westview Press, 1992.

Steward, Dick. *Trade and Hemisphere: The Good Neighbor Policy and Reciprocal Trade*. Columbia: University of Missouri Press, 1975.

Trask, David F., Michael C. Meyer, and Roger R. Trask (eds.). *A Bibliography of United States–Latin American Relations since 1810*. Lincoln: University of Nebraska Press, 1968.

Tulchin, Joseph S. *The Aftermath of War: World War I and U.S. Policy toward Latin America*. New York: New York University Press, 1971.

Weintraub, Sidney (ed.). *Integrating the Americas: Shaping Future Trade Policy*. Miami: North-South Center, 1994.

———. *NAFTA: What Comes Next?* Westport: Praeger, 1994.

Whitaker, Arthur P. *The Western Hemisphere Idea: Its Rise and Decline*. Ithaca: Cornell University Press, 1954.

Williamson, John (ed.). *Latin American Economic Adjustment: How Much Has Happened?* Washington, D.C.: Institute for International Economics, 1990.

Wood, Bryce. *The Dismantling of the Good Neighbor Policy*. Austin: University of Texas Press, 1985.

———. *The Making of the Good Neighbor Policy*. New York: Columbia University Press, 1961.

Latin America: Politics, Strategies, and Policies

Atkins, G. Pope. *Latin America in the International Political System*, 2nd ed. Boulder: Westview Press, 1989.

Bethell, Leslie, and Ian Roxborough (eds.). *Latin America between the Second World War and the Cold War, 1944–1948*. Cambridge: Cambridge University Press, 1993.

Bradford, Colin L. (ed.). *Strategic Options for Latin America in the 1990s*. Paris: Organisation for Economic Cooperation and Development, 1992.

Burns, E. Bradford (ed.). *Nationalism in Brazil: A Historical Survey*. New York: Praeger, 1968.

Castañeda, Jorge. *Utopia Unarmed: The Latin American Left after the Cold War*. New York: Alfred A. Knopf, 1993.

Constable, Pamela, and Arturo Valenzuela. *A Nation of Enemies: Chile under Pinochet*. New York: W. W. Norton, 1991.

Davis, Harold Eugene, and Larman Wilson (eds.). *Latin American Foreign Policies: An Analysis*. Baltimore: Johns Hopkins University Press, 1975.

Devlin, Robert. *Debt and Crisis in Latin America: The Supply Side of the Story*. Princeton: Princeton University Press, 1989.

Domínguez, Jorge. *Making the World Safe for Revolution: Cuba's Foreign Policy*. Cambridge: Harvard University Press, 1989.

Drake, Paul W. (ed.) *Money Doctors, Foreign Debts, and Economic Reforms in Latin America from the 1890s to the Present*. Wilmington: Scholarly Resources, 1994.

Goodman, David, and Michael Redclift (eds.). *Environment and Development in Latin America*. New York: Manchester University Press, 1991.

Grabendorff, Wolf, and Riordan Roett (eds.). *Latin America, Western Europe, and the U.S.* New York: Praeger, 1985.

Hilton, Stanley E. *Brazil and the Great Powers, 1930–1939: The Politics of Trade Rivalry*. Austin: University of Texas Press, 1975.

———. *Hitler's Secret War in South America: German Military Espionage and Allied Counterespionage in Brazil*. Baton Rouge: Louisiana State University Press, 1981.

[Instituto de Relaciones Europeo-Latinoamericanas]. *Prospects for the Processes of Sub-Regional Integration in Central and South America*. Madrid: Instituto de Relaciones Europeo-Latinoamericanos, 1992.

Kuczynski, Pedro-Pablo. *Latin American Debt*. Baltimore: Johns Hopkins University Press, 1988.

Lincoln, Jennie K., and Elizabeth G. Ferris. *The Dynamics of Latin American Foreign Policies: Challenges for the 1980s*. Boulder: Westview Press, 1984.

———. *Latin American Foreign Policies: Global and Regional Dimensions*. Boulder: Westview Press, 1981.

Liss, Sheldon B. *Marxist Thought in Latin America*. Berkeley and Los Angeles: University of California Press, 1984.

Lowenthal, Abraham F., and Gregory Treverton (eds.). *Latin America in a New World*. Boulder: Westview Press, 1994.

Mesa-Lago, Carmelo (ed.). *Cuba After the Cold War*. Pittsburgh: University of Pittsburgh Press, 1993.

Moreira Alves, Maria Helena. *State and Opposition in Military Brazil*. Austin: University of Texas Press, 1985.

Mujal-León, Eusebio (ed.). *The USSR and Latin America: A Developing Relationship*. Boston: Unwin Hyman, 1989.

Muñoz, Heraldo, and Joseph S. Tulchin (eds.). *Latin American Nations in World Politics*. Boulder: Westview Press, 1984.

Ojeda, Mario. *Alcances y límites de política exterior de México*. Mexico: El Colegio de México, 1976.

————. *México: el surgimiento de una política exterior activa*. Mexico: Secretaría de Educación Pública, 1986.

Oppenheimer, Andrés. *Castro's Final Hour: The Secret Story behind the Coming Downfall of Communist Cuba*. New York; Simon & Schuster, 1992.

Palmer, David Scott (ed.). *Shining Path of Peru*. New York: St. Martin's Press, 1992.

Pike, Fredrick B. *Chile and the United States, 1880–1962: The Emergence of Chile's Social Crisis and the Challenge to United States Diplomacy*. Notre Dame: University of Notre Dame Press, 1963.

————. *Hispanismo, 1898–1936: Spanish Conservatives and Liberals and Their Relations with Spanish America*. Notre Dame: University of Notre Dame Press, 1971.

Poppino, Rollie E. *International Communism in Latin America: A History of the Movement, 1917–1963*. New York: The Free Press, 1964.

Portales, Carlos (ed.). *El mundo en transición y América Latina*. Buenos Aires: Grupo Editor Latinoamericano, 1989.

Puig, Juan Carlos (ed.). *América Latina: Políticas exteriores comparadas*, 2 vols. Buenos Aires: Grupo Editor Latinoamericano, 1984.

Rock, David (ed.). *Latin America in the 1940s: War and Postwar Transitions*. Berkeley and Los Angeles: University of California Press, 1994.

Saborio, Sylvia (ed.). *The Premise and the Promise: Free Trade in the Americas*. New Brunswick: Transaction Publishers, 1992.

Sanderson, Steven E. *The Politics of Trade in Latin American Development*. Stanford: Stanford University Press, 1992.

Schoenhals, Kai P., and Richard A. Melanson. *Revolution and Intervention in Grenada: The New Jewel Movement, the United States, and the Caribbean*. Boulder: Westview Press, 1985.

Sigmund, Paul E. *The Overthrow of Allende and the Politics of Chile, 1964–1976*. Pittsburgh: University of Pittsburgh Press, 1977.

Skidmore, Thomas E. *The Politics of Military Rule in Brazil, 1964–85*. New York: Oxford University Press, 1988.

Skidmore, Thomas E., and Peter H. Smith. *Modern Latin America*, 3rd ed. New York: Oxford University Press, 1992.

Stepan, Alfred (ed.). *Americas: New Interpretive Essays*. New York: Oxford University Press, 1992.

Thomas, Hugh. *The Cuban Revolution*. New York: Harper & Row, 1977.

Tomassini, Luciano (ed.). *Nuevas formas de concertación regional en América Latina*. Buenos Aires: Grupo Editor Latinoamericano, 1990.

Turner, Frederick C. *The Dynamic of Mexican Nationalism*. Chapel Hill: University of North Carolina Press, 1968.

Index